D0986173

LAST TIME OUT

LAST TIME OUT

Big-League Farewells of Baseball's Greats

Updated Edition

JOHN NOGOWSKI

LYONS
PRESS

Essex, Connecticut

Very special thanks to Santo Labombarda at the Elias Sports Bureau. Thanks also to Alex Bonilla from Sports-Reference.com. And thanks, finally, to Rick Rinehart, for bringing this project back to life, and Joshua Rosenberg and Jehanne Schweitzer for their expert help. It takes a whole ballclub.

An imprint of Globe Pequot, the trade division of The Rowman & Littlefield Publishing Group, Inc.
4501 Forbes Blvd., Ste. 200
Lanham, MD 20706
www.rowman.com

Distributed by NATIONAL BOOK NETWORK

Copyright © 2022 John Nogowski
First edition 2004

Statistics courtesy of the Elias Sports Bureau
Topps® trading cards used courtesy of The Topps Company, Inc.

All rights reserved. No part of this book may be reproduced in any form or by any electronic or mechanical means, including information storage and retrieval systems, without written permission from the publisher, except by a reviewer who may quote passages in a review.

British Library Cataloguing in Publication Information available

Library of Congress Cataloging-in-Publication Data
Names: Nogowski, John, 1953– author.
Title: Last time out : big-league farewells of baseball's greats / John Nogowski.
Description: Updated edition. | Guilford, Connecticut : Lyons Press, 2022.
Identifiers: LCCN 2021060776 (print) | LCCN 2021060777 (ebook) | ISBN 9781493066537 (paperback) | ISBN 9781493068470 (epub)
Subjects: LCSH: Baseball—United States—History. | Baseball players—United States—Biography.
Classification: LCC GV863.A1 N64 2022 (print) | LCC GV863.A1 (ebook) | DDC 796.357092/273—dc23/eng/20220126
LC record available at https://lccn.loc.gov/2021060776
LC ebook record available at https://lccn.loc.gov/2021060777

To John Jr.:

I will always see you, running across the lawn, arms wide open after your very first catch of a flyball. On Father's Day. For me, getting a chance to grow up again in the game, through your eyes, has been magical. Sort of like that first catch. You've always understood—better than anyone I've ever known—to play this game right, you have to love it. Like a father loves a son.

Love, Dad
Summer 2004
P.S.: August 16, 2020—You MADE it, kid. You're a Big Leaguer!

CONTENTS

Introduction: Last Time Out

Finding the right ending is a problem equally shared by writers, filmmakers, poets, songwriters, and, thanks to Ted Williams of the Boston Red Sox, maybe even baseball players.

Unleashing that flawless swing one last time on a dark, nasty fall afternoon in Boston, Williams's perfect parting shot, launching a majestic home run into the Fenway Park bullpen in his final appearance at the plate, set a standard for baseball farewells that has rarely been equaled. It was as if Williams himself was saying to the game—take that!

Gracefully walking away from the game is a trick managed by only a few. The great Babe Ruth, stuffed into an unfamiliar Boston Braves uniform, walked off the field for the last time with no fanfare. Ty Cobb left before his final season was even over, his final bid for a World Series title gone after a Yankees sweep of Connie Mack's Philadelphia A's. And so it goes: Bob Gibson cursing out a mediocre player who'd just reached him for a grand slam on his final pitch, the extraordinary Willie Mays stumbling in the outfield in a World Series, Nolan Ryan unable to get out of the first inning of his final start, and on and on. Considering that all these men had been so triumphant in the game—just making it to the major leagues is an extraordinary achievement, even for one game—that when it all ended, whether by their choice or not, it was something worth looking at, worth remembering, like the dramatic final scene of a movie.

And of course, the mystique of Williams's final home run started with the work of an author, the great John Updike, who, the story goes, came to Boston anticipating a romantic liaison. Instead, Updike turned his disappointment into a trip to Fenway Park and brilliantly captured the final moments of a historic career. His legendary *New Yorker* piece, "Hub Fans Bid Kid Adieu," made a nation reconsider Williams's career and made me, eventually, come up with the idea for this book. Working for the local newspaper, I'd had a chance to meet and chat with Updike after his appearance at a Florida State workshop in 2000, and we chatted about his oft-discussed essay.

"Looking back," he said, "I'm still surprised that it was his last game and there was nobody there." He was right. Fenway Park had just 10,453 fans—and Updike—that September afternoon. On the way home, I wondered about how other great players had left the game.

I remembered Babe Ruth had hit three homers in a game: Was it his finale? And, teary-eyed, I remembered Carl Yastrzemski's last game in Boston, his trot around the field, slapping hands with watery-eyed Fenway Faithful. What about Hank Aaron, Lou Gehrig, Jackie Robinson . . . I'd have to look. And did.

Times have changed, of course, since Williams's finale in 1960. The final games of recent stars, like so many other events in professional sports, have become important. Sometimes they become a scripted, carefully planned, media circus like the departures of Derek Jeter, Mariano Rivera, David Ortiz, and a few others. Sometimes, they just leave.

Thanks to YouTube, you can go back and take a look at these final trips to the plate or mound. But you don't get the circumstances surrounding them, the backstory. That's what *Last Time Out* is all about.

In this, an updated edition of my original book with 20 new chapters, I've looked back at the departures of some of the most memorable players in my lifetime, all of whom I watched play, some of whom I even got to interview in my 25-year career as a sportswriter. There are even a few personal moments sprinkled in. As my connection to the game has deepened in a way I couldn't have anticipated—only dreamed about—I had another renewed interest in our national pastime.

My son, the kid you see leaning on my shoulder on the back jacket of my original book, is now 28. After a long, sometimes bumpy stint in the minor leagues, John is a player in the Atlanta Braves organization, selected in the minor-league phase of the Rule 5 Draft a couple weeks before Christmas. And he can testify to the mercurial nature of professional baseball these days. He made his major-league debut with the St. Louis Cardinals a week before my birthday in 2020, was traded to the Pittsburgh Pirates in July 2021, moved on to the San Francisco Giants organization in September, and in December, on to the world champion Braves. I share the story of his big-league debut in the concluding chapter. I'm hoping that *his* final at-bat is a few years away.

As a writer and fan, what has been truly fascinating in the intervening 16 years since the first publication of *Last Time Out* is suddenly how accessible everything is. Writing and researching that original book pre-internet, I remember spending hour after hour in Florida State's Strozier Library, eyes blurry from the trusty microfilm machine, sifting through ancient box scores, game stories, and newspaper columns. For this edition, almost all the material was found online or in books I had in my own library.

As far as the drama of Ted's farewell home run in his very last trip to the plate, the internet showed me there were a bunch of those dramatic farewells, even a guy who homered in his first *and* his last at-bat. According to what I could find online, there were 59 other guys, who, like Ted, left with a home run. Only John Updike wasn't there to immortalize any of those. One of them I even know; I covered him in high school (David Ross).

Familiar names like Ian Kinsler, Dan Uggla, Nyjer Morgan, Jim Edmonds, Todd Zeile, Troy O'Leary, the delightful Albert Belle, Willie Mays Aikens, Joe Rudi, Ken McMullen, Tony Kubek, and Hall of Famer Mickey Cochrane all left the game with a home run in their final turn at the dish. According to the online stats, Ted was just the 18th major leaguer to bow out with a round-tripper, not the first, which Updike's piece may have implied.

There is so much information available to you if you know where to look. I started every time with my personal Hall of Fame reference site, Baseball-Reference.com, which I found invaluable. Before, when I did the work for the first *Last Time Out*, all I had was a *Baseball Encyclopedia* to tell me when the guy retired. It was in those days of intensive research when I came upon stories I'd never heard before that, to me, were simply irresistible. Somehow, they'd been untold.

Here was Dizzy Dean, leaving the broadcast booth for a one-dollar contract and a dare to pitch the season finale for the pitiful St. Louis Browns. Here was Stan Musial, winding up an amazing career with a single, ending with exactly the same number of hits at home and on the road—3,630 perfectly split down the middle. Here was Satchel Paige, at 59 or more, coming back to pitch three innings in an end-of-the-season publicity stunt against Carl Yastrzemski's Boston Red Sox.

Little did I suspect that years later, I'd become friends with the last batter Satchel Paige faced in the majors, a journeyman big leaguer named Jim Gosger, who Paige got to bounce out to end the third inning and his major-league finale. I didn't know Gosger at the time I wrote the book but was excited to chat with him about it later on when I took him to a Detroit Tigers game years after he'd retired. He remembered Paige's delivery perfectly. "Everything was low and hard," Gosger recalled. "He was so smooth. You could imagine what he was like when he was young."

Watching my son grow up in the game with me in the multiple roles of dad, hitting coach, writer, and baseball fan brought some unusual surprises.

When John was eight, we attended an Atlanta Braves spring training game in Orlando and in the late innings, with the crowd thinned out, a stray foul ball wound up in the press box.

"Go up and get it," I said and John did, climbing to the back row of the bleachers, raising his hands, flashing a freckle-faced smile. Suddenly, Tom Seaver stood up, ball in hand, autographing it, peeking out at the row of eager faces below him. He pointed at John and flipped him the ball. We still have it.

Four years later, we're both in Cooperstown during Induction Week; I'm doing a book signing for *Last Time Out*, and he is competing in a travel tournament at the amazing Cooperstown Dreams Park. (John still has the record for hits in a week: 30-for-39!) As we pull into town, John spots a banner: "Bob Feller: Autographs." "Dad," John says, "he's in your book. Let's go see him."

We walked over, I introduced myself, mentioned my book and my chapter on Feller's final game—a complete-game loss in which, amazingly, he didn't strike out anyone. We chatted for a moment, then he eyed John, age 12, in full uniform and says "Who's this young man? I bet he doesn't know who the hell I am."

"Oh yes I do, Mr. Feller," John shot back. "You're Rapid Robert Feller in my Cooperstown Heroes video game and Mr. Feller, you still throw gas!"

Feller and Seaver are gone now. And so are some of the other baseball legends profiled here. But the memory of their careers, their time on that major-league stage, will always linger. Thanks to Baseball-Reference.com, I can look back to just about any game. In Satchel Paige's finale, for example, Paige threw 58 pitches in three innings, and only 9,289 people found nothing better to do on a Saturday night in Kansas City. Bill Valentine was behind the plate, opposing pitcher Bill Monbouquette was Paige's last strikeout victim, and my friend Gosger was not only Paige's last out, he was also the first, popping out to first base opening the game. In looking back, there were so many things I watched happen but had forgotten about: Mickey Lolich picking off Lou Brock and Curt Flood *in the same inning* in the 1968 World Series; Tom Seaver leaving the mound in his final start with the 1986 Red Sox, me realizing that if they made it to the postseason, he wouldn't be able to help them, then seeing the Series go to a Game 7; Nolan Ryan's 298th win—in person—in Detroit, talking to the Tiger players afterward, several of them suggesting retirement was a great option for the Ryan Express; or recounting the story of a friend and I hollering at Reggie Jackson in his one season with the Orioles and his response, verbally and otherwise . . . it was fun.

I know that for the original *Last Time Out* there were a few die-hard baseball fans who found the stories of their heroes' final games sad or disappointing and gave me hell for bringing those stories up. But I think they were shortsighted. All of the men had been so successful, so dominant over this most difficult of games, it was a way, as a friend wrote, of seeing them in a different, more human light. For me, it was also a way to celebrate and file away their magnificent careers, how it started, how it ran, and how it finally came to a halt, sometimes with tears, sometimes with laughter, sometimes with both. As fans, we shared in their lives, their moments of triumph and disappointment and here, in *Last Time Out*, their goodbyes.

John Nogowski
Tallahassee, Florida
July 4, 2021

BABE RUTH

MISSING THE PROPER EXIT

DATE: May 30, 1935 (first game of Memorial Day doubleheader)

SITE: Shibe Park, Philadelphia, Pennsylvania

PITCHER: Jim Bivin of Philadelphia A's

RESULT: Groundout to first baseman Dolph Camilli

The one and only George Herman "Babe" Ruth. Though Ruth did manage a dramatic three-home-run game at Pittsburgh's Forbes Field in his final season playing for the Boston Braves, his remarkable career ended on May 30 in Philadelphia's Shibe Park. Babe's final at-bat resulted in a weak groundball to first baseman Dolph Camilli. After missing a ball hit by Lou Chiozza, Ruth took himself out of the Memorial Day twinbill. He never played again.

COURTESY OF THE NATIONAL BASEBALL HALL OF FAME LIBRARY

The final swing of the game's greatest player did not result in a long, soaring home run. There was none of the mincing majesty of a Ruthian trot around the bases or even the extraordinary drama of a mighty whiff from the Sultan of Swat.

"No home run that Babe Ruth ever hit managed to hint at the energy, power, effort, and sincerity of purpose that went into a swing as much as one strikeout," Paul Gallico once wrote. "Just as when he connected the result was the most perfect thing of its kind, a ball whacked so high, wide, and handsome that no stadium in the entire country could contain it, so was his strikeout the absolute acme of frustration. He would swing himself twice around until his legs were braided. Often he would twist himself clear off his feet. If he had ever connected with that one. . . ."

There was none of that here. When Babe Ruth came to bat for the 8,399th and final time of his magnificent career, he was, finally, harmless. The Braves' aging slugger had an aching knee, the result of an embarrassing fall on the left field incline at Cincinnati's Crosley Field a few days earlier.

What hurt just as much, perhaps, was Ruth's unsightly .183 batting average with just six home runs in the team's first 27 games. It was a sad way for the game's greatest home-run king to wind up. Everyone around the game knew he was done. Ruth's teammate on the Braves, 19-year-old rookie Albie Fletcher, watched with sadness.

"He couldn't run, he couldn't bend down for a ball," Fletcher told Donald Honig in his book *Baseball America.* "And of course, he couldn't hit the way he used to. It was sad watching those great skills fading away. To see it happening to Babe Ruth, to see Babe Ruth struggling on a ballfield, well, you realize that we're mortal and nothing lasts forever." A contemporary of Ruth's, Hall of Fame third baseman Fred Lindstrom, put it even more plainly: "It was like watching a monument beginning to shake and crack," he said. "You know, when I think back on it, it was an awful thing to see."

So here he was, stepping into the batter's box in the first game of a Memorial Day doubleheader at Philadelphia's Baker Bowl, the stands barely half-full. Ruth looked out at the guy on the mound, a guy about as nondescript as it gets. He saw a 26-year-old rookie right-hander named Jim Bivin, who finished 2-9 in this, his only big-league season, allowing 220 hits in 162 innings of work. When Ruth came up with two outs and nobody on in the first, a roar, of course, went up from the crowd. It was Babe Ruth, after all. Ruth swung mightily and topped a slow roller to first baseman Dolph Camilli.

Running down to first, he felt the pain in his knee from his fall at Crosley Field. But he trotted out to left field, to try to make a go of it. The double-header had just started. There might be some kid who hadn't gotten there yet. As he trotted to left, he had to be thinking about when he should have quit, when he really wanted to, about a week earlier. He knew how he should have gone out. Nobody ever had a greater sense of the dramatic than Babe Ruth.

Who hit the first All-Star Game home run? Who hit the first home run in Yankee Stadium? Who hit a home run the first time he walked up to the plate wearing his famous number 3? What about his called shot in the 1932 World Series, whether he did it or not? Was there another player in baseball history who might even have dared do such a thing? And, Ruth thought, he had the perfect finish. He blew it.

Just five days earlier, Ruth had one of the finest games of his remarkable 22-year romp through the big leagues, swatting three home runs against the Pittsburgh Pirates. That included an extraordinary parting shot—the 714th of his career—a belt that cleared the entire stadium, the first fair ball ever hit over the right field roof at Forbes Field. Ruth left that game to a thunderous ovation. Why the hell didn't he keep on walking?

Former Red Sox outfielder Duffy Lewis, the Braves' traveling secretary, told the Babe right after that home run that he should quit and go out on top. Ruth's wife, Claire, told him the same thing. But Braves president Emil Fuchs, dangling the possibility of a managerial position over Ruth's head, lured him back. "There are people who want to see you, Babe," he'd tell him. He knew how badly Ruth wanted to be a big-league manager. And he knew his Braves, the worst team in baseball history, were an even worse draw without a fading Babe Ruth. Ruth had already threatened retirement two weeks before that magnificent day in Pittsburgh.

On May 12, with his average at a sickly .154 with only three home runs in 21 games, Ruth told Fuchs what he already knew—that he was washed up and wanted out right then and there. Fuchs insisted that Ruth go on the team's upcoming road trips to Pittsburgh, Cincinnati, and Philadelphia, all National League cities that were planning Babe Ruth Days for the former American League star. According to Fuchs, they'd already sold a lot of tickets. Since Ruth, a career American Leaguer, had never played in National League cities Pittsburgh or Cincinnati during the regular season, reluctantly, he agreed to make the trip.

But now, his knee aching, his batting average below .200, he knew it was a bad idea. Just like leaving New York.

When, in 1935, the New York Yankees dealt the aging Ruth to the worst team in baseball, the Boston Braves, just a few days after his 40th birthday, it seemed like the end was near. Ruth wanted to manage, but all the Yankees would offer him was a spot managing their Newark farm club. Ruth wasn't interested in that. So when Fuchs hinted that Ruth might be in consideration for a managerial role—if he earned it with a season of good behavior—that was all the Babe needed to hear.

When Ruth opened the 1935 season with a long home run off future Hall of Famer Carl Hubbell of the New York Giants in his first National League game—incidentally, Ruth's first game against Hubbell since Ruth was part of Hubbell's memorable All-Star Game whiff streak—Braves fans may have thought the old boy could turn back the clock.

Though Ruth had slid to a .288 average with 22 home runs and 84 RBI in his final year with the Yankees, maybe there was some kick left. The Braves—and Ruth—found out quickly that there wasn't. He was old, out of shape, and couldn't hit anymore. His teammates wanted no part of him. Had it been put to a vote, there's no question that Ruth's teammates on the Braves would have told him to leave.

He reported to spring training in St. Petersburg, Florida, at least 25 pounds overweight. He'd been wining and dining in Europe in the offseason. And at 40, he couldn't move or field his position. As the season continued, two Braves pitchers even planned to mutiny over his poor defensive play.

But as warm weather hit the Northeast in mid-May, Ruth's final week showed a bit of an upturn. The Babe rolled into Pittsburgh on May 23, a day that the Pirates chose to honor longtime Ruth pal Rabbit Maranville. Ruth went hitless in three trips in a 7–1 loss, but once sent Paul Waner to the fence where he made a leaping catch of Ruth's bid for a home run. As Waner trotted in, Ruth passed the 5-foot-8 "Big Poison" on the way out to his position and shook his head.

"Say, you're a mighty little fellow to be such a big thief," Ruth told Waner. The next afternoon, the Braves fell again, 7–6, and Ruth managed a single, his ninth hit of the season, but Waner again robbed him with a one-handed catch of a 400-foot drive.

But on that last great Saturday, Ruth had the last laugh for the last time. He homered off Pirates starter Red Lucas in the first, then singled off reliever Guy Bush, then homered again and in the seventh, hit one of the longest home runs of his career, a true grand finale—number 714—that cleared the right field pavilion. "He still had that swing," Bush remarked years later. "You could hear it go 'swish.'" Newspapers were ecstatic. "A prodigious clout that carried clean over the right-field grandstand that bounced into the street and rolled to Schenley Park," one account said.

Even the staid *New York Times* was gushing: "Rising to the glorious heights of his heyday, Babe Ruth, the Sultan of Swat, crashed out three home runs against the Pittsburgh Pirates Saturday afternoon but it was not enough."

Ruth was so excited by his third home run of the afternoon, he swung by the Pittsburgh dugout after rounding the bases. "Fellas," he told the stunned Pirate players, "that one felt good." It was only the second time in Babe's career that he had homered three times in a regular-season game—he also did it twice in the World Series. The only other time Babe hit three during the season was in Philadelphia's Shibe Park in 1930. On that day, in his fourth at-bat, Ruth waggishly took the first two strikes batting right-handed, before switching back to lefty and whiffing.

But the moment didn't linger. The following Sunday, the Braves played in Cincinnati and Ruth showed that Saturday's game was truly his last hurrah. He whiffed three times in a 6–3 loss on Babe Ruth Day before 24,300 fans. The next day, Ruth pinch-hit in the ninth inning of a 9–5 loss and walked. On that Tuesday, he went 0-for-2 in a 13–4 loss but scored a run, the 2,174th of his career, just 71 fewer than Ty Cobb, then the all-time leader. It was in that game that Ruth also stumbled, trying to go back and field a ball on the strange Crosley Field incline in left field. He fell flat on his face and left the game in a huff. The knee continued to bother him.

After an off-day, the Braves came into Philadelphia on Wednesday for Babe Ruth Day and Ruth went 0-for-1 in a rare 8–6 Braves win. Here he was the next afternoon, out in left field, his knee sore. He looked up and here was a shot off the bat of Philadelphia's Lou Chiozza in the gap. He tried to lunge after it but missed it and fell. The ball squirted to the wall, and Chiozza got to third. And suddenly, here was Ruth, walking in with a limp, calling for a replacement. The Babe never came back.

With Ruth trying to mend his knee, the Braves headed back to New York for a weekend series with the Giants. And in the meantime, Ruth got an invitation to go to a grand party for the new ocean liner *Normandie*. He wanted to go. The Braves said no. And the fight resulted in Ruth getting his unconditional release from the Braves on Sunday night in Boston.

It was headline stuff in Monday's *New York Times*: "Babe Ruth 'Quits' Braves and Is Dropped by Club." "The blow-off came today when Judge

Fuchs refused my request that I be allowed to go to New York Tuesday night for the Normandie celebration," Ruth told the *New York Times* Sunday night in Boston. "Here's my argument. I've got a bad leg, threatened with water on the knee unless I keep off it and can't play ball. We have an exhibition game [in Haverhill, Massachusetts] scheduled for tomorrow. I'm willing to go and hobble around in that to please the crowd. The game and my appearance have been advertised for a long time—and the Braves need the money.

"But I am not fit to play in a league game. . . . So when I received this special invitation . . . I thought it would be a great honor and that it would mean a great deal to the Braves if I attended. . . . When I put it up to the Judge, he said, 'Nothing doing!'

"Yes, I have just received my unconditional release from the Braves and I am mighty glad of it. . . . Now I'll go to the Normandie celebration on Tuesday night, and represent baseball—but not the Braves."

Braves president Fuchs sounded happy to get rid of him. "The matter came to a head today when Ruth requested permission to go to New York," Fuchs told the *Times*. "[Braves manager Bill] McKechnie felt, and I agreed with him, that Ruth's place was here, as we have games with the Dodgers on Tuesday and Wednesday. When permission was refused, Ruth did not take the refusal in a sportsmanlike way at all," Fuchs concluded. "For the sake of discipline, we could not give him the extra privileges he asked for."

At the same time Fuchs was announcing he was releasing Ruth, he also took advantage of the front-page publicity to announce that the struggling team was for sale. "I am willing to sacrifice the large equity I have in the Braves if some sportsman (who will get his reward, in my opinion, both financially and otherwise), or group of sportsmen, will come along and retain the outstanding players on our club, promise me they will not sell them to other cities, and that they will protect our small stockholders."

The newspapers were not kind to Babe regarding the matter. Gallico, generally a Ruth supporter, mocked the Babe in a nasty farewell column that ran in the *Chicago Tribune*. "There are two minor notes of appealing pathos in the quitting of Babe Ruth," he wrote. "The matter that brought this long-brewing retirement from the Boston Braves to a head was a little boy's fit of pique and disappointment because Judge Fuchs wouldn't let him go to what looks like a pretty swell party, the welcome to the S.S. Normandie.

"And in the Boston clubhouse, Ruth was quoted as saying, 'The team and [Manager Bill] McKechnie are swell. They are giving me a ball autographed by all the members of the team.' There is laughter in the first and tears in the second." If that's all the Braves had for one of the greatest players in the game's history, an autographed ball, Gallico hinted, shame on them.

"They call him Babe, and Babe he is," Gallico concluded. "Life to him is very often the life of a child and bosses are not bosses at all but grownups who interfere with his fun the way grownups always do. The greatest masters of men are those who treat them like well-loved children. Poor Babe. He wanted to go to a party where all the other kids were going."

Even crusty old John Kieran of the *New York Times* took a shot at both parties. "It seems that they won't stop swinging in baseball's Boston team party until everyone around the place has had a chance to come to bat and hit a loud foul," he wrote. "Let it go. Too much has been said on all sides. The Babe should have smiled and walked away. Judge Fuchs should have sent him off with a bouquet of flowers. Bill McKechnie should have gone on quietly without popping off. Each one had been doing his best with a plan that didn't pan out. The mistake they all made was to fill the parting of ways with the sound and sight of battle."

Fuchs's Braves finished the 1935 season with a record of 38-115, the worst record in the history of baseball until 1962's Amazin' Mets lost 120 games. The next night, The Babe went to the *Normandie* party.

This is what should have happened on May 25 at Pittsburgh's Forbes Field. The great Babe Ruth, then playing for the Boston Braves, clubbed the final three home runs of his glorious career, including number 714, the first ball hit out of Forbes Field. Instead, the Babe hung in for five more games, retiring after failing to chase down a drive by Lou Chiozza of the A's in Shibe Park. Babe's finale could have been so much better.
COURTESY OF THE NATIONAL BASEBALL HALL OF FAME LIBRARY

Babe Ruth by the Numbers

YEAR	TEAM	G	AB	R	H	TB	2B	3B	HR	RBI	BB	SO	SB	BA	SLG	OBP
1914	BSA	5	10	1	2	3	1	0	0	--	0	4	0	.200	.300	.200
1915	BSA	42	92	16	29	53	10	1	4	--	9	23	0	.315	.576	.376
1916	BSA	68	138	18	37	57	5	3	3	--	9	23	0	.268	.413	.313
1917	BSA	52	123	14	40	58	6	3	2	--	12	19	0	.325	.472	.385
1918	BSA	95	317	50	95	176	26	11	11	--	59	58	6	.300	.555	.413
1919	BSA	130	432	103	139	284	34	12	29	--	101	58	7	.322	.657	.456
1920	NYY	142	457	158	172	388	36	9	54	136	150	80	14	.376	.849	.534
1921	NYY	152	541	177	204	457	44	16	59	168	144	83	17	.377	.845	.511
1922	NYY	110	407	94	128	273	24	8	35	97	84	79	2	.314	.671	.433
1923	NYY	152	520	151	205	399	45	13	41	130	170	94	17	.394	.767	.546
1924	NYY	153	529	143	200	391	39	7	46	124	142	81	9	.378	.739	.513
1925	NYY	98	359	60	104	195	12	2	25	67	59	68	2	.290	.543	.393
1926	NYY	152	495	139	184	365	30	5	47	153	144	76	11	.372	.737	.516
1927	NYY	151	540	158	192	417	29	8	60	165	137	89	7	.356	.772	.486
1928	NYY	154	536	163	173	380	29	8	54	146	137	88	5	.323	.709	.463
1929	NYY	135	498	121	172	348	26	6	46	154	72	59	5	.345	.699	.431
1930	NYY	145	518	150	186	379	28	9	49	153	136	61	10	.359	.732	.493
1931	NYY	145	534	149	199	374	31	3	46	162	128	51	5	.373	.700	.495
1932	NYY	133	457	120	156	302	13	5	41	137	130	61	2	.341	.661	.489
1933	NYY	137	459	97	138	267	21	3	34	104	115	90	4	.301	.582	.443
1934	NYY	125	365	78	105	196	17	4	22	84	105	63	1	.288	.537	.449
1935	BSN	28	72	13	13	31	0	0	6	12	20	24	0	.181	.431	.359
TOTALS		2504	8399	2173	2873	5793	506	136	714	1992	2063	1332	124	.342	.690	.474

1916

CHRISTY MATHEWSON

"BIG SIX" MAKES A GREAT ESCAPE

DATE: September 4, 1916 (second game of Labor Day double-header)

SITE: Weeghman Park, Chicago, Illinois

OPPONENT: Mordecai "Three-Finger" Brown of the Chicago Cubs

RESULT: Complete-game 10–8 victory

The word "dashing" might well apply to the great Christy Mathewson, shown here in his New York Giants uniform. Mathewson's final pitching performance came in a Labor Day matchup between Mathewson, now managing the Cincinnati Reds, and the Chicago Cubs' Mordecai "Three-Finger" Brown. Both were well past their prime. Mathewson had three hits himself off Brown and gave up 14—including two to Brown—but Mathewson ended up a 10–8 complete-game winner.
COURTESY OF THE NATIONAL BASEBALL HALL OF FAME LIBRARY

Christy Mathewson stood on the mound quietly at Weeghman Park, watching Vic Saier trot around the bases. It was a helpless feeling, a feeling the great Mathewson rarely experienced on the hill. It was now 10–8, Cincinnati. But he still needed an out.

The home run was the seventh Saier had hit—more than any other player of Mathewson's time—off the fading ace right-hander. Though the game was winding down, Mathewson could hear 17,000 Cub fans let him know exactly how far his fadeaway had faded. What a way to wind up.

Barely two months into his new job as player-manager of the lowly Cincinnati Reds, the season nearly done, Mathewson hadn't really figured on pitching at all. He was trying to learn what it took to be a successful manager, like his old boss John McGraw.

With the team out of the pennant race, he considered the gate for his Labor Day doubleheader with the Chicago Cubs. Both teams were well out of pennant contention, so somebody—history doesn't record exactly who it was—had the wise idea to match up Mathewson one last time with his old Cubs rival, Mordecai "Three-Finger" Brown, then also playing out the string with the Cubs.

It was a stunt, sure. But the Mathewson-Brown matchup was the Ali-Frazier duel of their time. The two future Hall of Famers had faced off against each other many times through the years, and Brown had won 11 of them, including the famous playoff duel of 1908, the one caused by the infamous (Fred) Merkle boner, when he failed to touch second base on what appeared to be a game-winning hit during a key regular-season game. Mathewson had been the winning pitcher in 12 of their one-on-one contests.

So with a win, Brown would finally square the account with Mathewson, who was a fine pitcher and gentleman but also the darling of the New York media. They wrote about "Big Six" like he was a living legend, and their glowing words only served as fuel for Brown's competitive furnace. You didn't have to be a psychiatrist to read the envy in Brown's words as he talked about dueling the Giants great.

"I can still see Christy Mathewson making his lordly entrance," Brown wrote in his autobiography. "He'd always wait until about 10 minutes before game time, then he'd come in from the clubhouse across the field in a long linen duster like auto drivers wore in those days. At every step the crowd would yell louder and louder."

Brown never heard that kind of cheering, even though his 1908 season, the year he beat Mathewson in that playoff, was one of the finest in baseball history. He was 29-9, appeared in a league-leading 50 games, 32 complete games with nine shutouts, a league-leading five saves, working 312 innings, allowing just 214 hits and a glittering 1.31 ERA. He earned his money that year. With the end of the season approaching, Brown had pitched both ends of a doubleheader the day before the Giants' Fred Merkle failed to touch second base on a potential game-winning hit, a mistake that ended up propelling the Cubs into a neck-and-neck race with the slumping Giants.

In order to win the pennant for the Cubs, Brown had to pitch (and win) in 11 of the team's final 14 games to tie McGraw's Giants. He did.

It was Brown, too, who saved the Cubs in that 1908 playoff game and beat Matty.

It was a loss after which, some said, Mathewson wept. With the game set at New York's Polo Grounds, Cubs manager Frank Chance had the lame-brained idea to start little-known Jack Pfiester in that game. After the Giants pounced on him for one run and had the bases loaded with no outs, Chance had to frantically wave in Brown from the bench. Without so much as a warmup, Brown shut the Giants out the rest of the way to get the Cubs into the World Series. He would never forget what it was like at the finish of that game.

"As the ninth ended with the Giants going out one-two-three, we all ran for our lives, straight for the clubhouse with the pack at our heels," Brown wrote in his autobiography. "Some of our boys got caught by the mob and beaten up some. Pfiester got slashed on the shoulder by a knife. We made it to the dressing room and barricaded the door.

"Outside wild men were yelling for our blood—really. As the mob got bigger, the police came up and formed a line across the door. We read the next day that the cops had to pull their revolvers to hold them back. When it was safe we rode to our hotel in a patrol wagon, with two cops on the inside and four riding the running boards and the rear step.

"That night when we left for Detroit and the World Series, we slipped out the back door and were escorted down the alley in back of our hotel by a swarm of policemen."

Mathewson, a pitcher of such personal integrity that baseball legend has it that umpires sometimes would consult with him on a close play, seemed above that sort of thing. But he wasn't that September afternoon, standing on the hill as hits rained all over Weeghman Park.

As he looked around, seeing a game that he once had at his fingertips turning on him, he remembered the words he'd written for *Baseball Magazine* just a couple years earlier. "Strange impulses can grip a man as he stands on the pitcher's mound," Mathewson wrote. "There may be thousands of people in the stadium but for all practicable purposes the pitcher is alone. I mention this in relation to another subject that has been more or less a sore point with me. It has to do with those occasions when a pitcher, who has been working well all afternoon, will suddenly surrender a series of hits in a late inning."

This was a particularly sensitive spot with Mathewson, who was famous for "coasting" in one-sided games, much to the consternation of Giants manager John McGraw. "Often, at this point, the fans will start demanding that the manager take him out," he continued in the *Baseball Magazine* article. "I have heard more than one manager severely criticized by the fans for going along with a pitcher under these circumstances. It is my theory that the fans in instances such as this are too severe on both the pitcher and the manager.

"They are, in fact, ignoring the rules of chance that dominate the game. It is a mathematical certainty that over the course of any given season, batsmen including pitchers and weak hitters, will compile an over-all average of .250 against pitchers (take or give a few points). I am a great believer in these averages. Sooner or later they catch up with all of us."

They had caught up with him now. And he knew it. With old Mordecai over in the other dugout, itching for a chance to have the last laugh, Mathewson had to find a way to get out of this. Had to. He just needed one more out. It might have been Mordecai who pushed for the matchup. Maybe he figured he had one more game in him. A right-hander with a once-wicked curveball—he lost part of the index finger and thumb of his right hand in a farm accident as a child—he was a single game shy of breaking even with the great right-hander.

Nobody, it seemed, ever realized that. If he won this game, even with both of them washed up, they'd each have 12 wins against the other. Now, wouldn't that be a nice stat for Mathewson's adoring New York media? Brown had a point. He had beaten Mathewson 11 times in head-to-head meetings, including that memorable Cubs-Giants playoff game of 1908, a game played right in the Polo Grounds, Mathewson's home turf. But all you ever heard was Matty, Matty, Matty.

Tall, handsome, and college educated, Mathewson was always above the fray. But a win would not only deadlock their head-to-head matchups, it would also send Matty into retirement on a loss.

Weeghman Park was roaring. Mathewson looked around him. After Saier's home run, two more men were on. A home run would win it. Would this game ever end? He thought about what he read in the Chicago paper that day. There was an almost morbid fascination in watching how time had dealt with these two once-great hurlers.

"Gone are the days when Matty and Brownie could give the greatest batsmen in the game a winning argument nine times out of ten and when shutout scores were frequent when they performed," wrote I. E. Sanborn in the *Chicago Tribune*. "Gone was the fearsome and deadly hook with which the veteran of the Cub slab used to mow down his antagonists in the pinches; gone was the effectiveness of Matty's far famed fadeaway.

"Still, a great group of baseball rooters stood in the rain for an hour before time to start the games and, soon after it was decided to play, filled the plant. The dollar sign has not driven all the sentiment out of the nation's pastime."

He thought back over the game, one of the ugliest he was ever involved in. While the Reds were pounding Brown for 19 hits, with Mathewson (a career .215 hitter) collecting three of them, including a double, the Cubs responded by ripping 14 hits off Mathewson. Brown (a career .206 hitter) had two of them.

Though the Cubs jumped on Mathewson, pitching his first and only game for the Reds, for a pair of runs in the first, the Reds scored eight runs in the next six innings off Brown, sending Mathewson into the ninth with a 10–6 lead. One out away from a career-ending win, he faltered. It must have been a humbling feeling for a pitcher who had been so masterful for so many years.

How far he seemed from the pitcher Ring Lardner wrote about this way: "There's a flock o' pitchers that knows a batter's weakness and works accordin'. But they ain't nobody else in the world that can stick a ball as near where they want to stick it as he can. I bet he could shave you if he wanted to and if he had a razor blade to throw instead of a ball. If you can't hit a fast one inch and a quarter inside, and he knows it, you'll get three fast ones an inch and a quarter inside, and then, if you swang at 'em, you can go get a drink o' water.

"Take him in a common, ordinary ballgame, agin' an average club, and everyday pitchin' and what he's tryin' to do is stick the first one over so's he won't have to waste no more'n one ball on one batter. He don't stick it over right in the groove, but he puts it just about so's you'll get a piece of it and give the Giants a little easy fieldin' practice. If the Giants get a flock o' runs and goes way out in front, he'll go right on sticking that first one over, an' maybe he'll allow a little scorin'."

Well, there was plenty of scoring here. What would Ring Lardner have written about it? Mathewson, maybe for one of the few times in his career, was frightened. This was no way to end a career. A few years earlier, former Pittsburgh star Max Carey had written a piece about Mathewson that talked about his passion for the game.

"Mathewson has the ability and all that," Carey said. "But I believe the main factor that has held him up so long has been his love of the game. Thirteen years is a long time to be under fire. . . . But I've watched Mathewson closely and I've never seen him pitch a ballgame in which he didn't look as if he were having a lot of fun. He always looks as if he had rather be out there pitching than doing anything else. It doesn't look to be work with him, but only pure sport—an afternoon's romp as a businessman might go out to play golf or tennis. He either likes it immensely or is the greatest actor I ever saw."

He wondered what ol' Max would say now. Mathewson could already imagine the headlines in the next day's paper. "Washed-up Matty Collapses at Finish." "'Three-Finger' Gets Last Laugh." "Even Matty Can't Rescue Last-Place Reds."

But the Cubs weren't in the strong part of their batting order. He looked over at the dugout to see a pinch-hitter, Fritz Mollwitz, coming up for light-hitting Charlie Pechous (.145). Earlier, Pechous had hit his only double of the 1916 season off the once-great Mathewson. But Cubs manager Joe Tinker had a hunch and wanted to try Mollwitz, who was dealt from the Cincinnati club 65 games into the season. He was a light hitter (.241) with only one home run in a seven-year career as a part-time first baseman. But maybe he could keep the rally alive.

He wasn't on the Cincy club in July when Mathewson, outfielder Edd Roush, and infielder Bill McKechnie were dealt from the Giants for outfielder Red Killefer and former manager Buck Herzog. But Mathewson knew him. He had no power. He just wanted to make him hit it at somebody and get this endless game over with.

The big right-hander wound and threw the final pitch of his career. Mollwitz swung and lifted a harmless flyball to the outfield. The duel—and Mathewson's career—was over.

Christy Mathewson never pitched again. He managed the Reds until midway through the 1918 season, then left to fight in World War I. While in France, he inhaled some mustard gas and never fully recovered his health. Mathewson died at New York's Saranac Lake on October 7, 1925, just as the

World Series between the Pittsburgh Pirates and Washington Senators was getting under way.

A nation mourned the loss of the man who was probably baseball's first true superstar.

"While the captains and the kings of baseball were gathered here last night after the first game of a World Series, there died at Saranac the best loved of all the baseball players and the most popular of all American athletes of all time—Christy Mathewson," wrote W. O. McGeehan, sports editor of the *New York Tribune*. "Let none of us insult the memory of Christy Mathewson by making of him one of those sanctimonious and insufferably perfect heroes. He was a real man and essentially, a man's man. . . . He was the exalted man from whom every man wants to play the game straight and to carry his head high as a man who could learn something. He played for all that was in him, he fought the good fight and the clean fight. He was the incarnation of all those virtues with which we endow the ideal American."

Mathewson's death, coming as it did at the start of the World Series, seemed to jolt baseball fans far and wide. In the game stories of the World Series, there was more attention to Matty's death than to the game itself.

"John McGraw's gray head was tilted back as his eyes, wrinkled with the years, tried in vain to blink back the tears that came up with a rush. Billy Evans, who started his career soon after Matty started as a pitcher, bowed his head to the memory of a man who never had questioned a decision.

"Hughey Jennings, who was a grass-eating, fiery-haired manager of the Detroit Tigers when Matty was in his prime, made no pretense of hiding his handkerchief.

"Other thrills came later, as the innings went by and the crisis came and was passed. Through the innings the multitude's mind was on the action before them, but in the hearts of the throng was a deep, dull, dormant ache was that the still and silent Matty gone home."

Twenty years later, Mathewson was an original—and posthumous—inductee in the very first election for the new Baseball Hall of Fame in Cooperstown, New York. The perennially overlooked Mordecai "Three-Finger" Brown made the Hall, too. He was elected 10 years later, in 1949, just about exactly a year after he died in Terre Haute, Indiana, on Valentine's Day, 1948, at the age of 72.

Christy Mathewson by the Numbers

YEAR	TEAM	W	L	PCT	ERA	G	GS	CG	SHO	SV	IP	H	R	BB	SO
1900	NYG	0	3	.000	--	6	1	1	0	0	34.0	38	32	20	15
1901	NYG	20	17	.541	--	40	38	36	5	0	336.0	288	131	97	221
1902	NYG	14	17	.452	--	34	32	29	8	0	277.0	241	114	73	159
1903	NYG	30	13	.698	--	45	42	37	3	0	367.0	321	136	100	267
1904	NYG	33	12	.733	--	48	46	33	4	0	366.0	307	120	78	208
1905	NYG	31	9	.775	--	43	37	32	8	0	340.0	252	85	64	206
1906	NYG	22	12	.647	--	38	35	22	6	0	265.0	261	100	77	128
1907	NYG	24	12	.667	--	41	36	31	8	0	315.0	249	88	52	179
1908	NYG	37	11	.771	--	56	44	34	11	0	391.0	282	85	42	259
1909	NYG	25	6	.806	--	37	33	26	8	0	274.0	192	57	36	149
1910	NYG	27	9	.750	--	38	35	27	2	0	319.0	291	98	57	190
1911	NYG	26	13	.667	--	45	37	29	5	0	308.0	303	102	38	143
1912	NYG	23	12	.657	2.12	43	34	27	0	0	310.0	311	107	34	134
1913	NYG	25	11	.694	2.06	40	35	25	4	0	306.0	291	94	21	93
1914	NYG	24	13	.649	3.01	41	35	29	5	0	311.0	314	133	23	80
1915	NYG	8	14	.364	3.58	27	24	11	1	0	186.0	199	97	20	57
1916	NYG	3	4	.429	2.35	12	6	4	1	0	65.0	59	27	7	16
1916	CIN	1	0	1.000	8.00	1	1	1	0	0	9.0	15	8	1	3
1916	ALL	4	4	.500	3.04	13	7	5	1	0	74.0	74	35	9	19
TOTALS		373	188	.665	2.62	635	551	434	79	0	4779.0	4214	1614	840	2507

1928

TY COBB

THE LAST ANGRY MAN LEAVES QUIETLY

DATE: September 12, 1928

SITE: Yankee Stadium, New York, New York

PITCHER: Henry Johnson of the New York Yankees

RESULT: Popout to shortstop Mark Koenig

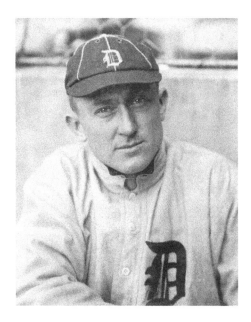

Ty Cobb had a different letter on his cap for his final season in the majors in 1928. He played for Connie Mack's Philadelphia A's along with future Hall of Famers Lefty Grove, Tris Speaker, and Eddie Collins. The Athletics made a good run at Babe Ruth's first-place Yankees, but faded in mid-September and dropped out of the race after losing a series in New York. Mack sent Cobb up as a pinch-hitter in the ninth and Cobb fouled out to third in his final at-bat. There were two weeks left in the season, but Cobb hung 'em up. He never played again.

COURTESY OF THE NATIONAL BASEBALL HALL OF FAME LIBRARY

Connie Mack, the gentlemanly manager of the Philadelphia Athletics, sitting ramrod stiff in his high celluloid collar and immaculate suit, motioned with his ever-present scorecard to the older man, sitting on the bench at the other end of the dugout.

"Ty, go up and hit for Jimmy," he said. Heads turned in the Philadelphia A's dugout. For one thing, Mack almost always called everyone "Son." For another, here was arguably baseball's greatest hitter, now being sent up as an afterthought pinch-hitter in a game, and now a season, lost.

Ty Cobb nodded and went up to pick out his bat. Dykes was supposed to lead off the ninth inning of a game the A's already trailed, 5–3. Cobb couldn't think about that now. His long and difficult career was finally at the end. The flame that had burned so hot and so brilliantly for so long was nearly out. He wasn't going to get back to a World Series.

He stepped out of the dugout on a Friday afternoon at Yankee Stadium, and the crowd of 50,000 erupted. Once the greatest player in baseball, he strode to the plate with the catcalls, the insults, the boos burning in his always sensitive ears. There was a time when their hatred fueled him and drove him to colossal, monomaniacal heights of baseball excellence. Not now. There was a bitterness in his mouth as he waited for a pitch. Denied again.

Maybe New York had had an extraordinary start to the 1928 season, winning 39 of its first 49 games—those 1927 Murderers' Row Yankees were still mostly intact. But once Mack's A's began to find themselves, they took over.

A clever blend of youth and experience, Mack's club put on a magnificent run, catching fire in July. Sparked by Lefty Grove's league-leading 24-win season and the combination of promising youngsters like Mickey Cochrane, Jimmie Foxx, and Al Simmons—all Hall of Famers—and old pros (and eventual Hall of Famers) like Cobb, Tris Speaker, and Eddie Collins, the A's came roaring back. By early September, they had taken over first place from Ruth and Gehrig and the mighty Yanks.

For Cobb, who came to Philadelphia only because he felt as though Mack could get him in one last World Series, this was what he'd hoped for. But when the A's couldn't hold their ground and the Yankees climbed back into first place, it all changed. Heading into this make-or-break series in New York, the A's, a game and a half out and a tough road schedule ahead, needed a sweep to have a chance to catch the Yankees. And in the morning, on paper, it looked good.

The A's started 24-game winner Grove, the best pitcher in baseball, while the Yanks started Henry Johnson, a marginal right-hander who, in the old phrase, had left no footprints on the sands of time. Johnson, in fact, had missed the entire 1927 season with arm trouble and had just four big-league starts prior to this season. But when the most important series of the season began in the Big Apple on a sunny September afternoon, Cobb and Speaker found themselves where Mack had put them since the middle of summer. On the bench. It made them sick.

Cobb had wanted to hang it up two seasons ago, after a difficult finish in Detroit as a player-manager and a betting controversy with the commissioner. Cobb and Speaker had been accused of betting on (and fixing) games in 1919 in a letter written by former pitcher Dutch Leonard.

The way the story went, Leonard told American League president Ban Johnson in the spring of 1926 that Cobb and Speaker had allegedly fixed a game late in the 1919 season. Perhaps fearing a Cobb outburst, Johnson waited until the season was over before he told Commissioner Kenesaw Mountain Landis of Leonard's charges. Landis suspended Cobb and Speaker for a while, then let them back on their respective rosters. Neither player was ever a manager again.

As a result, Cobb was ready to sue Landis. But when Mack came and visited him, the old man was able to convince Cobb that he had a team that could make a real run at the pennant. He also told him that he'd pay him a dollar more than Babe Ruth. Cobb couldn't say no.

Cobb and Mack got along surprisingly well. But the early moments had all the elements of a sparring session between two wary champions. Former Philadelphia sportswriter Al Horwits recalled in Jerome Holtzman's fine *No Cheering in the Press Box* that "Cobb hated to be told what to do. At first, when he was playing right field and Connie (Mack) waved his scorecard at him, Cobb acted as though he didn't see it. But finally Connie got him over there, and the very next batter hit the ball right at Cobb. He didn't have to move to catch it. He said afterwards he would never challenge the old man again."

That was just how Mack remembered it, too. "When Ty Cobb played his first game for the A's, I felt somewhat embarrassed," Mack wrote in his memoir, *My 66 Years in the Big Leagues*. "Here was the greatest player of his time, twenty-two years as the star fielder with Detroit and six years its able manager. He was noted as an expert on the strong and weak points of all the batters of all the other teams. I hesitated in giving orders to this great of the greats.

"However, I realized that I was responsible for the strategy of the game. A rival batter came to the plate. I felt that Ty knew where to play him, but it seemed to me that he was playing too far to the right of the batter. I was about to signal my pitcher to put the ball where, if hit, it would go far to the left of where Ty was standing.

"Standing up in the dugout, I waved to Ty with my scorecard to move over to the left. Everybody saw the signal. Even the pitcher turned and looked. What would the great Cobb do? Would he follow his judgment, or would he accept my decision? He saluted me as a soldier salutes a general and followed orders.

"Now I was on the spot. If the batter hit the ball to where Ty had been standing, I'd certainly look silly. Ty had barely reached the position I had designated when the batter walloped the ball. Where did it go? Right into the hands of Ty Cobb! Did I feel relieved? I'll say I did."

To Horwits, bringing Cobb and Speaker together for that 1928 season was a wise move—for business. "Bringing Cobb and Speaker together in 1928 for their last year was a great piece of showmanship. They didn't win the pennant for Connie. In fact, they didn't even finish the season as regulars. But they did a lot of business and were a great draw on the road, too."

Cobb had himself a fine 1927 season, playing in 134 games, hitting .357, fifth in the league. He drove in 93 runs, not bad for a 41-year-old. He tried for an encore in 1928 and hit decently. But the A's, like the rest of baseball, were no match for the Yankees. This series, at Yankee Stadium, was their last chance.

As expected, Mack's surging A's reached Yankees' no-name starter Johnson for two runs in the first, then added an unearned run in the fifth to stake the great Grove to a commanding 3–0 lead.

But after the Yanks got to Grove for one run in the seventh, Cobb suspected what would happen next. He'd seen it too many times before.

While the two old war eagles, he and Speaker, had to sit and squirm, the A's just collapsed behind the tempestuous Grove in the bottom of the eighth. There was a Grove walk, a groundball that bounced off Dykes's shins, then a wild throw past Jimmie Foxx at first to put a runner on third. The knot was tightening.

Grove wild-pitched the second run in, making a 3–2 game. When Lou Gehrig tried to duck out of the way of a Grove inside pitch, it clicked off his bat into left field for a lucky single. The crowd was electric. After Gehrig went to second on a bad throw, up stepped Ruth with a chance to break it open. Nobody hated Ruth more than Cobb, who hollered at him from the bench. This was it right here.

First, Ruth tried to cross up Grove by dropping down a surprise sacrifice bunt. It rolled foul by inches. On Grove's next pitch, Ruth drove the ball high and deep into the right field seats for his 49th home run—he went on to whack 54 that season—and the race was all but over. The Yankee Stadium crowd burst into cheers for the Babe. Cobb sat and sizzled.

Ruth had always gotten the better of Cobb. Once, in 1921, when Cobb was really giving it to Ruth from the Tiger dugout, Ruth clubbed seven home runs in a five-game series. To top it off, The Babe volunteered to come in and pitch in the last game of the series. He struck Cobb out.

Cobb had always hated the way Ruth's long-distance hits changed the game Cobb seemed to have mastered. What bothered him more was the way Ruth was loved everywhere he went, by fans, newspapermen, everybody.

One year, Cobb, fed up with all the attention going to Ruth, told the newspapermen that he could play that game if he wanted to. With his Tigers stuck in last place having lost 14 of its first 19 games and Ruth grabbing headlines every day, the Tigers star pulled *Detroit News* writer H. G. Salsinger and a few others aside before a May 5 game at Sportsman's Park in St. Louis. He told them to watch. He was going deep.

"Gentlemen," Cobb said, "I would like you to pay particular attention today because for the first time in my career, I will be deliberately going for home runs." He got them, too. Cobb whacked three home runs and went 6-for-6 in a Tiger win. The next day, he hit two other balls out of the ballpark, giving him five in two games and a major-league record for total bases (16) that stood for years. His point illustrated, Cobb then went back to his usual slashing style and hit just 17 more home runs over the remaining three and a half seasons of his career.

Here, in Yankee Stadium, he could hear the bench jockeys as he approached the plate. Cobb took a long look around at the House Ruth Built. Why didn't anybody build a house for him? Cobb had more hits, more batting titles, more steals, more runs. As he stepped in, Cobb knew he was hitting .324 in 95 games, which wasn't bad. But he and Speaker had barely played down the stretch as Mack went with the younger men. It was somebody else's team now. And Cobb was starting to realize there would be no World Series. It had been nearly 20 years since his last one in 1909, the last of three straight Series losses for Cobb's Tigers. He was just a kid then. He'd have lots of World Series ahead of him, he figured. Wrong.

Over his shoulder, he could see Mack had sent another veteran, future Hall of Famer Eddie Collins, out to the on-deck circle to hit next. Must be Old Home Week, he thought. Cobb looked out at Henry Johnson and waited for the next pitch. He stood there, flexing his strange hands-apart grip on the bat, staring out at the young right-hander who was born in 1906, the year Cobb really hit the big time with Detroit.

With the pitch heading his way, Cobb swung for the final

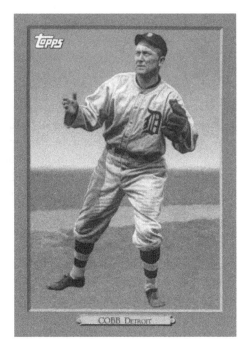

time, chasing a high pitch, lifting a popup into foul territory over and behind third base. Yankee shortstop Mark Koenig drifted over and made the catch. When Collins also fouled out to Koenig, a carbon copy of Cobb's final out, pinch-hitter Walt French followed with a flyball to Bob Meusel and the game—and the race—was over. The Yanks' lead went to 2½ games and stayed there for the rest of the season. After 3,034 games, 11,447 at-bats, and 4,192 hits, Cobb never played in the majors again.

Though there were two weeks left in the season, Cobb had vowed that once the A's were out of the race he would leave the team. Once the team sadly left New York, their World Series hopes gone for good, that's just what he did.

Ty Cobb by the Numbers

YEAR	TEAM	G	AB	R	H	TB	2B	3B	HR	RBI	BB	SO	SB	BA	SLG	OBP
1905	DET	41	150	19	36	45	6	0	1	—	10	—	2	.240	.300	.287
1906	DET	98	358	45	113	144	14	7	1	—	19	—	23	.316	.402	.355
1907	DET	150	605	99	212	286	29	15	5	—	24	—	54	.350	.473	.380
1908	DET	150	583	88	188	276	36	20	4	—	34	—	39	.322	.473	.366
1909	DET	156	574	115	216	296	33	10	9	—	48	—	78	.376	.516	.430
1910	DET	140	511	106	196	281	35	13	8	—	64	—	65	.384	.550	.456
1911	DET	146	592	148	248	367	47	24	8	—	44	—	83	.419	.620	.466
1912	DET	140	553	119	227	324	30	23	7	—	43	—	61	.410	.586	.458
1913	DET	122	429	70	167	229	18	16	4	—	60	31	52	.389	.534	.469
1914	DET	98	345	69	127	177	22	11	2	—	58	22	35	.368	.513	.467
1915	DET	156	563	144	208	274	31	13	3	—	118	43	96	.369	.487	.486
1916	DET	145	543	113	201	267	31	10	5	—	78	39	68	.370	.492	.451
1917	DET	152	588	107	225	335	44	24	6	—	63	34	55	.383	.570	.446
1918	DET	111	421	81	161	217	19	14	3	—	41	21	34	.382	.515	.440
1919	DET	124	498	92	191	256	36	13	1	—	40	22	28	.384	.514	.430
1920	DET	112	429	87	143	193	28	8	2	65	59	29	15	.333	.450	.415
1921	DET	128	507	124	197	302	37	16	12	101	56	19	22	.389	.596	.452
1922	DET	137	526	99	211	297	42	16	4	99	56	23	9	.401	.565	.462
1923	DET	145	556	103	189	261	40	7	6	90	66	14	9	.340	.469	.413
1924	DET	155	625	114	211	281	38	10	4	79	85	18	23	.338	.450	.418
1925	DET	121	415	97	157	248	31	12	12	103	67	12	13	.378	.598	.470
1926	DET	79	233	48	79	119	18	5	4	62	26	2	9	.339	.511	.408
1927	PHA	133	490	104	175	236	32	7	5	94	67	11	22	.357	.482	.440
1928	PHA	95	353	54	114	151	26	4	1	40	34	16	6	.323	.428	.389
TOTALS		3034	11447	2245	4192	5862	733	298	117	733	1260	356	901	.366	.512	.433

JACKIE ROBINSON

FIRE'S OUT FOR TRAILBLAZER ROBINSON

DATE: October 10, 1956 (Game 7 of the 1956 World Series)

SITE: Ebbets Field, Brooklyn, New York

PITCHER: Johnny Kucks of the New York Yankees

RESULT: Strikeout to end game, series, season

WHen he stepped out of the Ebbets Field dugout, the stadium was emptying and it seemed like he could hear most of the city crying.

Brokenhearted Dodger fans were again cursing their World Series luck, heading home sadly to a lousy dinner and another lousy offseason. As it turned out, Brooklyn's very last World Series game in cozy Ebbets Field was just about to come to a close. Jackie Robinson, due up third, couldn't have known what lay ahead for him or his franchise. Not just the last at-bat of the World Series and the last at-bat of the 1956 season. It would also be his final at-bat in the big leagues.

The journey that had begun with so much drama so long ago was finally about to end. What a rotten ending. To think that the night before, early Tuesday evening, his dramatic 10th-inning hit against the New York Yankees—repaying them for an earlier insult—had forced a Game 7 here in Brooklyn, lifting the hearts of Dodger Nation. That title last year wasn't a fluke; they were going to win it again. After all those losses to the Yankees, Brooklyn was going to start a dynasty of its own. There was going to be one more game for the baseball championship.

Yeah, Dem Bums were coming back, starting 27-game winner Don Newcombe in ol' Ebbets Field against whomever the Bronx Bombers would trot out. Didn't matter. Brooklyn was going to do it again and send that stuck-up, pinstriped mob back across town to stew on a Game 7 loss all winter.

Except it didn't quite work that way. Not at all. Robinson knelt down in the on-deck circle and could hear how quiet the park was. Ebbets Field wasn't usually like that. Even in a loss. The hurt was palpable. And constant, it seemed, when the Yankees were involved.

After the Dodgers had jumped out to a 2–0 Series lead, the Yanks won the next two games. Then in Game 5, New York's Don Larsen had thrown a perfect game, completely silencing the already near-dead Dodger bats and moving the Yankees within a victory of the title.

But in Game 6, the Dodgers fought back with one of the most stirring triumphs in franchise history to set the stage for this dramatic Game 7.

On Tuesday, Dodgers manager Walt Alston had sent reliever Clem Labine to the mound to face New York fireballer Bob Turley, and the two of them put on a pitching display to nearly rival Larsen's brilliance. Labine hadn't started a game since the second game of the 1951 playoffs vs. the Giants, and Turley was razor sharp. And neither team was hitting.

Through nine pressure-packed scoreless innings, the tension rose over Ebbets Field like a magnetic field. In the bottom of the eighth, Labine himself clouted a double, the only extra-base hit of the day for the weak-hitting Dodgers. After two outs, Yankees manager Casey Stengel ordered Duke Snider walked to put it all on Jackie Robinson's shoulders, to see if the proudest Dodger could force a Game 7 with a clutch hit.

The Brooklyn fans were aghast. True, it hadn't been that great a season at the plate for Robinson—he hit only .275 and in the World Series, he was just 6-for-24 (.250). But walking someone to face Jackie Robinson? This time, the Yankee fireballer won the battle, getting Robinson to pop out, preserving the scoreless tie.

The situation repeated itself in the 10th inning with the game still scoreless. Again, Stengel ordered Snider walked to face Robinson once again with the game on the line. Triumphantly, Robinson came through, lashing a rocket over the head of Yankees left fielder Enos Slaughter—his final big-league hit—and Junior Gilliam came all the way around to give the Dodgers a 1–0 10-inning thriller and set up a Game 7 back in Brooklyn with their 27-game winner on the hill.

After a victory like that, how could the Dodgers not win? Robinson quietly shook his head. He looked up at the scoreboard and saw all zeroes on the Brooklyn side.

The Yankees had a run for every inning, leading 9–0. It all seemed a cruel joke.

He took one last long look around the ballpark, the signs along the left field wall, "Brass Rail," and "Luckies Taste Better," and "Stadlers," and, of course, the "Van Heusen Shirts" sign out in right-center field. He could see the two-tiered stands, the World Series banners ruffling emptily in the cool October breeze, all nearly deserted now. There had been so much optimism in the place just a couple hours ago. Where did it all go wrong?

In his very first big-league season—1947—Jackie Robinson had led the Dodgers into the World Series, and they lost to New York in seven games. Here he was, leaving the same way. Well, almost the same.

In that 1947 World Series, the Yankees broke it open at the finish of that Game 7 to take a 5–2 win and take the title. At least, it was close for a while. Wednesday's box score wouldn't be as kind.

At first, it looked so good for the Dodgers. They were going to start 27-game winner Don Newcombe, while New York manager Casey Stengel decided to bypass veteran ace Whitey Ford to go with skinny right-hander Johnny Kucks, an 18-game winner during the regular season. Kucks wasn't bad, but he hadn't been able to win a game in over a month.

Though Newcombe bore the tag of a man who couldn't win the big one, surely he'd shake that 0-3 World Series mark here. This was a different Dodger team, wasn't it? Maybe not.

There were other off-the-field indications that Newcombe might not have been the Dodgers' best choice. When he had been shelled earlier in the Series, he was so upset about it that he got into a brawl with a parking lot attendant on the way home. His final World Series start wasn't much better.

Hank Bauer opened the game with a single and stole second. Newcombe fanned Billy Martin and then Mickey Mantle. He got an 0-2 count on Yogi Berra, just one strike away from getting out of the inning unscathed. But his third pitch to the little catcher was one he'd always regret. He fired a high fastball, a fat one, and Berra lined it over the right field fence. 2–0, New York.

In the third, Berra did it to him again, ripping another two-run homer to make it 4–0, Yankees. The Brooklyn fans were crestfallen. When Elston Howard blasted a Newcombe pitch into the seats in the fourth to make it 5–0, Alston had seen enough and gave him the hook. So, from the sound of it, had Brooklyn's faithless.

As Newcombe slowly walked off the mound, the Dodger fans cut loose with such a chorus of boos, even the Yankees were appalled. "I feel great that we won," Whitey Ford said afterward, "but it was awful the way the fans booed him. Why should they boo a guy who did so much for them this year?"

Newcombe was a good symbol for the Dodgers on this day, Robinson could see that. He was one of the best pitchers in baseball, everybody knew that. And the Dodgers were one of baseball's best teams. But they weren't quite as good as the Yankees. And never would be. This final time the Yankees would triumph in a World Series over the Dodgers during Robinson's career—this 1956 title—assured that.

Writing for the *New York Herald Tribune*, the famed columnist Red Smith began his column with the departure of Newcombe, too.

"This is a game for boys, and Don Newcombe is no kid," Smith wrote. "He is large and grumpy and not necessarily the most cuddly character in baseball. He is mean to hitters and a soft touch for gossips who have made him the victim of a cruel slander. Because the Dodgers' big pitcher can win 27 games in the National League but has never won one in a World Series, they call him a coward, a choke-up guy.

"It isn't true, but now he may never have a chance to prove it false. . . . They booed Newcombe out of the park."

"'Calling all parking lot attendants,' the funnymen in the press box were shouting as the big guy shambled off. 'All parking lot attendants—take cover!' It wasn't exactly hilarious."

Robinson could feel that anger, that sense of betrayal, kneeling in the on-deck circle, looking at Kucks. Thanks to that 9–0 score, the same as a forfeit, Robinson wondered how many sarcastic sportswriters would note it in their dispatches the next day. Many did.

Robinson thought about the other times he'd faced the Yankees in the World Series. Five different times in a 10-year career. He lost in five games in 1941 and 1949 and lost in seven in 1947 and 1952. Now this. A Game 7 loss in 1956. Damn.

He looked up to see Snider rifle a shot back through the box, only the Dodgers' third hit off Kucks. It was now up to him. He dug in, looked out at the right-hander, saw Berra behind him, Newcombe's tormentor, and tried to focus. It went by too quickly.

Suddenly he had two strikes on him and Kucks's pitch was on its way, sinking and twisting. Robinson swung and missed. The ball hit the dirt, Berra trapped it and Robinson had to run. He got a couple steps off, saw Berra's throw snap into Bill Skowron's mitt, and stopped. It was over.

All over.

The Yankees were world champs again. Brooklyn's reign as world champs lasted but a year. A fluky year. Robinson's heart ached as he watched the Yankees celebrate again. On his field.

A little over two months later—64 days to be exact—the Dodgers, figuring it was time to break up their aging club, dealt Robinson—with no warning or previous discussion—to the New York Giants for Dick Littlefield and $30,000. Everyone, including Jackie, was shocked by the move.

Jackie ROBINSON
second base BROOKLYN DODGERS

"It is impossible to think of Robinson except as a Dodger," wrote Red Smith in the *Herald-Tribune*. "Other players move from team to team and can change uniform as casually as the Madison Avenue space cadet sheds his weekday flannels for his weekend Bermuda shorts. His arrival in Brooklyn was a turning point in the history and the character of the game; it may not be stretching things to say it was a turning point in the history of this country."

One month later, Robinson had decided to retire. Instead of sharing the news with the New York press, he cashed in his chips and sold his exclusive story to *Look* magazine, stiffing the voracious newspapermen who, throughout his career, had built him into a folk hero.

Smith, naturally, was one of the first to let off steam. "The fact that he gave [the Dodgers] full value on the field and the fact that after 11 years, they sold his contract without consulting him, these do not alter the fact that everything he has he owes to the club," he wrote. "If it is true that Jackie Robinson has, for a price, deliberately crossed his friends and employers past and present, then it requires an eloquent advocate, indeed to make a convincing defense for him. From here, no defense at all is discernible."

That was nothing. The next year, the team left Brooklyn forever.

The strikeout by the way, was somewhat unusual for Robinson, a player who fanned just 291 times in 4,877 big-league at-bats. It was a heck of a way to end a World Series, a season, a career. It was also, some fans noted later, Kucks's only strikeout of the game.

Jackie Robinson by the Numbers

YEAR	TEAM	G	AB	R	H	TB	2B	3B	HR	RBI	BB	SO	SB	BA	SLG	OBP
1947	BRK	151	590	125	175	252	31	5	12	48	74	36	29	.297	.427	.383
1948	BRK	147	574	108	170	260	38	8	12	85	59	37	22	.296	.453	.369
1949	BRK	156	593	122	203	313	38	12	16	124	86	27	37	.342	.528	.432
1950	BRK	144	518	99	170	259	39	4	14	81	80	24	12	.328	.500	.423
1951	BRK	153	548	106	185	289	33	7	19	88	79	27	25	.338	.527	.429
1952	BRK	149	510	104	157	237	17	3	19	75	106	40	24	.308	.465	.440
1953	BRK	136	484	109	159	243	34	7	12	95	74	30	17	.329	.502	.425
1954	BRK	124	386	62	120	195	22	4	15	59	63	20	7	.311	.505	.413
1955	BRK	105	317	51	81	115	6	2	8	36	61	18	12	.256	.363	.378
1956	BRK	117	357	61	98	147	15	2	10	43	60	32	12	.275	.412	.382
TOTALS		1382	4877	947	1518	2310	273	54	137	734	742	291	197	.311	.474	.409

WALTER JOHNSON

THE BIG TRAIN REACHES THE STATION

DATE: September 12, 1927

SITE: Griffith Park, Washington, DC

OPPONENT: Sam Jones of the St. Louis Browns

RESULT: Knocked out of box in fourth inning

Washington Senators great Walter Johnson might well have gone down in history the way Boston Red Sox great Ted Williams did—with a home run in his final at-bat. Johnson had homered off Sad Sam Jones in his final pitching effort (against the St. Louis Browns), a game he was unable to finish. A few days later in New York, teammate Tom Zachary surrendered Babe Ruth's record-setting 60th home run and was due up in the ninth. Fearing an overwhelming—and literal—Bronx cheer, Senators manager Bucky Harris sent Johnson up to hit for him. The Senators great stepped to the plate one last time and hit a fly ball to—you guessed it—Babe Ruth.

COURTESY OF THE NATIONAL BASEBALL HALL OF FAME LIBRARY

He could see Bucky Harris get up from the bench. Walter Johnson sighed. It was over. He looked over at St. Louis Browns outfielder little Harry Rice at first, saw the 6–1 Browns lead on the scoreboard, and waited for Senators manager Harris to get to the hill.

After all those innings—5,925—stretched over 21 mostly brilliant seasons, the Big Train had reached the station. Johnson had faced his final big-league hitter, just two years after he'd pitched the Senators to their only World Series title.

Here, the lowly Browns had chased him with a three-run fourth on hits by Spencer Adams, doubles by Wally Gerber and pitcher "Sad" Sam Jones, and Rice's RBI single. The express train of the Johnson fastball had slowed like a trolley. After 802 games, after nine straight 300-inning seasons—and just 13 innings away from a dozen straight years of 300-plus innings of work—the arm was finally gone. The numbers in this final outing—nine hits and six runs in 3⅓ innings of work—were just not the kind of thing you expected from Walter Johnson.

Two weeks from the end of the year, everyone could see that this would be his final season. His numbers—a 5-6 record, a 5.08 ERA, nearly three runs per game higher than his career totals (2.17), only 48 strikeouts in 107.2 innings—those weren't Walter Johnson numbers.

Remember, this was a guy who, in 1913, amassed one of the most extraordinary pitching records in baseball history, a 36-7 record with 29 complete games, 11 shutouts, 346 innings of work, and most amazing of all, just 38 walks—in the entire season!

His last season hadn't been much fun for the veteran. A line drive off the bat of Joe Judge had broken his leg in preseason and thanks to the combination of that injury and his age, Johnson never regained his old form. Though Harris gave him one last shot to even his record after a lengthy rest, Johnson didn't have enough stuff left to squeeze by the Browns, one of the weakest teams in the American League. He found that out early.

St. Louis reached Johnson for a run in the second inning, thanks to errors by Harris and Goose Goslin, Spencer Adams's single, and Gerber's sacrifice fly. The Browns added two more in the third on a single by Homer Rice, a George Sisler double, and a Ken Williams single. Once Johnson was chased in the third, he heard the crowd applauding politely as he walked into the dugout. It wasn't much of a way to wind up a career.

He didn't get the loss, though, thanks to St. Louis's atrocious defense, by far the worst in the majors in that 1927 season. The Browns made 248 errors and committed four against the Senators that afternoon, allowing Harris's club to rally for a win. By then, Johnson was just an onlooker.

Happily, his teammates rallied right away after he was knocked out of the box, making sure that he would not go out as the losing pitcher. The Senators pounced on St. Louis starter "Sad" Sam Jones for six runs to take back the lead.

There was one nice thing about what would be the final pitching performance of Johnson's career. When he stepped up to the plate in the third inning, he belted a Jones pitch into the left field seats, his second home run of the season and 24th and last of his big-league career.

So if this was to be his final season, he had homered in what looked like his final at-bat, just like Ted Williams would do—to considerably more fanfare—33 years later. At the time, Johnson was batting .350 and ranked second among American League pitchers in hitting. He played 15 games as an outfielder for the Senators throughout his long career. As it turned out, that wasn't Johnson's final at-bat.

His very last big-league appearance came in a historic game against the New York Yankees on September 30, when Johnson was sent up as a pinch-hitter for Senators starter Tom Zachary in the ninth inning.

The Senators were 85-68, a respectable third-place club, facing the Murderers' Row Yankees, who had won a record 109 ballgames. The Senators had to close out the season in New York while Babe Ruth was on a home-run rampage. With a typically dramatic finish, Ruth had been clubbing home runs at a record pace. He came into the next-to-last game of the regular season having tied his own major-league mark of 59 home runs.

Senators' left-hander Zachary was the man charged with trying to keep Ruth from breaking the record. And he made it through seven innings without giving Ruth anything worth hitting. The Babe had managed two scratch singles and a walk.

But in the eighth, Ruth came up for what surely would be the final time that next-to-last day of the regular season. Amazingly, he picked a Zachary screwball off his shoetops and put it in the right field bleachers for his record-setting 60th. The Yankee Stadium crowd erupted.

As W. B. Hanna described it in the *New York Tribune*, "This one broke over the plate and was a screwball until it met the Babe's unruly bat. After that, it was a minie ball. It didn't go high and it did go on a line. Bill Dineen, the umpire, crouched on the foul line and peered carefully into the distance to see whether it was fair or foul. It buried itself in the bleachers 15 rows from the top and was fair by not more than six inches. Still, it was fair, and the record was broken."

After Ruth had crossed home plate, the Bronx crowd started in on Zachary, a 31-year-old left-hander who'd been traded to the Senators from the Browns. They didn't let up, even after he got the third out and headed for the Senators dugout. He was due up in the ninth but Harris spared him any further humiliation.

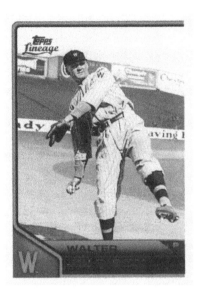

"Walter, go up and hit for him," Senators manager Bucky Harris said. And Johnson went to get his bat. He lifted a medium-range flyball to the guy who had just gotten the New York crowd into a frenzy, Babe Ruth. Two outs later, the game was over and so was Johnson's big-league playing career.

When he retired, he was second in lifetime wins (417) behind Cy Young's unapproachable 511, first in shutouts (110) and strikeouts (3,509), seventh in earned run average (2.17), fifth in complete games (531), third in innings pitched (5,914), and fourth in games pitched (802).

Some 80-plus years after his 110th shutout, he still has a 20-shutout lead on his closest rival, Hall of Famer Grover Cleveland Alexander, who threw 90. Of modern era pitchers, Warren Spahn heads the list with 63.

Johnson went on to manage the Senators from 1929 to 1932 and the Cleveland Indians from 1933 to 1935. He was elected to the Baseball Hall of Fame in 1936 and died of a brain tumor 10 years later.

In his prime, his peers said there was nobody better. "Did you ever see those pitching machines they have?" asked former Detroit Tigers outfielder Sam "Wahoo" Crawford in *The Glory of Their Times*. "That's what Walter Johnson always reminded me of, one of those compressed air pitching machines. Boy, what a pitcher [he] was. He was the best I ever faced."

His Tiger teammate, Davy Jones—the first batter to face Johnson in a big-league game—agreed.

"Boy, could he fire that ball. He had those long arms, absolutely the longest arms I ever saw. They were like whips; that's what they were. He'd whip that ball in there."

Yet he had a gentle spirit. Shirley Povich, the esteemed baseball writer of the *Washington Post* who had seen Johnson's entire career, said this at his passing. "Walter Johnson, more than any other ballplayer, probably more than any other athlete, professional or amateur, became the symbol of gentlemanly conduct in the battle heat. Here was the man who never argued with an umpire, never cast a frowning look at an error-making teammate, never presumed that it was his right to win, was as unperturbed in defeat."

Povich marveled at his kindness with fans with a story that has lived on—just like the Big Train. "Joe Judge, Johnson's roommate, had persuaded the 'Big Train' to go to a movie after dinner," he wrote. "Leaving the dining room, Johnson was button-holed by a fan in the lobby. Judge, standing apart, watched them talk for 15 minutes.

"When Johnson finally broke away, Judge was exasperated. 'We might not make the last show now. What on earth were you two talking about?' 'That fellow,' said Johnson, 'said he was from Kansas and was asking about my sister. I had to be nice to him.'

"'I never knew you had a sister,' Judge said. 'That's right,' said Johnson, 'I don't, but I had to be nice to him.'"

Walter Johnson by the Numbers

YEAR	TEAM	W	L	PCT	ERA	G	GS	CG	SHO	SV	IP	H	R	BB	SO
1907	WAS	5	9	.357	--	14	12	11	2	0	110.1	100	35	20	71
1908	WAS	14	14	.500	--	36	30	23	6	0	256.1	194	75	53	160
1909	WAS	13	25	.342	--	40	36	27	4	0	296.1	247	112	84	164
1910	WAS	25	17	.595	--	45	42	38	8	0	370.0	262	92	76	313
1911	WAS	25	13	.658	--	40	37	36	6	0	322.1	292	119	70	207
1912	WAS	33	12	.733	--	50	37	34	7	0	369.0	259	89	76	303
1913	WAS	36	7	.837	1.14	48	36	29	11	0	346.0	232	56	38	243
1914	WAS	28	18	.609	1.72	51	40	33	9	0	371.2	287	88	74	225
1915	WAS	27	13	.675	1.55	47	39	35	7	0	336.2	258	83	56	203
1916	WAS	25	20	.556	1.90	48	38	36	3	0	369.2	290	105	82	228
1917	WAS	23	16	.590	2.21	47	34	30	8	0	326.0	248	105	68	188
1918	WAS	23	13	.639	1.27	39	29	29	8	0	326.0	241	71	70	162
1919	WAS	20	14	.588	1.49	39	29	27	7	0	290.1	235	73	51	147
1920	WAS	8	10	.444	3.13	21	15	12	4	0	143.2	135	68	27	78
1921	WAS	17	14	.548	3.51	35	32	25	1	0	264.0	265	122	92	143
1922	WAS	15	16	.484	2.99	41	31	23	4	0	280.0	283	115	99	105
1923	WAS	17	12	.586	3.48	42	34	18	3	0	261.0	263	112	73	130
1924	WAS	23	7	.767	2.72	38	38	20	6	0	277.2	233	97	77	158
1925	WAS	20	7	.741	3.07	30	29	16	3	0	229.0	217	95	78	108
1926	WAS	15	16	.484	3.63	33	33	22	2	0	260.2	259	120	73	125
1927	WAS	5	6	.455	5.10	18	15	7	1	0	107.2	113	70	26	48
TOTALS		417	279	.599	2.17	802	666	531	110	0	5914.1	4913	1902	1363	3509

JOE JACKSON

SHOELESS JOE GETS CALLED OUT

DATE: September 27, 1920

SITE: Comiskey Field, Chicago, Illinois

PITCHER: George Hauss of the Detroit Tigers

RESULT: Game-winning double

Joseph Jefferson "Shoeless Joe" Jackson wound up what might have been a Hall of Fame career with a game-winning two-bagger off George "Hooks" Dauss in the sixth inning of a scoreless game against the Detroit Tigers on September 27, 1920. The hit made a winner out of Dickie Kerr, the White Sox hurler who won two games in the infamous 1919 World Series, dumped by the White Sox to the Cincinnati Reds. Jackson, along with seven other White Sox teammates, was banned for life by Commissioner Kenesaw Mountain Landis the day after their acquittal in a 1921 trial. COURTESY OF THE NATIONAL BASEBALL HALL OF FAME LIBRARY

By now, the noise was deafening. So persistent, so unmistakable, there seemed to be no way to keep it quiet any longer. "Shoeless Joe" Jackson stepped out of the dugout at Comiskey Park and looked around him. He could just feel it.

The season was almost over. They were just a game behind the Cleveland Indians, just one game, and they could do it. Here it was, the sixth inning of a scoreless duel with Detroit and a win might put them right at the top of the standings.

He hefted his trusty 48-ounce bat, "Black Betsy," and looked out at George "Hooks" Dauss, the Detroit Tigers' starter, who had just hit Buck Weaver with a pitch. With number three hitter Eddie Collins up next, maybe Collins could get Weaver into scoring position and Jackson would get a chance to give his club, charging hard at the American League pennant, the lead. Not only in this game but also in the American League race.

Jackson hefted the bat again. It was hard to think about only baseball. He wasn't reading the newspapers, that was for sure. Shoeless Joe couldn't read. But he could hear the talk. Everywhere he went. He knew this kettle was about to boil over.

Ever since Jackson and the rest of Kid Gleason's heavily favored Chicago "Black Sox" had fumbled away the 1919 World Series to the Cincinnati Reds, there had been talk in town that things weren't on the square. Of course, they weren't. And now, thanks to the damn Cubs and their gambling talk, it was everywhere. It wouldn't go away. Ever.

Back at the start of the month, there was a story in the *Chicago Tribune* about an attempted fix of a midweek game between the Cubs and Phillies. Cubs management, eager to dispel the notion that there was anything shady about that game—they'd seen the World Series the year before—pitched ace Grover Cleveland Alexander out of turn and even offered him a $500 bonus if he won. But Alexander lost. The stench from the story seemed to linger in the Windy City.

A week later, with the White Sox surging, the *Tribune's* I. E. Sanborn was able to write like a prophet. "Procrastination has proven the thief of something more valuable than time in the case of professional baseball versus gambling," he wrote. "It has cost the game a considerable portion of its good reputation. . . . If the promoters of professional baseball had heeded the warnings dinned into their ears for years against the inroads of the betting fraternity on their business they would have headed off much of the trouble that has come to them, and which is still coming to them."

Jackson heard the talk in the locker room. He was worried. He knew he shouldn't have come to the big league all those years ago. He first played in Philadelphia. He was 19. Why, it took him three tries to get to the big city.

Playing for the Greenville, South Carolina, team, he was summoned to play for the Philadelphia Athletics. Jackson was scared by the size of the town, the *Chicago Tribune* said. "The Athletics' scout, on the first attempt to get Jackson north, succeeded in piloting him as far as Charlotte, North Carolina, when the boy decided he has gone far enough and leaving the train, he hid from Ossee Schreckengost." A day later, the boy showed up in Piedmont country. "What's the matter, Joe? Don't you want to be a big leaguer?" friends of the young star asked.

"No, them places is too big," Jackson said. "Pelzer, Piedmont, and Newberry just about suits me." On the second trip, the A's scout got Jackson 200 miles closer, getting him into rural Virginia. But one look around at the cotton fields and smokestacks and Joe got lonesome for South Carolina again and left.

On the third try, he made it to Philadelphia and played for Connie Mack, who let him go to Cleveland the next year. He'd been in Chicago since 1915. Hell, he thought, I should of stayed in South Carolina. What a jam he was in now.

It wasn't the first time that shady things had happened in baseball. There had always been talk about gamblers and players laying down. Hal Chase himself was good for a scandal or two a year. There was always that kind of talk around the game, gamblers asking who was hurt, whose arm was ailing, who was hitting? Sure, sometimes strange things happened at the end of a season.

Just nine years earlier, Cleveland's Napoleon Lajoie thought he won himself a car (and the American League batting title) by collecting eight hits, including seven straight bunts in a final-day doubleheader to slip past Ty Cobb of the Detroit Tigers, who chose to sit out the last two games and protect his lead. Or so he thought.

It turned out that Lajoie tripled his first time up. Then St. Louis Browns third baseman Red Corriden, a rookie, and Browns manager Jack O'Connor got the word to him that he should simply bunt. He didn't have to go through all the trouble of hitting triples. It was also hinted that the Browns' strategy was greeted with the strong encouragement of the rest of the Detroit Tigers, who didn't want the hated Cobb to get the car.

So Lajoie got his hits and was so eager for the car and the batting title that after the game, he actually called the game's official scorer Richard

Collins, to ask him if he didn't think one of the fumbled bunts by Corriden should have been ruled a hit, which would have given him nine on the afternoon. According to a story in the *Chicago Tribune*, Harry Howell, a former Browns pitcher, even offered Collins a $40 suit if he'd change the call to help Lajoie out. Collins refused.

Ultimately, Cobb was declared the winner, thanks to a clerical error by the American League office, where one of Cobb's games was counted twice. Lajoie's hits—legit or not—stayed on his lifetime record. Corriden, a rookie, was forgiven. Manager O'Connor got himself suspended indefinitely.

Jackson knew about all that stuff. There was plenty more. All the stuff Hal Chase did. There were so many. But the one he was involved in, he couldn't shake.

Blowing a World Series was a different story. And for most of the season, it seemed that guilt hung over the White Sox players like a shroud. Though it had four eventual 20-game winners and Joe Jackson was hitting .382, a 31-point improvement, the White Sox struggled early in 1920. Buck Weaver was up 37 points to .333 and Hap Felsch and Jackson were among the top 10 in the league in home runs: Felsch had 14, Jackson 12.

Yet for most of the season, it was Cleveland and New York battling it out for the lead. The reigning American League champion White Sox, with the whole team back, were having a tough time. Near the end of the season, as the rumors grew louder, something clicked. Maybe it was a shot at redemption.

Nobody knows for sure, but Gleason's club took off and made a run at Tris Speaker's eventual pennant winners in Cleveland, winning 10 of its last 11 games, climbing within a half-game of the American League lead. Why, if they could just get back to the Series, they could make it all right again. In mid-September, the last time Jackson played against Babe Ruth and his Yankees, Eddie Cicotte, the same Eddie Cicotte who let himself get lit up in the World Series as part of the fix held Ruth (who'd hit 54 homers that year) to a harmless single and the White Sox pounded New York, then the AL leaders, 15–9. The Yankees were worried.

Nothing, it seemed, could stop these Black Sox. They all talked about getting back into the World Series, winning the damn thing and it'd be done with. It seemed as if that was indeed fueling Gleason's club, who were roaring. But a grand jury investigation had begun. Everybody on the Black Sox got nervous. They knew someone would talk about gambling and baseball. Their dirty not-so-secret would soon be out.

"Baseball is more than a national game," the jury foreman said at the time, "it is an American institution, (our great teacher of) respect for authority, self confidence, fair-mindedness, quick judgment, and self-control." And as the trial gathered, the talk in town was rampant.

A few days later, a letter to the *Chicago Tribune* from Fred Loomis, a heartsick White Sox fan, seemed to speak for all of Chicago. And you can imagine how the hearts of these Black Sox sank as his letter hit the press. Jackson heard all the guys talking about it. They weren't a close bunch, really, but now, this was going to be troublesome. "Widespread circulation has been given to reports from various sources that the World Series of last fall between the Chicago White Sox and the Cincinnati Reds was deliberately and intentionally lost through an alleged conspiracy between certain unnamed members of the Chicago White Sox and certain gamblers . . ." Loomis wrote. And the buzz continued.

By September 20, Gleason's White Sox had passed the Yankees and were within a game of trying to win themselves an American League pennant by outdueling the red-hot Cleveland Indians, taking two out of three.

In that last game in Cleveland, where Jackson first became a big-league regular, the crowd was nasty. Jackson had hit his final big-league homer in the fifth inning and with the crowd chanting nastily "Shipyard, shipyard"—mocking Jackson for refusing to enlist in the Army for World War I, preferring instead to work in a shipyard in Cleveland.

Feeling the pressure of everything mounting on him, Jackson lost his cool and made an obscene gesture when he hit third base, then did it again when he crossed home plate. Things were turning ugly.

On September 23, the dam broke. The banner headline in the *Chicago Tribune* would echo through history. "'Fixed' World Series. Five White Sox Men Involved Hoyne Aid Says." The investigation of the Alexander fix attempt had stirred a hornet's nest. It turned out too many people were asking too many questions. Cubs infielder Charles Herzog and Art Wilson, a Boston Braves reserve catcher, were the first two players to give affidavits about the rigged series.

Meanwhile, the White Sox kept playing against a clock they knew was running out. Next up were these Tigers here in a midweek series. If they could just catch Cleveland, maybe they could put off this trial.

Back at the ballpark, Jackson heard the Comiskey Park crowd roar as Collins's single drove Weaver over to third. Here was his chance. It was up to him and "Black Betsy." He looked over in the dugout to the White Sox pitcher that afternoon, fresh-faced Dickie Kerr, who was working on a six-hitter.

Kerr, Jackson remembered, was the guy who didn't know the fix was on in the Series and won two games against the Reds in spite of it.

Now he had a chance to win one for him—legitimately. He unleashed that picture-perfect swing one last time and launched a shot into the right-center-field gap, just beyond Ty Cobb's reach. Weaver came charging around and when Cobb botched the relay throw, so did Collins. Jackson pulled into second, the noise of the Comiskey Park crowd ringing in his ears one last time. It was the 1,774th and

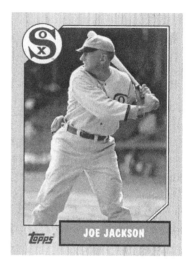

JOE JACKSON

final hit of Jackson's career, his 120th and 121st RBI of the season, the only time in his career he drove in more than 100 runs.

The game, a 2–0 White Sox win and Shoeless Joe Jackson's last big-league game, was over in just 75 minutes. When he got into the clubhouse at the end of the game, the guys were reading the papers from Philadelphia, where the story broke. Billy Maharg had talked and explained the whole deal. This wasn't good. The next day, Jackson, like the other seven White Sox players involved in the World Series scandal, was ordered to appear before the grand jury. They were just one game out. They could win this thing and get them all off their back. Why now? Why now?

When he got his turn before the grand jury, Jackson was blunt. "I wanted $20,000 for my part in the deal and (Chick) Gandil told me I could get that much out of it," he said. "After the first game, (Lefty) Williams came to my room at the hotel and slipped me $5,000. He said the rest would come as soon as we showed the gamblers we were on the square with them. But that is all I ever got. I raised a howl several times as the games went on but it never got anywhere. I was hog-tied."

And when he talked about the games themselves, he explained how easily a game could be rigged. "I am left fielder for the Sox," he told the jury. "When a Cincinnati player would bat a ball in my territory, I'd muff it if I could. But if it would look too much like crooked work to do that, I'd be slow and would make a throw to the infield that would be too short. My work netted the Cincinnati team several runs that they would never have made had I been playing on the square."

Once the players were on the grand jury list, White Sox owner Charles Comiskey had to indefinitely suspend those eight players for the rest of the regular season. The team didn't win another game.

Other teams around baseball offered to lend Comiskey their players for the rest of the season. It was quite a show. Cleveland won the pennant and went on to thump Brooklyn in the World Series.

The jury ended up acquitting the "Black Sox," but it was a hollow victory. There had been so much dirt unearthed from the testimony that new commissioner Kenesaw Mountain Landis, hired to clean up the sport, had no choice. He banned all eight of them—for life.

"Regardless of the verdict of juries," Landis wrote, "no player who throws a ball game, no player that undertakes or promises to throw a ballgame, no player that sits in confidence with a bunch of crooked players and gamblers where the ways and means of throwing a game are discussed and does not promptly tell the club about it, will ever play professional baseball."

Shoeless Joe Jackson's .382 final season was the fourth-highest of his career and strongest season in eight years, and raised his career mark to .356, ranking him third on the all-time list. The 1920 campaign was the 33-year-old Jackson's final one in the big leagues. His 13th season.

"Shoeless" Joe Jackson by the Numbers

YEAR	TEAM	G	AB	R	H	TB	2B	3B	HR	RBI	BB	SO	SB	BA	SLG	OBP
1908	PHA	5	23	0	3	3	0	0	0	--	0	0	0	.130	.130	.130
1909	PHA	5	17	3	3	3	0	0	0	--	1	0	0	.176	.176	.222
1910	CLE	20	75	15	29	44	2	5	1	--	8	0	5	.387	.587	.446
1911	CLE	147	571	127	233	337	45	19	7	--	56	0	41	.408	.590	.468
1912	CLE	153	572	121	226	331	45	26	3	--	54	0	37	.393	.579	.456
1913	CLE	148	528	109	197	291	39	17	7	--	80	26	26	.373	.551	.460
1914	CLE	122	453	61	153	210	22	13	3	--	42	33	22	.338	.464	.400
1915	CLE	83	303	42	99	142	16	9	3	--	28	11	10	.327	.469	.389
1915	CHW	45	158	21	43	63	4	5	2	--	24	12	6	.272	.399	.378
1915	ALL	128	461	63	142	205	20	14	5	--	52	23	16	.308	.445	.385
1916	CHW	155	592	91	202	293	40	21	3	--	46	25	24	.341	.495	.393
1917	CHW	146	538	91	162	231	20	17	5	--	56	25	13	.301	.429	.374
1918	CHW	17	65	9	23	32	2	2	1	--	8	1	3	.354	.492	.425
1919	CHW	139	516	78	181	261	32	14	7	--	61	10	9	.349	.506	.422
1920	CHW	146	570	105	218	335	42	20	12	123	56	14	9	.382	.588	.422
TOTALS		133	1481	873	1772	2576	309	168	54	123	520	157	205	.356	.517	.422

1947

DIZZY DEAN

OL' DIZ SHUTS 'EM UP ONE LAST TIME

DATE: September 28, 1947

SITE: Sportsman's Park, St. Louis, Missouri

OPPONENT: Eddie Lopat of the Chicago White Sox

RESULT: Four scoreless innings

"It ain't bragging if you can do it" was one of Dizzy Dean's most famous quotes. Challenged by Browns owner Dick Muckerman to start the final game of the 1947 season, the 37-year-old Dean, not exactly in game-shape, fired four scoreless innings against the Chicago White Sox—and got himself a single in his final big-league at bat—and left with a rare Browns lead. The bullpen gave it up and the Browns lost. Diz had made his point. COURTESY OF THE NATIONAL BASEBALL HALL OF FAME LIBRARY

The phrase has roared through history like a Dizzy Dean fastball: "It ain't bragging," he once reasoned, "if you can do it."

As he strode out to the mound at Sportsman's Park, home of the worst team in baseball—the St. Louis Browns—for the final game of the 1947 season, it's a safe bet Dizzy Dean, one of the greatest pitchers in St. Louis Cardinals history, was laughing.

What was he doing in a Browns uniform? What was he doing, about 40 pounds over his playing weight, on a baseball mound? Was he a baseball announcer or a pitcher? What had that big mouth of his gone and gotten him into this time?

As great a character as ever strode across a big-league stage, Jerome Hanna "Dizzy" Dean was Davy Crockett in spikes, a twinkle-eyed braggart with a prodigious talent and a personality that jumped out of America's sports pages. There didn't seem to be anything that he wouldn't do or say. The stories, apocryphal or not, have been out there for 50 years.

After his younger brother, Paul, fired a no-hitter in the second game of a doubleheader—Dizzy won the opener—he quipped, "If I'd have knowed Paul was going to have throwed a no-hitter, I'd have throwed one, too." Or, the day after he was struck in the head by a throw in a World Series game, "They X-rayed my head and didn't find nothing." Or when he was criticized for his grammatical mistakes as an announcer. "Never went fur in school," he said, wryly. "Didn't get out of the third grade, you know; didn't want to pass my father." Or confronted with the fact that he gave three different writers three different birthdays and birthplaces on the same day: "Them ain't lies," he said. "Them's scoops."

Well, now it was Dizzy's time to do it. After retiring from baseball in 1940, Dean had gone into radio broadcasting and been a hit. He won a wide following throughout St. Louis for his colorful expressions and folksy manner. But on January 11, 1947, St. Louis Cardinals owner Sam Breadon had decided to go to a two-state, six-station network to do Cardinals games live. And he chose the announcing team of Harry Caray and Gabby Street.

Dean, despite his popularity in St. Louis, was relegated to doing the worst team around, covering the St. Louis Browns with John O'Hara. Dean went after Breadon on and off the air. He once described the Cardinals owner as "a shameless skinflint, so tight he even sends paper towels to the laundry and schemes to save further money by requiring the players to hitchhike between cities."

He was just as tough on the sad Browns, ripping their hitters, their strategy, and the fans. Once, with the stands nearly empty, Dean quipped, "The peanut vendors is going through the stands. They is not doing so good because there is more of them than there is of customers."

He saved his toughest criticism for the beleaguered Browns pitching staff (a league-worst 4.33 team ERA) suggesting time and again that he could go down there and do as well. "I can beat nine of ten who calls themselves pitchers today."

With the season winding down, the offer to do just that came from Browns owner Dick Muckerman, who was desperate to help attendance. The Browns had drawn just 350 fans a few days before Dean's stunt. So here came a $1 contract and a chance to pitch the home finale. Dizzy Dean jumped at it.

There was a bit of a brouhaha in the Browns' front office over the stunt. Muddy Ruel, the Browns manager, refused to sit on the bench and actually left town. But Dizzy was going to have his day.

On September 17, the *St. Louis Post-Dispatch* ran a droll brief with a little more editorializing than usual, announcing that Dean would return. "Trying to brighten the waning days of the American League season for their cash customers, the Browns today signed Jerome Hanna 'Dizzy' Dean to a player contract. Ed Smith, publicity director for the club announced that Dean, who recently in his baseball broadcasts had expressed the wish to test his arm against the hitters of today, would be given the chance in a Brownie uniform.

"According to Smith, the Browns, before signing Dizzy, had checked with American League president Will Harridge. Nothing was said about the company carrying Dean's insurance or Dizzy's beneficiaries."

A *St. Louis Post-Dispatch* columnist was somewhat kinder—if as noncommittal. "That fans were interested in Dizzy's view is evident from the fan mail so voluminous, we're told, that the Browns decided to sign Dizzy for a one-game test—with more to follow if, perhaps Diz can prove his point.

"At 37, defying Father Time, bursitis, and six or more years absence from a major-league uniform, probably neither the club nor Diz is expectant. . . . But his appearance will make a very interesting 'pot-boiler' to help swell a last-day attendance.

"Many of us will be present to again view this assertive and aggressive fellow who provided this city more baseball thrills and baseball color than any player since the days of Sisler and Hornsby."

Those were the days for Dizzy Dean, a 30-game winner for the Cardinals in 1934 and one of the most entertaining players in the history of the sport. A pitcher with untold confidence—and matchless results—he blew onto the scene like a Missouri twister, wreaked havoc for a few years, and was gone.

Columnist Red Smith was there the September day in 1934 when Dean won his 30th game, pitching the Cardinals to the National League championship, beating the Cincinnati Reds. "It was Dean's ballgame," he wrote. "He, more than anyone else, had kept the Cardinals in the pennant race throughout the summer. He had won two games in the last five days to help bring the Red Birds to the top of the league."

Here, with the championship apparently hinging on the outcome of this game, was his chance to add the brightest jewel to his crown, and at the same time, achieve the personal triumph of becoming the first National League pitcher since 1917 to win 30 games in a season. "And it was Dizzy's crowd. . . . They whooped when he rubbed resin on his hands. They yowled when he fired a strike past a batter. They stood and yelled when he lounged to the plate, trailing his bat in the dust. And when, in the seventh inning, with the game already won by eight runs, he hit a meaningless single, the roar that thundered from the stands was as though he had accomplished the twelve labors of Hercules."

That was the way Dizzy Dean captivated a crowd. And even though he'd been away from the game for a long time, he was confident he could do it again. While Dean worked out, preparing himself for the game, he was met with more than a few scornful looks, some of which, no doubt, came from the Browns pitching staff itself, who hardly wanted to stand for criticism from a washed-up big leaguer.

The day of the game, the *Post-Dispatch* advance was similarly tart. "If you like track and field events with your baseball and if you're interested in seeing Dizzy Dean try to pitch again, then Sportsman's Park's the place this afternoon, starting at 1:30 o'clock."

After five field events and a 60-yard sprint (won by White Sox outfielder Thurman Tucker), the game began and Dean toed the rubber against the White Sox, a 70-84, sixth-place club that had Rudy York (15 home runs) as its only power threat. Future Hall of Famer Luke Appling (.306) was at shortstop and Taffy Wright, who finished tied for third in the AL batting race with Boston's Johnny Pesky (.324), was in left.

Once the game began, Dean, looking strange in a baggy Browns uniform, turned back the clock. He pitched effortlessly and worked through the White Sox lineup—Don Kolloway, Bob Kennedy, Dave Philley, Rudy York, the whole bunch—without a hit or a run. The 15,916 on hand—by far the biggest Browns crowd in months and third-largest of the season—were loving it. He didn't have much velocity, but he sure knew how to pitch.

As they reported in the *St. Louis Post-Dispatch* the next morning, it was impressive. "Not so fast as when he pitched 30 victories for the Cardinals in 1934, Dean was remarkably free and easy in his motion. He kept the ball so close to the strike zone that he forced the White Sox batters to swing. As a result, he made only 39 pitches in the four innings [he worked]."

And that wasn't all. When Dean came up in the third inning against White Sox left-hander Eddie Lopat, a roar rose through the stands. Dizzy was carrying a bat painted black and white. He called it his "Zebra model."

Home plate umpire Cal Hubbard called time and ordered Dean to go get another one. Dizzy nodded, walked back to the Browns' dugout, and came back with a different bat, this one "grotesquely painted with red bands on it." Hubbard laughed, let Dean use it, and on Lopat's first pitch, the veteran right-hander lashed a single, then later slid theatrically into second base.

His wife, Pat, seated next to the Browns' dugout, hollered in: "He proved his point. Now get the damned fool out of there before he kills himself."

Dean returned to the mound and worked one more scoreless inning. But in between innings, he told Coach Fred Hofmann, running the team in Ruel's absence, that he'd pulled a muscle running out his single and was through pitching for the afternoon. Dean got a terrific ovation from the crowd. His big-league career was over. It wasn't a bad way to go out.

In true Browns fashion, reliever Glenn Moulder surrendered five runs in the ninth to ruin Dean's good work. The White Sox were 5–2 victors.

Dean wasn't about to make a comeback, though. "I still think I could pitch well enough to win up here but I don't intend to try it," he said after the game. "I have a contract as a radio announcer and I intend to stick to that job."

Which, of course, he did, eventually going all the way to nationwide fame, working for NBC Television, doing their Game of the Week baseball telecasts. Not bad for a guy who didn't get through third grade.

His pitching career was mighty brief by Hall of Fame standards—a 12-year run but only six seasons where he appeared in more than 20 games. Though he's most often compared to Sandy Koufax, the Dodgers' Hall of Fame great who retired at 30 from arm miseries, Koufax actually pitched in 80 more games—397 to Dean's 317.

Yet Dizzy Dean was elected to Baseball's Hall of Fame in 1953, going into Cooperstown in the very same year that Joe DiMaggio appeared on the ballot for the first time. DiMaggio finished a distant eighth in the balloting.

In his induction speech, Dizzy Dean left the Cooperstown audience the way he left everybody throughout his 12-year run in the big leagues—laughing. "The Good Lord was good to me," Dean said, winding up his talk. "He gave me a strong body, a good right arm, and a weak mind."

Dizzy Dean by the Numbers

YEAR	TEAM	W	L	PCT	ERA	G	GS	CG	SHO	SV	IP	H	R	BB	SO
1930	SLN	1	0	000	1.00	1	1	1	0	0	9.0	3	1	3	5
1932	SLN	18	15	.545	3.29	46	33	16	4	0	287.0	280	122	102	191
1933	SLN	20	18	.526	3.04	48	34	26	3	0	293.0	279	113	64	199
1934	SLN	30	7	.811	2.65	50	33	24	7	0	312.0	288	110	73	195
1935	SLN	28	12	.700	3.05	50	36	29	3	0	325.0	324	126	77	190
1936	SLN	24	13	.649	3.17	51	34	28	2	0	315.0	310	128	53	195
1937	SLN	13	10	.565	2.70	27	25	17	4	0	197.0	200	76	33	120
1938	CHC	7	1	.875	1.80	13	10	3	1	0	75.0	64	20	8	22
1939	CHC	6	4	.600	3.38	19	13	7	2	0	96.0	98	40	17	27
1940	CHC	3	3	.500	5.17	10	9	3	0	0	54.0	68	35	20	18
1941	CHC	0	0	--	18.00	1	1	0	0	0	1.0	3	3	0	1
1947	SLA	0	0	--	0.00	1	1	0	0	0	4.0	3	0	1	0
TOTALS		83	83	.644	3.02	317	230	154	26	0	1968.0	1920	774	451	1163

SATCHEL PAIGE

NOTHING WAS GAININ' ON SATCHEL

DATE: September 25, 1965

SITE: Municipal Stadium, Kansas City, Missouri

OPPONENT: Bill Monbouquette of the Boston Red Sox

RESULT: Three scoreless innings

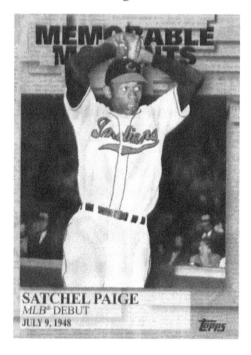

He stood out on that little hill that to enemy hitters over the past 30 years always looked like a mountain. For Satchel Paige, the view was always majestic. He could hear the buzz in the stands. Satchel always could. Right now, he laughed to himself, they were probably wondering how old he was.

Was he 59? Or 62? Or 64? Had it been any other 59-year-old man, somebody surely would have asked, "What are you doing on a major-league mound?" Nobody was going to ask Satchel Paige that. Not even at 59.

Another baseball season had come and almost gone. Only a couple regular-season games left. The A's were out of it. So were their visitors, the Boston Red Sox. The owner of the Kansas City A's, Charles Finley, had noticed the lagging attendance at Municipal Stadium and decided to do something about it.

He contacted Paige, who hadn't pitched in the big leagues since 1953—he'd retired after a 3-9 record in 117 innings for the St. Louis Browns in 1953 at age 47— and asked him if he'd like to come back to the big leagues and pitch the regular-season finale. Paige, who was always up for making a dollar, said sure.

Finley did the act up big-time. When Paige went out to the bullpen to warm up, there was a nurse there and a rocking chair. Ever the showman, Paige sat down in the chair and commenced to rocking as the crowd of 9,289 began trickling in. The nurse even started rubbing liniment on his limber right arm and Paige went along with the gag.

But once his warmups were complete, the fans hooting and hollering, the lanky Paige, 6-foot 3-inches, all arms and legs, strode deliberately to the mound for the very last time. This time, it was just baseball.

There were nights where he'd tell the outfield to sit down so he could strike out the side, like he'd do in his barnstorming days. There were other nights he'd put up a 2x4 behind home plate with 10-penny nails in it and proceed to nail the board to the backstop with his pitches from the mound.

Tonight, he'd just pitch. He'd been doing this for a very long time, spanning baseball generations. He once struck out the great Rogers Hornsby five times in a single barnstorming game. Hornsby won his first batting title in 1920, his last in 1928. He had long since retired.

Then there was Joe DiMaggio. He'd called Satchel "the fastest pitcher I ever batted against. And the best." DiMaggio had been retired for nine years. Former Cubs slugger Hack Wilson said Satchel's fastball "started out like a baseball but by the time it got to the plate, it looks like a marble."

"(He) must be talking about my slowball," Paige replied. "My fastball looks like a fish egg."

Wilson had died in 1948. Satchel pitched on.

Why, Dizzy Dean, who used to barnstorm with Ol' Satchel, hadn't been on a major-league mound in 18 years. Now he was an announcer. Dizzy said Satchel was the best pitcher he ever saw, adding "my fastball looks like a change of pace compared to that pistol bullet that ol' Satchel sends up there."

Dean, Hornsby, Wilson, DiMaggio—all of them were gone now. Yet here was Satchel Paige, a baseball in that long, spidery hand, standing on the mound at Municipal Stadium, staring in at a stocky left-handed hitting rookie, Jim Gosger.

Paige was back in the big leagues. One last time. For the longest time, he wondered if he'd ever get the chance that Jackie Robinson did. From the late 1920s on, the name Satchel Paige was known all across America. He'd been wowing them in the Negro Leagues and in barnstorming tours.

Some of that was because of his undeniable talent. Some of it was because he understood how to be colorful. He called his pitches different names: his be-ball ("because it be where I want it to be"), his jump ball, trouble ball, Little Tom, Long Tom, his midnight rider, and his four-day creeper. Whether the hitter could actually distinguish between any of the pitches didn't matter. Paige could and the lore grew.

"I'm the easiest guy in the world to catch," Paige once told a rookie receiver. "I don't take to signals too good. All you have to do is show me a glove and hold it still. I'll hit it."

When barnstorming, Paige used to guarantee to strike out the first nine hitters. He was willing to go anywhere and pitch for a dollar. He jumped teams, jumped leagues, went wherever there was a little more money. Despite his magnificent talent, not all the Black newspaper writers were sympathetic to his cause.

As Chester Washington wrote in the *Pittsburgh Courier*, "No player is bigger than a baseball club, and no player is certainly more important than the National Association of Negro Baseball Clubs.

"And this goes for Satchel Paige, too. . . . Despite his contract, Paige, who has in the past set a bad example for Negro baseball by his 'gallivantin' tactics, repeatedly refused to join the Pittsburgh Crawfords training camp at Hot Springs; instead, he joined the Bismark [*sic*] [North Dakota] Club, where he expects to play 'free-lance' baseball."

Later, when Paige joined the Crawfords, then took off again in a contract dispute, Black baseball's greatest pitcher was rapped by the Black press. "Some owners and fans are genuinely glad to have Paige leave," they wrote then. "Others are sorry. Negro baseball has been very good to Paige. His phenomenal, well-publicized pitching ability could not be expressed in terms of finance. No colored club drew enough cash customers to pay him a salary commensurate with his ability. Then again, his unreliability was a factor which at all times kept him from being a valuable asset to any team."

Because of that reputation, when it came time to break the color barrier several years later, major-league owners weren't all that tempted to bring Paige along, even though, at his advanced age, he could probably still win.

Finally on July 9, 1948, the Cleveland Indians' maverick owner Bill Veeck signed the 42-year-old Paige. When he made his first big-league appearance, relieving Bob Lemon in the fifth inning of a game with Cleveland trailing the St. Louis Browns, 4–1, all of baseball was watching to see how the legend would fare. Paige threw two scoreless innings.

He made his first start a month later, and the Indians drew 72,000 to watch him pitch a night game against the Washington Senators. He won, 4–3.

Some baseball folks still talk about a game that Paige pitched on August 6, 1952, when he was at least 46 years old. For 12 innings, the ageless Paige shut the Detroit Tigers out, finally winning the 0–0 game in the bottom of the 12th. He won 12 games that season.

But he retired after the 1953 season with a 3-9 record. But 3-9 for the Browns, that might have been the equivalent of a 15-win season for some teams. Even that year, when Paige maybe was 49 years old, he had his moments. In June, the sad Browns, losers of 14 straight, stumbled into New York to face the Yankees, who were riding an 18-game win streak.

With Duane Pichette inexplicably pitching superbly one Wednesday afternoon, holding a 3–1 lead into the eighth, Browns skipper Marty Marion had a hunch to bring in ol' Satchel to try to close it out.

A New York AP sportswriter caught the moment perfectly. "A lone figure disentangled itself from the little group out there, stepped over the low fence and headed for the mound. It wasn't exactly a march, although there was a certain dignity in the shuffling advance. His pants legs dangled almost to his ankles, his shirt hung on his bony shoulders like tired bunting the day after a celebration. Old Satch never was much for sartorial splendor on a ballfield. He took his warm-up pitches, then stood back and rubbed his hands with the rosin bag. You could almost hear his mind ticking, as if he was thinking 'Well, so you want a little action, hey boys?'"

"Paige was magical. He got Joe Collins and Irv Noren to pop out to end the eighth, then in the ninth, got Mickey Mantle to hit a foul, trying to bunt a third strike ("Why for that boy to try that?" was Satch's quote the next day), induced Yogi Berra to pop out, gave up a single to Gene Woodling, then retired Gil McDougald on a popup to preserve the Browns win.

An ancient Satchel Paige (approximately mid-40s) pitching to a 22-year-old Mantle. Seems like a mismatch. But it wasn't.

Magically, it all came back for Satchel one last time this night 12 years later. Leading off the game, Boston outfielder Jim Gosger popped Paige's pitch up into foul territory. One out.

Next was another young lefty, Dalton Jones. He topped a slow roller to first baseman Santiago Rosario, who bobbled it. Next up was Boston's talented Carl Yastrzemski, twice an American League batting champion. Paige's next pitch was in the dirt, scooting past catcher Bill Bryan, letting Jones go to second. When Paige's second pitch was also in the dirt, Jones lit out for third. Bryan threw him out. Two down.

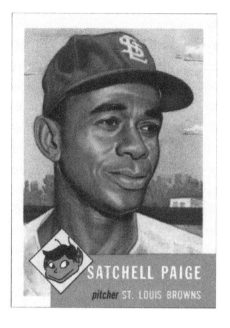

When the next pitch missed, Paige was behind in the count, 3-0, an unusual predicament for a guy whose control was so extraordinary, he convinced Cleveland Indians owner Bill Veeck to sign him by throwing five straight pitches over the stub of Veeck's ground-out cigarette.

Paige fired a fastball on the outside corner, and Yastrzemski swung and bounced it off the left field wall. It was the last hit off the great Negro League legend. It also prompted much teasing in the Yastrzemski house. Yaz's dad, Carl Sr., had also gotten a hit off the great Paige, except he did it about 20 years earlier. Carl Sr. hit a triple.

Paige got 20-year-old Tony Conigliaro, who led the league in home runs that year, to end the inning. The Red Sox scoring threat had passed.

Before the night was out, Paige faced six more hitters—Lee Thomas, Felix Mantilla, Ed Bressoud, Mike Ryan, Boston's pitcher Bill Monbouquette, and Gosger, one last time on a groundball—and got 'em all.

When he himself came to bat, the whole Municipal Stadium crowd rose and cheered him. Cheered him even louder when he struck out. And when A's manager Haywood Sullivan sent out Diego Segui to relieve Paige to begin the fourth inning, the cheers grew the loudest of all.

As Satchel went into the clubhouse to change, the fans in Municipal Stadium were urged to light matches in tribute, and by the time Satchel came out of the locker room to the dugout in his regular clothes, the stadium lights had been turned down and thousands began to sing, "The ol' grey mare she ain't what she used to be."

One of the greatest careers in the game was over. A little later than usual. Better late than never.

In the clubhouse afterward, Paige sat in his long A's underwear and chatted with the newspapermen. It had been a cool night, but Paige said he handled it OK.

"Naw, the cold was nothing," he told the *Kansas City Star*. "It ain't like it is when you're sitting around. When I got goin' I got hot, and there was nothing on my mind but baseball."

It didn't sound as if Paige planned on just sitting around. "Everybody doubted me on the ballclub," he said. "They'll have more confidence in me now. Before, they only took my word for it. Don't forget, I ain't been up in this league for 15 years (actually, it was 12 years). Now I'll stay in shape because they know what I can do."

Satchel Paige never did come back to pitch. But don't think it was because he couldn't. One of the greatest careers in the game was finally over. Better late, much better late, than never.

Satchel Paige by the Numbers

YEAR	TEAM	W	L	PCT	ERA	G	GS	CG	SHO	SV	IP	H	R	BB	SO
1948	CLE	6	1	.857	2.47	21	7	3	2	0	73.0	61	21	22	43
1949	CLE	4	7	.364	3.04	31	5	1	0	0	83.0	70	29	33	54
1951	SLA	3	4	.429	4.79	23	3	0	0	0	62.0	67	39	29	48
1952	SLA	12	10	.545	3.07	46	6	3	2	0	138.0	116	51	57	91
1953	SLA	3	9	.250	3.54	57	4	0	0	0	117.0	114	51	39	51
1965	KC	0	0	--	0.00	1	1	0	0	0	3.0	1	0	0	1
TOTALS		31	31	.475	3.29	179	26	7	4	0	476.0	429	191	180	288

1951

JOE DIMAGGIO

ONE LAST JOLT FROM JOE

DATE: October 10, 1951 (Game 6 of the 1951 World Series)

SITE: Yankee Stadium, New York, New York

PITCHER: Larry Jansen of the New York Giants

RESULT: Double to right-center

Of course, it really wasn't a secret. Anybody that had been watching the New York Yankees really closely already knew that The Yankee Clipper, literally, was on his last legs. But they didn't have to go and tell the whole world. Was that anyway to treat somebody like DiMaggio? The New York papers sure didn't ever treat him that way. Louie wasn't like that. And he was with the *New York Times*.

DiMaggio couldn't believe that *Life* magazine was going to go and blab it all. Why the hell couldn't they leave him alone and let him go quietly? Was it the Dodgers way of getting back at the Yankees for beating them in all those World Series? *Life* magazine could go to hell. He still got mad when he remembered that profile they did on him back in 1939, just as he was taking over as the Yankees' marquee player following Lou Gehrig's retirement.

"Instead of olive oil or smelly bear grease, he keeps his hair slick with water," the profile said. "He never reeks of garlic and prefers chicken chow mein to spaghetti." Or how about "Joe DiMaggio's rise in baseball is a testimonial to the value of general shiftlessness? His inertia caused him to give up school after one year in high school. He is lazy, rebellious, and endowed with a bad stomach."

Even the caption of a photo of DiMaggio with then heavyweight champion Joe Louis was insulting. "Like Heavyweight Champion Joe Louis, DiMaggio is lazy, shy, and inarticulate."

Yeah, that was a nice story, wasn't it? But nobody remembered that stuff now. DiMaggio had gotten past it. He had 'em, all of the New York media, eating out of his hands. Jimmy Cannon listed DiMaggio as one of his best friends. Same thing for Red Smith. But *Life* magazine? What was this?

As Joe DiMaggio walked out of the dugout and knelt in the on-deck circle in the eighth inning of Game 6 of the 1951 World Series, there was a lot going through his mind. He was coming to the end of something. He knew it. Nobody else did. Yeah, he wasn't hitting anything when the Series started. He talked to his friend, the *Times* reporter Louie Effrat about it, didn't he? He owned up. Louie handled it right, too. It looked good; it looked OK the way he did it. What was *Life* magazine doing? Was this any way to treat somebody like DiMaggio? After all he'd done? How would it look? That was the thing with Joe. Yankee players would talk about it, about how when DiMaggio came back to the dugout after making an out, he might ask, "How'd I look?"

The answer was always one thing: "Great, Joe, great." DiMaggio tried to clear his mind.

He knew this was it. And the moment meant a little more to him than he imagined. Hampered by injuries ever since he came back from World War II, he'd struggled and played in just 116 games in 1951, hitting a career-low .263. He could see it all coming to a close. Then this *Life* magazine crap. What would people say?

Hefting his bat, he looked out at the Giants' Larry Jansen, a 23-game winner, on to pitch the eighth, trying to keep his club still alive in the Series that the Yankees had stolen away once again. He watched him carefully, saw the delivery, imagined the ball and how it'd look coming out of his hand. Then he was distracted again. If only he'd had a chance to say something to that little bastard, Andy High. *Life* magazine, too. Since when did *Life* magazine give a good goddamn about whether a guy could hit a high fastball or not? Or maybe he'd give him the DiMaggio stare, a spine-tingling look that made even the toughest reporter wince. Who did he think he was, writing like that about DiMaggio?

All these years, all the effort he put into being the perfect Yankee, the perfect ballplayer, the guy that nobody ever saw argue a call or dive for a ball or find himself looking bad in any way. And now this?

He hefted the bat again and swung it, still on one knee. Jansen, a 6-foot-2 right-hander with a new pitch, a slider, had held him hitless in Game 2. How did he work him? He thought about the pitch sequence, how Jansen's ball moved. He was going to miss this part of the game. Damn.

DiMaggio could see who would be the next star. That was OK. He took over for Babe Ruth and Lou Gehrig. Now someone would take over for him.

Bolstered by the arrival of a broad-shouldered, free-swinging rookie named Mickey Mantle, Casey Stengel's Yankees sailed through the regular season, winning by five games over Al López's Cleveland Indians. DiMaggio, for once, didn't have much to do with this pennant. Vic Raschi and Eddie Lopat each won 21 games, the Yankees led the league in pitching and homers, and were one point away from leading the AL in batting average, too.

At first it looked as if Bobby Thomson's dramatic "Shot Heard 'Round the World" was going to propel Leo Durocher's Giants past the Yankees in the Series, as the Giants grabbed two of the first three games. Stengel's club had come around, led by—who else? DiMaggio.

Thank God, he did. The Yankees came back to take the next two to lead, 3–2. A win here would clinch it. They were almost there. Then Joe could walk away in style, looking good. That would show that High son of a bitch. When he read what High, the Dodgers' key scout, had to say about his fading skills in the latest issue of *Life* magazine, he burned inside. The bastard.

What happened was this: The Dodgers had been leading the National League most of the year. So they sent High, their top scout, to watch the Yankees in the latter part of the season. They were expecting to play them in the World Series. High took his job seriously, wrote copious notes, noticing exactly what DiMaggio's game had fallen to. But when Thomson's dramatic home run knocked the Dodgers out of the World Series, High's report was going to be filed somewhere, never to be read. Except an out-of-work writer named Clay Felker had heard about it. He knew the Dodgers had scouted the Yankees, and he was trying to get a job with *Life* magazine. The brass at *Life* told him that if he got a copy of the report, he was in.

"So I went to Andy High's hotel room," Felsker said. "I asked him, and he gave me a copy of the report." High's assessment of the fading star was scalding. Fielding: "He can't stop quickly and throw hard. Take the extra base on him if he is in motion. He won't throw on questionable plays. Challenge him even though he may throw a man out."

DiMaggio seethed when he read it. Somebody going to take an extra base on him? The great DiMaggio? Louie didn't get into that crap in the *Times*. He told them how poorly he was hitting and how he'd brought Lefty O'Doul in to help him fix it. They didn't need to know that other crap. Not after all Joe D. had done for the Yankees. Hell, all he'd done for baseball. What was wrong with the way his pal Louie did it in the *New York Times*? Wasn't that good enough?

"Sympathy is merely a word in the dictionary to Joe DiMaggio," Louis Effrat wrote in the *Times* that week. "Powerless, hitless, runless in the series so far, the Yankee Clipper is not feeling sorry for himself. What's more, he doesn't want fans feeling sorry for him. 'I've just been lousy.'

"Such self-censure by the man who many acknowledge as the greatest baseball player since Babe Ruth, the man who currently is playing in his 10th series, the man who has carried the Yankees to so many glorious victories, was characteristic of Joseph Paul DiMaggio.

"Always a perfectionist, with a burning desire to succeed, Joe cannot excuse himself. So far, he has flopped and no one is more aware of it than DiMaggio himself." Louie's story went on to talk about Lefty O'Doul coming in and advising Joe he was swinging too hard, trying too hard. . . .

"Warm, friendly throughout the hour-long interview [Gee, Joe D. gave you an hour?], DiMaggio, comfortable in pajamas and lounging robe, sipped coffee and appeared to be completely at ease.

"He has been sleeping well, eating well, and is in the best physical condition of the year. He looks great everywhere except at the plate and that is a matter he hopes to correct."

That was how to write a story, DiMaggio thought. He said I wasn't hitting, that I had help, that I was trying. What more did they want? Do people need to read Andy High's crap? The *Life* magazine article was comprehensive. "Speed: He can't run and won't bunt." Awful, he thought. And people are going to read this tripe? "Hitting vs. Right-Handed Pitchers: His bat is slow and he can't pull a good fastball . . . throw him nothing but good fastballs. Don't slow up on him."

What kind of crap was that to write about a guy? Louie understood how to play the game between writers and players. Why Joe D. remembered the night he and Louie were out at Toots Shor's and Louie started to ask him about his contract.

"What are ya, trying to play newspaperman?" DiMaggio sneered at him. That ended that. You just had to put these newspaper guys in their place. It was great to hang around with 'em—off the record. You could get 'em to write great stuff about you, never any negative stuff. If they got negative, they were done. Gone. Cut off. That was DiMaggio's way. If you were late for a dinner date, mentioned something he didn't want to hear, whatever, you were done. Gone. Forgotten.

For the first three games of this 1951 World Series, High looked like a prophet, which drove Joe even more. He could feel his ears burning every time he walked back to the bench. With the Giants taking two of the first three games, beating both Raschi and Lopat, he wondered if the Yanks could turn it around, especially without Mantle, the heir apparent who'd gotten injured in the fifth inning of Game 2, trying to back up the elder center fielder.

Willie Mays had ripped one into the gap and DiMaggio was slow to react to it. Mantle, playing right field, saw that DiMaggio got a slow start and with his tremendous speed, dashed into the gap to try to get to the ball. At the last second, without calling for the ball, DiMaggio came in and reached up to make the catch. Mantle, frantically turning away to avoid colliding with the Clipper, caught his knee in an outfield drain, tearing ligaments. He was out for the rest of the Series. The Yankees seemed poised to stumble.

Finally, in Game 4, DiMaggio found a way to kick himself—and his team—back into gear. In the fifth inning, he slashed a two-run homer off Sal Maglie—his eighth and final in World Series play—and the blow seemed to lift the Yankees. They'd won two more games. And now, the Yanks up 4–1 in the eighth, his club three outs from a title, it was down to that little game he loved so, pitcher vs. hitter: he and Jansen. Maybe he wasn't hitting much in this Series (just 5-for-22) but hey, he was still DiMaggio. That still meant something.

He settled into the batter's box and looked out at Jansen. He was good. He was pitching his 10th inning of World Series work, and during the season was fourth in strikeouts (145), fifth in innings pitched (278.1), and tied for fifth in ERA (3.04.) The Giants had left their season up to him. But even he couldn't rescue them.

DiMaggio heard his name announced over the stadium loudspeakers for the last time, and the applause rumbled through the stands. Of course, they would have been so much louder had they only known what they were witnessing. He looked out at the mound, the great green expanse of center field that was his territory, the monuments out there, then took his stance, that spread-legged, erect pose, bat held way back, head unmoving, eyes focused on the pitcher.

Then without thinking, he swung one last time and connected and the ball roared off his bat out into the alley in right-center field. He knew it was two bases the minute he hit it and as he came hard around first base, the crowd's excitement ringing in his ears, he slowed to a magnificent trot as he approached the base.

By the time Joe DiMaggio actually got to second, the ball was still being relayed in from the outfield. So there he was, in the middle of the diamond, one last time. He stood and looked around him. He was going to miss all this.

Many years later, friends of DiMaggio admitted that he got as much of a bang out of that last at-bat as any hit in his career. "I bowed out with a two-bagger," he'd say, smiling happily. It was something DiMaggio didn't do very often.

A few pitches later, the game was over. The Yankees celebrated once again, and DiMaggio headed for the locker room a champion once more. What would *Life* magazine have to say about that?

Though he didn't want to say anything publicly—and wouldn't for a couple months—once he was in the clubhouse, he finally did say something about it. The guys in there, they could just tell it was the end of something. Reliever Spec Shea asked him point-blank. "What about it, Joe?" DiMaggio's voice was even, well thought out. "This is it," he told him. "I've played my last game of ball."

Two months later, after a farewell trip to Japan, Joe DiMaggio made it official. In Red Smith's column the next day, he called DiMaggio "The Real Amateur." "'When baseball is no longer fun, it is no longer a game. . . . And so, I have played my last game of ball,'" Smith wrote, quoting DiMaggio. "That is the amateur view. It is the feeling which prevents a great commercial enterprise like baseball from ever becoming a commercial enterprise exclusively. Joe DiMaggio made a great deal of money playing baseball. Most of all, though, he played for fun, and now that it is no longer any fun, he isn't going to play anymore."

Later on, Smith even got a little maudlin. "This is a meandering way of approaching the simple flat fact that the greatest ballplayer of our day and one of the greatest of any day quit baseball yesterday. . . .They know he's quitting because he cannot stand mediocrity in anything, and least of all in himself. They [the fans] couldn't stand it either, not in Joe. On him, it couldn't look good."

Joe DiMaggio by the Numbers

YEAR	TEAM	G	AB	R	H	TB	2B	3B	HR	RBI	BB	SO	SB	BA	SLG	OBP
1936	NYY	138	637	132	206	367	44	15	29	125	24	39	4	.323	.576	.352
1937	NYY	151	621	150	215	418	35	15	46	166	64	37	3	.346	.673	.412
1938	NYY	145	599	129	195	349	32	13	32	139	59	21	6	.326	.583	.388
1939	NYY	120	462	108	176	310	32	6	30	126	52	21	3	.381	.671	.448
1940	NYY	132	508	93	179	318	28	9	31	132	61	30	1	.352	.626	.425
1941	NYY	139	541	122	193	348	43	11	30	125	76	13	4	.357	.643	.440
1942	NYY	154	610	123	186	305	30	13	21	114	68	36	4	.305	.500	.376
1946	NYY	132	503	81	146	257	20	8	25	95	59	24	1	.290	.511	.367
1947	NYY	141	534	97	168	279	31	10	20	97	64	32	3	.315	.522	.391
1948	NYY	153	594	110	190	355	26	11	39	155	67	30	1	.320	.598	.396
1949	NYY	76	272	58	94	162	14	6	14	67	55	18	0	.346	.596	.459
1950	NYY	139	525	114	158	307	33	10	32	122	80	33	0	.301	.585	.394
1951	NYY	116	415	72	109	175	22	4	12	72	61	36	0	.263	.422	.365
TOTALS		1736	6821	1389	2215	3950	390	131	361	1535	790	370	30	.325	.579	.398

LOU GEHRIG

SAD FINISH FOR THE IRON HORSE

DATE: May 1, 1939

SITE: Yankee Stadium, New York City

PITCHER: Pete Appleton of the Washington Senators

RESULT: Flyball to center fielder George Case

When New York Yankees great Lou Gehrig pulled the plug on his 1939 season just eight games in, he had only a single RBI: a groundout to first off Philadelphia A's hurler Lynn Nelson that allowed Tommy Henrich to score from third. A few days earlier, Gehrig's final major-league hit came off the Senators' Ken Chase. Just two years after taking himself out of the Yankee lineup for good, the great Gehrig was dead from the disease that went on to carry his name. COURTESY OF THE NATIONAL BASEBALL HALL OF FAME LIBRARY

He watched carefully as the ball came whistling out of the left hand of Washington Senators pitcher Joe Krakauskas and headed toward the plate. He was always really focused up there. Now it was a matter of survival. Literally.

"Inside," Lou Gehrig told himself in the split second as the pitch bore in on him. "It's going to be inside. Gotta back up."

Snap! He heard the ball plop into the catcher's glove and felt it whistle as it went by. How did it miss him?

After his groundout, Gehrig trotted back to the bench, shaking his head slowly from side to side. How could this be happening to him? Two more stranded runners. Another failed at-bat. How could this be? He couldn't be washed up at 35, could he? And geez, look at that scoreboard. We're losing to the Senators? Every time up there were men on. Every time, he left 'em out there. The greatest RBI guy in baseball history.

He looked up and it was the eighth inning already. The guys were getting to this reliever, this well-traveled right-hander named Pete Appleton. "I knew him when he was Pete Jablonowski," Gehrig laughed to himself, remembering back in 1933 when Appleton decided to change his name.

As Gehrig walked to the plate, he kept telling himself to be quick, to see the ball hit the bat. The bases were loaded, just the way Lou liked 'em. With a home run, Gehrig would have himself 24 grand slams, an all-time baseball record, more even than The Babe. He remembered that last shot, a grand slam off Lee Ross of the A's last August. That gave him 23.

Even a nice sharp hit here, maybe that'd get him back on track. How could a reasonably young, almost impossibly strong, extraordinarily durable athlete weaken so? He could hardly rest, he was so worried. There was talk in the locker room that something was seriously wrong with him. He couldn't wrestle with anybody anymore. They talked in spring training about watching him walk across the grass, working as hard as a man on roller skates.

Grantland Rice, one of the country's most famous sportswriters, saw Gehrig couldn't even lift a large coffeepot with one hand the night before. What was wrong? Why now?

Appleton looked in at the forlorn figure there in pinstripes. Once the most feared man in baseball history with runners on base, now he was an easy out. Appleton fired one in and Gehrig swung weakly at it and lifted it to center. George Case trotted in, reached up, and made the catch. Gehrig trotted back to the dugout quietly. How many men was that left on today? Six? Eight?

He didn't know his stats exactly, but he knew he'd only struck out once. Nobody got him today, either. But gee, what did he have, four hits—all singles—in the team's first eight games? A grand .143 average. Worst of all, the number he knew that they were talking about up in the press box. One measly RBI. One.

Suddenly, the game was over. He could see the batboys gathering the bats, lining them up in front of the dugout. He could see the Senators looking over at the Yankee dugout, talking. It was all slipping away. And damn, he couldn't stop it.

In the other clubhouse, the Senators' first pitcher of the day, Joe Krakauskas, was shaking his head, talking to a sportswriter. "They better get that Gehrig out of there before somebody kills him," he said. "I pitched him inside, across the letters today—just once! If Gehrig saw that ball he couldn't move away from it. The ball went through his arms. Not over or under 'em but through his arms."

Gehrig just couldn't get out of the way. And sitting in front of his stall across the way, smoking a cigarette—his one vice—he knew what he would have to do. The team was traveling to Detroit in a few hours to start a series with the Tigers. He knew what he was going to have to do. Maybe he hadn't missed a game since 1925. Maybe that streak was important and everything. But Lou Gehrig just wasn't Lou Gehrig anymore. In his mind, he kept hearing the voices of his teammates congratulating him on this routine play he made in the ninth inning, flipping the ball to Johnny Murphy. "Great play, Lou!" they told him. Great play, my butt.

Losing to the Washington Senators on a rainy Sunday afternoon was unsettling for Gehrig. How exactly did Krakauskas, who had a record of 11-17 that season or Appleton, who went 5-10 that year, get him out four times? And all four times with men on base, a Gehrig specialty. That'd be in the paper tomorrow, for sure.

It was, too. Sure enough, the next morning, he noticed that the *New York Times* duly noted "Lou Gehrig was up four times with men on base yesterday and didn't drive in a single run." That hurt. That was Gehrig's pride in being a Yankee, driving in runs. Maybe he couldn't hit 'em as far as The Babe. Or as often. Except for that one game he whacked four, which he knew was kind of a fluke. His specialty was reliability, consistency, the guy you could always count on. Why, he wouldn't even play golf. Was afraid it'd hurt his swing.

Sitting there at his locker, he knew the saddest truth of all. The Yankees couldn't count on him anymore.

In his prime, his numbers were amazing. Seven times he drove in more than 150 runs in a season, including his American League record 184 in 1931, a record that he figured would last a long time. In 34 World Series games, he drove in 35 runs. Only Yankee successors Mickey Mantle and Yogi Berra would surpass Gehrig's total. It took Mantle 65 games to drive in 40 runs. Berra played in a record 75 World Series games and drove in 39 runs. Gehrig was clutch, too, hitting .361 to Ruth's .326 in World Series games, twice hitting over .500. But he never was a headline guy, that's just how it was. Heck, the day he swatted the four homers it wasn't even big news because New York Giants manager John McGraw decided to retire that day. This would be headline news. The streak, Gehrig's 2,130-game monstrosity, had to end. He knew it. He had to do something to help the team. He'd make the trip, sure. He wanted to be with the fellas. He was part of the team, still. But he knew he had to talk to Yankees manager Joe McCarthy. He knew McCarthy would never take him out of the lineup. Why, he was careful about moving him down to number five in the order, even with Gehrig hitting .142 with one measly RBI.

When he got to Detroit, he went up to McCarthy's room at the Box Cadillac Hotel and told him he was taking himself out of the lineup. It was time, he said. At first, they thought it was lumbago, because if Gehrig had to bend over to catch a throw or field a ball, sometimes, he had a tough time straightening up. Yankee infielders resigned themselves to make sure they threw the ball around neck high, so Gehrig wouldn't have to stoop over to field the throw.

But now, he knew it was time. He had to wait in Detroit for McCarthy to arrive from Buffalo by plane. Once McCarthy arrived, Gehrig met with him and told him he was taking himself out of the lineup. McCarthy met immediately with the New York press and broke the news. "Lou just told me he felt it would be best for the club if he took himself out of the lineup," McCarthy told the *New York Times*. "I asked him if he really felt that way. He told me he was serious. He feels blue. He is dejected. I told him it would be as he wished. Like everybody else, I'm sorry to see it happen. I told him not to worry. Maybe the warm weather will bring him around.

"He's been a great ballplayer. Fellows like him come along once in a hundred years. I told him that. More than that, he's been a vital part of the Yankee ballclub since he started with it. He's always been a perfect gentle-man, a credit to baseball."

Gehrig met with the press, too. And it was hard to talk. "I decided last Sunday night on this move," Gehrig told the *Times*. "I haven't been a bit of good to the team since the season started. It would not be fair to the boys, to Joe or to the baseball public for me to try to go on. In fact, it would not be fair to myself.

"It's tough to see your mates on base, have a chance to win a ballgame and not be able to do anything about it. . . . I knew in Sunday's game that I should get out of there. I went up there four times with men on base. . . . A hit would have won the game for the Yankees but I missed. . . . Maybe a rest would do me good."

The next day, May 2, Gehrig officially ended his consecutive games streak. He brought the lineup card out to home plate before the game and tipped his cap to the Detroit crowd, who cheered wildly when they understood what was happening. And one of the game's greatest records was brought to a solemn end.

A little over a month later, on June 19, his 36th birthday, Gehrig got the news from the Mayo Clinic that he had a degenerative, incurable nerve disease. His teammates were stricken, especially when the newspapers caught wind of it. They called the illness "infantile paralysis—polio" and many of the Yankees were petrified that Gehrig's disease was contagious. One overzealous New York sportswriter even penned a column that said that the reason the Yankees were slumping in June was the team had contracted polio from Gehrig. He was later sued by several Yankees and ultimately settled out of court. Gehrig never returned to the lineup.

On July 4, the Yankees held Lou Gehrig Day at the Stadium. Mayor Fiorello La Guardia was on hand to speak. Postmaster General James Farley and many of Gehrig's teammates on the 1927 Yankees were present. And Ruth. Yes, Babe Ruth was there, retired for four years himself. He went up and threw his big meaty arms around Gehrig, a teammate and ex-pal. The two hadn't spoken in years, not since Ruth inadvertently criticized Gehrig's mother. After the speeches were concluded, it was Gehrig's turn to talk, but he was too choked up. He couldn't do it. Master of Ceremonies Sid Mercer saw it and spoke up. "I shall not ask Lou Gehrig to make a speech. I do not believe that I should." They started to take the microphones away and Gehrig started toward the Yankee dugout. Then, suddenly, he stopped and walked back toward the microphone. The crowd of 60,000 hushed. He held up a hand and spoke from his heart.

"Fans, for the past two weeks, you have been reading about a bad break I got. Yet today, I consider myself the luckiest man on the face of the Earth. I have been in ballparks for 17 years and I have never received anything but kindness and encouragement from you fans.

"Look at these grand men. Which of you wouldn't consider it the highlight of his career just to associate with them for even one day? Sure I'm lucky. Who wouldn't have considered it an honor to have known Jacob Ruppert? Also, the builder of baseball's greatest empire, Ed Barrow? To have spent six years with that wonderful little fellow Miller Huggins? Then to have spent the next nine years with that outstanding leader, that smart student of psychology, the best manager in baseball today, Joe McCarthy?

"Sure, I'm lucky. When the New York Giants, a team you would give your right arm to beat and vice versa, sends you a gift, that's something. When everybody down to the groundskeepers and those boys in white coats remember you with trophies, that's something. When you have a mother and father who work all their lives so that you can have an education and build your body, it's a blessing.

"When you have a wife who has been a tower of strength and shown more courage than you dreamed existed, that's the finest I know. So I close in saying that I might have been given a bad break, but I've got an awful lot to live for."

Gehrig died two years and one month from the very day his 2,130-game streak ended in Detroit—June 2, 1941.

Lou Gehrig by the Numbers

YEAR	TEAM	G	AB	R	H	TB	2B	3B	HR	RBI	BB	SO	SB	BA	SLG	OBP
1923	NYY	13	26	6	11	20	4	1	1	8	2	5	0	.423	.769	.464
1924	NYY	10	12	2	6	7	1	0	0	5	1	3	0	.500	.583	.538
1925	NYY	126	437	73	129	232	23	10	20	68	46	49	6	.295	.531	.365
1926	NYY	155	572	135	179	314	47	20	16	109	106	73	6	.313	.549	.421
1927	NYY	155	584	149	218	447	52	18	47	173	109	84	10	.373	.765	.474
1928	NYY	154	562	139	210	364	47	13	27	147	94	67	4	.374	.648	.467
1929	NYY	154	553	127	166	323	32	10	35	125	124	71	4	.300	.584	.433
1930	NYY	154	581	143	220	419	42	17	41	173	102	63	12	.379	.721	.474
1931	NYY	155	619	163	211	410	31	15	46	184	117	56	17	.341	.662	.446
1932	NYY	156	596	138	208	370	42	9	34	151	108	38	4	.349	.621	.451
1933	NYY	152	593	138	198	359	41	12	32	140	92	42	9	.334	.605	.424
1934	NYY	154	579	128	210	409	40	6	49	166	109	31	9	.363	.706	.465
1935	NYY	149	535	125	176	312	26	10	30	120	133	38	8	.329	.583	.467
1936	NYY	155	579	167	205	403	37	7	49	152	130	46	3	.354	.696	.478
1937	NYY	157	569	138	200	366	37	9	37	158	127	49	4	.351	.643	.473
1938	NYY	157	576	116	170	301	32	6	29	114	107	74	6	.295	.523	.410
1939	NYY	8	28	2	4	4	0	0	0	1	5	1	0	.143	.143	.273
TOTALS		2164	8001	1889	2721	5060	534	163	493	1994	1512	790	102	.340	.632	.448

CAL RIPKEN JR.

SWEET FINALE FOR CAL

DATE: October 6, 2001

SITE: Camden Yards, Baltimore, Maryland

PITCHER: David Cone of the Boston Red Sox

RESULT: Flyout to left fielder Trot Nixon

How do you say goodbye to a legend? It wasn't an easy thing for the Baltimore Orioles to do. Cal Ripken, in many ways, was the embodiment of the Oriole franchise. The guy who never missed a game was going to play his last one. This would be a night to remember. Former president Bill Clinton showed up to say thanks. David Letterman sent in a video tribute, a Top 10 list that included the bulletin that Ripken ended his consecutive game streak at 2,632 so he could catch a *Golden Girls* marathon on the Lifetime Network.

There was baseball stuff there, too. The kind of gesture that showed just how Ripken had touched everyone who'd worn the Orioles uniform. Just as he was about to run onto the field for his 3,001st and final game, the entire Orioles lineup from his very first big-league game (August 12, 1981) emerged from the third base dugout, wearing 1981 Orioles uniforms. That is, all of them except for Mark Belanger, the O's shortstop who'd died of cancer a few years back. His place was taken by his son.

By the end of the night, Cal had been treated to a chauffeured trip around the ballpark in the back of a cherry-red Corvette, and given a spotlighted Farewell Address that General MacArthur would have approved of. There were fireworks, music, and more sentimentality than *Terms of Endearment*.

The only way Cal Ripken could have correctly finished off this magnificent final night would have been to climb aboard a rocket ship and fly directly to the moon, where first, he'd unfurl a giant Orioles logo, then inscribe the numbers 2,632 with a Cal Ripken–model Louisville Slugger on the lunar surface.

Was this the right way to say goodbye? Was it too much? What do you do for a cultural monument who happens to still be alive when you want to honor him? The Orioles did about everything they could think of. There wasn't much else left in their season. Why not make an event out of it? Cash in. The media did the same thing, with TV specials and memorial editions, and hour-long tributes. If Channel 5 did it, Channel 2 had to.

The thing is, what do you do? You can't ignore someone who lasted as long and played as well as Ripken did. But where do you draw the line? Or do you draw a line? Speaking strictly from a baseball standpoint, Ripken's career had been on a downslide for five years. He hadn't been the same player and had slowed quite a bit. But he loved playing. The age-old question that plagues every superstar was starting to get asked around the Orioles offices. Who was going to ask him to leave?

In mid-June, Ripken solved that problem nicely. He off-handedly slipped word of his impending retirement to Dave Sheinin of the *Washington*

Post. Ripken, hitting just .132 over his previous 10 games, was beginning to feel the pressure to move on. But he wanted to finish what he started. When you've played in 2,632 consecutive games, you're not about to quit in midseason. Maybe this move—get it off his chest—would help.

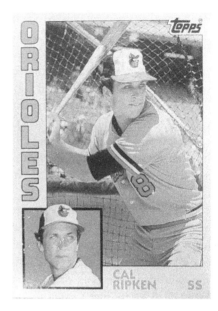

Within minutes, it seemed word of Ripken's retirement at the end of the season was out. Front page of the *Baltimore Sun.* Top story on ESPN's *Baseball Tonight.* Talk radio. Everywhere.

The next day, there was a hastily assembled press conference in Baltimore. Ripken, wearing a bright blue short-sleeved shirt and black slacks with a portable microphone pack on his waist, seemed glad to see everyone and talk on his own terms. He walked in with wife, Kelly, at his side. He had the air of someone who'd just won an election. He stole her line to open things. "I don't have a formal statement," he told the media. "I do have an observation, though. I guess maybe I'll give Kelly the credit for it. She said 'It feels like we're getting married all over again.' That's my statement."

It all happened so fast, his teammates found out about Cal's decision from the newspapers or TV. With three full months of baseball left, including the All-Star Game, it was an open invitation for America to show Cal their love. America came through.

First, he and Tony Gywnn, who was also retiring at the end of the season, were invited to the All-Star Game and given awards right in the middle of the game. Then Ripken, with his flair for the dramatic, like so many of the game's all-time greats, gave everyone something to smile about.

In his final All-Star at-bat, he had barely stepped into the box and stared out at Dodgers starter Chan Ho Park when the ball was on its way. Ripken cut loose with a mighty swing. Before you could say "Goodbye," Ripken caught a belt-high fastball in front of the plate with a resounding crack. There was no doubt about where it was headed.

And as he trotted toward first base, watching it all the way, he saw it descend into the bullpen. Home run. And he smiled. Ripken had also homered on the night he broke Lou Gehrig's record. He'd also been a hero in several All-Star Games, including winning MVP in the 1991 All-Star Game, the night after he hit 12 home runs out of 22 swings in the Home Run Derby to win that title. This was a guy who knew how to step up. Now he was showing he could step down, too.

Named the All-Star Game's Most Valuable Player, Ripken seemed nourished by the love of a nation. The next day, the Ripken Farewell Tour began in earnest. Ripken seemed revitalized.

Though there were endless autograph sessions—which he initiated—endless interview requests before and after games, somehow he never got tired of it. Amazingly, he also began to hit. In one game against the Atlanta Braves, he collected six hits in six trips, including a pair of homers. His batting average climbed all the way to .261. He continued to play well in the field and looked as if he were enjoying every single inning, like he had in the old days.

That was something people didn't understand about Ripken's consecutive game streak. Everybody around him saw it as work. He saw it as play. Even as hard as he worked, it was still play to him.

By late September, though, Ripken was worn out. The crowds didn't care, of course, and he wasn't about to come out of the lineup. The average dipped. As he came out of the dugout for his first at-bat on that final Sunday night, Ripken had managed just two hits in his previous 45 at-bats, an .044 batting average. His seasonal mark had dipped to .242. Maybe he would rise to the occasion on this final night. He had so many times before. Both teams were excited about it.

Why, Boston's David Cone had skipped a turn in the rotation just to pitch this game. He decided to throw Ripken nothing but fastballs. "I didn't throw him any cookies, though," Cone said later.

In his first trip, after taking ball one, Ripken crushed Cone's second pitch, scorching a shot to left field that was gloved. One out. "I really, really hit that ball hard," Ripken said later.

His next time up, still facing Cone, Ripken let a fastball get in on his hands and popped up to shortstop, angrily flinging the bat away like some guy who'd just spent a fortune on batting lessons and somehow forgot Lesson One: Hit a strike.

Ripken came up one last time, in the eighth, and everyone at Camden Yards knew, finally, this was going to be it. Flashbulbs were going off all over the stadium from the instant he stepped out of the dugout like a Hollywood premiere. It amazed him. Hadn't everyone who wanted a picture of him already taken one? Surely, they'd already had an autograph. Or two or three. What more could they want? What could he do in this last at-bat that would send everyone home happy?

He stood there calmly, acknowledging the cheers that filled the park. How was he going to leave this game, after all? So many other great players had left quietly. Lou Gehrig with a flyball. Babe Ruth with a nubber to first. Mickey Mantle a popout to short. Ripken stepped in and swung the bat back and forth. He'd come a long way since 1981. He'd had 3,184 hits, 431 home runs, 1,695 RBIs. Pretty nice numbers. This was game number 3001.

Cone wound and gave him a medium-height fastball that he swung at and just missed. The high, harmless flyball dropped in Trot Nixon's glove in left-center field. Ripken peeled off back toward the Oriole dugout. There was an inning to go. Three more outs.

Amazingly, in the bottom of the ninth, these dead-in-the-water Orioles rallied in a game that Boston seemed to have salted away. Trailing by a run, with one out, Brady Anderson moved into the on-deck circle. He turned to Ripken, who was next. "You want to hit again?" Ripken smiled and nodded. Of course, he wanted to hit again. He was Cal Ripken, wasn't he? "OK," Anderson told him. "I'll make that happen."

Boston's Ugueth Urbina was throwing hard and when Anderson stepped in, there were two out. A "We Want Cal!" chant rose up from the crowd. Flashbulbs still popped. Ripken knelt in the on-deck circle and waited. Would he get three last swings?

Anderson put up a mighty fight. With a full count, he chased a fastball in his eyes to end it. Urbina pumped a fist on the mound. Ripken stood and greeted his teammate. It was OK, he said.

A little while later, no one had left. With the stadium darkened, except for a spotlight on him, Ripken walked back out to a podium, as if giving a State of the Union Address. Which, in a way, he was. Who better to speak for the state of the game than its most celebrated participant?

"As a kid, I had this dream," Ripken said. "And I had parents that encouraged that dream.

"Then I became part of this organization that helped me fulfill this dream. Imagine playing for my hometown team for my whole career. Tonight, we close the chapter on this dream, my playing career."

What was strange was his voice. So calm. So collected. So . . . reasoned. He was ready to retire. And it was hard to believe. Harder to accept. "I've been asked, how do I want to be remembered?" Ripken said, the words echoing through the ballpark and hearts of every true baseball fan all across America. "My answer has been simple. To be remembered at all is pretty special."

Cal Ripken Jr. by the Numbers

YEAR	TEAM	G	AB	R	H	TB	2B	3B	HR	RBI	BB	SO	SB	BA	SLG	OBP
1981	BAL	23	39	1	5	5	0	0	0	0	1	8	0	.128	.128	.150
1982	BAL	160	598	90	158	284	32	5	28	93	46	95	3	.264	.475	.317
1983	BAL	162	663	121	211	343	47	2	27	102	58	97	0	.318	.517	.371
1984	BAL	162	641	103	195	327	37	7	27	86	71	89	2	.304	.510	.374
1985	BAL	161	642	116	181	301	32	5	26	110	67	68	2	.282	.469	.347
1986	BAL	162	627	98	177	289	35	1	25	81	70	60	4	.282	.461	.355
1987	BAL	162	624	97	157	272	28	3	27	98	81	77	3	.252	.436	.333
1988	BAL	161	575	87	152	248	25	1	23	81	102	69	2	.264	.431	.372
1989	BAL	162	646	80	166	259	30	0	21	93	57	72	3	.257	.401	.317
1990	BAL	161	600	78	150	249	28	4	21	84	82	66	3	.250	.415	.341
1991	BAL	162	650	99	210	368	46	5	34	114	53	46	6	.323	.566	.374
1992	BAL	162	637	73	160	233	29	1	14	72	64	50	4	.251	.366	.323
1993	BAL	162	641	87	165	269	26	3	34	90	65	58	1	.257	.420	.329
1994	BAL	112	444	71	140	204	19	3	13	75	32	41	1	.315	.459	.364
1995	BAL	144	550	71	144	232	33	2	17	88	52	59	0	.262	.422	.324
1996	BAL	163	640	94	178	298	40	1	26	102	59	78	1	.278	.466	.341
1997	BAL	162	615	79	166	247	30	0	17	84	56	73	1	.270	.402	.331
1998	BAL	161	601	65	163	234	27	1	14	61	51	68	0	.271	.389	.331
1999	BAL	86	332	51	113	194	27	0	18	57	13	31	0	.340	.584	.368
2000	BAL	83	309	43	79	140	16	0	15	56	23	37	0	.256	.453	.310
2001	BAL	128	477	43	114	172	16	0	14	68	26	63	0	.239	.361	.276
TOTALS		3001	11551	1647	3184	5168	603	44	431	1695	1129	1305	36	.276	.447	.340

1993

CARLTON FISK

THANKS FOR THE MEMORIES, CARLTON

DATE: June 22, 1993

SITE: Comiskey Park, Chicago, Illinois

PITCHER: Kenny Rogers of the Texas Rangers

RESULT: Flyout to Dave Hulse

Y ou can see him sitting at his stall in his underwear, feet in stirrups, baseball undershirt and jock on, scanning that morning's *Tribune*. "That
pissant," he would say, reaching down for a paper cup, spitting with extra
emphasis, though the Chicago White Sox locker room was mostly empty.
The game with the Texas Rangers wouldn't begin for a few hours yet.

As Carlton Fisk read the remarks from the California Angels' diminutive
outfielder Luis Polonia one more time, he could feel the back of his neck getting hot. If he had only known this when that little son-of-a— came to the
plate last night. "You know, he's not the same," Polonia said in the *Tribune*.
"You lose a lot when you get old. He's almost done, ready to retire." There was
that word again, retire. Even on a day that would put Fisk into the record
books—Most Games Caught, Lifetime, Carlton Fisk, Boston (A), Chicago
(A) 2,225—there was no escaping it.

At 45, with a batting average well below the Mendoza line (.200), teams
were running against him at will. Hell, 20 steals in a row, the newspaper
cheerfully pointed out. What else could anybody say?

He straightened up in his canvasback chair—his extraordinarily erect
posture always made him look two inches taller—and ran a hand through
his thick brown hair, still parted in the middle like some 18th-century black-
smith or Methodist minister.

He was a native New Englander and looked it, too. He was just as stubborn as ever. Maybe they wanted to retire him, but Carlton Fisk would retire
when he was good and ready and not a second before. He wasn't ready. The
White Sox management had been trying to get him to retire for years now.
How many times had he fought back? There were too many to count.

He remembered back when Jim Fregosi was the White Sox manager.
Once in mid-August, Fregosi said that Fisk, then 38, would be benched for
the rest of the season so they could get a look at Ron Karkovice, the 23-year-
old prospect who'd moved up from Double-A. Fisk was hitting just .215,
so there wasn't much he could say, Fregosi thought. But management knew
better. They knew Fisk.

Through the cooperation of former *Tribune* baseball writer Jerome
Holtzman, the White Sox brass sent Fisk a hint in Holtzman's notes column
the next day. "What happens to Carlton from here on," Holtzman's unnamed
source said, "will depend on his reaction...." Fisk's reaction? Give me a break.
He laughed as he remembered the way he handled it.

"Why they are doing this now, I have no idea," he said in a story that
ran on the top of the page in sports the next day. "What have I done? I've
played hard and I've worked hard. It's been fairly evident for close to a year

that they thought I should be somewhere else. I don't understand why. I feel like from Day One, my situation has been approached less than honorably." That was seven years ago. He was still here. But for how much longer? What is management supposed to do when they have an icon that has outlasted his usefulness? Or somebody who simply won't go along with what they tell him he should do for the team?

Even before the season started, the White Sox management tried to get Fisk to accept a minor-league contract for $500,000 so they could protect another prospect on their 40-man major-league roster. Most 44-year-olds, happy to have a major-league job, would have agreed. Fisk said no.

He'd hit more home runs than anyone in White Sox history, had been essential in reestablishing the franchise as a viable contender in the 1980s after coming over from Boston when Red Sox management blundered and let an angry Fisk get away. So no, he didn't trust management. Still. Not after 24 years in the major leagues. He knew how it all worked, what a meat market it was.

He could hear the noise rising around him as the clubhouse began to fill up with young millionaires.

"Today, one, two, three-million dollar salaries are assumed," he would say a couple years later. "Some of the guys would kid me because I grew up in such a different era. They can't even fathom what it was like to be expected to do chores and work for the family and not get paid for it."

He felt very distant from just about all of them, and that made this management crap worse. Fisk didn't have anything in common with any of these guys. He clearly came from a different time.

"I enjoyed coming out and hitting," he said later. "Even warming up the pitchers, talking to those who would listen . . . but the rest, it became difficult." He didn't like the way the game was turning, either. The last blitz of national media Fisk got before this, for the games caught record, was back in 1990 when he dressed down then New York Yankee outfielder Deion Sanders for not running out a popup at Yankee Stadium, The House That Ruth Built.

Sanders, a National Football League All-Star defensive back in the off-season, barely moved toward first and had peeled off toward the Yankee dugout when he heard Fisk, mask balanced on top of his head, screaming at him (and really every other overpaid rookie hotshot who was ruining his game). "Run it out, you piece of shit," Fisk said.

Sanders was shocked. Unlike his usual manner, he didn't say anything back. On his next trip to the plate, Deion couldn't help himself. He muttered something to Fisk.

"What?" Fisk shot back, hoping, maybe even praying for a confrontation. "The days of slavery are over," Sanders, a two-sport millionaire, said.

Fisk stood up and was at full bellow before you could say "Go." "Let me tell you something, you little son-of-a—. There is a right way and a wrong way to play this game. You're playing it the wrong way. And the rest of us don't like it. Someday you're going to get this game shoved right down your throat." Or up somewhere else, he had to be thinking. The umpire leaped between the two players and both benches emptied. All over Fisk's moral crisis.

To some, he was a hero for that. And frankly, he hadn't given them much to cheer about for some time now. And when he came up out of the dugout for the pregame ceremony that night, he could hear the cheers from all corners of Comiskey Park. Cheers of relief.

He saw a few signs. "The Commander" and "Fisk Forever." Forever. Well, at 45, he almost got there, he laughed. When the team and management gathered around him out in front of the mound a little while later, he was proud and as always, unyielding. His teammates gave him a motorcycle; Bo Jackson himself rode it in from center field. The White Sox gave him a shadow box of home plate, gave his wife, Linda, a diamond bracelet, and had some orchids (one of his off-field hobbies) planted in Fisk's name at Chicago's Botanical Garden.

But the unpleasant undercurrent between him and management was still there, and you could hear it in Fisk's voice when he began to speak. "This record isn't something that just happened," he said. "It is more an example of perseverance and endurance. I always dreamed and expected it to end on a productive note." White Sox management looked around, at the ground, preparing for the other spike. And here it came.

"I find it has been increasingly difficult to maintain a competitive edge," Fisk said, his voice strong and defiant. "I feel as though I've played hard, played with intensity, and played with enthusiasm. But most importantly, I've played to win. I've given a lot to this game and the game has taken a lot. The game has been fun sometimes and sometimes it hasn't. When the old rooster crows, the young rooster learns, and I've crowed a lot in my life."

Which was part of what made Carlton Fisk such an extraordinary figure in baseball history. He was a modern-era player with old-school values. And, as that 12th-inning "wave it fair" World Series home run showed, someone who understood that baseball was meant to be *played*, not performed.

And he could be cranky. "I really resent that old phrase about the 'tools of ignorance,'" Fisk told writer Roger Angell one spring late in his career. "No catcher is ignorant. I've caught for pitchers who thought that if they won it's because they did such a great job, and if they lost, it's because you called the wrong pitch. A lot of pitchers need to be led—taken to the point where they're told what pitch to throw, where to throw it, when to throw it and what to do after they've thrown it. I worked with Luis Tiant as well as anybody, and if he threw a fastball waist-high down the middle—well, it was nobody's fault but his own and he was the first to say so. Not many fans know the stats about catchers, but smart pitchers notice after a while that they'll have a certain earned-run average with one catcher and that it'll be a point and a half higher with another catcher on the same club. Then they've begun to see that it isn't just their talent that's carrying them out there."

At 45, though, his sermons were mostly falling on ears already plugged with headphones or adorned with earrings. He felt as much of an outsider as a rookie. It was a relief to get the game going.

When Fisk stepped to the plate in the second inning, the plane he'd hired flew over Comiskey Park carrying a banner that read "Thanks for your support, Sox fans No. 72." Facing Texas lefty Kenny Rogers, he lifted a flyball to deep center to Dave Hulse.

In the fifth, he put down a nice sacrifice bunt to move Lance Johnson to second base. Johnson then scored on Craig Grebeck's single. In the seventh, Fisk came up for the final time that night—and the final at-bat of his career, as it turned out. He again lofted a deep flyball to Hulse in center field.

When White Sox manager Gene Lamont sent out Mike Lavalliere, another New Hampshire boy, to catch for Fisk in the eighth, his night was over. So was his career.

Though there had been plenty of hints dropped in the Chicago papers about the White Sox needing to make a roster move and that the aging Fisk was a likely candidate, he read over it.

He sat on the bench the next five nights. Then, six days after he'd set the record for most games caught, lifetime, a testament to his stubborn pride and extraordinary endurance and persistence, the White Sox pulled into Cleveland to begin a series with the Tribe.

Fisk was summoned to General Manager Ron Schueler's room on the 13th floor of the team hotel as soon as the White Sox arrived in town. He told him that the White Sox had given him his release.

"He thought I was calling him to talk about his role on the team," Schueler told the press. "I don't think he expected it. He still thought he was going to be here all season. It was a rough thing to do but I feel I owe it to the fans, the city of Chicago and the White Sox organization to try and bring home a winner."

The White Sox, then battling the Kansas City Royals for the American League West lead, did go on and win the West but fell in six games in the American League Championship Series to Toronto.

Carlton Fisk never played again. Though he ended up playing longer in Chicago than he did in Boston, when he was inducted to the Baseball Hall of Fame in the summer of 2000, he chose to go in as a member of the Red Sox.

Carlton Fisk by the Numbers

YEAR	TEAM	G	AB	R	H	TB	2B	3B	HR	RBI	BB	SO	SB	BA	SLG	OBP
1969	BOS	2	5	0	0	0	0	0	0	0	0	2	0	.000	.000	.000
1971	BOS	14	48	7	15	25	2	1	2	6	1	10	0	.313	.521	.327
1972	BOS	131	457	74	134	246	28	9	22	61	52	83	5	.293	.538	.370
1973	BOS	135	508	65	125	224	21	0	26	71	37	99	7	.246	.441	.309
1974	BOS	52	187	36	56	103	12	1	11	26	24	23	5	.299	.551	.383
1975	BOS	79	263	47	87	139	14	4	10	52	27	32	4	.331	.529	.395
1976	BOS	134	487	76	124	202	17	5	17	58	56	71	12	.255	.415	.336
1977	BOS	152	536	106	169	279	26	3	26	102	75	85	7	.315	.521	.402
1978	BOS	157	571	94	162	271	39	5	20	88	71	83	7	.284	.475	.366
1979	BOS	91	320	49	87	144	23	2	10	42	10	38	3	.272	.450	.304
1980	BOS	131	478	73	138	223	25	3	18	62	36	62	11	.289	.467	.353
1981	CHW	96	338	44	89	122	12	0	7	45	38	37	3	.263	.361	.354
1982	CHW	135	476	66	127	192	17	3	14	65	46	60	17	.267	.403	.336
1983	CHW	138	488	85	141	253	26	4	26	86	46	88	9	.289	.518	.355
1984	CHW	102	359	54	83	168	20	1	21	43	26	60	6	.231	.468	.289
1985	CHW	153	543	85	129	265	23	1	37	107	52	81	17	.238	.488	.320
1986	CHW	125	457	42	101	154	11	0	14	63	22	92	2	.221	.337	.263
1987	CHW	135	454	68	116	209	22	1	23	71	39	72	1	.256	.460	.321
1988	CHW	76	253	37	70	137	8	1	19	50	37	40	0	.277	.542	.377
1989	CHW	103	375	47	110	178	25	2	13	68	36	60	1	.293	.475	.356
1990	CHW	137	452	65	129	204	21	0	18	65	61	73	7	.285	.451	.378
1991	CHW	134	460	42	111	190	25	0	18	74	32	86	1	.241	.413	.299
1992	CHW	62	188	12	43	58	4	1	3	21	23	38	3	.229	.309	.313
1993	CHW	25	53	2	10	13	0	0	1	4	2	11	0	.189	.245	.228
TOTALS		2499	8756	1276	2356	3999	421	47	376	1330	849	1386	128	.269	.457	.341

ROGERS HORNSBY

RAJAH LEAVES ON A SOUR NOTE

DATE: July 20, 1937

SITE: Sportsman's Park, St. Louis, Missouri

PITCHER: Frank Makosky of the New York Yankees

RESULT: Groundout to pitcher Frank Makosky

There were two things about the great Rogers Hornsby that were sure bets: He was going to hit—he owned a .358 lifetime career average, including three seasons over .400, including a high of .424 in 1924—and he was going to go to the racetrack. Though he was banned from going to the racetrack many times and had his job threatened again and again, Hornsby went anyway. Once Browns business manager Bill DeWitt, father of the Cardinals' current owner, found out he had gone again, Hornsby was fired midway through the 1937 season.

COURTESY OF THE NATIONAL BASEBALL HALL OF FAME LIBRARY

The trouble had started about a month ago with a quote. It was a pithy, brutally honest assessment of the bat-handling capabilities (or liabilities) of the ragtag collection of ballplayers under his direction. It was exactly what one would expect Rogers Hornsby to say. That was the problem.

Presently his St. Louis Browns were one-half game out of the American League cellar. Back in early July, player-manager Hornsby, in talking with an out-of-town newspaper guy named Pat Robinson over breakfast, reportedly called his team "a bunch of banjo hitters." It was true. That was the thing.

But in those days, a manager, even one as crusty as Hornsby, wouldn't come right out and say such a thing. And if he did say it, no writer worth his salt would dare write it. Certainly no St. Louis writer. No manager rips his own players, deserved or not, and expects to read it in that afternoon's newspaper. Not when there's a whole season of baseball ahead and that writer planned to keep on covering the team. But that's just what happened. And the mess wouldn't disappear.

In his fifth season with the Browns and 12th overall as a player-manager, everybody knew Hornsby, one of the game's greatest hitters, didn't have a lot to work with. The team was going nowhere. There wasn't much else to write.

Somehow, this "banjo hitters" controversy wouldn't go away. It was everywhere you went.

Finally, on July 2, Hornsby addressed the issue with the *St. Louis Post-Dispatch*. "That story from New York in which I was quoted about 'banjo hitters' was signed by Pat Robinson," he said. "I haven't seen Robinson in at least a year. The last time I saw him he was in a group that included Dan Daniel of the *New York World-Telegram*, Frankie Graham of the *New York Sun*, Charlie O'Leary, and myself.

"We were talking about the pennant race and somebody brought up the subject of umpires. I said that perhaps umpires made an occasional mistake, but that so did we. . . . O'Leary said something about umpires who always favored the home team and the next day, Robinson wrote a story quoting me as saying the American League umpires were 'a lot of homers. . . .'"

Ah yes, the old "I was misquoted" trick. Except that anyone who knew the caustic old National Leaguer Hornsby didn't doubt for a second that he probably said that about American League umpires. And "banjo hitters."

Heck, as one of the game's greatest right-handed hitters, Hornsby could speak with some authority on who was a banjo hitter and who wasn't. The thing was, nobody was used to insults at that time, not in the newspaper, anyway.

The next day, the talk was still all around. So Hornsby went into greater detail with a guy he'd known from his Cardinal years, J. Roy Stockton, the *Post-Dispatch*'s baseball writer. "I never said anything about banjo hitters," he said. "You know me long enough that I don't care what anybody writes or says about me, but I would like to clear up that story. . . ."

This time, he told a different story, one about having breakfast with a New York writer who noted that the Browns weren't getting many big hits. "I told him that yes, we were getting lots of hits," Hornsby said, "but that our best hitters were having trouble getting long ones right then and that it was tough to win when you were getting mostly singles and them scattered through a lot of innings. I told him Clift was the only one on the club getting his share of extra-base hits. . . ."

In other words, Hornsby was saying, "No wonder we're losing. I've got a bunch of banjo hitters here, whattya expect?" He just never actually came right out and said those actual words.

"I never had used the expression 'banjo hitters,'" Hornsby explained. "I hadn't put the slug on any of my players and I didn't know what that 'banjo hitter' stuff was all about until I got back to St. Louis and they showed me a clipping of a story in which another New York writer, whom I didn't talk to about it at all, quoted me as saying I had a bunch of 'banjo hitters' on my club."

The Rajah was turning a one-day story into the elephant in the living room. Or maybe the clubhouse. Now, it was true that sometimes, writers would spread the word and it would get out. There might be three or four of 'em sitting around talking over beers and one of them might pipe up and say "Talked to Hornsby the other day. He's getting fed up managing the Browns. He can't get decent pitching and he's got a bunch of banjo hitters on his team, so how can you win with a lineup like that?" Something like that.

Then one of those guys would get back to the office, has nothing else— he's covering the Browns, remember?—and write it up. Even though he never actually heard Hornsby say those words himself. Happened all the time.

The hullabaloo even got Donald Barnes, the president of the Browns, going. "I'd like to spike these rumors that are being circulated," Barnes told the *Post-Dispatch*, "to the effect that Hornsby is in trouble with us and is going to be released. . . . Of course, when a man has been in the public eye as long as Hornsby has, he usually has a few enemies. . . . There are a few snipers right here in St. Louis who welcome every chance to take a shot at Hornsby. But he has been 100 percent with us and we are backing him the same way. We are well satisfied with the way things are going this year. Naturally, we'd like to win more games but we don't blame Hornsby. . . . In fact, I personally am pleased to find that we have a better ballclub than the one we bought."

It was a vote of confidence. The sure kiss of death. A little over two weeks later, the Browns were still struggling. They'd lost 12 of 14 games and with the New York Yankees in town for a Tuesday afternoon game, things came to a head.

The "banjo hitters" were getting to him. Hornsby was really agitated. Nobody could get a big hit for them when it counted. They could get singles all right, heck they had 11 hits through nine, the Yankees just four.

Yet here was poor Oral Hildebrand, pitching probably one of his best games of an 8-17 season, holding the Yankees to just four hits, the big blow a three-run homer by Joe DiMaggio in the fifth. And the Browns finally got him three runs in the eighth to tie it, but no more. Here we were in the 10th.

Hildebrand opened the inning by walking Frank Crosetti, but got Red Rolfe to bounce one right at Tim "Scoops" Carey at second, Hornsby's old spot, a nice spot for a double-play ball. But Carey kicked it. Hildebrand got DiMaggio to bounce out and next up was Lou Gehrig. And wouldn't you know it? Gehrig tops a slow roller to Carey who again, can't make a play. Crosetti comes around to score to break the tie.

In the Browns dugout, Hornsby was irate. Though he wasn't remembered as a great fielding second baseman, he could get an out when he needed it, for cryin' out loud. He looked down the lineup and saw that Carey was up in the 10th. He couldn't wait.

Now, Carey was generally a decent glove man; he only made eight errors all season, tops in the league for second basemen. But Hornsby was hot. When the team came in, he told Hildebrand that they'd get that run back for him. Hornsby was still seething. Beau Bell led off with a single and moved to third on Bill Knickerbocker's double off Yankee reliever Frank Makosky. Maybe they could do it after all.

Yankee manager Joe McCarthy didn't like the looks of that, so he had Makosky walk "Sunny Jim" Bottomley, a pinch-hitter, to load the bases. Let's see how the Browns' "banjo hitters" would do in a tough spot.

"Carey, sit down," Hornsby cried out to his second baseman, who was ready to go up and hit.

There was quiet in the dugout as Hornsby picked out his bat and walked to the plate for the 8,173rd time of his 23-year career. He'd show his team what clutch hitting was like. Let's see Makosky get him out.

Sportsman's Park grew quiet with anticipation as Hornsby dug in. He was, after all, not only a career .358 hitter, he'd led the National League with lifetime grand slams with 12.

But this at-bat was a letdown. He took a mighty cut at Makosky's first pitch and topped it in front of the plate. Yankee catcher Bill Dickey pounced on it and stepped on home. One out.

Pinch-hitter Ethan Allen rocketed one right at right fielder Tommy Heinrich for out number two. Knickerbocker tagged and tried to score but a fine throw had him easily at the plate to end the ballgame. The final was New York 5, St. Louis 4.

The next day, Hornsby was called to meet with Browns business manager Bill DeWitt. He knew what it was. And it didn't have anything to do with baseball. He'd been warned against spending too much time and money at the horse tracks.

Once, when he was strictly a player, he'd gotten himself into debt and had to borrow money from some disagreeable people. So the word was out there. Problem was, when it came to gambling, Hornsby couldn't help himself. Besides, nobody was going to tell Rogers Hornsby what to do.

"Have you been playing the horses again?" DeWitt asked when Hornsby got to his office. Hornsby didn't flinch. "I have," he said. "You're through," DeWitt said. And that was that. Goodbye, Rogers Hornsby.

It was announced that Jim Bottomley would take over Hornsby's 46-108 club. Bottomley went 21-58 for the rest of the year. "Sunny Jim," who likely wouldn't have earned that nickname had he only been a St. Louis Brown, never managed again.

In the days to come, the St. Louis papers tried to get Barnes to say why Hornsby was let go but Barnes wouldn't say. "Just say he was released for cause," he said. "Draw your own conclusions."

Some time later, Hornsby spoke his piece. "My betting at no time interfered with my handling of the club," he said. "Hell, I never promised anybody I wouldn't play the horses. The money is as good as the money you take from the loan shark business [Barnes's principal line of work]. It's better than taking interest from widows and orphans."

A few months later, Hornsby pulled a writer aside. He sounded worried. "I don't know what I'll do," he said. "Maybe there's still a place for me in the game. I don't know any other business. I don't want to. Baseball is the best. But it's like everything else, I guess, some players for you, some against you.

"I'm a tough guy, a gambler on horses, a slave driver and in general, a disgrace to the game. I wish I knew why. I only wanted to win."

On the field and at the horse track. He was great at one of them.

Rogers Hornsby by the Numbers

YEAR	TEAM	G	AB	R	H	TB	2B	3B	HR	RBI	BB	SO	SB	BA	SLG	OBP
1915	SLN	18	57	5	14	16	2	0	0	--	2	6	0	.246	.281	.271
1916	SLN	139	495	63	155	220	17	15	6	--	40	63	17	.313	.444	.369
1917	SLN	145	523	86	171	253	24	17	8	--	45	34	17	.327	.484	.385
1918	SLN	115	416	51	117	173	19	11	5	--	40	43	8	.281	.416	.349
1919	SLN	138	512	68	163	220	15	9	8	--	48	41	17	.318	.430	.384
1920	SLN	149	589	96	218	329	44	20	9	94	60	51	12	.370	.559	.431
1921	SLN	154	592	131	235	378	44	18	21	126	60	48	13	.397	.639	.458
1922	SLN	154	623	142	250	450	46	14	42	152	65	50	17	.401	.722	.459
1923	SLN	107	424	89	163	266	32	10	17	83	55	29	3	.384	.627	.459
1924	SLN	143	536	121	227	373	43	14	25	94	91	31	5	.424	.696	.509
1925	SLN	138	504	133	203	381	41	10	39	143	83	39	5	.403	.756	.489
1926	SLN	134	527	96	167	244	34	5	11	93	61	39	3	.317	.463	.388
1927	NYG	155	568	133	205	333	32	9	26	125	86	38	9	.361	.586	.448
1928	BSN	140	486	99	188	307	42	7	21	94	108	41	5	.387	.632	.499
1929	CHC	156	602	156	229	409	47	8	39	150	87	65	2	.380	.679	.459
1930	CHC	42	104	15	32	45	5	1	2	18	12	12	0	.308	.433	.385
1931	CHC	100	357	64	118	205	37	1	16	90	56	23	1	.331	.574	.421
1932	CHC	19	58	10	13	18	2	0	1	7	10	4	0	.224	.310	.357
1933	SLN	46	83	9	27	39	6	0	2	21	12	6	1	.325	.470	.423
1933	ALL	11	9	2	3	7	1	0	1	2	2	0	0	.333	.778	.455
1933	SLA	57	92	11	30	46	7	0	3	23	14	6	1	.326	.500	.426
1934	SLA	24	23	2	7	12	2	0	1	11	7	4	0	.304	.522	.484
1935	SLA	10	24	1	5	8	3	0	0	3	3	6	0	.208	.333	.296
1936	SLA	2	5	1	2	2	0	0	0	2	1	0	0	.400	.400	.500
1937	SLA	20	56	7	18	24	3	0	1	11	7	5	0	.321	.429	.397
TOTALS		2259	8173	1580	2930	4712	541	169	301	1319	1041	678	135	.358	.577	.434

1986

PETE ROSE

A LATE SCRATCH

DATE: August 17, 1986

SITE: Riverfront Stadium, Cincinnati, Ohio

PITCHER: Rich "Goose" Gossage of the San Diego Padres

RESULT: Strikeout

He got up from his spot in the dugout and went to the bat rack in the bottom of the ninth. Nobody said a word.

Here it was, mid-August, and Pete Rose's fourth-place Cincinnati Reds were trailing the San Diego Padres, the worst team in the National League, 9–5. It didn't look as if things were going to improve any time soon. Padres reliever Rich "Goose" Gossage was in his second inning of relief and still throwing aspirin tablets.

Looking down the dugout, it was hard to find any volunteers. Earlier in the game, Rose, in his second year as player-manager, had already made some moves. He'd already sent Tony Pérez and John Milner up as pinch-hitters. He was running out of choices.

With the top of the order coming up here in the ninth, he needed somebody else to get on base. Why not him? Nobody else was offering.

The dog days of August were setting in, and Rose's Reds seemed to be going nowhere. They were already 10½ games behind Houston, five games under .500. Following Rose's encouraging second-place finish last year—he took over the team after being dealt from Montreal in midseason—many thought this year's club would win it all.

But the year was a bust. Rose was on the disabled list when the year began. The Reds couldn't sort out their pitching, dropped 19 of their first 25 games, and for months, couldn't seem to get rolling.

Worse, Rose, now 45 years old, couldn't step in and help. He'd played in just 72 of the team's first 116 games and seemed relegated to pinch-hitting and playing the occasional day game after a night game.

At the start of the month, Rose's skidding average had bottomed out at a miserable .204. Had he not been the manager, there's no doubt he would have been shamed into retirement. This was not the way a Hall of Famer ought to go out. Yet Rose had one surprise left.

One marvelous Monday night, Rose turned back the clock for the last time. He found his stroke and went 5-for-5 (including the final extra-base hit of his career, his 746th double), off three different San Francisco Giants pitchers—Mike LaCoss, Mark Davis, and Frank Williams. While Rose's five hits mattered little in a 13–4 San Francisco win, how could you not write about Pete Rose?

Author Roger Kahn, at work on a book on Rose, was there to document the scene. It was like feeding drugged canaries to a manic cat. A sportswriter asked Rose if he knew how many five-hit games he'd had.

"That would be 10," Rose said. What about the National League record, someone else asked?

"I got it now, if I'm not mistaken," Rose said. "The old record was nine. Belonged to Max Carey."

"And the major-league record?" came a third voice.

"Again, if I'm not mistaken," Rose said, "that would be Cobb. You guys remember Cobb. Supposed to have been a mean guy, but he got a lot of hits."

A reporter asked what this achievement meant to him. Rose smiled.

"A slightly larger stone on my grave," he said.

It was his first five-hit game since April 28, four years earlier. It raised his average to a grand .218. The Reds were still 10 games out.

Fueled by his big night, Rose kept himself close to the bat rack for what would be his final active week. Tuesday night, Rose sent himself up as a pinch-hitter against the Giants' Scott Garrelts in a 2–1 loss and grounded out. He did the same thing the next night in an 8–6 win.

Yet as he sat in his office, making out his lineup every night, it was beginning to be hard to know when to play and when to sit. When does a manager bench himself? Both Joe Torre (with the Mets) and Frank Robinson (with the Indians) took a brief shot at playing and managing at the same time. But neither one lasted many games. As a manager, there were too many distractions. And Rose found he was sensitive to criticism.

He knew that not everybody recognized all that went into his job, but handling the second-guess, that was a pitch he wasn't ready to foul off. He explained as much to a visiting writer over batting practice one afternoon, after receiving a particularly nasty letter from a fan.

"Guy's writing that I should have brought in Ron Robinson to replace Ted Power," he said, "Well, I didn't have Ron Robinson to bring in. He couldn't pitch but the guy writing it 1,200 miles away doesn't know that.

"Same as the people who wrote that I put Ty Cobb's record ahead of the team last year. I play in only 119 games, but I'm second in the league in walks. I don't start myself against left-handers and I hit .354 against them. And I'm putting myself ahead of the Cincinnati Reds? I don't let that stuff annoy me but, man, I don't understand it."

As this final week finished, Rose collected what would be the final hit of his career. Facing the Giants' Kelly Downs and reliever Greg Minton, he batted second, played first base, and had three hits as John Denny threw a three-hit shutout against the Giants. Rose even drove in the game-winning run with a fifth-inning single.

By the weekend, something changed in the clubhouse and in Rose's mind. His old pal Tony Pérez, back with the Reds, had already announced he'd retire at the end of the season. He wanted to play first. Rose also had promising Nick Esasky, a strong right-handed power hitter, in the dugout too.

With just 50 games to play, Rose knew he had to do something to get the Reds' attack rolling.

In Friday's twi-night doubleheader vs. the Padres, Rose did pinch-hit and make an out in the first game, a 7–2 win, then played first base against his old pal Eric Show, the Padres pitcher who had surrendered Rose's 4,192nd hit to surpass Cobb the previous summer, and went 0-for-4.

He played on Saturday against Ed Whitson and Lance McCullers in a 4–1 Reds win. But his 0-for-4 dropped his seasonal average to .219 and his career average to .303. The guy who'd won four National League batting titles, three of them with averages over .330, well, that guy wasn't stepping into batter's boxes these days. With another out or three, he'd be below .300 for his career, just like Mickey Mantle.

He'd been at this for so long now. There were so many other things to deal with as a manager. And distractions away from the field too. After all this time in fame's fast lane, Pete Rose wasn't about to stop taking chances. But the batting average? That was history. You didn't screw with that.

There were other things tugging at Rose now, not just age. The fans could sense it, perhaps, but still hoped their hero would come through. They didn't realize the gambling fever was taking over.

Rose, like a lot of other baseball people from Rogers Hornsby all the way to Don Zimmer, loved to spend every spare moment at the track. It wasn't hard to figure why. They liked the action, the excitement, anything that got the adrenaline going.

But there were rumblings that this wasn't just gambling there. It wasn't only wagers on college football and basketball. Or the NFL. If the talk was right, this was more serious. There was talk that Rose was betting on his own sport, baseball.

There would be talk that when the Riverfront Stadium out-of-town scoreboard was out of action for a couple months, Rose had a pal in the stands keeping tabs on all the other games Pete had supposedly bet on. Supposedly, the two exchanged signals throughout the game so Pete could keep tabs on his bets.

Gambling on baseball is a sore subject in Cincinnati. It was the underdog Redlegs who were the beneficiaries of the 1919 World Series title supposedly thrown by the Chicago "Black Sox," and the town has understandably been sensitive on the subject ever since.

But if there were any questions about Pete's off-the-field behavior when he played for the Reds or when he came back to manage, nobody said a word about it. He was a folk hero in Cincinnati.

When Rose let it be known he wanted out of Montreal in 1984, Cincinnati president Bob Howsam got a call from Rose's agent Reuven Katz and the two talked about Rose becoming manager.

There were problems. One was Rose's $500,000 salary, which was more than the Reds could afford, Howsam said. The other was Howsam didn't think Rose could hit anymore. Rose, never one to back down from a challenge, knew what he wanted to have happen. Like he explained to writer Roger Kahn some time later, Rose knew how to get things his way.

"There aren't many things I back away from," he said. "If they wouldn't let me play back home in Cincinnati, then I was damned if I was going to manage. I'd hang in at Montreal and take my chances, as a free agent, it looked like, the following year. But I wanted to come home to be with the Reds when they won a pennant. I wanted to come home like a kid who forgot his school lunch somewhere and is standing in the yard smelling his mother's cooking through a window. . . ."

There was another problem. The Major League Players Union has an across-the-board rule that no player's salary may be reduced more than 20 percent at one time. Howsam was offering Rose $225,000, less than half his salary in Montreal. But Rose really wanted to come home. He applied to the union for a dispensation and they agreed.

The next day, Rose was in uniform and in his very first at-bat against the Phillies' Dick Ruthven, ripped a single to center field. When the ball was misplayed, Rose came around second and flew into third with a wonderful belly whomping, headfirst slide. Yesssssireeeee. Pete Rose was back.

That was two years earlier. A lot can happen in two years. Rose looked around at the middling crowd of 27,175. There was no huge reaction from the crowd when he was announced. He'd stayed long enough to be overlooked.

Rose walked up to the plate, took his familiar crouch in the left-hand batter's box against Gossage, and got ready for his 14,053rd and final major-league at-bat. Zing. . . . Gossage's fastball blistered past Rose's feeble swing. Home plate umpire Ed Montague signaled strike one. Gotta be quicker, he thought. Damn. Quicker. Gossage wound and with that wild, tottering delivery, fired again. Zing. . . . Rose swung through another fastball. Goose was bringing it.

Rose stepped out of the batter's box. I'm not going to catch up with that, he thought. Nobody had gotten a hit off Gossage yet. Or a walk. Didn't look like anybody would. Rose peered out at the mound in that crouch, his chin tucked behind his right shoulder, trying to pick the ball up out of Gossage's windmill motion. He saw Gossage rock and let the ball go. There was no way, just no way to get a bat on it. He swung and missed and the ball popped into catcher Bruce Bochy's glove.

He never batted again.

A week later, the Reds rolled into Chicago and *Tribune* columnist Bob Verdi asked him why he wasn't playing.

"Want to get Esasky in there," Rose said. "My decision to retire or not depends on how I finish up and how we finish up. There's no hurry. I don't want to make it before the season ends so I can have a night in Riverfront. I've had enough hullabaloo in my career."

So there would be no Pete Rose Farewell Tour?

"If I knew that was going to happen to me, I would have done that," Rose told Kahn. "But I didn't know and I had my philosophy. You see, play, or manage, I was going to the ballpark every day. I was putting my uniform on. It was not like I was going to be away from it."

Besides, as we would find out later, Rose had many other problems at the time. Concentrating on managing and hitting and keeping up with all the off-the-field nonsense was too much.

Years later, Rose explained his sudden benching to author Roger Kahn this way. "My buddy Tony Perez had shared first base with me. Tony was in his last year. He had announced his retirement. He was a couple of home runs behind Orlando Cepeda as the most productive home run hitter of all the Latin players.

"He did end up tying that record," Rose said. "As a matter of fact, in the last week of the season Tony played and he was player of the week in the National League. I let him play the whole month of September because he was swinging the bat good and I wanted him to get the record."

But Rose's term as manager was short-lived. The off-the-field stuff escalated to the point where it became scandalous. A *Sports Illustrated* story blew it wide open.

Three years and one week later, he was sent away from the game for good. Four months after it was alleged that Rose had been betting on baseball (among other things), then-commissioner Bart Giamatti ended a long investigation with Rose signing an agreement that would permit him to step away without admitting to gambling. Then Giamatti made an announcement.

"The banishment for life of Pete Rose from baseball is the sad end of a sorry episode," Giamatti said. "One of the game's greatest players has engaged in a variety of acts which have stained the game and he must now live with the consequences of those acts...."

In the press conference afterward, Rose felt double-crossed. Giamatti and he had agreed on a deal, that the commissioner's office wouldn't say that Pete Rose

bet on baseball and that Rose himself would leave quietly. Yet when a reporter asked Giamatti if he believed that Rose bet on baseball, the commissioner said he believed Rose had.

Nine days later, Giamatti was dead of a heart attack. Rose stuck to the statements he made after the lifetime ban—namely, that he never bet on baseball. As the ban pushed on, Rose, baseball's all-time hit leader, could see his chances for Hall of Fame induction vanishing. A player remains on the Baseball Writers Association ballot for 20 years.

Since Rose was confident that many of the writers were in favor of him being elected to the Hall, if he could get himself off the permanently ineligible list and on their ballot, they might vote him in. If the writers didn't put him in, it'd be up to the Veterans Committee to select him and Rose wasn't sure how that would go. Many of those players are on record as being against Rose's induction. Some have even threatened to boycott future induction ceremonies if he's elected.

So Rose found someone to float the word *confession* to the commissioner's office: his old teammate, Joe Morgan. Back in November of 2002, he was summoned to a meeting with then-commissioner Bud Selig in

Milwaukee. Selig asked Rose the question he finally understood he had to answer. As recounted in Rose's 2004 book *My Prison without Bars* and excerpted in *Sports Illustrated's* January 12, 2004, issue, the meeting went like this: "Mr. Selig looked at me and said, 'I want to know one thing. Did you bet on baseball?'"

"Yes," Rose said. "I did bet on baseball."

"How often?" Selig asked.

"Four or five times a week," Rose replied. "But I never bet against my own team and I never made any bets from the clubhouse."

"Why?" Selig asked.

"I didn't think I'd get caught," Rose said.

Pete Rose by the Numbers

YEAR	TEAM	G	AB	R	H	TB	2B	3B	HR	RBI	BB	SO	SB	BA	SLG	OBP
1963	CIN	157	623	101	170	231	25	9	6	41	55	72	13	.273	.371	.334
1964	CIN	136	516	64	139	168	13	2	4	34	36	51	4	.269	.326	.319
1965	CIN	162	670	117	209	299	35	11	11	81	69	76	8	.312	.446	.382
1966	CIN	156	654	97	205	301	38	5	16	70	37	61	4	.313	.460	.351
1967	CIN	148	585	86	176	260	32	8	12	76	56	66	11	.301	.444	.364
1968	CIN	149	626	94	210	294	42	6	10	49	56	76	3	.335	.470	.391
1969	CIN	156	627	120	218	321	33	11	16	82	88	65	7	.348	.512	.428
1970	CIN	159	649	120	205	305	37	9	15	52	73	64	12	.316	.470	.385
1971	CIN	160	632	86	192	266	27	4	13	44	68	50	13	.304	.421	.373
1972	CIN	154	645	107	198	269	31	11	6	57	73	46	10	.307	.417	.382
1973	CIN	160	680	115	230	297	36	8	5	64	65	42	10	.338	.437	.401
1974	CIN	163	652	110	185	253	45	7	3	51	106	54	2	.284	.388	.385
1975	CIN	162	662	112	210	286	47	4	7	74	89	50	0	.317	.432	.406
1976	CIN	162	665	130	215	299	42	6	10	63	86	54	9	.323	.450	.404
1977	CIN	162	655	95	204	283	38	7	9	64	66	42	16	.311	.432	.377
1978	CIN	159	655	103	198	276	51	3	7	52	62	30	13	.302	.421	.362
1979	PHI	163	628	90	208	270	40	5	4	59	95	32	20	.331	.430	.418
1980	PHI	162	655	95	185	232	42	1	1	64	66	33	12	.282	.354	.352
1981	PHI	107	431	73	140	168	18	5	0	33	46	26	4	.325	.390	.391
1982	PHI	162	634	80	172	214	25	4	3	54	66	32	8	.271	.338	.345
1983	PHI	151	493	52	121	141	14	3	0	45	52	28	7	.245	.286	.316
1984	MTL	95	278	34	72	82	6	2	0	23	31	20	1	.259	.295	.334
1984	CIN	26	96	9	35	44	9	0	0	11	9	7	0	.365	.458	.430
1984	ALL	121	374	43	107	126	15	2	0	34	40	27	1	.286	.337	.359
1985	CIN	119	405	60	107	129	12	2	2	46	86	35	8	.264	.319	.395
1986	CIN	72	237	15	52	64	8	2	0	25	30	31	3	.219	.270	.316
TOTALS		3562	14053	2165	4256	5752	746	135	160	1314	1566	1143	198	.303	.409	.375

1984

JOE MORGAN

STAYING UNDER THE RADAR

DATE: September 29, 1984

SITE: Oakland Coliseum, Oakland, California

PITCHER: Mark Gubicza of the Kansas City Royals

RESULT: Double to left-center

He could hear the mitt popping. Kansas City's Mark Gubicza, a 6-foot 5-inch rookie fireballer, was bringing the high, hard one as he took his warmup pitches for his 29th and final regular-season start. You could hear the pop of fastball after fastball all over Oakland Coliseum as a trickle of die-hard A's fans trekked in for Fan Appreciation Day.

Some, maybe, came to say goodbye to Joe Morgan.

Inside the Oakland dugout, the old-timer was watching Gubicza's every pitch, smiling to himself. One more hard-throwing kid who thinks he can throw the ol' pill past Joe. We'll have to see about that.

His long haul through a 22-year major-league career was over. This was going to be Joe Morgan's last game. It'd be nice to go out with a hit. With his mother and father in the stands, along with 23,036 other fans on a sunny Sunday afternoon just down the street from where he grew up, Joe wanted to wrap things up right. That's how he did things.

He had his dad, Leonard, throw him the ceremonial first pitch. He had friends and family in the stands to see him bow out in his hometown, the place he left some 20-odd years ago with the crazy notion that a 5-foot 5-inch, 150-pound high schooler could play major-league baseball and have a major impact.

Morgan did. Way more than his relatively modest (by Hall of Fame standards) career numbers would ever show.

On this final Sunday, Morgan's departure was hardly front-page news. There was no mention of his impending retirement in any of the country's major newspapers. No big feature stories bidding him a fond farewell. There was no ESPN, of course, no live up-to-the-minute coverage of his departure.

Heck, by the time the game was over and the Oakland reporters hit the A's locker room, all that Joe Morgan left behind was an empty locker. At 5-feet 7-inches (maybe), Morgan made a career out of flying under the radar. That's how he liked it.

Coming out of Oakland's Castlemont High, a baseball-rich area that produced big leaguers like Frank Robinson, Vada Pinson, and Willie Stargell, Morgan was a fine high school player. But nobody would look at him because of his size, or lack of it. Only the National League expansion team from Houston, the Colt .45s, later the Astros, were interested. They signed him out of junior college for $3,000. They were so desperate for talent, Morgan found himself in the big leagues for eight games at age 20. He wasn't ready.

Two years later, he was back with the big club and stayed seven seasons with the Astros, all well under the radar. He was a solid major-league player, and Houston liked him. But Cincinnati saw something in him, something the Astros didn't suspect. They thought Morgan just might be the catalyst for the gathering collection of talent that would become the Big Red Machine.

He was smart, he was fast, he was always on base and better than anybody else in the game; he was one step ahead, mentally. But he was little. How long would he last?

The Astros now know the answer to that question. In leading the Reds to two world championships in 1975 and 1976, Morgan won himself two MVP awards, and amassed five Gold Gloves and seven All-Star berths. He played until he was 40.

But he never forgot that it all could have been different. He couldn't help but remember. Tony Pérez was always reminding him, "If you had stayed in Houston," Perez would laugh, "nobody would know who you are."

Under the radar, indeed. Luck and timing had always been a key part of baseball. What if Babe Ruth had stayed in Boston? What if Stan Musial hadn't hurt his arm pitching and turned to outfielding? The history of the game was filled with "what ifs." Joe Morgan was one more.

After all the games and the end-of-career jumping around, from Cincinnati to Houston to San Francisco to Philadelphia, he'd finally landed back in Oakland. It hadn't been a wonderful year. His average hovered in the low .240s and the team—well, they would never really get it together.

Morgan had thought about retiring after teaming up with old Reds teammates Pete Rose and Tony Pérez to lead the Philadelphia Phillies into the 1983 World Series. He was going to retire on top. He wanted to wrap things up right.

But in the offseason, Morgan struck up a friendship with Oakland club president Roy Eisenhardt. Eisenhardt wanted Morgan to play with the A's, offered him a two-year deal. He figured Joe could bring some maturity and wisdom to a team in tatters after the Billy Martin regime. Morgan wasn't sure it was the right thing to do. He'd been a career-long National Leaguer. Could he handle being a part-time player, being a designated hitter?

In the end, though, Morgan decided to play. Plus, there was one pretty big carrot out there for him. The all-time record for home runs by a second baseman was 264 by Rogers Hornsby. Morgan was two away. Now, he'd never been a real big stats guy. But Rogers Hornsby? That was tempting.

So, Morgan signed on with the A's and manager Steve Boros and his cast of excitables like Rickey Henderson, Dwayne Murphy, the always-cheery Dave Kingman, and the fiery Tony Phillips.

Problem was, all of the A's weren't as focused on the things Joe Morgan was. They were a second-division team with first-division talent.

On this, the final day of the season, the team in the other dugout, the Kansas City Royals, had an eight-game lead. They were thinking ahead to their playoff series with Detroit, which would start in Kansas City on Tuesday. The Royals had beaten Oakland 6–5 on Friday night, clinching the West title behind Charlie Leibrandt and Dan Quisenberry. Morgan, who'd played about twice a week down the stretch, pinch-hit and grounded out. Boros gave him Saturday off against Royals ace Bret Saberhagen.

Here on Sunday, he was back in his number two spot in the batting order. He heard his name announced and strode toward the plate. Even though it had been six years since he'd worn a Cincinnati Reds uniform, somehow the number 8—chosen in honor of friend Willie Stargell—didn't look right on the green uniform shirt. He waved the bat back and forth and did that strange little elbow flip with his arm, the one that always got people talking and pointing.

Then here it came—a fastball—and Morgan swung, a full, healthy cut, and the ball screamed out into left-center. Morgan, as always, was out of the box quickly, and he sailed into second base with a double, the 449th of his career. His 2,517th hit.

The Coliseum faithful stood and cheered for the small man in green and white, who waved to them all, flashed that winning smile. He looked up and here came his protégé, another smallish second baseman, Tony Phillips, in to run for him. The baton was passed. Morgan headed for the dugout, his mission completed.

He wound up with a career batting average of .271, some 87 points lower than the career average for second-base icon Rogers Hornsby. Yet, five years later, Morgan was a first-ballot Hall of Famer, something Joe DiMaggio couldn't boast of.

"To make it in on the first ballot is unbelievable," Morgan said then. "Only players who are deemed great make it on the first ballot. I guess that makes me a great second baseman. I'm appreciative [the writers] took the time to look beyond the numbers."

To those who played with him, there was little debate about that issue. "He did it all and he did it all the time," teammate Johnny Bench said. "I always thought Joe was the best player I ever played with, and that takes in a lot of ground."

Oddly, Morgan had never thought about the Hall of Fame until about midway through his career. Then Sparky Anderson, his old Cincinnati Reds manager, said something to him.

"In 1975, at the end of the season," Morgan recalled, "Sparky said 'You're going to be Most Valuable in the league. Joe, you need one of those to get in the Hall of Fame.' That was the first time I thought about going to the Hall of Fame," Morgan said on the eve of his election in 1990. "I started thinking, maybe. I never thought for sure."

Funny enough, the guy who had everything in his career work out just about right was thrown a curve on his big day. The 1990 Hall of Fame Induction Ceremony was rained out. It ended up being held the next day in the Cooperstown High School gym. That was OK with Morgan. He had education on his mind, anyway. He'd just completed his bachelor's degree, fulfilling a promise he'd made to his mother way back when he first signed a pro contract.

"It took me 22 years in the major leagues to get a plaque in the Hall of Fame and it took me 27 years to get my degree. But I'm thrilled to have them both."

When he finally was handed his Hall of Fame plaque, the little guy from Oakland who flew under the radar was amazed by his own ability to make such a perfect landing.

"Mays, Musial, and Morgan in the same breath," he said. "I'm not sure I'll ever get used to that."

Joe Morgan by the Numbers

YEAR	TEAM	G	AB	R	H	TB	2B	3B	HR	RBI	BB	SO	SB	BA	SLG	OBP
1963	HOU	8	25	5	6	8	0	1	0	3	5	5	1	.240	.320	.367
1964	HOU	10	37	4	7	7	0	0	0	0	6	7	0	.189	.189	.302
1965	HOU	157	601	100	163	251	22	12	14	40	97	77	20	.271	.418	.373
1966	HOU	122	425	60	121	166	14	8	5	42	89	43	11	.285	.391	.410
1967	HOU	133	494	73	136	203	27	11	6	42	81	51	29	.275	.411	.378
1968	HOU	10	20	6	5	7	0	1	0	0	7	4	3	.250	.350	.444
1969	HOU	147	535	94	126	199	18	5	15	43	110	74	49	.236	.372	.365
1970	HOU	144	548	102	147	217	28	9	8	52	102	55	42	.268	.396	.383
1971	HOU	160	583	87	149	237	27	11	13	56	88	52	40	.256	.407	.351
1972	CIN	149	552	122	161	240	23	4	16	73	115	44	58	.292	.435	.417
1973	CIN	157	576	116	167	284	35	2	26	82	111	61	67	.290	.493	.406
1974	CIN	149	512	107	150	253	31	3	22	67	120	69	58	.293	.494	.427
1975	CIN	146	498	107	163	253	27	6	17	94	132	52	67	.327	.508	.466
1976	CIN	141	472	113	151	272	30	5	27	111	114	41	60	.320	.576	.444
1977	CIN	153	521	113	150	249	21	6	22	78	117	58	49	.288	.478	.417
1978	CIN	132	441	68	104	170	27	0	13	75	79	40	19	.236	.385	.347
1979	CIN	127	436	70	109	164	26	1	9	32	93	45	28	.250	.376	.379
1980	HOU	141	461	66	112	172	17	5	11	49	93	47	24	.243	.373	.367
1981	SF	90	308	47	74	116	16	1	8	31	66	37	14	.240	.377	.371
1982	SF	134	463	68	134	203	19	4	14	61	85	60	24	.289	.438	.400
1983	PHI	123	404	72	93	163	20	1	16	59	89	54	18	.230	.403	.370
1984	OAK	116	365	50	89	128	21	0	6	43	66	39	8	.244	.351	.356
TOTALS		2649	9277	1650	2517	3962	449	96	268	1133	1865	1015	689	.271	.427	.392

1968

MICKEY MANTLE

A QUIET FAREWELL FOR THE MICK

DATE: September 27, 1968

SITE: Fenway Park, Boston, Massachusetts

PITCHER: Jim Lonborg of the Boston Red Sox

RESULT: Popout to shortstop Rico Petrocelli

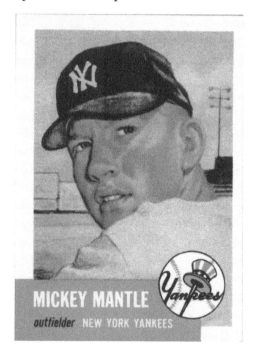

For years, they hated and admired him, all at the same time. Another season was almost over. Boston's long-suffering Red Sox fans had suffered so much over the years, thanks to these New York Yankees, the idea of applauding for one of them, under normal circumstances, was grounds for hanging.

But clap by clap, row by row, Fenway Park began to erupt in sound. The sound of applause. They all could see the Yankees' Golden Boy was old and hobbled and failing. Finally, Mickey Mantle was harmless.

Hell, he was hitting—what was it now, .237? When Mantle saw it in the Sunday paper, the day they list all the averages, he wondered if he was hung over or just in some bad dream.

Once, not so long ago, Mantle had hit .353. Another year, he hit .365. With his speed—his speed was magical when he was young—they predicted some year he'd hit .400. That year never came. Over time, injuries took his speed away. Finally, he was done.

As their cheers, the rousing, heartfelt cheers from the Fenway faithful, washed down around him as he walked to the plate, Mantle smiled to himself.

"I get a better hand here than I did in The Stadium."

It was true. It was one of the mysteries of the fickle New York crowd. Nobody could quite understand why New Yorkers would cheer for Billy Martin and Whitey Ford and Yogi Berra as if they were their own children. But Mantle, for the longest time, drew little but boos.

Ty Cobb, who knew a thing or two about being booed, once dropped by the Yankee dugout in the middle of all the noise and was asked about it. He was remarkably prescient. "They've got to cheer when he's as good as he can be," Cobb said. The implication, of course, was that he wasn't. And never would be.

That was the problem with Mantle. Forget the 500-plus home runs, the Triple Crown, the MVP awards, all the great plays. Forget all of it, he could have done more. At least, that's how it seemed to everyone who watched him play. Mantle himself sensed it.

"Me and the fans really had a go-round the first couple of years," he said once. "I didn't like them and they didn't like me." And Mantle's failed potential was evident to everyone.

The *New York Times*'s Arthur Daley would say as much just a few months after his final season ended. "Did he really accomplish all that his extraordinary physical gifts had once indicated he would? He did not. His legs bothered him throughout his stay with the Yankees, hobbling him so cruelly that he never really reached the heights that had been ordained for him."

The fans knew it wasn't all physical. There was a stubbornness about Mantle that frustrated some in the game. Ted Williams said as much. "Mantle had the power, and he wouldn't concede with two strikes," Williams said. "He didn't know what the heck you were talking about. He would swing the same way with no strikes as he was with two strikes. If he had ever got it in his mind, 'All I want to do is make contact with two strikes—swing as hard but choke up an inch or two'—if he had not struck out 2,000 times and got 400 more balls to hit, I guarantee he'd have had another 150 hits (raising his career average to .317). Well, he was the great Mantle, but he just ticked .300."

Actually, the great Mantle, career-wise, was just below .300 now. He had been since late August. There was no way to get it headed back in the other direction. Not now.

For this final season, Mantle had been around the .240s until that damn Cleveland Indians staff came to The Stadium to close out the Yankees' home schedule in late September. This was not a staff to be facing when you were losing your ability to hit a fastball.

Mantle's plummet began. A switch-hitter, he went 0-for-4 batting righty against the Tribe's fearsome "Sudden" Sam McDowell, one of the game's hardest throwers. Except on this night, Sam had struck out a career-low: one. That was the first game of a twi-nighter. Mantle pinch-hit in the second game and popped out.

The next day, he got the Yankees' only hit against the Indians' sensational Luis Tiant in his final game at Yankee Stadium, but his batting average kept sinking. While Tiant fanned 11, winning his 21st game of the season in the Year of the Pitcher, lowering his American League–leading ERA to 1.60, Mantle was headed in the other direction.

The Yankee great drew a ninth-inning walk in his final plate appearance in the Bronx that night before a grand crowd of 5,723. Some farewell.

For the year, the Yanks drew just 1,185,666, the fewest since the war years. The fans didn't miss much. Mantle wound up his final three games in New York 1-for-8. It was on to Boston to wrap things up.

And that first night in Boston, what a surprise. There was no announcement or anything, no Mickey Mantle Farewell Tour where everybody could trot out rocking chairs and motorcycles and parting gifts and make a big show, a staged production out of saying goodbye. Mantle came out of the dugout and the place started clapping. That was respect. That was genuine.

On that night, Mantle went 0-for-3. Yankee manager Ralph Houk, wanting to acknowledge the Boston crowd, had Mantle in the lineup Saturday afternoon against the American League's defending Cy Young Award winner, Boston's Jim Lonborg. Lonborg had injured his knee in a skiing accident over the winter and was trying to round back into form. There was reason for optimism in the Mantle camp when they found out who Boston was starting. Turns out the Mick had had some success against him 10 days earlier in New York, hitting his 536th and final career homer off him batting left-handed.

So when his name was announced to the Fenway crowd one last time, a cheer went up, as it had the night before. He was going to miss all this.

Mantle looked down. Here he was, in the same place Ted Williams stood eight years earlier, almost to the day, when Williams had swatted one into the bullpen, trotting around the bases hurriedly, head down, running off into the sunset with a dramatic home run.

It was a nice thought. Mantle looked out to Lonborg and waved the bat back and forth. Hard thrower. Gotta be quick. Like last time. He thought about that last home run. The great thing about it was nobody made anything out of it, like they did with number 535. Mantle had hit that home run left-handed, too, off the 1968 Pitcher of the Year, the Tigers' Denny McLain, Mr. 31 wins himself. It had happened in Detroit 10 days ago.

Here it was, mid-September and McLain was pitching a shutout when Mantle hobbled to the plate in the eighth inning. Denny was up, 6–0, and felt something for the aging Yankee star.

McLain gestured in to his catcher, Jim Price, trying to get Mantle's attention. He was going to groove a fastball for him.

"Where do you want it?" McLain asked.

Mantle gestured with his bat, about shoulder high, then laughed. Not quite believing his good fortune, Mantle was a bit late and fouled the pitch off. McLain had delivered it just where Mantle had asked.

McLain laughed and gestured he'd do it again. Mantle, laughing, nodded.

Sure enough, the pitch came and Mantle got this one. He hit it into the seats in right field. That was number 535.

When Joe Pepitone, up next, did the same thing to McLain, gesturing where he wanted the ball, McLain knocked him flat on the seat of his pinstripes.

Back in Fenway, they were still clapping. Maybe Mickey Mantle wasn't through. He hadn't made up his mind about retirement yet. His leg hurt like hell and he'd been at this for so long. Yet it all went by so fast. Just because all his pals were done didn't mean he had to be, did it?

His old partner in off-the-field high jinks, Whitey Ford, had retired after a painful—and ugly—inning in Detroit in May. Roger Maris, now playing out the string with the St. Louis Cardinals, was going to quit too. At least Roger would get to go out in a World Series like DiMaggio did. Like Mick, Roger wasn't hitting much either, around .255 in his final campaign.

His last career home run was a couple days before Mantle's 535th off McLain. It was Roger's fifth of the season. He got me in average, Mantle thought, but I got him in home runs (Mantle finished with 18). He was looking for one more.

Lonborg wound and threw and as the fastball tailed in, Mantle swung from his heels and lifted a high popup toward short. Boston's Rico Petrocelli drifted under it and Mantle peeled off from his trot down the first base line and headed back to the dugout, his 8,102nd and final at-bat completed. He walked to the end of the dugout and put his helmet and bat back. Then he saw Houk go over and tell Andy Kosco that he was in at first base for him. His season was over and so, it turned out, was his career.

With his right knee hurting and his 36-year-old body worn down from the year, Houk put him on a plane back to Dallas Saturday night. On Sunday, the Yankees won their regular-season finale at Fenway, 4–3. The Mick would never be back.

About two weeks later, his old outfield mate Roger Maris, playing in Game 7 of the World Series against Detroit's Mickey Lolich, got to take his final swings. At 34, two years younger than Mantle, Maris was all through too. He'd broken a bone in his hand during the season and never let it heal properly. Like Mantle, he had to play his final season in the big leagues unable to hit the fastball.

Mantle was watching when Maris's final at-bat came in the seventh inning of Game 7 vs. Detroit in the World Series. The Cardinals trailed, 3–0 against Mickey Lolich. Like his ol' pal Mantle, Maris popped out to short-stop, too. Mickey Stanley made the catch.

A little later, Maris got around to discussing his final season. Maris could have been talking for the both of them. "It got so this year, I couldn't hit a home run, even in batting practice," Maris said. "That was the toughest part to swallow—to watch those fastballs go by or foul them off. It's tough to real-ize that you're not able to do what you hope to be capable of doing. . . . Now you know you don't have the good whip to the bat. . . . You hate to continue

MICKEY MANTLE   *outfield NEW YORK YANKEES®*

on in the same circumstances because you're just pressing your luck. Keep it up and you go out the way you don't want to be remembered."

After all that mess, Maris decided then and there he was all done. Over the winter, Mantle considered retirement and didn't report to spring training until March 2, three days after the regulars. When he did, his mind was made up.

He had a long talk over breakfast with Yankees president Mike Burke, then on a Saturday afternoon, called a press conference at the Yankee Clipper Motel in Fort Lauderdale.

"I can't hit any more," Mantle said flatly, announcing his retirement as an active player. "I feel bad that I didn't hit .300 [for his career, finishing at .298] but there's no way I could go back and get it over .300 again. I can't hit when I need to. I can't go from first to third when I need to. There's no use trying."

Though some thought he might hang around to try to get 3,000 hits—he finished with 2,415—or 550 home runs [he was 14 away], Mantle was never big on numbers.

"They said Mickey was a great team man," Mantle said proudly years later. "If I could have one thing on my tombstone, I wouldn't want 536 home runs. I'd rather have 'He was a great friend and teammate.'"

All the same, Mantle knew what opportunities he missed. In the late 1980s, there was a story going around about Mantle meeting then-A's power-and-speed sensation José Canseco in a bar. Mantle offered to toast him on his big season.

"Nice goin' Jose," Mantle said. "Forty homers. Forty stolen bases. If I'd have known it was going to be such a goddamned big deal, I'd have done it three or four times."

Mickey Mantle by the Numbers

YEAR	TEAM	G	AB	R	H	TB	2B	3B	HR	RBI	BB	SO	SB	BA	SLG	OBP
1951	NYY	96	341	61	91	151	11	5	13	65	43	74	8	.267	.443	.349
1952	NYY	142	549	94	171	291	37	7	23	87	75	111	4	.311	.530	.394
1953	NYY	127	461	105	136	229	24	3	21	92	79	90	8	.295	.497	.398
1954	NYY	146	543	128	163	285	17	12	27	102	100	107	5	.300	.525	.406
1955	NYY	147	517	121	158	316	25	11	37	99	113	98	8	.306	.611	.431
1956	NYY	150	533	132	188	376	22	5	52	130	112	100	10	.353	.705	.464
1957	NYY	144	474	121	173	315	28	6	34	94	146	75	16	.365	.665	.512
1958	NYY	150	519	127	158	307	21	1	42	97	129	123	18	.304	.592	.443
1959	NYY	144	541	104	154	278	23	4	31	75	95	126	21	.285	.514	.391
1960	NYY	153	526	119	145	294	17	6	40	94	111	124	14	.276	.559	.400
1961	NYY	153	514	131	163	353	16	6	54	128	126	112	12	.317	.687	.448
1962	NYY	123	377	96	121	228	15	1	30	89	122	78	9	.321	.605	.486
1963	NYY	65	172	41	54	107	8	0	15	35	40	33	2	.314	.622	.441
1964	NYY	143	465	91	141	275	25	2	35	111	99	102	6	.303	.591	.423
1965	NYY	122	361	44	92	163	12	1	19	46	73	78	4	.255	.452	.379
1966	NYY	108	333	40	96	179	12	1	23	56	57	76	1	.288	.538	.389
1967	NYY	144	440	63	108	191	17	0	22	55	107	114	1	.245	.434	.391
1968	NYY	144	435	57	103	173	14	1	18	54	106	98	6	.237	.398	.385
TOTALS		2401	8101	1675	2415	4511	344	72	536	1509	1733	1719	153	.298	.557	.420

WILLIE MAYS

SAY IT AIN'T SO, WILLIE

DATE: October 15, 1973 (Game 3 of the 1973 World Series)

SITE: Shea Stadium, New York, New York

PITCHER: Paul Lindblad of the Oakland A's

RESULT: Groundout to shortstop Bert Campaneris

The very last time Willie Howard Mays walked up to home plate with a bat in his hands was in Game 3 of the 1973 World Series. It was a cursory at-bat. Manager Yogi Berra had sent him up to pinch-hit for pitcher Tug McGraw in the 10th inning of a tie game. He was hoping for one more shot of Mays's magic.

Maybe he wasn't hitting much over .200, but the Old Man had come through the day before in a similar spot. He was still Willie Mays, wasn't he? But here, Mays, batting against left-hander Paul Lindblad, rapped a routine groundball to Oakland shortstop Bert Campaneris, who easily threw him out.

Though the series went the full seven games, Mays never played again. Imagine Willie Mays on the bench. In a World Series! The reason was Game 2. At 42, everybody knew Mays's best days were long behind him. The San Francisco Giants tried to ease him into retirement two years earlier, but Willie found it hard to let go. San Francisco never seemed to warm to him anyhow.

Funny how New York was unduly hard on center fielder Mickey Mantle and San Francisco was never quite satisfied with their star. Through a trade in May a year before, Mays found a way to come back to the city where he'd started with such flair and drama two decades earlier. And who thought he'd find himself in the middle of one more pennant race?

A year before, he'd won the first game he played against his Giants with a solo home run. But now his reflexes were gone. He was hitting just .211, and pitchers just threw it past him with regularity. For those who had watched him in previous seasons, it was a tough thing to see.

In September, he cracked a rib chasing a flyball in Montreal and had to sit out and watch the Mets contend for a pennant through the final three weeks of the season. The rest gave him time to think.

On September 19, Mays told the New York press that he'd decided to retire. "It's been a wonderful 22 years and I'm not just getting out of baseball because I'm hurt," Mays said. "I just feel the people of America shouldn't have to see a guy play who can't produce. I have three cracked ribs and at 42, you can't play the way you could at 20 anyway. If the Mets get in the World Series, I'm playing—I don't know how but I'm playing. But I got to face facts. I've been in a lot of slumps and come out of them but now I'm running out of time.

"It was my decision alone," Mays continued. "The way the ballclub is going now, I don't have to say you have to play me. I'm not ashamed the way things have gone the last couple of months. They didn't run me out. In San Francisco, I don't think I would have played this year; the people would have run me out of the city. In New York, they let me hit .211."

Mays was quiet for a moment. Then he smiled. "I thought I'd be crying right now," he said, "but so many people love me that I don't hurt too bad. Maybe I'll cry tomorrow."

The next night, he did. Facing a full house at Shea Stadium, Mays said goodbye. "I didn't ever feel that I would quit baseball," he said, standing at the microphone next to the pitcher's mound in a dark blue Mets jacket with NY in gold letters over his heart. "But as you know, it always comes a time for someone to get out. These kids over here, the way they are playing, tells me one thing. 'Willie, say goodbye to America.' Thank you very much."

He stepped back from the microphone and tears welled up in his eyes, just like everybody else in Shea Stadium. There were signs all over the place. "A Giant among Mets" and "Say Hey Belongs to Shea" and "The Hour Has Come for No. 24." On the scoreboard, it read: "So long, yes. Good-bye, never."

Two weeks later, when the Mets won the pennant and reached the World Series against the Oakland Athletics, Mays pronounced his cracked ribs healed enough for him to play. But the "Say Hey Kid" had grown into an old man. We saw it for ourselves.

After Oakland won the Series opener, Mays found his way into Game 2 as a pinch-runner and actually fell down rounding second base. For the most spectacular baserunner of his era, it was only a hint of what was to come. At the time, the Mets held a 6–4 lead heading to the ninth, hoping to even the Series. Mays trotted out to his domain—center field—in the ninth to try to wrap it up.

What baseball fan didn't remember the first time he or she likely heard of Willie Mays, the Giants' wunderkind? It had to be in the 1954 World Series, when Willie's Giants came up with a startling four-game sweep of the mighty Cleveland Indians, a team that had won more games in a single season than anyone in baseball history. America was watching when Mays improbably found himself at the descending part of a long, majestic drive off the bat of Vic Wertz, way, way out in the deepest center field in all of baseball at New York's Polo Grounds. With his back to home plate, the number 24 stretched across his back in white flannel, he made the catch, losing his cap, and gaining a nation of breathless fans, all in one sweeping grab. Then he spun and made a wonderful throw back to the infield and suddenly, everybody was talking about it as if it were the greatest catch in World Series history.

Years later, Mays would shrug off the catch and talk about the throw as if that were the real feat. But America thought differently. Even though he was 42 now, nobody worried about him trotting out to center field to start the inning. Even if he were too old to get around on a fastball, Willie Mays would always be able to catch a flyball, wouldn't he?

Suddenly, there was a line drive off the bat of Deron Johnson, a twisting, sinking shot to left-center that Mays started slowly after. Everything seemed to be in slow motion.

The ball kept drifting and Mays looked as if he was stuck on flypaper. He couldn't move the sleek, silky way he used to; instead, his hands lowered, Mays scuttled across the outfield grass, then lunged for the ball with both hands in front of him and missed it by two feet. The ball skittered past him and rolled to the wall. This was not the way America wanted to remember Willie Mays. Not the player that seemed to be able to do anything on a base-ball field. Except look mortal. Cleon Jones retrieved the ball and fired it in and the stadium was nearly silent, even as the Athletics mounted a stirring comeback that tied the game. Willie Mays, falling down chasing a flyball? In the World Series? Who would believe it?

"I didn't see the ball," Mays said later, describing the blinding sun field at Oakland-Alameda County Stadium. "I tried to dive for it at the last second. We had a two-run lead and I shoulda played it safe."

Safe? Mays? Nobody ever went after a flyball with more vengeance than Willie Mays. A ball sailing into his domain? It was his, always his, landing easily into that wonderful Mays basket catch. An out? From the time it left the bat.

Happily for Mays's fans—and what baseball fan wasn't in that category?—he had a chance to redeem himself a few innings later. The game had stretched into the 12th inning and with two runners on and two outs, the Old Man came up against the A's ace reliever Rollie Fingers. He dug in with that odd, open stance, his huge hands still twitching on the knob of the bat as Fingers wound and threw. Mays threw the head of his bat at the ball and caught it on the end of the barrel.

The ball hopped once midway to the mound, then bounded high over Fingers's head into center field. Bud Harrelson trotted in to give New York a lead it was able to hold onto.

"I think it was a fastball, up," Mays said later. "I'd seen Fingers a lot on television and he likes to work inside and outside, up and down. Yesterday was the test. He threw me a fastball, then gave me a breaking pitch and came back with a fastball so I knew he'd feed me 80 percent fastballs."

Give the Old Man the hard stuff. He can't get around anymore. Willie showed 'em. By the end of the inning, New York had scored three more times on Oakland errors. With a 10–6 lead in the 12th, Mays trotted out to center field to see if he could help his Mets win the longest World Series game ever.

There was one more embarrassing moment. Reggie Jackson was up first, and he swung mightily, blasting a shot right at Mays, watching carefully from deep center field. Mays retreated on the sound of the hit, right to the fence, then ran along brushing up against the wall, almost like a blind man,

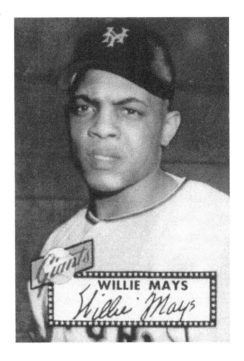

making sure he was going in the right direction. He raised up his glove and the ball dropped in front of him on the warning track, two feet away.

"I saw it," Mays said later, trying to brush it off. "In a close game, I might have had a chance on it, but we had a four-run lead then and I didn't want to kill myself because we got a lot more games to play."

He didn't, as it turned out. Just that one pinch-hitting appearance in Game Three. A week later, the Series ended with Mays watching from the bench. Who'd believe that Willie Mays would ever be benched for a Game 7? The Mets lost 5–2, losing the Series to the A's, four games to three.

America suddenly felt very old. Was it that long ago that Mays scooted across that endless outfield at the Polo Grounds to flag down that long drive off the bat of Vic Wertz? After 660 home runs, all those marvelous, gravity-defying catches, was the thrilling ride over? Willie Mays, whose visible exuberance for the game of baseball was always contagious, was finally worn out.

He had to sit and watch a Game 7. Say Hey, it was time to go. "I didn't think about (retiring) during the game or anything," Mays said after, sitting before his locker as the A's celebrated their world title. "I didn't play but just because it was my last game, it didn't make any difference to me if I played or not. If it was to help the ballclub, fine, but not because it was my last game. I didn't come in that way," Mays said quietly. "I don't want to go out having people feel sorry for me. I don't need that."

Willie Mays by the Numbers

YEAR	TEAM	G	AB	R	H	TB	2B	3B	HR	RBI	BB	SO	SB	BA	SLG	OBP
1951	NYG	121	464	59	127	219	22	5	20	68	56	60	7	.274	.472	.354
1952	NYG	34	127	17	30	52	2	4	4	23	16	16	4	.236	.409	.326
1954	NYG	151	565	119	195	377	33	13	41	110	67	55	8	.345	.667	.412
1955	NYG	152	580	122	185	382	18	13	51	127	79	60	24	.319	.659	.400
1956	NYG	152	578	101	171	322	27	8	36	84	69	65	40	.296	.557	.370
1957	NYG	152	585	112	195	366	26	20	35	97	77	62	38	.333	.626	.408
1958	SF	152	600	120	208	350	33	11	29	96	78	56	31	.347	.583	.419
1959	SF	151	575	125	180	335	43	5	34	104	66	58	27	.313	.583	.382
1960	SF	153	595	107	190	330	29	12	29	103	61	70	25	.319	.555	.381
1961	SF	154	572	129	176	334	32	3	40	123	81	79	18	.308	.584	.393
1962	SF	162	621	130	189	382	36	5	49	141	78	86	18	.304	.615	.384
1963	SF	157	596	115	187	347	32	7	38	103	66	83	8	.314	.582	.380
1964	SF	157	578	121	171	351	21	9	47	111	82	72	19	.296	.607	.383
1965	SF	157	558	118	177	360	21	3	52	112	76	71	9	.317	.645	.398
1966	SF	152	552	99	159	307	29	4	37	103	70	81	5	.288	.556	.368
1967	SF	141	486	83	128	220	22	2	22	70	51	92	6	.263	.453	.334
1968	SF	148	498	84	144	243	20	5	23	79	67	81	12	.289	.488	.372
1969	SF	117	403	64	114	176	17	3	13	58	49	71	6	.283	.437	.362
1970	SF	139	478	94	139	242	15	2	28	83	79	90	5	.291	.506	.390
1971	SF	136	417	82	113	201	24	5	18	61	112	123	23	.271	.482	.425
1972	SF	19	49	8	9	11	2	0	0	3	17	5	3	.184	.224	.394
1972	NYM	69	195	27	52	87	9	1	8	19	43	43	1	.267	.446	.402
1972	ALL	88	244	35	61	98	11	1	8	22	60	48	4	.250	.402	.400
1973	NYM	66	209	24	44	72	10	0	6	25	27	47	1	.211	.344	.303
TOTALS		2992	10881	2060	3283	6066	523	140	660	1903	1467	1526	338	.302	.557	.384

1976

HANK AARON

ONE LAST SWING FOR HANK

DATE: October 3, 1976

SITE: County Stadium, Milwaukee, Wisconsin

PITCHER: Dave Roberts of the Detroit Tigers

RESULT: Infield single to shortstop

There was barely a ripple from the paltry County Stadium crowd when Hank Aaron came out of the Brewers dugout one last time. Only 6,858 fans had showed up to watch these last-place Brewers, some 32 games out, face the next-to-last-place Detroit Tigers, who were 24 games out on this final Sunday of the regular season.

Since the Green Bay Packers were on TV that Sunday afternoon playing the Seattle Seahawks, apparently many Milwaukeeans stayed home to watch that instead. The drama had been drained out of the Brewers' season long ago.

It was the sixth inning of a 5–1 game the Brewers were losing. There hadn't been much to cheer about all season long. Though it was well known all around town that this would be the final major-league game—number 3,298—of Aaron's 23-year career, Milwaukee fans knew there wasn't going to be much to see.

Not now. Not from this team. Not from the 42-year-old Aaron. Like the other two peerless players from his era—Willie Mays and Mickey Mantle—Aaron hung on longer than he should have. He was in his second season as a designated hitter for the American League's Milwaukee Brewers, and he was awful.

He played—that is, batted—in just 85 games, about half the season. Worse, he batted just .229, five points lower than he'd batted in 1975, his first year as an American Leaguer. He hadn't been able to hit a home run since hitting one off California Angels reliever Dick Drago back on July 20. That was number 755. He was staying on that number.

Yeah, he was back in the town he'd asked to be traded to, the town he began his big-league career in, just like Mays did in 1973. And like Mays, he was pretty lousy at the finish too. Had Aaron known he'd fade like this, though, he wouldn't have played. He'd managed just 10 home runs, only 35 RBI—a rookie's numbers.

Unlike Mantle, though, Aaron's sad decline in batting average in his final two seasons didn't lower his career average below the prestigious .300 mark. He began the day at .305 and almost regardless of what happened today, he'd finish at .305.

The Tigers starter on this final afternoon of the season was left-hander Dave Roberts, midway through a mediocre career (103-125), but winding up what would be his winningest season (16-17) ever in the majors. Roberts had already gotten Aaron out twice and had allowed just one run, walking no one. Even with a runner on third, he wasn't worried watching old number 44 walk to the plate in his slow, deliberate way. He quietly watched Aaron pause, as he always did when he stepped into the batter's box, to fit the batting helmet over his head.

Aaron's once-whippet-like body had thickened with age. His pronounced backside was even more noticeable as he turned his head to the mound and wiggled the bat back and forth, those great wrists guiding it with confidence and ease. He'd done a lot of great things in this town for the first 11 years of his career. The home run he hit in 1957 to give the Braves the pennant—that was the hit he'd always talk about.

Even after hitting number 715, a clout that gave him one more home run than Babe Ruth. That home run in 1957, now that was exciting. The chase of Ruth, all those letters, the publicity, the hate mail, none of it was much fun. Though Aaron hung around long enough to play two more seasons after swatting that historic home run, he hit just 40 more home runs over that span.

The Brewers hyped up Aaron's return when the 1975 season started—the same sort of thing San Francisco did a couple years earlier, unloading a fading Willie Mays on the Giants—but there was even less left of Aaron's game. At least Mays got to jump into a pennant race. Many American League fans welcomed a chance to see the guy who passed Babe Ruth the first time around the league. But his game was long gone. So was whatever mystique Aaron had.

As Aaron stepped in this last time, he wondered about what he could do with these final swings. He would have loved to go out like Ted Williams did, with a long, majestic home run. Or maybe even like Stan Musial, with a pair of hits. Or maybe like Joe DiMaggio, he could slam a quiet double in the late innings of a World Series game, never saying a word to anyone that this was going to be it. Not until the game was all over.

But then all of a sudden, Roberts's pitch was on him, tailing inside and Aaron flipped those magnificent wrists one last time. He caught the ball on the handle and drove it in the gap between short and third. It bounced once, twice, three times as George Scott lumbered in toward home from third base.

Shortstop Jerry Manuel chased it deep in the hole and saw it skip off his glove. Aaron was safe at first. The run scored. The ball hadn't left the infield. Brewers manager Alex Grammas sent out infielder Jim Gantner to pinch-run for Aaron. A cheer went up from the crowd as Aaron walked back to the dugout, his career now officially over. The game's biggest home-run hitter had checked out with an infield hit.

In the locker room afterward, Aaron seemed relieved the long run had ended. "I guess this is the last press conference, boys," he smiled. "But at least I'm going out a little better than Nixon did. I've had enough. It's sad in a way that it's over. But in another way, I'm glad it's over." All the nights of the one-on-one struggles with that pitcher had finally worn him down. And he wasn't afraid to admit it, now.

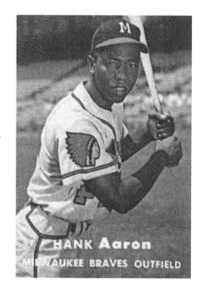

"Since I came over from the National League two years ago and acted as a DH here, I've sort of been preparing for this day," Aaron said. "I've lost my desire to compete and I could feel it at the start of this season. It just wasn't there anymore. Wasn't hungry anymore. The routine, the traveling, it finally got to me. And when you don't have the hunger anymore. . . ."

His honesty was disarming. How many other players, great ones, would step down with such frank analysis? Aaron, the guy who always seemed aloof, sort of removed from everyone, well, he wondered about how he'd fit into the outside world. Now.

"You know, this is one of the things I'll really miss, the clubhouse. It was always one place I could find peace, get away from the outside world. In Atlanta, when the Babe Ruth thing was going on, I came to the park at two in the afternoon to sleep for a couple hours. Only place it was quiet."

Now, the quiet beckoned. "I'm not going to the World Series—not unless they play it in my backyard," he said, laughing. "I may not even watch it on TV. I don't know whether I'll ever be able to go in a restaurant and eat in peace, but I hope I'll have a little more privacy."

Finally, Hank Aaron was famous. Just when the spotlight hit him, he was ready to go back to being anonymous.

"I didn't get much recognition at the beginning," he said, finally, "but when it did come, man, it came in waves. I'm totally fulfilled."

Though later on in the locker room after the Brewers' 5–2 loss, the team's 95th defeat of the season, Hank did grouse a little at being pulled for a pinch-runner, preventing him from having a chance to score a run and break the flat-footed tie between he and Ruth for second place in all-time runs scored (2,174); the truth was, the slow-footed Aaron wasn't likely to score from first on anything but a home run.

And if he had to settle for one tie with Ruth, that wasn't so bad, was it? Interestingly, though Aaron's pursuit of Ruth brought him his first real headlines, when it came time for Cooperstown to make a place for him, Aaron never mentioned The Babe in his induction speech. He did mention Jackie Robinson, though.

"I also feel especially proud to be standing here where some years ago Jackie Robinson and Roy Campanella proved the way and made it possible for Frank [Robinson] and me and for other blacks hopeful in baseball. They proved to the world that a man's ability is limited only by his lack of opportunity.

"Twenty-three years ago, I never dreamed this high honor would come to me. For it was not fame I sought, but rather to be the best baseball player that I could possibly be."

For almost all of his long, productive major-league career, Aaron was exactly that. You could look at those last few years with Milwaukee and say Henry stayed too long. Maybe so, but it seemed exactly long enough for all of us—even Hank—to appreciate all that he had done. He played too long, sure. But how nice it would be if every retiring big leaguer could say what Aaron did: I'm totally fulfilled. Nobody deserved it more.

Hank Aaron by the Numbers

YEAR	TEAM	G	AB	R	H	TB	2B	3B	HR	RBI	BB	SO	SB	BA	SLG	OBP
1954	MIL	122	468	58	131	209	27	6	13	69	28	39	2	.280	.447	.322
1955	MIL	153	602	105	189	325	37	9	27	106	49	61	3	.314	.540	.366
1956	MIL	153	609	106	200	340	34	14	26	92	37	54	2	.328	.558	.365
1957	MIL	151	615	118	198	369	27	6	44	132	57	58	1	.322	.600	.378
1958	MIL	153	601	109	196	328	34	4	30	95	59	49	4	.326	.546	.386
1959	MIL	154	629	116	223	400	46	7	39	123	51	54	8	.355	.636	.401
1960	MIL	153	590	102	172	334	20	11	40	126	60	63	16	.292	.566	.352
1961	MIL	155	603	115	197	358	39	10	34	120	56	64	21	.327	.594	.381
1962	MIL	156	592	127	191	366	28	6	45	128	66	73	15	.323	.618	.390
1963	MIL	161	631	121	201	370	29	4	44	130	78	94	31	.319	.586	.391
1964	MIL	145	570	103	187	293	30	2	24	95	62	46	22	.328	.514	.393
1965	MIL	150	570	109	181	319	40	1	32	89	60	81	24	.318	.560	.379
1966	ATL	158	603	117	168	325	23	1	44	127	76	96	21	.279	.539	.356
1967	ATL	155	600	113	184	344	37	3	39	109	63	97	17	.307	.573	.369
1968	ATL	160	606	84	174	302	33	4	29	86	64	62	28	.287	.498	.354
1969	ATL	147	547	100	164	332	30	3	44	97	87	47	9	.300	.607	.396
1970	ATL	150	516	103	154	296	26	1	38	118	74	63	9	.298	.574	.385
1971	ATL	139	495	95	162	331	22	3	47	118	71	58	1	.327	.669	.410
1972	ATL	129	449	75	119	231	10	0	34	77	92	55	4	.265	.514	.390
1973	ATL	120	392	84	118	252	12	1	40	96	68	51	1	.301	.643	.402
1974	ATL	112	340	47	91	167	16	0	20	69	39	29	1	.268	.491	.341
1975	MIL	137	465	45	109	165	16	2	12	60	70	51	0	.234	.355	.332
1976	MIL	85	271	22	62	100	8	0	10	35	35	38	0	.229	.369	.315
TOTALS		3298	12364	2174	3771	6856	624	98	775	2297	1402	1383	240	.305	.555	.374

1956

BOB FELLER

SLOW FINISH FOR RAPID ROBERT

DATE: September 30, 1956

SITE: Municipal Stadium, Cleveland, Ohio

OPPONENT: Detroit Tigers

RESULT: Complete-game 8–4 loss

The season was gone, the game was gone, and so, Bob Feller figured, was his arm. After 20 big-league campaigns in a Cleveland uniform, the 37-year-old right-hander stood on the mound on the final Sunday in September and readied his final pitch to Detroit center fielder Bill Tuttle. He needed just one more out to get the Indians into the ninth.

Then, with the Tribe trailing 8–4, three more outs would put them into the offseason and Feller, probably, into retirement. He looked over at the scoreboard again. Detroit 8, Cleveland 4. It wasn't quite riding off into the sunset. They had announced the final day's attendance at 5,910, and many of them had left already. So much for saying a sweet goodbye.

To tell you the truth, it was an odd day. All season long, Feller was the forgotten man in the bullpen, the guy that hung on long enough to make everyone uncomfortable when he came around and started throwing. For a player of his magnitude to be relegated to mop-up duty or worse, batting practice, something was unseemly about it.

As columnist Red Smith was quick to note the week before his finale, quoting Hank Greenberg: "'There's something wrong with the picture of him warming up in the bullpen.' Of course the picture is wrong," Smith wrote. "So are those figures: no victories, three defeats. It always seems wrong when this happens, though there never could have been a moment's doubt that the year would come when Feller wouldn't win a game. When Cy Slapnicka led him off the Iowa sandlots, he started the boy toward this year."

After noting that Feller's record would leave him shy of the coveted 300-win club, Smith went on. "To be sure, there is meat enough in Feller's record to feed any man's pride. In 1938 he struck out eighteen Tigers in nine innings. In 1946 he fanned 348 batsmen, smacking a record that Rube Waddell had held for 42 years. He pitched three no-hit games. In one four-year span, he struck out 1,007 batters in 1,238 innings. He was, simply, the greatest pitcher of his time."

But his time was long past. And considering he wasn't the easiest fella in the world to get along with, Feller took the whole thing pretty well. Since everybody knew he was about to be out of a job, as was Indians manager Al López, who, after six years as the Tribe's manager had announced his resignation the day before. *Cleveland Plain Dealer* photographer Marvin Greene got Feller to pose with López and also retiring Western Union press box chief Al Brandeis for a photo that they ran on the front of the paper's sports section.

Here were the three of them thumbing through the help wanted ads. There was something a little strange about the greatest pitcher in Cleveland history going out as comic relief. Considering he came into the game with a won-loss record of 0-3 with an earned-run average of 4.41, it's a wonder he could laugh at all. Well, correct that.

Feller's 4.41 ERA was before the Detroit Tigers had pounded him for eight runs in these eight innings. (It would wind up at 4.78.) He'd only had one other start the whole year and sure wasn't fooling anybody.

Why, he came into this game having worked just 50 innings all season long—about nine innings per month—and the former strikeout king had fanned just 18 batters or one more than he'd fanned in a single game against Philadelphia back when he was 17 years old. With López leaving and the Indians locked into second place, there really wasn't anything to play for. Except trying to help Feller leave with a win. López gave him the ball even though he knew, Detroit knew, and probably even Feller himself knew it wasn't going to happen.

From his opening inning, Feller had a pretty good idea how it was going to go. After he'd gotten leadoff hitter Harvey Kuenn out, Feller gave up a home run to somebody named Wayne Belardi, the sixth of his season and 28th and final home run of Belardi's career. Belardi retired, a .242 career hitter, over the winter.

But his home run let Detroit go ahead to begin with. Cleveland never could catch up. There was plenty of chatter in the Detroit dugout, though. Kuenn and the Tigers' Boy Wonder, Al Kaline, were battling for the American League lead in hits and Feller settled it for 'em.

Kuenn got three hits; Kaline managed just a triple. Kuenn's three hits got his average up to .332, but that still left him a distant third in the AL batting race behind Triple Crown winner Mickey Mantle (.356) and runner-up Ted Williams (.345).

In the fourth, the Tigers kept after Feller, bunching three hits in the fourth to make it 4–1, then added four more runs off the old-timer in the sixth. Though Feller had allowed 14 hits, walking three, López never moved off the bench. He was going to let him finish his final game. He'd done that much for the Cleveland Indians. He'd earned that.

Why, Feller couldn't ever have imagined he'd complete a game where he'd allowed 14 hits. Wasn't he the guy who'd thrown 12 career one-hitters and three no-hitters? Wasn't he the guy who, in his most magnificent season, returned from World War II to pitch a whopping 371 innings for Lou Boudreau's Indians, fanning a record 348 (a record later broken by Sandy Koufax, then Nolan Ryan), pitching 36 complete games, posting a 26-15 record with an amazing 2.18 ERA for a sixth-place Indians team?

But that amazing workload took its toll. Though Feller was only 27 years old at the time and would go on to pitch for 10 more years, he never again fanned more than 200 batters in a season. Still, he won.

At 36, he went 13-3 for the 1954 Indians, the winningest team in baseball history with four 20-game winners (Bob Lemon, Herb Score, Mike Garcia, Early Wynn). Oddly, he never got to pitch in that World Series. The Tribe was swept in four games by the New York Giants.

There was talk that Feller was going to retire because his 1955 season was a big dropoff. He appeared in just 25 games, only 83 innings, 11 starts, with just 25 strikeouts. Since the Indians were well stocked with pitchers, retirement seemed to make sense. But Feller, always keen with a dollar, was involved in trying to set up baseball's pension plan. The players didn't want him to go.

"I probably should have retired in 1955," Feller said many years later. "But we were working on the pension plan. In those days, you had to have continuity. If I'd have retired, someone else would have taken over as the player representative with no continuity and no background in working on the pension plan. The owners did have continuity. So the players asked me to stay another year."

He did. It sure wasn't much fun. The Tribe seemed to continue to skid after that World Series sweep two years earlier. They won just 88 games, the fewest they'd won since 1947 and had only hit .244 as a team, their worst since the war years. And their failures were clear to everyone.

Cleveland was a combined 51-15 against the league's three worst teams—Baltimore, Washington, and Philadelphia—a pretty impressive won-lost record. But against the AL champion Yankees, they were 10-12.

On that mound for the final time, the Tribe's greatest hurler was down to his last out and that'd be it. Feller wound and delivered and just from the sound of the swing, Feller knew it'd be a groundball. He started walking with that familiar plowboy walk toward the Cleveland dugout. His day, his career, was over. López sent Gene Woodling up to pinch-hit for Feller leading off the ninth. When the game ended a moment later and the Indians' season closed with a defeat, Feller felt a sense of relief.

So, you can bet, did Cleveland management.

"I know they don't want me on the team another year," Feller said, candidly, after his 162nd career loss. "And I doubt that there's any job in the front office that will interest me."

And managing? Somebody asked Feller that on Saturday, after hearing of López's resignation.

"No thanks," he said.

Though he surely knew the truth, he still tried to sound brave at the finish when the sportswriters came around one last time.

"I'm not yet convinced I'm all through," he said. "I want to talk to (Indians' players) Jim (Hegan) and (Mel) Harder in the next few weeks and see what they say. Maybe I'll be pitching somewhere else next year."

How did it feel to go out like that?

"I've had better stuff," Feller said in possibly the understatement of the century. "But my arm felt good and I didn't tire. That's the important thing."

Yet in his final appearance in a big-league game, one of the game's greatest strikeout artists had left his sport in most unusual fashion.

Bob Feller faced 41 hitters that final afternoon at Municipal Stadium. He didn't strike out a single one.

Bob Feller by the Numbers

YEAR	TEAM	W	L	PCT	ERA	G	GS	CG	SHO	SV	IP	H	R	BB	SO
1936	CLE	5	3	.625	3.34	14	8	5	0	0	62.0	52	29	47	77
1937	CLE	9	7	.563	3.44	26	19	9	0	0	149.0	116	68	106	150
1938	CLE	17	11	.607	4.11	39	36	20	2	0	278.0	225	136	208	241
1939	CLE	24	9	.727	2.85	39	35	24	4	0	297.0	227	105	142	246
1940	CLE	27	11	.711	2.56	43	37	31	4	0	320.0	245	102	118	261
1941	CLE	25	13	.658	3.15	44	40	28	6	0	343.0	284	129	194	260
1945	CLE	5	3	.625	2.50	9	9	7	1	0	72.0	50	21	35	59
1946	CLE	26	15	.634	2.18	48	42	36	10	0	371.0	277	101	153	348
1947	CLE	20	11	.645	2.68	42	37	20	5	0	299.0	230	97	127	196
1948	CLE	19	15	.559	3.66	44	38	18	2	0	280.0	255	123	116	164
1949	CLE	15	14	.517	3.75	36	28	15	0	0	211.0	198	104	84	108
1950	CLE	16	11	.593	3.43	35	34	16	3	0	247.0	230	105	103	119
1951	CLE	22	8	.733	3.46	33	32	16	4	0	250.0	239	105	95	111
1952	CLE	9	13	.409	4.73	30	30	11	0	0	192.0	219	124	83	81
1953	CLE	10	7	.588	3.58	25	25	10	1	0	176.0	163	78	60	60
1954	CLE	13	3	.813	3.09	19	1	9	1	0	140.0	127	53	39	59
1955	CLE	4	4	.500	3.47	25	11	2	1	0	83.0	71	43	31	25
1956	CLE	0	4	.000	4.97	19	4	2	0	0	58.0	63	34	23	18
TOTALS		266	162	.621	3.26	570	484	279	44	0	3828.0	3271	1557	1764	2583

BOB GIBSON

BAD TIME FOR A SLAM

DATE: September 3, 1975

SITE: Busch Stadium, St. Louis, Missouri

OPPONENT: Pete LaCock of the Chicago Cubs

RESULT: Allowed grand slam to LaCock in seventh, which helped Cubs go on to win. Gibson left the game and took the loss.

The count ran full. Bob Gibson took a deep breath and fingered the white baseball in his long, calloused fingers as he stood on the hill and took the sign from St. Louis Cardinals catcher Ted Simmons. So many pitches. So many innings.

He looked around and saw the bases were full of Chicago Cubs. Gibson stared in at a left-handed hitter, who waved the bat at him eagerly. Who was this kid? What was his name again? LaCock. Quite a name.

That's it. Standing at the plate with a three-ball, two-strike count on him was Ralph Pierre LaCock Jr., the so-so hit, no-field son of *Hollywood Squares* host Peter Marshall. A 23-year-old rookie, itching, as he would put it to an adoring news media a little bit later, to break into the Cubs' lineup, Cubs manager Jim Marshall had sent LaCock to the plate against the 39-year-old Gibson, hoping to break open a close game.

Here was a classic baseball matchup, an eager rookie against a wily old pro, a fading veteran, still trying to hang on. Except the fierce Gibson didn't see himself as fading. Not really. He should have been starting, that's the way he figured it. Manager Red Schoendienst saw it another way.

When the right-hander began the 1975 season, he was still penciled in as a starter. Coming off an 11-13 season where he posted a career-high 3.83 ERA in 33 starts, the famous Gibson fastball was slowing. He fanned just 129 in 240 innings, the lowest per-game strikeout ratio (4.8) of his career. He struggled in three of his first five starts and was 1-5 on May 31 when he was demoted to the Cardinal bullpen. He won just twice more the rest of the season, making only four more starts.

But to Gibson, standing on the same mound where he'd been so dominating for so many years, it was impossible for him to see things had changed that much. No matter what his numbers said.

Five years later, on the eve of his induction to Cooperstown, he told writer Roger Angell that he never let age back him down. "I always threw hard," he said then. "They didn't use me much my final season, after I'd announced I was going to retire—I never did understand that.

"But once, when I hadn't pitched in three weeks, they brought me into a game against Houston in extra innings—I was the last pitcher we had—and I struck out the side on nine pitches that were nothing but fastballs. So I still had something left, even at the end...."

It didn't feel like that right now, though. The score had been tied at 6 when Gibson came on in relief of Cardinals starter Ron Reed, who had been pinch-hit for in the Cards' five-run sixth. It was the eighth relief appearance of Gibson's final season.

Gibson retired the Cubs' Bill Madlock, that season's batting champion (.354) with his first pitch. But the game's momentum quickly swung back to the Cubs when Gibson walked José Cardenal and an infield error let Champ Summers get on. A walk to Andre Thornton loaded the bases. Though Gibson retired Manny Trillo on a sharp grounder right back at him, forcing Cardenal at the plate, the veteran righty then fired a wild pitch past Simmons to let the Cubs score the tie-breaking run from third. Relievers aren't supposed to do that.

So, fearing further trouble, with first base open, pinch-hitter José Morales was intentionally walked, bringing up the nine-spot in the order and pinch-hitter LaCock. If you weren't really paying attention, it was easy to see the big red "45" underneath "Gibson" on the back of the bright white Cardinal jersey and imagine that it was 1968 all over again.

That was Gibson's extraordinary season, perhaps the finest single season by a pitcher in the long history of baseball. Gibson recorded a 1.12 earned-run average that year, throwing 13 shutouts, completing 28 of 34 starts, posting a 22-9 record for the NL champs. His was the most dominant season of all in the Year of the Pitcher, a year that prompted Major League Baseball to uniformly lower the mounds across both leagues the following spring.

And Gibson's dominance wasn't just limited to National League performances. When he worked the opening game of the 1968 World Series against the Detroit Tigers, all of America got to see what National League hitters had been flailing at all season long.

Facing a Tiger team that led the American League in runs (671) and home runs (185), Gibson scorched them with a brilliant, World Series record 17-strikeout performance in the opener on this very mound seven years earlier. Had there ever been a more dominating Series performance? Well, maybe Don Larsen's perfect game.

But Larsen didn't strike out 17 hitters, including the last three in the ninth, the way that Gibson did. The Cardinal catcher in that Series was broadcaster Tim McCarver, who didn't need much encouragement to remember the specifics of that game. Gibson fanned the side in the ninth inning, including retiring slugger Willie Horton on a called third strike to end the game on a sharp-breaking slider, his 144th pitch.

"I can still see that last pitch," McCarver told writer Roger Angell, "and I'll bet Willie Horton thinks to this day that the ball hit him—that's how much that ball broke. Talk about a batter shuddering!"

Gibson's third baseman in that game was Mike Shannon, who also marveled at what he saw in that ballgame. Gibson was so dominating that only two batters managed so much as a groundball off his electric stuff. Neither came Shannon's way.

In the years since that game, Shannon has talked with Tiger batters who can't help but talk about what it was like, batting against Gibson at his absolute peak. "Most of them had never seen Gibby before," Shannon told Angell, "and they had no idea what they were up against. It's as if they can't believe it to this day. I've never seen major-league hitters overmatched that way. It was like watching a big-league pitcher against Little League batters. It was frightening."

But by the end of that season, the strain on Gibson was showing. You could get a sense of where he was in a bylined piece that ran in the *St. Louis Post-Dispatch* during an off-day near the end of the 1968 World Series with Detroit.

"All day yesterday reporters kept coming up to me, asking if it was true that I was thinking about retiring and if it is true that my arm hurt so much I would not be able to pitch a seventh game.

"Apparently, somebody wrote a story to that effect, adding that I need an operation and that arthritis in my elbow would shorten my career. If I need any operation, I wish somebody would tell me. Sure, my arm hurts. It hurts every time I pitch. I don't think there's a pitcher alive whose arm does not hurt, if he has pitched long enough.

"The way this probably got started is that I said I hoped I didn't have to pitch again and I do . . . I don't want to pitch again. I want this thing to finish up today. But if I have to, I will pitch. If I had to, I would have pitched yesterday."

It turned out Gibson did pitch in Game 7. He and eventual Series MVP Mickey Lolich matched each other for six scoreless innings. But after Gibson got two outs in the seventh, he faltered and allowed four hits, turning the Series. Gibson, possibly the greatest of all postseason pitchers, lost his final World Series game.

A lot can change in seven years. Gibson was now 39. His Cardinal team was in the middle of the pack in the National League. With 119 hits allowed in 109 innings, he wasn't overmatching anybody anymore.

Still, he was Bob Gibson, as arrogant, as confident, as bold a pitcher as any who ever stood on a mound. He had reason to be, didn't he? "He was the most intimidating player in the league," Ted Simmons, Gibson's former catcher, recalled in Daniel Okrent's *Nine Innings*. "He'd stare in at the batter, and I could feel his eyes burn. Every pitch was a war for him, every hitter a threat. He never gave in and he never gave up. He won by force of his personality and by his concentration."

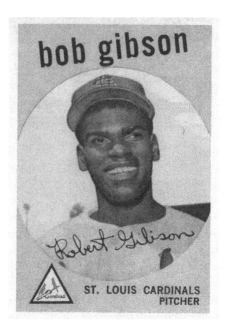

But here, finally at the end, Gibson stared in at LaCock. Who was this guy? Was he ready to hit against Bob Gibson? *The* Bob Gibson? Didn't he win 11 straight postseason games, including seven straight in a World Series? Didn't he win two Game 7s, vs. the New York Yankees in 1964—in Yankee Stadium!—and vs. the Boston Red Sox in 1967—at Fenway Park! And had the usually reliable Curt Flood made the kind of catch that he normally did in Game 7 in 1968, he might have won that one too. Wasn't he the greatest big-game pitcher in modern times? Who is this joker?

He wound and fired. LaCock saw the ball come out of Gibson's hand, saw the tall, athletic form lunge to the right, to the first base side as the white baseball flew plateward. He swung and the crack was unmistakable. The ball soared toward right field, over right fielder Willie Davis's head into the seats. Grand slam. The first of LaCock's career as a professional or an amateur. A grand salami!

Gibson swallowed hard, then walked around the base of the mound, hollering at LaCock in that high, squeaky voice that always seemed surprising, coming from such an imposing man. The St. Louis fans, booing loudly as LaCock ran around the bases, couldn't hear what he said. Fortunately.

When Gibson got to the other side of the mound, Schoendienst was waiting for him. Reliever Mike Wallace, a lefty, was on his way in to take over.

Gibson, who'd been honored by the St. Louis fans with Bob Gibson Night two days earlier, stalked off silently. It was not exactly walking off into the sunset.

Reading the *St. Louis Post-Dispatch* the next day, Cardinal fans had to bite their lip. "Cubs' Lucky Seventh Slams Door on Gibby" read the headline on the day's top story. Down below, though, in Dick Kaegel's story, was a quote from Madlock, one that was even more troubling than the grand slam. "A few guys on the bench said he looked like he was just going through the motions," Madlock said, adding (figuring he might have to still face him sometime) "now I didn't say that—that's just what I heard."

Bob Gibson? Going through the motions? Maybe it was, indeed, time to go. Though he never pitched again, Gibson hung with the Cardinals for two more weeks. On Wednesday night, as the Cardinals were getting ready to face the Montreal Expos, Gibson cleared out his locker and left the team.

He did take time to talk to the *Post-Dispatch*. "I was a little disappointed at the way they used me," Gibson said. "I think I could have pitched better if it hadn't been for the way they did. The biggest disappointment I've ever had in baseball was being taken out of the starting rotation this year. I really didn't pitch any differently than I had, but they just didn't want me any more."

Bob Gibson by the Numbers

YEAR	TEAM	W	L	PCT	ERA	G	GS	CG	SHO	SV	IP	H	R	BB	SO
1959	STL	3	5	.375	3.32	13	9	2	1	0	76.0	77	35	39	48
1960	STL	3	6	.333	5.59	27	12	2	0	0	87.0	97	61	48	69
1961	STL	13	12	.520	3.24	35	27	10	2	0	211.0	186	91	119	166
1962	STL	15	13	.536	2.85	32	30	15	5	0	234.0	174	84	95	208
1963	STL	18	9	.667	3.39	36	33	14	2	0	255.0	224	110	96	204
1964	STL	19	12	.613	3.01	40	36	17	2	0	287.0	250	106	86	245
1965	STL	20	12	.625	3.07	38	36	20	6	0	299.0	243	110	103	270
1966	STL	21	12	.636	2.44	35	35	20	5	0	280.0	210	90	78	225
1967	STL	13	7	.650	2.98	24	24	10	2	0	175.0	151	62	40	147
1968	STL	22	9	.710	1.12	34	34	28	13	0	305.0	198	49	62	268
1969	STL	20	13	.606	2.18	35	35	28	4	0	314.0	251	84	95	269
1970	STL	23	7	.767	3.12	34	34	23	3	0	294.0	262	111	88	274
1971	STL	16	13	.552	3.04	31	31	20	5	0	246.0	215	96	76	185
1972	STL	19	11	.633	2.46	34	34	23	4	0	278.0	226	83	88	208
1973	STL	12	10	.545	2.77	25	25	13	1	0	195.0	159	71	57	142
1974	STL	11	13	.458	3.83	33	33	9	1	0	240.0	236	111	104	129
1975	STL	3	10	.231	5.04	22	14	1	0	2	109.0	120	66	62	60
TOTALS		251	174	.591	2.91	528	482	255	56	2	3885.0	3279	1420	1336	3117

1966

SANDY KOUFAX

SHORT AND OH SO SWEET

DATE: October 6, 1966 (Game 2 of the World Series)

SITE: Dodger Stadium, Los Angeles, California

OPPONENT: Andy Etchebarren of the Baltimore Orioles

RESULT: Koufax got Etchebarren to hit into an inning-ending double play in the sixth.

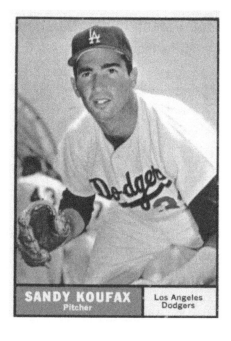

He needed an out. Just one out. Since when could the dominant pitcher of his time, heck, maybe *any* time, be humbled into praying for a little out?

Sandy Koufax stood on the mound at Dodger Stadium in Chavez Ravine on a sunny Thursday afternoon, staring in at the Baltimore Orioles' beetle-browed catcher Andy Etchebarren. Koufax had to wonder what he had done to deserve this.

Here it was, Game 2 of the 1966 World Series and his Dodgers were looking like a bunch of rookies on the first day of spring training. What was it, five errors? Six? He'd lost count. This was the World Series, what they'd been fighting for all season long, chasing a second-straight title. Koufax, pitching for the third time in eight days with an aching arm, was now into his 329th inning of the season. What more did he have to do?

Etchebarren waved his bat. This was the guy who started it all last time up, Koufax thought. How unlikely was that? A career .235 hitter in his first full big-league season with the Orioles, Koufax had whistled three faster-than-fast fastballs past a stunned Etchebarren in his first at-bat. His battery mate that day, Baltimore's 20-year-old future Hall of Famer Jim Palmer, kneeling in the on-deck circle at the time, called Koufax's pitches to Etchebarren "radio fastballs." "You could hear them," Palmer said, "but you couldn't see them."

But when Etchebarren batted again in the fifth, Koufax needed some help. He needed a routine play that suddenly wasn't so routine after all. All hell broke loose and the game—and maybe the World Series—turned.

One of the beauties of the game of baseball is even all-time greats still need routine plays made behind them. It's never a one-man show, no matter how dominating a pitcher can be. It's a game that looks easy enough. We've all played it, imitated big-league stars by making those great catches in our front yards and Little League parks, taking those mighty swings and hitting dramatic home runs.

But under the indiscriminate magnifying glass of history, the game's magic can turn on the most unsuspecting performer at the most shocking times. Fine players can become remembered more for their gaffes than the achievements of a long and distinguished career. From Fred Merkle's boner to the time Johnny Pesky held the ball to Mickey Owen's dropped third strike to Bill Buckner's bobble, goats are a part of baseball lore too.

As Koufax toed the rubber for the first pitch to Etchebarren, he knew that all-time champion World Series goat—Dodgers outfielder Willie Davis, his teammate—would never live this down. The inning before, the speedy

Davis set a World Series record with three errors as Baltimore mounted a 2–0 lead off Koufax while Dodger hitters flailed haplessly at relentless Palmer fastballs. What were the odds of Cy Young winner Sandy Koufax, a 27-game winner at the peak of his powers, being outpitched by a 20-year-old rookie fireballer in his first World Series start?

It all seemed so shocking, like watching a classical pianist break into "I've Got a Lovely Bunch of Coconuts" in the middle of a Carnegie Hall recital. A virtuoso all season long—a 27-game winner, an ERA of 1.73—Koufax's pitching performances were like perfectly conducted baseball symphonies. But this sounded like Spike Jones.

A year earlier, Koufax had wrought one of the game's masterpieces, retiring 27 batters in a row. It was only the second perfect game in Major League Baseball in the decade following Don Larsen's perfecto in the 1956 World Series. (This is not counting Harvey Haddix's 12 perfect innings, a game he lost in the 13th.)

Last October, Koufax had made national headlines by refusing to pitch the World Series opener because it fell on Yom Kippur. The headlines this year would be different.

Koufax went to the stretch and cast a glimpse over at Orioles second baseman Dave Johnson, leading off first. After his flare single, the last hit ever off Koufax, Sandy was tired. He'd worked a lot of innings the past two seasons, nearly 700 of them, counting the 30 World Series innings. And there was a mighty price to pay for such overwork: pain.

Some experts concluded that Koufax's elbow problems stemmed from an incident in a game against the Braves where he jammed his elbow sliding back into the base on a pickoff attempt. Others maintain he simply threw too hard for his body to stand it for too long a time. Whatever the cause, Koufax's arm problems were relentless. Sometimes, after games, his arm would swell so much he wouldn't be able to bend it.

According to Jane Leavy's *Sandy Koufax, A Lefty's Legacy*, his arm was so often stiff before a game that Koufax would coat his arm with Capsolin, an old pitchers' salve that felt like a burn on his skin, distracting him from the arthritic ache in his elbow. Through the years, most players had learned to cut the substance with Vaseline or cold cream. Koufax applied it straight to his skin and the odor from it was so strong, it could bring tears to the eyes of any nearby players.

After the game, Koufax would plunge the arm into a bucket of ice and hope the cold would help keep the swelling down. Sometimes, the elbow would swell up to the size of Koufax's knee joint and was impossible to bend. His coats had to be retailored. It was no way to live. In between starts, Koufax would take Empirin for pain, sit for painful cortisone shots directly into the joint, even take his chances with an anti-inflammatory drug that some people insisted killed a few horses. The drug was called Butazolidin. It's now off the market.

In an era where fragile aces like Boston's Pedro Martínez and New York's Mariano Rivera have every pitch carefully monitored, their pitch counts carefully documented and consulted, it seems incredible that a pitcher with Koufax's extraordinary talent wasn't treated more cautiously by the team that owned his contract.

In *Legacy*, Leavy recounts a story of Koufax being allowed to pitch a complete game in spring training in 1965, an unheard-of occurrence, especially with a player of Koufax's value to the franchise. The next morning, Koufax showed his roommate, Dick Tracewski, what price he paid for pitching that game.

"The elbow was black," Leavy quotes Tracewski. "And it was swollen. There were muscles that were pulled and there was hemorrhaging. From the elbow to the armpit, it looked like a bruise. A black, angry hemorrhage. It was an angry arm, an angry elbow. And all he says is 'Roomie, look at this.'"

As the 1965 season wore down, so did Koufax. After consulting with Dr. Robert Kerlan, Koufax made the decision to play one more season—1966— but told no one save his friend, writer Phil Collier, who wrote the story, then filed it away in a drawer until Sandy gave him the OK.

After pitching a pair of shutouts in the 1965 World Series to give the Dodgers the world title (Koufax worked two complete games on two days' rest), the arm continued to give him problems. In April 1966, Kerlan advised Koufax that it was time to retire. Koufax nodded and pitched on. One more year.

So now, that year was about up. It was Game 2 of the 1966 World Series, his elbow aching as though an alligator had a hold of it. Trailing 4–0, he just wanted to get out of the inning. After 350 innings and who knows how much ice, how many shots, and how much suffering, Koufax looked at Etchebarren and thought about a double-play ball. That wasn't Sandy's style of pitching, but hey, at least it wouldn't be a flyball.

Koufax looked out at center fielder Willie Davis and thought about all the wonderful catches he'd made over the past few years, helping him save ballgames. It wasn't fair that the newspapers tomorrow would blister Davis just because he had trouble in a tough sun field. But baseball wasn't always fair—he knew that too. He looked over at the scoreboard and there were numbers for the Orioles. It didn't say how they got them, but for anyone who was there or watched on TV, it would be hard to forget. It happened so fast.

As the fifth inning began, Boog Powell, a lefty hitter, sliced a single to left to get things started. After Dave Johnson sacrificed him to second, Paul Blair lofted a high fly to Davis. But Davis, normally a solid outfielder, promptly lost the ball in the sun, allowing runners to go to second and third.

Next up was Etchebarren, the number eight hitter. Instead of walking him to load the bases and set up a force at any base—conventional baseball strategy with the pitcher batting next—Dodger manager Walt Alston was confident Koufax didn't need a force play to get out of any jam. He let him pitch to Etchebarren.

It was a bad call. One baseball truism is the ball will always find the person who doesn't want it. Sure enough, Etchebarren lofted a high, very catchable flyball to Davis in center again and once more, to the horror of Dodger fans everywhere, Davis lost the ball in the sun and it dropped. Then he panicked, picked up the bobbled ball, and promptly fired the ball past third. Error Number Three. A hat trick!

It was 2–0 Orioles. When Luis Aparicio followed by ripping a double past third, Etchebarren rumbled in with the third unearned run of the inning. In the sixth, Frank Robinson's long flyball to the wall was again misplayed by Davis (this one wasn't ruled an error), allowing him to get to third. Powell singled him in to make it 4–0, Baltimore. Then, after an out, Dave Johnson flared one into right-center. Which brought him to this spot. One more pitch. One more out. With one pitch, if he threw it in the right place, Koufax might get the slow-footed Etchebarren to chase it, hit it on the ground, and start an inning-ending double play. He wound and fired the pitch, a low fastball, and, sure enough, Etchebarren chased it, rapping a slow roller that was quickly turned into a double play to end the inning. The walk to the dugout seemed long and sad.

When manager Walt Alston sent up a pinch-hitter for Koufax in the bottom of the sixth, the great left-hander's career was over. Nobody knew it at the time.

Remember, the Dodgers had trailed in the 1965 World Series vs. the Minnesota Twins and came back to win. Maybe if the Series went long enough, Koufax would be back.

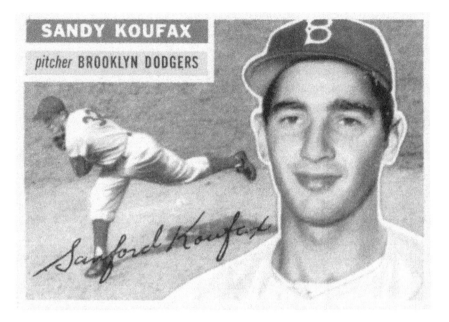

SANDY KOUFAX

pitcher BROOKLYN DODGERS

But it wasn't to happen. The Dodgers, hitting abominably, faded quickly against the young and sassy Baltimore staff and, suddenly, the Series had ended. The Orioles had won.

And the Dodgers, well, they'd ridden Koufax to a pair of World Series berths and one title. But by working him over 700 innings in his final two years, perhaps they made him into a bright and brilliant comet that was about to burn out. The last pitcher who had thrown more than 350 innings in a nonwartime season was Cleveland's Bob Feller, who returned from the service to throw a stunning 371 innings for the Tribe in 1946, fanning a then-record 348.

Apparently, the workload partially tamed him. Feller played another decade but never again struck out more than 200 batters in a single season. It was a long, slow, gradual fade. Koufax's numbers, despite the between-start suffering, kept getting better, even though elbow issues and circulation problems in his finger threatened to end his career at any time. Somehow, he battled through it all, never missed a start. On November 17, he officially announced his retirement.

With much of the Dodger brass on a trip to Japan and unrepresented at the noon press conference at the Beverly Wilshire, Koufax made it official. He was done.

"If there was a man who did not have the use of one of his arms," Koufax explained to the press that afternoon, "and you told him it would cost a lot of money if he could buy back that use, he'd give every dime he had, I believe."

There would be no more shots, no more pills, and no more potions. At the very tip-top of his game, he'd decided to say goodbye.

"I don't regret one minute of the last twelve years," he said softly, "but I think I would regret one year that was too many."

Five days after Christmas, three weeks into his retirement, Sandy Koufax turned 31.

Sandy Koufax by the Numbers

YEAR	TEAM	W	L	PCT	ERA	G	GS	CG	SHO	SV	IP	H	R	BB	SO
1955	BRK	2	2	.500	3.00	12	5	2	2	0	42.0	33	15	28	30
1956	BRK	2	4	.333	4.88	16	10	0	0	0	59.0	66	37	29	30
1957	BRK	5	4	.556	3.89	34	13	2	0	0	104.0	83	49	51	122
1958	LA	11	11	.500	4.47	40	26	5	0	0	159.0	132	89	105	131
1959	LA	8	6	.571	4.06	35	23	6	1	0	153.0	136	74	92	173
1960	LA	8	13	.381	3.91	37	26	7	2	0	175.0	133	83	100	197
1961	LAN	18	13	.581	3.52	42	35	15	2	0	256.0	212	117	96	269
1962	LAN	14	7	.667	2.54	28	26	11	2	0	184.0	134	61	57	216
1963	LAN	25	5	.833	1.88	40	40	20	11	0	311.0	214	68	58	306
1964	LAN	19	5	.792	1.74	29	28	15	7	0	223.0	154	49	53	223
1965	LAN	26	8	.765	2.04	43	41	27	8	0	336.0	216	90	71	382
1966	LA	27	9	.750	1.73	41	41	27	5	0	323.0	241	74	77	317
TOTALS		165	87	.655	2.76	397	314	137	40	0	2325.0	1754	806	817	2396

1972

ROBERTO CLEMENTE

INTO HISTORY

DATE: September 30, 1972 (final regular-season at-bat)

SITE: Three Rivers Stadium, Pittsburgh, Pennsylvania

PITCHER: Jon Matlack of the New York Mets

RESULT: Clemente doubled to left-center field in the fourth inning, his 3,000th career hit.

Empty seats. Standing on the top step of the Pittsburgh Pirate dugout off the first base side, Roberto Clemente took a long, slow look around the nearly empty Three Rivers Stadium. There was nobody here. Maybe 10,000 people. What did he have to do? Was this all he meant to them?

It was a cool Saturday in September, the last Saturday of the month. The defending world champion Pirates were once again headed for the postseason. They'd already clinched the National League East title against these same Mets about a week earlier at Shea Stadium. The suspense of the pennant race was over for now. The story on this day was Clemente. Or at least it was supposed to be. Except it didn't look that way in Pittsburgh. Not this afternoon.

To think that at this point only 10 men before him in the long history of the game had gotten this far. Babe Ruth didn't make it. Neither did Ted Williams, Joe DiMaggio, Jimmie Foxx, Lou Gehrig, or former Pirate greats Ralph Kiner, Pie Traynor, Lloyd Waner, or Kiki Cuyler—all of whom would eventually reach the Hall of Fame.

Now, with the regular season nearly over, the great Clemente was a single hit away from reaching 3,000. At home, yet. How excited was all of Pittsburgh about it? Only 13,117 were in the stands that afternoon, one of the smallest crowds of the season. A proud man, someone who seemed to seek out slights, unintentional or otherwise, Clemente felt hurt. As he so often did.

It wasn't like they didn't know about Clemente's quest for 3,000, either. The night before, a crowd of 24,193 showed up on a chilly Friday night to watch Pirate starter Nelson Briles battle New York's Tom Seaver. Since the race was over, you had to think they were there to see if Clemente could reach his milestone against the Mets great, who was going for his 20th win. They went home with something to talk about, almost from the first pitch.

After Pittsburgh's little lefty Vic Davalillo opened the game with a walk and Dave Cash grounded out, a roar rippled through the stands as Clemente walked to the plate. He waited for the cheers to subside, then stepped in and Seaver wound and fired and Clemente rapped a Seaver breaking pitch hard into the turf, bouncing it high over the mound. The ball skittered past Seaver's reach, out to second baseman Ken Boswell, who made a belated attempt to stop the ball, then kicked it. The Three Rivers fans roared, figuring that Clemente had his milestone hit.

But up in the press box, official scorer Luke Quay of the *McKeesport Daily News* quickly ruled it an error. Problem was, it took longer than usual to register that on the Three Rivers scoreboard. Mets first baseman Ed Krane-pool, who had just caught Boswell's late throw, assumed it was a hit, as did the Three Rivers crowd. He handed the ball to Pirates first base coach Don Leppert, figuring Clemente would want the keepsake, and the fans went wild for the Latin star.

It was then that the scoreboard flashed the "1" in the error column after the Mets' totals on the scoreboard. Pirate fans cut loose with a chorus of boos. On first base, Clemente seethed, as usual. More disrespect. The pressure of the 3,000-hit chase was starting to get to him. A player who was a career .300 hitter, he had at least a .400 average as a complainer and this gave him more ammunition.

The rest of the night wasn't productive. He took a called third strike, grounded out to Seaver, and lined out hard to right fielder Rusty Staub in the ninth. He wondered if he'd have enough games left in the season to make it to 3,000. In baseball, only regular-season records count toward those immense lifetime totals—500 home runs, 3,000 hits, 300 wins. Time was running out. Clemente felt it as far back as spring training.

"I've got to get those 3,000 hits," he said then. "I might get sick or die and no other Latin will do it." Immediately, Clemente thought about whether or not coming out of the game early in Philadelphia the night before was a good idea. On Thursday, Clemente had collected hit number 2,999 in his second at-bat, a single off the Phillies great Steve Carlton in what turned out to be Carlton's 26th win of the season. Since Clemente really wanted to collect hit number 3,000 at home, he got manager Bill Virdon to let him take himself out of the game, though Pittsburgh trailed 2–1 at the time. That 2–1 score held up for Carlton and the lowly Phillies. That's how much he wanted to achieve that milestone before the fans of Pittsburgh. If he'd only have known how they were to repay him Saturday afternoon.

After Friday night's controversial call, Clemente was bitter. "This is nothing new," Clemente sneered. "Official scorers have been robbing me of hits like this for 18 years. . . ." This was the Clemente the writers often heard. Instead of swallowing hard and muttering some typical baseball cliché about going out and getting 'em next time, the emotional Pirate star would lash out at the fans or the media or those who didn't understand what sort of physical price he was paying each and every time he pulled on a uniform. Though he could see for himself that on the field he was every bit the equal of Willie Mays or Hank Aaron or Mickey Mantle, he was nowhere near the national figure they were.

Well, at least not until the 1971 World Series against Baltimore, which Clemente made his personal showcase. Yet here it was, only a year later, and only 13,117 showed up to see him try for his 3,000th hit. What did he have to do?

Clemente never did find out. And years earlier, he'd made it clear that being overlooked truly bothered him. You could read that in a long feature story that appeared in *Sports Illustrated* in 1966, a season in which Clemente won the NL's MVP award for his .317 average and 119 RBI.

Veteran writer Myron Cope wrote a long profile on Clemente titled "Aches and Pains and Three Batting Titles" in which Cope introduced the Pirates right fielder to a national audience by mostly mocking the always-complaining Clemente. "Relatively small at 5-feet 10-inches and 180 pounds when able to take nourishment, the chronic invalid has smooth skin, glistening muscles, and perfect facial contours that suggest the sturdy mahogany sculpture peddled in the souvenir shops of his native Puerto Rico.

"Many Pittsburghers have concluded that the only thing that can keep Clemente from making them forget Paul Waner is a sudden attack of good health." Cope's piece made several good points. In it, a Clemente friend explains, "You have to understand that the Latin is touchy." And later on, talking with Cope about his image, Clemente was certainly that: "If a Latin player or even an American negro is sick," Clemente said, "they say it is all in the head. Felipe Alou once went to his team doctor and the doctor said 'You don't have anything.' So he went to a private doctor and the doctor said, 'You have a broken foot.'"

Consequently, Clemente concluded, his reputation as a malingerer clouded his on-field excellence. "With my eyes blind, I can throw to the base," he said. "I know that. If [Mickey] Mantle has the arm I have you will put it in headlines because he is an American. You never give me credit. How many players in history win three batting titles? The sportswriters don't mention that. They ask me, what you think about dis, what you think about dat?"

Remembering that Pittsburgh was a steel town, hearing a Latin player complain about how he hurt all the time—when his spectacular play on the field never showed any evidence of ill health—put Clemente in an awkward situation. In 14 of his 18 seasons, he'd played in at least 124 games and for nine years in a row, played more than 144 (out of 162). That's a pretty impressive track record for a guy who said he was hurting all the time.

Everybody could see what an extraordinary player he was. His 1971 World Series was one of the greatest sustained performances of any great player in baseball history. But there would never be the outpouring of love for him that there was for Papa Bear Willie Stargell, no matter what he did. There was a distance there. Roberto Clemente was just always out of reach. The language barrier didn't help such a sensitive soul, either.

For much of his career, the Pittsburgh press made him sound like a savage. Once, a female Pirate fan asked him if he wore loincloths at home. "I know I don't speak as bad as they say I speak," Clemente told Cope. "I know that I don't have the good English pronunciation because my tongue belongs to Spanish, but I know where the verb, the article, the pronoun, whatever it is, go. I never in my life start a sentence with 'me.' 'Me Tarzan, you Jane.'"

So when Clemente heard his name announced to lead off the fourth inning of Saturday's game, he walked quietly to the plate, never once looking around at the nearly empty stands, refusing to let himself measure the volume of their cheers or feel the excitement of those who were there.

New York Mets starter Jon Matlack, a left-hander with a good curveball, had gotten him in his first at-bat, striking him out with a sharp curve. Clemente thought about that as he carefully set up in the far corner of the batter's box, waving that unusually white bat back and forth as he trained his sights on Matlack. He took a pitch, then on Matlack's second offering, a low curveball, Clemente reached out with the fat part of the bat and drove the ball hard into the gap in left-center field. Just from the sound alone, he knew it would be a hit and Clemente took off quickly, easing into second base standing up as the relay throw from Mets outfielder Dave Schneck came in to shortstop Jim Fregosi. Fregosi gave the ball to umpire Doug Harvey, who then handed it to Clemente and shook his hand. The Three Rivers scoreboard flashed the news that Clemente was one of 11 players in major-league history who had reached 3,000 hits. The noise was considerable, despite the tiny crowd, and Clemente, standing on second base, raised his cap to all the fans.

He stayed in the game for one more inning, then retired to the dugout. Mets outfielder Willie Mays, who with Hank Aaron was the only other active player with over 3,000 hits, walked over from the other dugout to give Clemente a hug.

Afterward, Clemente was his usual self: complaining. He said that he'd had a sleepless night after his near-miss on Friday thanks to telephone calls from home. "Then my wife (Vera) had to be at the airport at six o'clock to meet some friends so we didn't even bother to go to bed," Clemente told the *New York Times*. "When I arrived at the ballpark, I had no sleep at all."

Clemente credited teammate Willie Stargell for helping him get hit number 3,000. "I haven't been swinging good lately so Willie picked out one of my bats . . . a heavier one than I have been using. He handed it to me and told me to 'go get it.'"

After the game, Clemente also told the writers that he'd take the next three regular-season games off so that he'd get a week of rest to be ready for the Pirates' postseason series with Cincinnati. "I play better when I am rested," he said.

As it turned out, Clemente didn't quite get the complete rest he wanted. After collecting his 3,000th hit, the Pirates' public relations staff noticed that Clemente had just tied Honus Wagner for the most games in a Pirate uniform, 2,432. With three games left in the regular season, Pirate staffer Bill Guilfoile urged Manager Bill Virdon to get Clemente into a game, to break Wagner's record. He did. Though at 38, Clemente had another fine season, and there was no talk of retirement, Virdon didn't want to wait until next season. Sure enough, he let Clemente play the ninth inning of the team's next-to-last game with the St. Louis Cardinals, breaking Wagner's record.

It turned out that the Pirates' season only went a little bit longer. Pittsburgh was knocked out of the postseason, losing a five-game series to the Cincinnati Reds in heartbreaking fashion. After the Pirates won two of the first three games (Clemente went hitless in the first two), Pittsburgh fell apart in Game 4, committing three errors and playing generally lousy baseball, falling 7–1 to lefty Ross Grimsley. Only Clemente did anything of note for Pittsburgh, collecting both of their hits, including a seventh-inning home run.

In Game 5 in Cincinnati, Pittsburgh carried a 3–2 lead into the bottom of the ninth, but reliever Dave Giusti gave up a solo home run to Johnny Bench, then a single to Tony Pérez and a single to pinch-hitter Denis Menke. Pirates manager Bill Virdon went to the bullpen, bringing in starter Bob Moose, hoping that he might work out of the jam. He nearly did. Moose got César Gerónimo to fly out to Clemente in right for one out (pinch-runner George Foster advanced to third), then got Darrel Chaney to pop out to shortstop Gene Alley for the second out.

But with the count 1-1, Moose's third pitch sailed past catcher Manny Sanguillén and Foster scampered home from third to win it for Cincinnati. They were on to the World Series. The Pirates were done.

By October 10, Clemente's season was over. He went back home to Puerto Rico, where, in December, he got involved with relief efforts to aid earthquake victims in Managua. On New Year's Eve, he boarded a plane leaving San Juan International Airport, fearing that profiteers were stealing the relief supplies that were intended for the earthquake victims. The DC-7 crashed shortly after takeoff. Clemente's body was never found.

Six years earlier, Clemente had talked about helping people, how important it was. "Anybody who have the opportunity to serve their country or their island and don't, God should punish them. If you can be good, why should you be bad?

"Today, life is moving too fast for these kids," he said. "You see 15-year-old boys and girls holding hands. They hang out on street corners. Maybe if I can keep them interested in sports, they will not always be talking about stealing and about gangster movies. I'm proud to do good for my island. I like to work with kids," Clemente told Cope, concluding his 1966 interview. "I'd like to work with kids all the time, if I live long enough."

Roberto Clemente, now honored with a statue and a bridge outside PNC Park in Pittsburgh, remains the only Puerto Rican player to have collected 3,000 hits, the milestone hit coming in what turned out to be his final regular-season at-bat.

Roberto Clemente by the Numbers

YEAR	TEAM	G	AB	R	H	TB	2B	3B	HR	RBI	BB	SO	SB	BA	SLG	OBP
1955	PIT	124	474	48	121	181	23	11	5	47	18	60	2	.255	.382	.284
1956	PIT	147	543	66	169	234	30	7	7	60	13	59	6	.311	.431	.330
1957	PIT	111	451	42	114	157	17	7	4	30	23	45	0	.253	.348	.288
1958	PIT	140	519	69	150	212	24	10	6	50	31	41	8	.289	.408	.327
1959	PIT	105	432	60	128	171	17	7	4	50	15	51	2	.296	.396	.322
1960	PIT	144	570	89	179	261	22	6	16	94	39	73	4	.314	.458	.357
1961	PIT	146	572	101	201	320	30	10	23	89	35	59	4	.351	.559	.390
1962	PIT	144	538	95	168	244	28	9	10	74	35	73	6	.312	.454	.352
1963	PIT	152	600	77	192	282	23	8	17	76	31	64	12	.320	.470	.356
1964	PIT	155	622	95	211	301	40	7	12	87	51	87	5	.339	.484	.388
1965	PIT	152	589	91	194	273	21	14	10	65	43	78	8	.329	.463	.378
1966	PIT	154	638	105	202	342	31	11	29	119	46	109	7	.317	.536	.360
1967	PIT	147	585	103	209	324	26	10	23	110	41	103	9	.357	.554	.400
1968	PIT	132	502	74	146	242	18	12	18	57	51	77	2	.291	.482	.355
1969	PIT	138	507	87	175	276	20	12	19	91	56	73	4	.345	.544	.411
1970	PIT	108	412	65	145	229	22	10	14	60	38	66	3	.352	.556	.407
1971	PIT	132	522	82	178	262	29	8	13	86	26	65	1	.341	.502	.370
1972	PIT	102	378	68	118	181	19	7	10	60	29	49	0	.312	.479	.356
TOTALS		2433	9454	1417	3000	4492	440	166	240	1305	621	1232	83	.317	.475	.359

1963

STAN MUSIAL

BACK FROM THE BENCH

DATE: September 29, 1963

SITE: Busch Stadium, St. Louis, Missouri

PITCHER: Jim Maloney of the Cincinnati Reds

RESULT: RBI single to right field (1,815th career hit at home, matching road total)

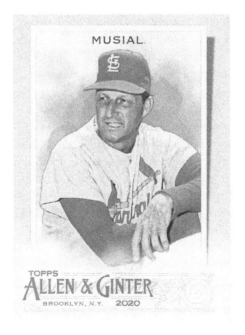

As long as I live," Stan Musial said softly, standing alone at the microphone in the middle of the diamond at Busch Stadium one sunny Sunday afternoon in late September, "this is a day I'll always remember. This is a day of both great joy and sorrow; the sorrow which always comes when we have to say farewell. My heart is filled with thanks for so many who made these 22 years possible."

He looked around at the 27,576 all around the stadium standing and cheering for him, a St. Louis monument to rival the great arch. He looked down. Stan "The Man" Musial thought quickly to himself, "Gee, if they all knew how close I was to becoming a Pirate a few years back. . . ."

Just four summers earlier, in 1960, the magnificent Musial, nearing 40, was riding the pine and thinking about retirement. It looked like it was going to turn into yet another sad story of a one-time great player hanging on until he was embarrassed into retirement.

Imagine the fiery Ty Cobb, wearing that Philadelphia A's uniform with the white elephant on it, sharing a corner spot in the dugout next to Tris Speaker as the final moments of his career trickled into late summer. Or the great Rogers Hornsby, stuck in a St. Louis Browns uniform, grumbling to himself on the bench, wondering if he should put himself back in the lineup, as he watched mishap after mishap occur on the field before him. Or Ruth, fat and slow in a Braves uniform, or Christy Mathewson, a startling sight in a Cincinnati uniform, throwing pitches that were pounded all over the yard. There didn't seem to be any kind, uplifting, considerate way to explain to these baseball giants that now it was time to go home.

Writer Roger Angell explained as much in *Late Innings* shortly after learning of Willie Mays's election to the Hall of Fame. It was hard, Angell noted, to forget how age had weakened the great one. "His enshrinement allowed me to remember Mays as he had been in his wonderful youth," he wrote. "The brilliant boy gliding across the long meadows of the Polo Grounds . . . and to forget the old, uncertain, querulous Willie Mays who came to the Mets in his final few seasons and clearly stayed too long in the game. The shift in my feelings (upon his election) was like the change that sometimes comes after we remember a close relative who has died . . . suddenly one morning, our sad last view of that person fades away and we are left instead with an earlier and more vivid picture—the one that stays with us."

For Stan Musial to regain that, to go back to where he was, where he would always be—forever, in memory—why, who would have bet on that?

Musial's troubles had their start in a 1959 season where he came to spring training a bit out of shape and, at the suggestion of management, didn't play much, trying to rest up for the season.

Problem was, Musial never did get into the kind of consistent groove that marked his extraordinary career, and he wound up the 1959 season at a grim .255, only a point higher than Boston's Ted Williams, who himself had a miserable, injury-plagued season over in the American League.

By year's end, the Cardinals were in seventh and Musial was on the bench. His numbers were the worst of his career. He'd hit just 14 home runs and drove in only 44 runs. Though Musial went through a rigorous offseason training regimen and reported to spring training in 1960 in better shape, he was still on the bench well into May.

That's when the talk of the Pirates started. St. Louis manager Solly Hemus, a former Musial teammate, was convinced that Stan was washed up after what he'd seen in 1959 and wasn't playing him. The team was going nowhere, and Hemus pushed for a trade to shake things up.

The Cards dealt lefty Wilmer Mizell and infielder Dick Gray to Pittsburgh for second baseman Julián Javier and pitcher Ed Bauta. The two teams weren't done talking. As the trade deadline approached, the Cardinals were still struggling and Pittsburgh had designs on the National League pennant (which it went on to win).

Noticing that Musial hadn't been in the lineup, Pirate manager Danny Murtaugh approached St. Louis writer Bob Broeg and asked about Musial's absence. He found out Musial was healthy but that Cards manager Hemus wasn't going to put him back in the lineup. Maybe the Pirates would?

Murtaugh scoffed. "Heck, Stan would never leave the Cardinals," Murtaugh said. "Until now, you would have been right" explained Broeg, who recounted this story in Musial's ghostwritten autobiography. "But Hemus is convinced Stan is through and the guy wants a chance to prove he isn't. He might be interested in going to his old hometown area and getting the chance at one more World Series" (a World Series that the Pirates went on to win).

When Musial admitted to Broeg that he'd consider it, Murtaugh was stunned. "Musial could mean the difference for us in the race," the Pirate manager said, trying to imagine Musial in gray and black. When Pittsburgh general manager Joe L. Brown caught wind of it, his sense of what was right for baseball overrode his sense of competition. "As much as we'd like to have Musial," he told Broeg, "I just can't do it to [Cardinals GM] Bing Devine . . . to offer too little [Pittsburgh would only grab him if Musial was unconditionally released] would be taking advantage of public sentiment. . . . Devine would be on a spot where I don't care to put him."

So Musial remained a Cardinal. And as the 1960 season continued, Musial finally worked his way back into the lineup and the team surged into second place, behind Pittsburgh. Guess who beat the Pirates three separate times with clutch home runs?

By the end of the year, St. Louis had fallen back to third. But Musial had worked his average up to .275, hit 17 home runs, and drove in 63 runs in 116 games, one more than he'd played the year before. He was back.

In 1961, Musial hit .288 and was productive the entire year. Once the Cardinals changed managers, Stan got better news. New Cards manager Johnny Keane wanted him to play more in 1962, not less.

Musial responded with his last great season. The whole year was like one long highlight reel.

After collecting his 3,000th hit as a pinch-hitter in a game in Chicago in May (Musial's success on the road was extraordinary—more on that later), he went on to break Honus Wagner's National League record for most hits, Ty Cobb's major-league record of total bases, and Mel Ott's National League RBI record.

Even better, Musial was having a golden year at the plate, leading the National League in hitting late into the summer. In the season's final weeks, the Dodgers' Tommy Davis and Cincinnati's Frank Robinson surged past Musial. But it was still a banner year for Stan, who finished third in the race with a .330 mark. He also hit 19 home runs and had 82 RBI in 116 games. Not bad for a 41-year-old.

Naturally, the Cardinals invited Musial back in 1963 for his 22nd big-league season. Finally, it appeared age had caught up with him. He played in only 86 games, batted just .255, a dip of 75 points from the year previous. Even so, he still had his moments.

In the final week of the season, the Dodgers' remarkable left-hander Sandy Koufax carried a no-hitter into the seventh inning against Musial's Cardinals. Guess who lined a single to center field to break up the no-hitter?

A few weeks earlier, facing Braves great Warren Spahn for the final time, Musial whacked a double, lifting his career batting average against the Hall of Fame lefty to .314 with 14 home runs.

As Musial's career wound down to its final days, somebody noted how consistent Stan was at home and on the road. For most players, playing at home meant a big difference in batting prowess. Ted Williams, Musial's contemporary, batted .361 for his career at Fenway Park and .327 on the road, collecting 1,406 hits in Boston and 1,248 in other parks.

That's the way it was for most players. Roberto Clemente hit .329 at home, .306 on the road. Carl Yastrzemski hit .306 at Fenway, .264 on the road.

Musial did hit 10 points higher at home (.336 to .326), but as Stan ran out on the field in St. Louis that late-September afternoon in 1963, the consistency of his career numbers was truly amazing. Of the 3,628 career hits he'd collected through his 22-year career heading into his final game, 1,815 of them came in other ballparks, 1,813 of them came in St. Louis. So ol' Stan had something unusual to shoot for in this finale against Cincinnati fireballer Jim Maloney, one of the game's hardest throwers. Maloney, chasing his 24th win, was matched with St. Louis ace Bob Gibson this sunny afternoon. Gibson had a target, too. He was chasing his 19th victory.

In Musial's first at-bat, with the St. Louis crowd bursting with noise on every pitch, Stan took a slow curveball on the outside corner and home plate umpire Al Barlick rang him up. It was the 696th and final strikeout of Musial's career, a span that would cover 10,972 official at-bats and 3,026 games. Despite being a power hitter (475 career home runs), Musial only fanned 40 or more times in a season three times—a good month for Reggie Jackson. Two of those 40-plus strikeout campaigns were the final two years of his career.

When Musial came up again in the fourth inning, Maloney still hadn't allowed a hit. Would Stan again spoil the no-hitter, as he'd done to Koufax a few days ago? Sure enough, he worked the count to 1-1, then got a belt-high Maloney fastball on the fat part of his bat and rifled it past Maloney and a diving Cincinnati second baseman for hit number 3,629. The Cincy second baseman turned out to be the man who later supplanted Musial as the NL's hit king, Pete Rose.

As Musial got to first, all of St. Louis, it seemed, was roaring for him. Manager Johnny Keane smiled and many expected to see him get the hook right there. But Keane left him in. The game was still scoreless. And you could always expect a little more from Musial, couldn't you?

He came up again in the sixth with one out. Curt Flood, who'd opened the inning with a double, was at second and once again, all of St. Louis stood and roared for number 6, who smiled and drank it all in—the applause, the warmth, the love. He had come back from the bench, defied age and skeptics, and last summer, nearly won his eighth batting title.

Maloney pitched carefully to Musial. He wound and fired a high fastball and Musial fouled it straight back. 0-1. Next, he tried the pitch that had fooled Musial in his first at-bat, the curve, and bounced it in the dirt. 1-1. He tried the heat and missed outside. 2-1. Trailing in the count, many fireballers would have gone to the fastball, trying to get the count back to even. Maloney had other ideas.

He broke off a sharp-breaking curve, low and inside, to the lefty Musial. Stan was ready. He picked up the spin, kept his hands back, and rifle-shot a groundball past first base into right field to score Flood and break the tie. It was Musial's 1,951st RBI, then an NL record.

With the Cardinals fans teary-eyed and tender, Keane sent out pinch-runner Gary Kolb and the fans booed, seeing Musial leave. There was a game to finish.

Talk about professionalism. Talk about consistency. Talk about rising to the occasion. Stan Musial may have been 42, but he knew what it meant to leave on the right note, exactly the right note. How was he able to get a pair of hits off one of the game's hardest throwers at the end of a long and difficult season? Because he was Stan Musial, that's how. He'd waited long enough, battled hard enough to turn the game back his way. He waited his turn, trusted his talent, that golden swing, knew it would return if he was patient enough.

Here, in his final moments as a player, it was all happening for him—and for St. Louis—one last time. Unlike many of his peers, Musial was keenly aware of his town, his fans, and the bond between the two. Having seen what Ted Williams's dramatic exit had been like in cantankerous Boston, he knew what he wanted for the fans of St. Louis. How wonderful and fortuitous that Manager Johnny Keane sensed that Stan had one more hit in that dime-store bat and kept him in the game after that fourth-inning single. Maybe he hated to imagine the Cardinal lineup without Musial in it.

Earlier in the afternoon, Commissioner Ford Frick described Musial this way: "Here stands baseball's perfect warrior. Here stands baseball's perfect knight." How could Stan not come through after a pronouncement like that.

As it turned out, there was more than two hours more of baseball ahead before a Dal Maxvill single to right scored rookie Jerry Buchek with the winning run in a 14-inning, 3–2 Cardinal victory. Musial had to wait all that time in the clubhouse, talking with writers, sipping beer, listening to the game on the radio.

When it was all finally over and the media crush surrounded Musial, waiting to hear what the one and only "Man" St. Louis would ever have had to say, he kept it simple. "I love to play this game of baseball," he said softly. "I love putting on the uniform."

He said he was headed to the World Series, where he'd throw out the first ball for the opener, then go down to Fort Riley to see his grandson. "And then . . ." Musial said, with the satisfied air of a man closing a book that he so loved to read, he dreaded coming to the final page, "I'll retire. Retire. And take things easy."

Now that's how to finish a career, isn't it? One thousand, eight hundred and fifteen hits on the road. One thousand, eight hundred and fifteen hits at home. Coming back off the bench out of that paralyzing limbo of age and self-doubt to say goodbye on his terms. Not one, not two, not three, but four seasons later when he was good and ready to go.

That's why they called Stan Musial "The Man."

Stan Musial by the Numbers

YEAR	TEAM	G	AB	R	H	TB	2B	3B	HR	RBI	BB	SO	SB	BA	SLG	OBP
1941	SLN	12	47	8	20	27	4	0	1	7	2	1	1	.426	.574	.449
1942	SLN	140	467	87	147	229	32	10	10	72	62	25	6	.315	.490	.397
1943	SLN	157	617	108	220	347	48	20	13	81	72	18	10	.357	.562	.425
1944	SLN	146	568	112	197	312	51	14	12	94	90	28	7	.347	.549	.440
1946	SLN	156	624	124	228	366	50	20	16	103	73	31	7	.365	.587	.434
1947	SLN	149	587	113	183	296	30	13	19	95	80	24	3	.312	.504	.398
1948	SLN	155	611	135	230	429	46	18	39	131	83	34	7	.376	.702	.453
1949	SLN	157	612	128	207	382	41	13	36	123	109	38	3	.339	.625	.440
1950	SLN	146	555	105	192	331	41	7	28	109	87	36	5	.346	.596	.437
1951	SLN	152	578	124	205	355	30	12	32	108	98	40	4	.355	.614	.449
1952	SLN	154	578	105	194	311	42	6	21	91	98	29	7	.336	.538	.434
1953	SLN	157	593	127	200	361	53	9	30	113	105	32	3	.337	.609	.437
1954	STL	153	591	120	195	359	41	9	35	126	103	39	1	.330	.607	.428
1955	STL	154	562	97	179	318	30	5	33	108	80	39	5	.319	.566	.408
1956	STL	156	594	87	184	310	33	6	27	109	75	39	2	.310	.522	.386
1957	STL	134	502	82	176	307	38	3	29	102	66	34	1	.351	.612	.422
1958	STL	135	472	64	159	249	35	2	17	62	72	26	0	.337	.528	.423
1959	STL	115	341	37	87	146	13	2	14	44	60	25	0	.255	.428	.364
1960	STL	116	331	49	91	161	17	1	17	63	39	34	1	.275	.486	.351
1961	STL	123	372	46	107	182	22	4	15	70	52	35	0	.288	.489	.371
1962	STL	135	433	57	143	220	18	1	19	82	64	46	3	.330	.508	.416
1963	STL	124	337	34	86	136	10	2	12	58	35	43	2	.255	.404	.325
TOTALS		3026	10972	1949	3630	6134	725	177	475	1951	1605	696	78	.331	.559	.417

1983

CARL YASTRZEMSKI

TO YAZ, WITH LOVE

DATE: October 2, 1983

SITE: Fenway Park, Boston, Massachusetts

PITCHER: Dan Spillner of the Cleveland Indians

RESULT: Popout to second baseman Jack Perconte

He looked down at his feet, planted in the same batter's box, maybe in the exact location where his predecessor had bowed out so memorably 23 years earlier.

Talk about following in Ted Williams's footsteps. Carl Yastrzemski literally did. Now, it was all over. After 23 years, 3,308 games, 11,988 at-bats—4,282 more than Ted Williams—3,419 hits, and 1,845 walks, he was finally through.

With this last at-bat against Cleveland reliever Dan Spillner, a nondescript right-hander finishing a grand 2-9 season, Yaz would wrap it all up. It was hard to focus the way he normally wanted to. The moment he stepped out of the Red Sox dugout, the crowd began to clap and wouldn't stop, even for the public address announcer.

Yastrzemski stood outside the batter's box, his bat by his side, his right arm waving his helmet to the overflow crowd that couldn't throw enough love his way. They knew this was it; they'd never see number 8 in that batter's box again. Then he had to step in and try to hit.

How different a finish it was for him compared to Williams. For Teddy Ballgame's final game—which wasn't announced in advance—there was a brief pregame ceremony on a September day 23 years ago. Williams then merely went through the motions of another drab ballgame. It only became electric when Williams came to bat for the final time, in the eighth.

Even after Ted's dramatic last at-bat home run, there was no nod to the fans, no final tip of the cap, nothing for them but the thrill of the moment, which, of course, has grown with the years.

Like the attendance, no doubt. But on this final day of reckoning, Yaz did beat Williams there. Ted drew just 10,454 to his Wednesday afternoon finale. There were 33,491 there for the Sunday afternoon farewell to Yaz.

In fact, Yaz's final weekend was a pure fan fest. Sure, there had been a time when Yaz had heard their boos, when he stuffed cotton in his ears when he ran out to left field. Boston's fans can be demanding and very hard to please. Some of them thought Yaz should have won the Triple Crown and been the American's League's MVP every season from 1967 to 1983.

Instead, after that Impossible Dream season of 1967, it took him eight years to get the Red Sox back into the World Series. So if he'd heard more than his share of boos and took more than his share of blame in the newspapers and on the radio talk shows over that time, he understood, at last, how much they cared. So did he.

Together, they came through the years, through all the stances and heart-ache and strains and bruises and disappointments. This hard-won audience finally loved him. He loved them, too.

You could see it as he stood there waving his helmet, turning as if to drink in all the sad and happy faces that showered him with such affection. They had noticed how long and how hard he'd kept at it. How much of himself—and his life, really—he gave to this team.

So the day of reckoning was healthy. No, he never quite matched Williams's standards of excellence at the plate. It wasn't for lack of trying. How he worked at it. All those hours and hours of extra hitting. At least a dozen different stances.

And worry. All those off-hours thinking about that next at-bat, that next game, that next pitch.

No, it was never easy for him. Never looked it, either. Maybe the great Ted Williams could study the enemy, declare that the dumbest guy in the ballpark was always the pitcher, come to the park, and get his two hits every day. You'd never hear Yaz say something like that. He could see the lines in his face when he got dressed before this last ballgame. Deep circles under his eyes. He could see the silver feathering in the sides of his thick brown hair. He looked like a man who worked hard for a living.

"The pervasive, unshakeable image of Carl Yastrzemski that I carry inside me," wrote Roger Angell in 1983, "is of his making an out in a game, in some demanding or critical situation—a pop-up instead of a base hit, or perhaps an easy grounder chopped toward a waiting infielder—with Yaz dropping his head in sudden disappointment and self-disgust as he flips the bat away and starts up the line, his chance gone again.

"No other great ballplayer I have seen was more burdened by the difficulties of this most unforgiving of all sports," Angell continued, "and by the ceaseless demands he made on his own skills, and by the expectations we had of him in every game and almost every at-bat. . . . Yaz wasn't glum, he was funereal."

Why? Why could someone who could play the game so well be so down-hearted about it? Well, he never came right out and said it, but how do you step into the batter's box that Ted Williams had made his for 20 seasons?

So now, here it was. His final at-bat. Everybody remembered how Williams went out. What would Yaz do?

All New England knew his mannerisms as he stepped in. The hitch at the back of the pants, the jamming of the blue batting helmet down on his head with the palm of his hand, the twirl of the bat, the front foot poised. . . .

He laughed as he thought about that unmistakable voice he used to hear all the time every spring . . . Williams.

"That damn Yastrzemski; he's always got 15 million things to do before he gets into the batter's box."

No, he wasn't another Ted Williams. But who the hell was? As you saw him standing at the plate on this sunny final Sunday, he was showing a little more of his back to the pitcher than he had before, the bat partially hidden by his body. Once he held the bat so high over his head, it looked as if he was trying to poke a cloud.

Now, it was as if age and gravity had finally brought his hands and tools down to a level more befitting a 44-year-old man. He didn't look threatening anymore.

There was a time when he cocked those hands and ripped that bat through the strike zone with a dramatic, back-bending flourish that would sometimes move classically understated Red Sox announcer Ned Martin to blurt, "Mercy!" One writer said Yastrzemski had a chiropractor's dream of a swing. That was it, ferocious, at his best, almost untamed, out of control.

After his sudden surge of power in 1967—he hit 44 home runs—the stance seemed to change annually, a concession to age, to the way they happened to be pitching him that season, to a whim.

That was another element that further separated him from Williams, whose stance was defiant, his swing classical, elegant, unchanging through the seasons. Unlike Williams who played left field except for his rookie season, Yastrzemski started in left but eventually moved to first base, then designated hitter, still hitting in the productive spots in the Red Sox lineup. Williams just about always hit third.

Like Williams, he wasn't able to bring home a World Series title, either. But, unlike Ted, in Yaz's two tries, 1967 and 1975, both were seven-game series and he hit like hell (.400 vs. the Cardinals, .310 vs. the Cincinnati Reds).

Like Williams, he was great in All-Star Games, too. Always found a way to raise his game when it counted. That's what Boston fans just knew. They didn't need stats to tell them. The Boston writers dug them up anyway. In the 22 most important games of his career—World Series, pennant races, playoffs—Yastrzemski batted .417, nearly 140 points higher than his lifetime average or about twice what Williams hit vs. St. Louis in his 1946 World Series against the St. Louis Cardinals.

Yaz was also the man at the plate when both those World Series ended. He flied out against Bob Gibson in Game 7 of the 1967 World Series and flied out against Will McEnaney in Game 7 of the 1975 World Series. His most famous final out came in the Red Sox-Yankees 1978 playoff game, when Goose Gossage got him to pop out to Graig Nettles, ending the game in utter heartbreak for Boston fans, who'd had a huge lead that season, then squandered it, losing a playoff game at home.

For stunned Red Sox fans, it just didn't seem as if it really happened, as if it should have counted. *Globe* columnist Ray Fitzgerald, writing moments after he saw the ball descend into Nettles's glove, said "Somewhere there should be a film director wearing a beret and shouting through the megaphone: 'Another take, gentlemen, and this time, let's get it right.'"

Angell, a Red Sox devotee, was wounded to the core. Writing about the moment in *Late Innings* he brought the moment back vividly.

"Two out and the tying run on third. Yastrzemski up. A whole season, thousands of innings, had gone into this tableau. My hands were trembling. The faces around me looked haggard. Gossage, the enormous pitcher, reared and threw a fastball. Ball one. He flailed and fired again, and Yastrzemski swung and popped the ball into very short left field foul ground, where Graig Nettles, backing up, made the easy out. It was over.

"Afterward, Yaz wept in the training room, away from the reporters. In the biggest ballgame of his life, he had homered and singled and had driven in two runs, but almost no one would remember that. He is 39 years old, and he has never played on a world championship team; it is the one remaining goal of his career. He emerged after a while, dry-eyed, and sat by his locker and answered our questions quietly. He looked old. He looked fifty."

The scene so moved Angell, he even directed a criticism upward. A Harvard professor had written: "The hero must go under at last, after prodigious deeds, to be remembered and immortal and to have poets sing his tale."

"I understand that," Angell wrote, "and I will sing the tale of Yaz always, but I still don't understand why it couldn't have been arranged for him to single to right center, or to double off the wall. I'd have sung that, too. I think God was shelling a peanut."

A couple years later, after Gossage had surrendered a game-winning home run to George Brett in the AL playoffs, writer Peter Gammons asked him about the pitch and Brett's final swing. What was it like, surrendering that game-winning home run?

He was surprised at Gossage's answer. "I think of Yaz," Gossage said. "I'd like to think of these moments as the best against the best, not winners and losers. The pitch to Yaz ran a little more than the pitch to Brett. Don't ask me why because I don't know. If time were called and we went back and I had to throw those pitches over again, George might pop up and Yaz might have hit the ball into the bleachers."

This was it. No time for a popup. His last at-bat, competing with the ghost of Williams. Ol' Ted had gotten it right in his final turn at bat. Could Yaz follow him there, too? That was on the mind of every soul inside Fenway Park. Every player on either team knew what was on Yaz's mind. So, of course, did Spillner, winding down a rotten season.

As reported in the *Boston Globe* the next day, Spillner already knew what the rules were for Yaz's last at-bat. "We were in the bar with the umpires Friday night and Rich Garcia told us, 'Look, fellows, if he doesn't swing, it's a ball,' said Tribe pitcher Lary Sorensen.

With all that going on around him, the emotion of the moment got to Spillner, not exactly a precision pitcher on his best day. Once Yaz stepped in, he couldn't find the plate.

Ball one. Cheers. Ball two. More cheers, some boos. Ball three. Boooooooos. "I could see Spillner was trying to aim the ball," Yastrzemski said later. "It was coming in at 80 miles per hour."

With a 3-0 count in his favor, 33,491 screaming for him to whack one, to go out like Ted did, Spillner wound and delivered.

The pitch, Yaz could see right off, was high. Up in his eyes. Williams would have taken it, no question. That was his way. If it was a fraction of an inch off the plate, he'd take it. Period. So he'd go out with a walk. Fine.

Yaz just couldn't. He and all those who came to cheer for him had too much riding on the pitch. He swung from his heels and lifted a high popup to second baseman Jack Perconte. He laughed as he ran down to first base.

"I was trying to jerk it out," he admitted later.

He trotted back out to his old post, left field, in the eighth and Red Sox manager Ralph Houk, like Mike Higgins had done with Ted Williams years earlier, sent a substitute out to take his position.

Yastrzemski left to deafening roars and stopped on his way to the dugout to give his hat to a youngster seated along the rail. In the locker room afterward, Yastrzemski ordered champagne for all the writers and even toasted them for their fairness as they stood around his locker. He even remembered some of the writers who'd covered him early in his career who had since passed away. Ted Williams might not ever have talked to him again if he knew that.

There was something going on inside Yastrzemski. Never a forthcoming interview, he suddenly opened up, as if it were a great relief to him to have this career thing over with.

"I'm just a potato farmer from Long Island who had some ability," Yaz said then. "I'm not any different than a mechanic, an engineer, or the president of a bank."

The emotions, he was astonished to see them keep coming. Earlier in the day when he had his turn at the microphone before the game began, he spoke with such feeling, he had to halt a couple times to collect himself.

"I saw the sign that read 'Say it ain't so, Yaz' and I wish it weren't. This is the last day of my career as a player, and I want to thank all of you for being here with me today. It has been a great privilege to wear the Red Sox uniform the past 23 years, and to have played in Fenway in front of you great fans. I'll miss you, and I'll never forget you."

The great thing was, for those who saw that final weekend in person or on TV, they won't need any final home run in his last at-bat to keep it in their memory.

Yes, the signature Yastrzemski moment came the day before when, without any warning, Yaz broke away from a sweet pregame ceremony around the pitcher's mound and impulsively began to trot along the fence down the right field line, reaching up to slap hands with a wildly excited Fenway crowd along the way.

Amazingly, he just kept going. All the way around the ballfield. No player had ever said goodbye like this. Organist John Kiley, catching the moment perfectly, soared through "My Way" while Yaz kept waving, slapping hands down the line. He finally reached the 380 sign on the right field bullpen wall where 23 years earlier, Williams had flied out in his next-to-last at-bat.

Then Kiley brilliantly swung into "The Impossible Dream," the unofficial theme song for Yaz and the Red Sox's improbable pennant drive 16 years earlier, his greatest year as a baseball player, and the joint melted. By the time Yaz crossed through right-center and center field, still waving, misty-eyed himself, Fenway was a sweet, soggy mess.

No, it didn't seem 16 years ago. Yaz and all of Red Sox Nation were young again. Finally, Yaz's trot got to his old workspace, left field. Seeing him jog across the worn grass, it had never occurred to Red Sox fans that someday he would leave that spot. It was as if he would always be out there, like a lawn ornament.

Once he got to the left field line, Yaz moved back along the edge of the wall, slapping hands with fan after fan while Kiley swung into his third number, an emotional "Auld Lang Syne." Yaz stopped to shake hands with a few Indians players, then stood at home plate, waving, his eyes wet, his lip trembling.

By the time he was back in the dugout, it didn't seem as if he'd be able to play. And that was only Saturday. Of course, Yaz did play

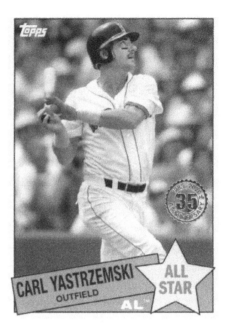

and went 0-for-4, grounding out four times, including the game's final out.

There was one great surprise left. On that final Sunday, after that glorious last at-bat popup, Yaz stayed in the dugout until the game and season ended. As fans were emptying Fenway feeling a little downhearted, he magically appeared again, in an undershirt, and trotted back out onto the field and gave them his own instant replay, starting down the right field line and taking the whole park in one last time.

With a thunderous roar from the Red Sox fans still there, Carl Yastrzemski took one final, triumphant tour around the field. Call it a victory lap.

Carl Yastrzemski by the Numbers

YEAR	TEAM	G	AB	R	H	TB	2B	3B	HR	RBI	BB	SO	SB	BA	SLG	OBP
1961	BOS	148	583	71	155	231	31	6	11	80	50	98	6	.266	.396	.324
1962	BOS	160	646	99	191	303	43	6	19	94	66	82	7	.296	.469	.363
1963	BOS	151	570	91	183	271	40	3	14	68	95	72	8	.321	.475	.418
1964	BOS	151	567	77	164	256	29	9	15	67	75	90	6	.289	.451	.374
1965	BOS	133	494	78	154	265	45	3	20	72	70	58	7	.312	.536	.395
1966	BOS	160	594	81	165	256	39	2	16	80	84	60	8	.278	.431	.368
1967	BOS	161	579	112	189	360	31	4	44	121	91	69	10	.326	.622	.418
1968	BOS	157	539	90	162	267	32	2	23	74	119	90	13	.301	.495	.426
1969	BOS	162	603	96	154	306	28	2	40	111	101	91	15	.255	.507	.362
1970	BOS	161	566	125	186	335	29	0	40	102	128	66	23	.329	.592	.452
1971	BOS	148	508	75	129	199	21	2	15	70	106	60	8	.254	.392	.381
1972	BOS	125	455	70	120	178	18	2	12	68	67	44	5	.264	.391	.357
1973	BOS	152	540	82	160	250	25	4	19	95	105	58	9	.296	.463	.407
1974	BOS	148	515	93	155	229	25	2	15	79	104	48	12	.301	.445	.414
1975	BOS	149	543	91	146	220	30	1	14	60	87	67	8	.269	.405	.371
1976	BOS	155	546	71	146	236	23	2	21	102	80	67	5	.267	.432	.357
1977	BOS	150	558	99	165	282	27	3	28	102	73	40	11	.296	.505	.372
1978	BOS	144	523	70	145	221	21	2	17	81	76	44	4	.277	.423	.367
1979	BOS	147	518	69	140	233	28	1	21	87	62	46	3	.270	.450	.346
1980	BOS	105	364	49	100	168	21	1	15	50	44	38	0	.275	.462	.350
1981	BOS	91	338	36	83	120	14	1	7	53	49	28	0	.246	.355	.338
1982	BOS	131	459	53	126	198	22	1	16	72	59	50	0	.275	.431	.358
1983	BOS	119	380	38	101	155	24	0	10	56	54	29	0	.266	.408	.359
TOTALS		3308	11988	1816	3419	5539	646	59	452	1844	1845	1395	168	.285	.462	.379

1960

TED WILLIAMS

PERFECT SWING, PERFECT FINISH

DATE: September 28, 1960

SITE: Fenway Park, Boston, Massachusetts

PITCHER: Jack Fisher of the Baltimore Orioles

RESULT: Home run into the right field bullpen

Okay, so maybe he wouldn't go out with a home run. That stubborn realization seemed to sink in slowly in the most stubborn of men as he walked out of the Boston Red Sox dugout and kneeled down in the on-deck circle. It was the eighth inning of a cool and overcast Wednesday afternoon in late September. This was it.

The Baltimore Orioles were in town and, after a good run at the New York Yankees, they'd fallen a little short in their pennant run. Like Boston, they were just playing out the schedule. After a walk and two long flyouts on this dank, damp day, it didn't look like Ted Williams, Boston's famed slugger, was going to go out the way he wanted to, the way he'd been planning to, with a home run.

He knew this kid Fisher, Jack Fisher, a right-hander with a good fastball, was going to go right after him, just like he did in his two previous at-bats. Hard stuff against the old man. He had thought he caught that last one in the fifth just right. The ball jumped off his bat and the fans rose to their feet. There was something about the sound of Ted Williams hitting one.

But the long, majestic flyball backed Orioles center fielder Al Pilarcik right to the 380 sign on the green wall of the bullpen in right-center in Fenway Park. Then he caught it.

When Williams got back to the dugout, he saw Vic Wertz, who knew a little bit about being robbed by a center fielder—Wertz's everlasting moment of glory came when Willie Mays had robbed him in the World Series six years earlier—and shrugged.

"Damn, I hit the living hell out of that one," Williams said. "I really stung it. If that one didn't go out, nothing is going out today."

Yeah, all these young pitchers were going at ol' Ted now, like you'd expect young pitchers would against a tired 42-year-old. Last week in Washington Chuck Stobbs had struck him out twice with men in scoring position.

Ted had the last laugh there. The next night, Pedro Ramos tried the same thing and Ted got his revenge with a two-run shot over the right field wall. It won the ballgame.

That was his 28th home run of the season, the 520th of his career, putting him third on the all-time list at that time behind Babe Ruth (714) and Jimmie Foxx (534).

Here he was, down to his last at-bat, and it looked like he was going out on 520. This last week hadn't been much fun. Tuesday night in Baltimore, Williams fouled a ball off his ankle in the first inning and had to leave the game. He caught a plane back to Logan Wednesday afternoon where he was met by the local press. Williams shrugged it off.

"You might think this was a broken leg with all this fuss," Williams told the media. "I expect to finish the season playing. There is no reason why I shouldn't."

He didn't get back into the lineup until the Yankees came into Fenway on the weekend and swept the Sox to clinch the pennant. Williams was still swinging the bat pretty well. On Friday night he had a double off Bob Turley. On Saturday, he had three hits against an assortment of Yankee pitchers. On Sunday, he had two hits off Ralph Terry.

But Williams had gone hitless in two trips in the previous day's embarrassing 17–3 loss to the Orioles. That was a reason to get out. Enough of those kinds of ballgames. His average? Well, he was still over .300. About .316. Not bad for 42 years old.

The afternoon crowd was pretty sparse, considering Williams was New England's most notorious—if not necessarily loved—professional athlete. There wasn't a lot of fanfare over his final game in Boston. Only a middling crowd of 10,454 showed up (even tiny Fenway can hold three times that), and there wasn't any big hullabaloo from the national media. It sounded like the Red Sox feared that might happen with a controversial star like Williams.

Williams broke the news that he was quitting on Sunday after the Yankees had clinched their 25th pennant by sweeping the Red Sox. You can bet Ted laughed when he read the front-page story in Monday's *Boston Globe*, a story that was played above the bold headline "Strike Vote Threatens to Idle All G.E. Plants." It read simply: "Ted Quits—as Player."

"It is the hope of the Boston management that Fenway Park will be filled on Wednesday to bid farewell to Ted," *Globe* writer Hy Hurwitz wrote. Fat chance of that, Williams laughed. These Red Sox didn't draw. There was no TV coverage, local or national, and none of the major papers had sent their columnists out to see Teddy's bye-bye.

One reason was the Red Sox were a lousy team and they'd been out of the pennant race for some time. Another was the team was going on to New York to close out the regular season. Maybe some expected Williams would wrap it up there.

Or it could be they didn't see it as a big deal. Nobody saw it as an event. Athletes retire all the time, usually with a whimper. Who'd want to see Ted Williams go out with a whimper? Williams had retired before—or so he had announced—five years earlier, taking $10,000 to write a magazine series for the *Saturday Evening Post*, "This Is My Last Year in Baseball."

He was heading into a divorce and ultimately didn't join the team until mid-May because of all the squabbling. But he could still hit. He hit .345 in 1956 and would have won the batting title if he'd had the necessary number of at-bats. The next year, 1957, he hit an amazing .388. So he played a little longer.

Now, though, this was the end of the line. The pennant race had already been decided—Williams sat in the dugout that Sunday afternoon knowing with another win, the Yankees had run off nine straight—including a sweep at Fenway—to clinch one more pennant.

He watched Yankees reliever Luis Arroyo come in and get Boston's Pete Runnels, the AL batting champion, to foul out to third with the game-tying run right there. That was the Red Sox for you. Close but no cigar.

With the pennant race officially over, Williams had given Red Sox owner Tom Yawkey the OK in the clubhouse to announce to the newspapers that he'd be retiring at the end of the season. The Red Sox said Williams would go to spring training as a batting instructor. Some thought he'd be Boston's new general manager.

During Wednesday's game, it had been announced in the press box during the game that Williams's number 9 would be retired after the game. That drew a few cracks from the peanut gallery about Williams playing in his undershirt at Yankee Stadium.

The official pronouncement that he wasn't going to New York hadn't been made yet, except to a few people in the Red Sox clubhouse. Williams had already given the word to manager Mike Higgins that he wasn't going back to New York. This was going to be it. He could just imagine the chatter in the press box right above him.

Hell, Williams thought, those idiots ought to be happy. They'd been trying to retire me for years. By now, Williams knew their ritual. Ted would come to spring training and see the "Is this it for Ted Williams?" stories, suffer through the "Williams's slow start may mean he's finished" stories that were sure to appear in the cold early months when Williams never hit his best, then expect the "Will Red Sox invite Williams back for one more year?" stories in the fall.

In a town with, at times, seven newspapers and a rabid—some might say unhealthy, baseball interest, Williams was always somebody worth writing about. Hell, at least one of them admitted it.

"The loss of Williams to a Boston sports columnist is like a bad case of athlete's fingers to Van Cliburn," wrote John Gillooly of the *Boston Daily Record*. "You just can't pound the keys any more. The song is ended."

"I am not going to crank through the microfilms of the Daily Record for the past year.... But I'll guess that if I wrote 280 columns in that 12-month [span] that 80 of them were about The Kid, the chromatic, bombastic, the quixotic—a demon one day and a delight the next. . . . Williams made columning easy."

Yeah, they were going to miss Ted Williams, all right. Even the bastards who hated him as much as he hated them. The thing was, nobody ever called them on any of the shit they wrote, even when they were dead wrong. Ever.

Williams thought back to Bill Cunningham's analysis of his swing, back when he was a rookie. Williams could remember it word for word. He had that kind of recall if something ticked him off enough. And many things did.

"The Red Sox seem to think Williams is just cocky and gabby enough to make a colorful outfielder, possibly the Babe Herman type," Cunningham wrote. "Me? I don't like the way he stands at the plate. He bends his front knee inward, he moves his feet just before he takes a swing. That's exactly what I do just before I drive a golf ball and, knowing what happens to the golf balls I drive, I don't think this kid will ever hit half a Singer midget's weight in a bathing suit."

What a horse's ass. But who ever called them on it?

Once Williams learned the newspaper game, Ted fought back in his own way from time to time. Like giving an exclusive interview to the out-of-town guy, knowing full well that the Boston guys would catch wind of it and be pissed off that he gave someone else the scoop. That was a real "Kiss my ass" to the boys on the beat.

Williams loved to do that. Or after a disagreeable article, maybe he'd get in their face, tell 'em he smelled something awful in the locker room, then tell 'em it must have been the shit that they were writing.

And the stuff they wrote in the offseason, why, it was unbelievable. Williams feuding with his brother, Williams refusing to visit his mother in the offseason, Williams not being at the hospital for the birth of his daughter—there were so many more. Why was he the only player anywhere who had to deal with that crap?

More than once Williams wondered why the hell didn't they write that stuff about DiMaggio? Hell, DiMaggio was a great player but also out until all hours at New York nightclubs, banging showgirls left and right, a different one every night, drinking and smoking with the New York newspaper guys, calling them his pals. They write about him like he's a god. Hell, DiMaggio had had his failed marriages, too. How come nobody ever wrote about that?

Even Red Smith, whom Williams liked, always fawned over DiMaggio. He remembered one time Smith wrote that DiMaggio was "excelled by Ted Williams in all offensive statistics and reputedly, Ted's inferior in crowd appeal and financial standing, (yet DiMaggio) still won the writers' accolade as the American League's most valuable in 1947. It wasn't the first time Williams earned this award with his bat and lost it with his disposition."

Well, that was true enough, Williams thought. But what does your personality have to do with what you do with a baseball uniform on? Can you play, can you hit or not? Was it a popularity contest or not? Writers, can kiss my. . . .

But his relations with the press cost him. In 1942, Williams won the Triple Crown and lost the MVP to one of the Yankees, Joe Gordon, who hit .322 to Williams's .356, drove in 103 runs to Ted's 137. Even in 1941 when Williams hit .406 with six hits on the final day of the season, DiMaggio got the award for his 56-game hitting streak.

Williams always tried to be gracious about it. Joe was a great ballplayer. But he had to wonder what the New York media blitz did for Joe on a regular basis. Even Red Smith, for chrissakes. "As a matter of fact," Smith continued in that same article, "if all other factors were equal save only the question of character, Joe would never lose out to any player. The guy who came out of San Francisco as a shy lone wolf, suspicious of Easterners and Eastern writers, today is the top guy in any sports gathering in any town. The real champ."

Were we supposed to bow when DiMaggio comes up? Williams laughed. Nobody ever puffed up Ted Williams that way. How much did DiMaggio do for charity, anyway? Anybody ever ask that question?

Ah, it didn't matter. The people at the Jimmy Fund knew who Ted Williams was and how much he cared and how much he helped kids. The hell with the New York press. The more Williams thought about what happened to him in Boston, it wasn't fair. Not that he could ever say it. Then they'd really let him have it.

Sure, he was a hot head and ill-tempered and childish and foulmouthed and ill behaved and you bet your life he'd go at those sons of bitches. But how come we never found out what kind of dad, what kind of son, what kind of husband DiMaggio was? The Boston writers all had to know all that about

Ted. Why didn't the New York writers want to know that about Joe? It was a fair question.

One year, a Boston writer called Williams's ex-wife to find out what he'd bought his kid for Christmas! They didn't pull that crap with DiMaggio. If any one of them wrote a single word that DiMaggio didn't like, he'd cut them off. And they'd be out of a job. Don't think DiMaggio didn't know it.

Hey, if you've got that kind of clout, why not use it? No knock on Joe. But you've got to wonder how would he have done with the Boston press? As nervous as he was? What would they have done with his legend? Especially near the end when he couldn't hit or play center field like he always had.

Many years later, the respected journalist David Halberstam, a Williams fan, talked with famed sportswriter W. C. Heinz about DiMaggio and how the New York press handled him. "I had been around DiMaggio a good deal," Heinz said, "I knew how most of the reporters played up to him, I knew how difficult he could be, and how coldly he could treat writers and how he would cut them off if he was displeased."

Contrast that with Williams's treatment by the voracious Boston press, as Halberstam would later note, not one of the shining moments in American journalism, and you have a much more complex picture. And when, in 1959, an assortment of injuries knocked Williams down to just .254—hell, he was under .200 until the midsummer—the writers were just savage. It got so bad that even Red Sox owner Tom Yawkey told Ted he ought to retire.

Nobody, not even Yawkey was going to tell Ted Williams what to do. He was still eight home runs short of 500 and he wanted to get there, for sure. He decided he'd take a pay cut, a pretty good one—$35,000—from his $125,000 annual salary (wonder if DiMaggio would ever do that?) and worked himself into good shape when the year began. He'd show those sons a bitches who was washed up.

He blasted a home run in his first at-bat and hit all year long. And so, well, it was all over now as he approached the Fenway Park batter's box for the final time. It had been quite a day, Williams thought, taking one long last look around Fenway Park. He knew the writers were grousing about him right now up in the press box, those "knights of the keyboard," as he'd called them in that brief pregame ceremony.

Screw 'em. There was no way he was going to let them off the hook at that pregame ceremony earlier today. They hurt too much. Too often. Somebody was going to call them on what they wrote. This was his last chance.

He knew it was supposed to be a happy, classy day but damn, he stood at the microphone by the pitcher's mound, sort of shifting his weight uneasily from one foot to the other and just let it go. He couldn't help it.

"Despite the fact of the disagreeable things that have been said of me—and I can't help thinking about it—by the knights of the keyboard up there, baseball has been the most wonderful thing in my life. . . .If I were starting all over and someone asked me where is the one place I would like to play, I would want it to be Boston, with the greatest owner in baseball and the greatest fans in America. Thank you."

That was his final shot in the war with the press. He was sure they'd fire back one last time. But Ted Williams just didn't know how to let anything go, and he wasn't going to start now. He heard his name announced for the last time and he started toward the plate. He could hear the crowd now, roaring, applauding, without a single boo in the house.

He laughed. He always used to be able to pick out that boo. He hefted the bat and thought to himself, "one more time, one more time." He'd started the season, this final season, with a home run in his very first at-bat, a 450-foot shot off Camilo Pascual. Wouldn't it be something if he could go out with one, too?

He stepped into the batter's box and Fisher deferentially waiting until the cheers died down, wound and threw. Ball one. Williams, who rarely swung at the first pitch, was ready for a fastball and here it came. He uncoiled and swung mightily at it. Plop. He heard the ball land in Gus Triandos's glove. Strike one.

The crowd rumbled and buzzed around him. This was a challenge. Take that, you old bastard.

"The pitcher's always the dumbest guy in the ballpark," that was one of Williams's favorite lines.

He dug in. He knew what he was going to get next. Just knew it.

Fisher snapped his glove at Triandos's return throw as if he was eager to get another pitch headed homeward. He wound and threw—it was another hard fastball—and Williams let loose with the final swing of his glorious career and caught it flush.

The crack of the bat, an unmistakable sound when Williams hit one right, rang through the park and the 10,000 came to their feet as the ball soared deeper and deeper toward the right field bullpen, toward Williamsburg, they used to call it.

Suddenly, it descended with a rush, clunking off the canopy over the bullpen. Home run. Goodbye.

Some time later, novelist John Updike, a Williams fan, wrote a piece about Williams's final game. He caught that moment perfectly: "He ran as he always ran out home runs—hurriedly, unsmiling, head down, as if our praise were a storm of rain to get out of. He didn't tip his cap. Though we thumped, wept, chanted, 'We want Ted!' for minutes after he hid in the dugout, he did not come back. . . . The papers said that the other players, even the umpires on the field, begged him to come out and acknowledge us in some way. But he refused."

Immediately after the game, though, Williams was in no sentimental mood—at least not to share with the newspapers. Reporter Ed Linn noted that Williams was pleasant enough with the first wave of reporters. Those he liked came to his locker first. They got the good Ted. "I was gunning for the big one. I let everything I had go. I really wanted that one," he said, smiling.

By the time those Williams wasn't as tolerant of arrived—including Linn—his mood had soured. What little goodwill he had toward the press had evaporated. Linn asked Williams if he'd thought about tipping his cap when manager Mike Higgins had sent him back out to left field at the start of the ninth inning, only to have Carroll Hardy immediately replace him amid a roaring, foot-stomping ovation. Wasn't that heartwarming?

It was the writer's way of asking, didn't Williams really want that ending where everybody goes home happy? Williams wasn't playing that game. "I felt nothing," Williams said. No sentimentality, the writer asked? "I said nothing. Nothing, nothing, nothing."

And he knew what they'd say in the papers, too. That he was going to go to New York until he hit that home run, then decided to quit then and there. The bastards. He told Higgins, he didn't pack for the trip to New York, he'd made up his goddamned mind before the game that this was it. Period. But they've got to have a little controversy.

And that Kaese, Harold Kaese from the *Globe*, he knew he'd find a way to go after him, too. He did too, in his column in Thursday's *Globe*. Sure enough, here was Kaese making sure to mention Harry "The Cat" Brecheen, who'd stopped Williams in his only World Series appearance against the Cardinals in 1946, a guy who happened to be standing and watching Baltimore's Steve Barber warm up. Gee, he was a key component of the final game story, wasn't he?

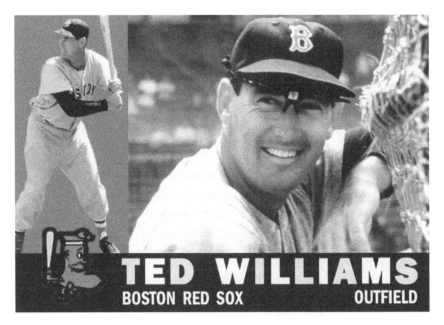

TED WILLIAMS

BOSTON RED SOX　　　　　　　　　　**OUTFIELD**

Then Kaese mentioned that more people had seen Williams play his first game at Fenway—his American League opener—or his first "farewell" in 1954 than this game. Then Kaese speculated on what some of his press box colleagues (including himself) might write for the next day's headlines, "Sox Pennant Hopes Soar, (Jackie) Jensen returns, Williams retires."

Then there was this. Low by even Kaese's standards. His description of Williams crossing the plate after his dramatic final home run. "For Fisher, Gus Triandos, and Umpire Ed Hurley, Williams had a smiling curtsy as he touched the plate. Was Fisher 'piping' the ball for Williams? Some wondered. He threw nothing but fastballs his last two times up, but one had so much on it that Williams fanned it just before he homered."

Williams started to get angry when he read it. Then he laughed. Kaese had questioned the purity of the home run, the timing of Ted's retirement, slammed him about the Red Sox's failing attendance and his own rotten World Series 14 years earlier, all in a single column.

Kaese left Ted Williams with a home run too. What did Williams really feel about it all? That wasn't going in some friggin' newspaper. Not a Boston newspaper, that's for sure.

It wasn't until years later that he lowered his guard with TV's Bob Costas. "I have to say that was certainly one of the more moving moments, the tingling in my body, that I ever had as a baseball player, that last home run," Williams said. "That it was all over and I did hit the home run."

Williams also explained that final at-bat in more detail. After he'd swung and missed that 1-0 fastball—the wire services ran a shot of Ted flailing at it, eyes closed, bat outstretched, his picture-perfect swing looking awkward and old—he saw something in Fisher's manner that flipped a switch.

"So here I am, the last time at bat," Williams told the Baseball Hall of Fame some years later, "I got the count one and nothing and Jack Fisher's pitching. He laid a ball right there. I don't think I ever missed in my life like I missed that one but I missed it. And for the first time in my life I said 'Oh Jesus, what happened? Why didn't I hit that one?' I couldn't believe it. It was straight, not the fastest pitch I'd ever seen, good stuff. I didn't know what to think because I didn't know what I'd done on that swing. Was I ahead or was I behind? It wasn't a breaking ball and right in a spot that, boy, what a ball to hit. I swung, had a hell of a swing, and I missed it. I'm still there trying to figure out what the hell happened. Then I could see Fisher out there with his glove up to get the ball back quickly, as much as saying 'I threw that one by him, I'll throw another by him.' And I saw all that and I guess it woke me up, you know. Right away, I assumed 'He thinks he threw it by me.' The way he was asking for the ball back quick, right away, I said, 'I know he's going to go right back with that pitch.'"

So Ted Williams, the greatest hitter who ever lived, sat back and waited for one more, one last, fastball. Then he hit it out of sight, ran around the bases and never tipped his cap, never looked back even when they screamed and clapped and stomped and hollered his name.

He heard them all right. But he sat in the dugout and pulled on his jacket. "Gods," John Updike famously wrote a few months later, "don't answer letters."

Months later, when Williams saw Updike's story, you can bet he was laughing. "Gee, I wonder if Joe D. saw that line about Gods and letters. . . ."

Ted Williams by the Numbers

YEAR	TEAM	G	AB	R	H	TB	2B	3B	HR	RBI	BB	SO	SB	BA	SLG	OBP
1939	BSA	149	565	131	185	344	44	11	31	144	105	64	2	.327	.609	.435
1940	BSA	144	561	134	193	333	43	14	23	113	96	54	5	.344	.594	.442
1941	BSA	143	456	135	185	335	33	3	37	119	147	27	2	.406	.735	.553
1942	BSA	150	522	141	186	338	34	5	36	137	145	51	3	.356	.648	.499
1946	BSA	150	514	142	176	343	37	8	38	124	156	44	0	.342	.667	.497
1947	BSA	156	528	125	181	335	40	9	32	114	161	47	0	.343	.634	.498
1948	BSA	137	509	124	188	313	44	3	25	127	126	41	4	.369	.615	.497
1949	BSA	155	566	150	194	368	39	3	43	159	162	49	1	.343	.650	.490
1950	BSA	89	334	82	106	216	24	1	28	97	82	21	3	.317	.647	.452
1951	BSA	148	531	110	169	295	28	4	30	126	144	45	1	.318	.556	.464
1952	BSA	6	10	2	4	9	0	1	1	3	2	2	0	.400	.900	.500
1953	BOS	37	91	17	37	82	6	0	13	34	19	10	0	.407	.901	.509
1954	BOS	117	386	93	133	245	23	1	29	89	136	32	0	.345	.635	.513
1955	BOS	98	320	77	114	225	21	3	28	83	90	24	2	.356	.703	.495
1956	BOS	136	400	71	138	242	28	2	24	82	102	37	0	.345	.605	.479
1957	BOS	132	420	96	163	307	28	1	38	87	120	44	0	.388	.731	.527
1958	BOS	129	411	81	135	240	23	2	26	85	98	49	1	.328	.584	.458
1959	BOS	103	272	32	69	114	15	0	10	43	52	28	0	.254	.419	.372
1960	BOS	113	310	56	98	200	15	0	29	72	75	41	1	.316	.645	.451
TOTALS		2292	7706	1799	2654	4884	525	71	521	1838	2018	710	25	.344	.634	.482

REGGIE JACKSON

A SAWED-OFF GOODBYE

DATE: October 4, 1987

SITE: Comiskey Park, Chicago, Illinois

PITCHER: Bobby Thigpen of the Chicago White Sox

RESULT: Broken-bat single

The smile on Reggie Jackson's face was more one of embarrassment than joy. After 20 major-league seasons, Jackson's final trip around the country came back where he started—in an Oakland A's uniform. You could call it a year-long curtain call.

On a sunny—if chilly—Sunday afternoon at Comiskey Park, a quick 2:29 let's-get-this-over final game of the season, a little over 15,000 fans watched Reggie Jackson complete his major-league run with a most un-Reggie-like final swing that was almost comical. It wasn't just the 5–2 White Sox win, which ended a disappointing A's season.

No, Reggie's final moment on center stage was about as far from vintage Jackson as it gets. That explained the somewhat sheepish smile under those dark aviator glasses, watching him stand on first base and look around him, as the visiting crowd respectfully clapped and hooted. It wasn't the kind of exit you might have expected from such a dynamic player. Age is undefeated, after all.

That final hit—more about that in a bit—was his 2,584th, which lifted his career batting average to .262. Low, perhaps for an eventual Hall of Famer. But Reggie was different. Has another Hall of Famer endured a .194 season and played for another five seasons?

With 563 home runs—some delivered in the most dramatic of circumstances—Jackson went on to punch his ticket to Cooperstown. He hadn't hit one since August 17—a seventh inning two-run shot off California's Mike Witt over a month and a half earlier. No, Reggie Jackson didn't own October anymore. This finale was Jackson's first full game in the A's lineup since an August 23 0-for-3 at Oakland Coliseum against his old team, the New York Yankees, a performance that dipped his average again perilously close to the Mendoza line.

From there, as the season wound down, Manager Tony LaRussa decided Reggie's role was to pinch-hit. One at-bat a game. He didn't do a bad job, going 5-for-14 (.357), but with only one extra-base hit coming into this final game. Nothing but three pinch-hit singles in September. Not going to stir many drinks with that straw.

Though he was 40, Jackson came back to Oakland with plenty of a Jackson staple—confidence. He re-signed with Oakland, where he began his Hall of Fame career two decades earlier. He signed on Christmas Eve. Thanks, Santa.

"I think I'm still a good ballplayer as far as statistical impact and contributing to the team are concerned," Jackson said at the Christmas Eve signing.

"If you're asking me to put a number on it, it'd probably be somewhere around 70 RBI and around 20 home runs."

Jackson had big plans to help LaRussa's talented A's team, particularly a promising power-hitting rookie named Mark McGwire.

"What I'll bring to the A's hopefully is what you feel after you've been around a certain type of person," he said then. "You feel better because you were around that person. I want the fans, the owners, and the other ballplayers to reap a dividend from having me on the ballclub.

"It will be nice to look around the clubhouse, into the stands, up into the mezzanine where the front office sit and feel wanted."

LaRussa had a strong team, including the opening season of the Bash Brothers, 20-game winner Dave Stewart, and eventually Hall of Famer Dennis Eckersley in the bullpen. But a rough July (12-15) and a fading September (12-15) pretty much guaranteed a .500 season (81-81). They made it to the World Series the next year—that was the Kirk Gibson series—and won the Series in four straight in 1989.

LaRussa, in his second year with the A's, had high hopes for Reggie and had given him the A's DH spot to start the year. With a 23-year-old José Canseco and rookie McGwire, the idea was, Reggie's left-handed power bat would offset the right-handed Bash Brothers. But Reggie couldn't get the bat around anymore. He actually dipped below the Mendoza line (.194) in May after an 0-15 stretch against Boston and Detroit. He considered retiring at the All-Star break, but the team talked him out of it.

LaRussa seemed to give up on him as a regular after that final groundout to second against Tim Stoddard that August 23 night. He gave him a pinch-hit at-bat pretty much every other game. Everybody knew this was it and wanted to say goodbye to one of the game's electric presences.

Watching him stalk his way to the plate that final time, the mind's eye brought back vintage Reggie, bespectacled, thickly muscled, he seemed to get as much strength out of his steely, springy thighs as any hitter ever. What kid wasn't impressed by Jackson's absolutely titanic homer off Pittsburgh's Dock Ellis—the year after the LSD no-hitter—in the 1971 All-Star Game in Detroit's old Tiger Stadium.

What first-time visitor to the park didn't look first for that right field transformer, way up above the playing surface, that Jackson dented with a baseball that had to have left Earth at supersonic speed? Stepping up in dramatic moments was something he always seemed to be able to do.

On July 19, his Fenway farewell, Red Sox organist Sherm Feller swung into "Auld Lang Syne" as number 44 stepped into the left-handed batter's box. The noise was too much, the emotion rising and Jackson, trying not to smile, stepped out of the box, raising his helmet, pointing to Feller up in the press box. Then, as he had the previous Fenway at-bat, Jackson drilled one off the Green Monster for his second double of the game. Jackson hit 51 of his 563 HR against Boston in 236 career games.

If you had been in the old Fenway bandbox alongside me on June 14 in 1969, you would have been awestruck—as were Red Sox pitchers—as Jackson single-bat-edly defeated the Red Sox 10–7. Well, the actual final score was 21–7, Oakland. Jackson was 5-for-6 in the game, with two HRs and a double and a stunning 10 RBIs. The home runs were impressive, but the double he hit off Ray Jarvis off the Green Monster was struck so hard, it nearly bounced all the way to second base. Stunning.

Later, it was suggested that Jackson used a bat that was flat on one side that afternoon. Some suggested Reggie was trying to pull a fast one. Nobody suggested that the force of Jackson's swing colliding with the baseball might have made one side of the bat flat. He did not take easy swings.

Fenway seemed to bring out something in Reggie. Maybe the closeness of the fans, the great tradition, who knows? There was the memorable—and for Red Sox fans, delightful—exchange between Jackson and Billy Martin in the Yankee dugout on June 18, 1977. You could see the whole thing from the center field bleachers. We loved it.

Jim Rice had singled to right field, Jackson sort of took his time going after the ball, Rice got to second, and Martin immediately yanked him from the game, sending Paul Blair out to right field. Jackson certainly hustled to the dugout, where the loudmouthed Martin was waiting for him. The two exchanged pleasantries—this was all on national TV—and Martin tried to go after Jackson only to be restrained—with not a little effort by supposedly retired Yankee catchers Elston Howard and Yogi Berra, each of whom had to employ their plate-blocking techniques one last time in the visitor's dugout at Fenway. Red Sox fans, years away from World Series triumphs, enjoyed the altercation as much as the game. We were yelling at Martin from center field, and I'm sure he heard us. If not, it wasn't as if we didn't give it our best try.

The Jackson moment that lingers, however, was a personal experience that took place at Fenway in the right field stands on the next-to-last day of the regular 1976 season. It had been the strangest of seasons for Jackson, who began the season as an A, then, appropriately enough was traded on

April Fool's Day—when A's owner Charlie Finley traded Jackson, lefty Ken Holtzman, and a minor-league pitcher (Bill VanBommel) for Don Baylor and righties Mike Torrez (later to join the Red Sox and Yankees) and Paul Mitchell. Jackson sat out the first 16 games, refusing to report until the Orioles agreed to up his salary to $200,000. That was the year Finley traded Vida Blue, Joe Rudi, and Rollie Fingers to the Red Sox, only to have Commissioner Bowie Kuhn void the deal.

Jackson did well for the Orioles, though it seemed so strange to see him in that uniform. He stole 28 bases, believe it or not, and came into that final series at Fenway with 26 home runs, 90 RBIs, and a .277 average. Considering he sat out the season's first 16 games, those were pretty good numbers. But the Orioles could do no better than second place behind the Yankees, and on this Friday night at Fenway, Reggie looked off.

He fanned against Red Sox starter Rick Wise in the first, hit a lazy fly-ball to center in the third, and with two on, one out, struck out again facing Wise and when the inning was over, dogged it out to right field. Two Red Sox fans from New Hampshire stood up in the right field stands and booed at Jackson's leisurely stroll out to his right field spot. And amazingly, Jackson walked toward the two booing fans. "What's your problem? Why are you on my ass?" "We came to see Reggie Jackson, great player, not some choke artist who can't even hustle," they shot back. He laughed. "So what do you want?" he asked. "What do you think we want?" they said. "We want to see Reggie Jackson hit a home run. Whattya think?" The fans around us joined in. Here we were, at an end-of-the-season, playing out the string game with one of the game's greatest players, who was surely going to go elsewhere next year for big bucks. He nodded. "OK," Jackson said. "OK. I hit a home run and you're going to stand up just like you are now, in Boston, and cheer." "Hell, yeah. We'll stand and cheer," we said, and those around us clapped in encouragement.

Jackson came to bat again with one out in the seventh against Wise. He swung, there was a mighty "thwack" that echoed through the evening air, and there it was, soaring way over the bullpen, way up into the right field stands.

Jackson always had that sort of a jaunty, side-to-side home-run trot but here, as he approached first base, he was looking down into the right field stands, right where those New Hampshire fans, Tom Lavoie and I, had ridden him. He wanted to see if they kept their part of the bargain, if they were standing and celebrating one of the most electric players the game had ever seen. We were. And we kept standing and cheering for the enemy player as he ran—not shuffled—out to his position. He looked over at us and tipped his cap. The home run had given the Orioles the lead.

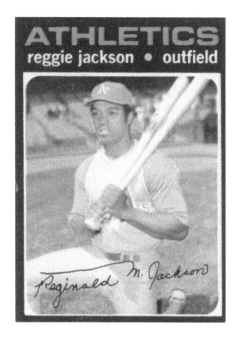

He came back up one last time in the ninth and the Orioles were trailing, 7–4. Rich Dauer was on first, Jim Willoughby on the hill. The New Hampshire fans stood once more and yelled, "We'll do it again." This time, Jackson rapped a sharp groundball to Denny Doyle, who threw to Rick Burleson covering second, who in turn fired to first baseman Carl Yastrzemski to end the game. The next day, Reggie came up in the ninth, the Orioles trailing 1–0 on a Jim Rice first-inning RBI triple. Tom House struck him out to end his stint in Baltimore.

A free agent on November 1, he signed with the Yankees and cemented his place in baseball history. Everyone remembers the three World Series home runs on three swings in 1977, clinching a championship for the New York Yankees. It was five tumultuous years in New York, then, we tend to forget, five more years playing for the California Angels, the numbers dipping radically from a .275, 39, 101 opening year in Anaheim to a horrid .194, 14, 49 year that would have driven most 37-year-olds from the game. Not Reggie. He hit 27 and 25 homers in consecutive seasons and at 40, decided he'd go for one last year in the California sun, returning to where he started, with the Oakland A's.

We all remember how unleashing Reggie Jackson on the world's greatest media market always made things interesting. "I'm the straw that stirs the drink"—which he claims he never said. "Fans don't boo nobodies," was a good one. "The magnitude of me"—which is on videotape. Or the quotes about Reggie—"One's a born liar and the other's convicted," Billy Martin talking *about* Reggie and Yankee owner George Steinbrenner or Darold Knowles's famous "There isn't enough mustard in the world to cover that hot dog."

There were so many more moments, quotes, controversies . . . you couldn't help but think about all of them as he walked out of the visitor's dugout that Sunday afternoon in Comiskey Park and headed for the plate. He had sliced a double to left field in the first inning off Floyd Bannister—after José Canseco stole third (with two outs!), then walked and flied out. Bobby Thigpen was on the mound and he seemed impatient as the crowd began to chant "Reggie, Reggie" loud enough for him to step out of the box, turn around, doff his helmet, and raise both arms to the crowd in every direction.

He seemed to dig in, waved the bat and bang, here was Thigpen's pitch, a fastball in tight, right on Reggie's hands. He swung, almost in self-defense, and the bat snapped like a toothpick, but the ball scooted out past the mound, hit just in front of second base, and trickled into center field. Reggie's final mighty swing had produced a broken-bat single. Oops. He stood on first base, a sheepish grin on his face like a man who had farted in church. There was a sign stretched out across the outfield wall that seemed to sum up how everybody felt. Well, maybe not Billy Martin. The sign read "So long, Reggie. We'll miss ya."

Reggie Jackson by the Numbers

YEAR	TEAM	G	AB	R	H	TB	2B	3B	HR	RBI	BB	SO	SB	BA	SLG	OBP
1967	KC	35	118	13	21	36	4	4	1	6	10	46	1	.178	.305	.269
1968	OAK	154	553	82	138	250	13	6	29	74	50	171	14	.250	.452	.316
1969	OAK	152	549	123	151	334	36	3	47	118	115	142	13	.275	.608	.411
1970	OAK	149	426	57	101	195	21	2	23	66	75	134	26	.237	.458	.359
1971	OAK	150	567	87	157	288	29	3	32	80	63	161	16	.277	.508	.352
1972	OAK	135	499	72	132	236	25	2	25	75	58	125	9	.265	.473	.349
1973	OAK	151	539	99	158	286	28	2	32	117	76	111	22	.293	.531	.383
1974	OAK	148	506	90	146	260	25	1	29	93	86	105	25	.289	.514	.391
1975	OAK	157	593	91	150	303	39	3	36	104	67	133	17	.253	.511	.329
1976	OAK	134	498	84	138	250	27	2	27	91	54	108	28	.277	.502	.351
1977	BAL	146	525	93	150	289	39	2	32	110	74	129	17	.286	.550	.375
1978	NYY	139	511	82	140	244	13	5	27	97	58	133	14	.274	.477	.356
1979	NYY	131	465	78	138	253	24	2	29	89	65	107	9	.297	.544	.382
1980	NYY	143	514	94	154	307	22	4	41	111	83	122	1	.300	.597	.398
1981	NYY	94	334	33	79	143	17	1	15	54	46	82	0	.237	.428	.330
1982	CAL	153	530	92	146	282	17	1	39	101	85	156	4	.275	.532	.375
1983	CAL	116	397	43	77	135	14	1	14	49	52	140	0	.194	.340	.290
1984	CAL	143	525	67	117	213	17	2	25	81	55	141	8	.223	.406	.300
1985	CAL	143	460	64	116	224	27	0	27	85	78	138	1	.252	.487	.360
1986	CAL	132	419	65	101	171	12	2	18	58	92	115	1	.241	.408	.379
1987	OAK	115	336	42	74	135	14	1	15	43	33	97	2	.220	.402	.297
TOTALS		2820	9864	1551	2584	4834	463	49	563	1702	1375	2596	228	.262	.490	.356

ROGER CLEMENS

ROCKET GROUNDED

DATE: October 7, 2007

SITE: Yankee Stadium, New York, New York

HITTER: Victor Martínez of the Cleveland Indians

RESULT: Strikeout

His nickname was "Rocket Man," and the on-the-field records were almost impossible to believe: seven Cy Young Awards, 354 wins, 4,672 strikeouts, 11 All-Star Games, an MVP, an All-Star Game MVP. You would think that in the Baseball Hall of Fame in Cooperstown, New York, Roger Clemens would have his own wing. Nope.

Thirteen years since he ended his career, leaving the mound with one out in the third inning of the American League Division Series in 2007, Roger Clemens is still waiting for the Hall to call. It may be a while yet. You see, in the end, there was a question about Rocket Man's fuel.

In a long and ugly chapter that will likely always shroud his magnificent on-field achievements, Clemens's extraordinary mid-career rebirth prompted not-so-subtle talk about steroids, performance-enhancing drugs, and cheating, even while he was winning Cy Young Awards, one right after another. While there was surely talk inside the game, the media—like many of the thousands of batters who stood in a batter's box 60 feet, six inches away—swung late.

Looking at Clemens's extraordinary numbers with the perspective of time, you wonder why somebody didn't raise a hand and say, "Wait a minute!" You can't really find another case where a 34-year-old pitcher who'd already logged these many innings (2,219 by age 30) suddenly rediscovered his fastball—and league-wide dominance—again.

"I remember the last few years he was with the Red Sox and I don't know if he had some arm problems or what," explained Cal Ripken Jr. to Jonathan Mayo in *Facing Clemens*. "(Clemens') fastball came back a little bit to more of a hittable speed so his control had to be more on."

"Maybe he went through a little bit of a dead-arm period," Ripken continued. "Maybe the innings he logged started to wear on him a little bit . . . then when he was with Toronto, he came back with his fastball a little and he maintained it for the rest of his career. I don't know what the situation was, but when he got to Toronto, his fastball was back. And also, he came up with the split-finger. Maybe it was the combination of the two that made his fastball better. But I think the miles-per-hour came back."

That's an understatement. Once he left Boston, Clemens's amazing eight-year run, four Cy Young Awards, a 148-61 record (from age 34 to 42) with 30-plus starts and seven years of 200-plus innings seemed simply too good to be true. Which, in retrospect, maybe it was. The Clemens steroids saga was long, drawn-out, and depressing. How could anyone believe this late-career resurgence was anything but chemically induced?

Clemens had his defenders. Yankee manager Joe Torre said he didn't think Clemens used steroids. "I saw him in there," Torre said, referring to the gym. "That's what I saw." Steroid king José Canseco, who cast a wide net across baseball with his own steroid accusations, denied Clemens was a user. But many others were skeptical, and after his name came up 82 times in the controversial Mitchell Report, a 20-month study on the impact of performance-enhancing drugs led by former Maine senator George Mitchell, Clemens was summoned to testify before Congress.

On the stand, Clemens denied he had anything to do with steroids, but as more and more people talked, particularly Clemens's former trainer Brian McNamee, Clemens found himself charged with perjury and obstruction of justice, facing a grand jury. Though found not guilty of lying to Congress after a depressing 10-week trial, this win sure felt like a loss. Clemens's reputation has never recovered.

In Ken Burns's *The Tenth Inning*—a sequel to his highly acclaimed *Baseball* series—the Clemens segment made it clear where Clemens stood in baseball history—*on* the field.

"We can forget about the debate between Walter Johnson and Cy Young and Lefty Grove. The greatest pitcher in the history of baseball is Roger Clemens," baseball historian John Thorn says. "Now there have been many, many great pitchers, but no one has ever done what Roger did. And there's the freak show accomplishment. There's 20 strikeouts in a game, twice, 10 years apart. This is a superhuman critter." Fueled *unlike* a human? Perhaps. We will never know.

What we do know is while on the mound, Clemens's hulking 6-foot-4, 250-pound frame was so prototypical "Power Pitcher," it almost seemed disappointing that someone so big, so hulking, so strong with such a powerful leg drive was throwing something as ordinary as a baseball. Clemens held it in his hand like an egg. The pitching motion was a bit modified, maybe even simplified as the years went on. In Boston, Clemens stood with his right foot on the middle of the rubber, shoulders squared, and as the motion began, would raise both arms—hand in glove—over his head, then swinging the powerful right arm back and launching the ball homeward.

By the time he arrived in New York after a trade from Toronto, an unshaven Clemens held the big black glove up in front of his glowering face, only his intense eyes visible above the rim of the glove. The glove would drop, Clemens's eyes would be downcast instead of staring at his target as pitchers are generally instructed, and he would tuck his chin behind his left shoulder with a slight backward turn, raise the left leg straight up, then launch a lumbering step toward home, bringing the thunderous right arm up and through, sending the sizzling fastball homeward.

Watching his fireballing rival and contemporary and fellow Texan Nolan Ryan on the mound was such a contrast for baseball fans. Whereas Clemens was all bulk and muscle, channeled into a smooth, bazooka-like delivery, he seemed the very opposite of Ryan's wiry build and whiplike delivery, that dangerous arm coming up over that almost impossibly limber high left leg kick—a chiropractor's friend—then a sizzling stream of white and a loud "pop" into the mitt.

Of the two, Clemens was a more reliable winner (Clemens: 354-184; Ryan: 324-292), perhaps because he typically played on stronger teams. Ryan had an edge in some areas, though. Clemens allowed over 20 home runs five times in a 24-year-career with a high of 26 in 2000, allowing a total of 363 HR in 4,916 innings, quite a few more than Ryan, who allowed 321 in his 27-year-career.

In Ryan's 5,386 innings, he only allowed 20 home runs in a season once, but over 27 seasons, things add up. As Clemens found out. Heading into the final weeks of the 2007 season, Clemens had allowed a home run in four straight starts Seattle's Ichiro Suzuki hit a leadoff home run in the third inning of Clemens's next-to-last regular-season start against the Mariners for number 362. The final home run Clemens allowed was to his old Boston teammate Trot Nixon, winding down his career with the Tribe, in the second inning of Clemens's final appearance in the majors, pitching in Game 3 in the American League Division Series.

Throughout Clemens's run in Boston, there almost always seemed to be disappointment lurking everywhere. Just when it looked like Boston would finally win the World Series in 1986 against a New York Mets team that seemed to be handing off the trophy, there was that bouncing ball and Bill Buckner and heartbreak. For a pitcher with his extraordinary numbers, Clemens generally struggled in postseason play until the end of his career. Closing out his career with Houston and an abbreviated final season with the Yankees, he won seven of his last nine decisions to get to 12-8 for his career.

But his postseason record early on was questionable. In his postseason debut against the California Angels in Game 1 of the AL playoffs in 1986, a year in which Clemens was named the American League's Most Valuable Player off a 24-4 record with 238 strikeouts, he was bombed in the opener vs. the Angels (7.1 innings, allowing 10 hits, seven earned runs) in an 8–1 loss.

In that memorable 1986 World Series, it was Clemens on the mound for the first seven innings of Game 6. That's where things get interesting. In an MLB Network special, "1986: A Postseason to Remember," then–Red Sox manager John McNamara claims Clemens asked out of the game, Boston up, 3–2.

"He came off the mound in the bottom of the seventh inning," McNamara said, "and we were waiting there at the steps to congratulate him you know, getting out of the seventh and he came down the steps and he said, 'That's all I can pitch.' Quote unquote. And my answer to him was, 'You gotta be shitting me.' And he said 'No,' and he showed us his finger . . . where he had the start of a paper tear on his middle finger and—well, correct this right here and now, he had no blister whatsoever, and how that got started I don't know. But it spread rapidly and it continued over the next two years that the blister took him out of the ballgame. And that is not the case. As sure as I'm sitting here."

So here's the most accomplished pitcher in Red Sox history, his team just six outs from a long-sought-after World Series win, and he asks out. Or not.

Clemens contends that he could—and would have—continued but McNamara decided to pinch-hit for him. "I think I was getting ready to hit," Clemens recalled. "And if I'm not mistaken, McNamara pinch-hit Mike Greenwell for me. Again, I don't know why McNamara would say something like that, if it was to deflect attention from the game. My recollection is, I was at the bat rack putting my gloves on or getting my bat, my helmet or whatever and getting ready to go hit. I think I had only given up four hits. I've pitched 100-pitch games, I've pitched 150-pitch games, I think I threw a 164-pitch game at some point in my career, so I don't know where that came from."

Clemens did say he had a problem with his finger. "Yes, again, (I had) a little problem with my finger. If they're saying they didn't see anything with my finger, I mean, there was blood on the baseballs and crazy things like that, but it wasn't going to affect me to continue."

McNamara disagrees. "That is not accurate. That is not the truth and I don't lie. Those words are indelibly imprinted in my mind."

However, the reliable Peter Gammons, writing for *Sports Illustrated* after his historic years at the *Boston Globe*, reported otherwise.

"Clemens held the lead in the bottom of the seventh, retiring the side on 17 pitches—giving him 135 for the game," Gammons wrote. "But while pitching to (Mookie) Wilson—naturally—he tore the fingernail on his middle finger, and when he got back to the dugout, he was bleeding from two fingers. McNamara and pitching coach Bill Fischer approached him. "Does it sting?" McNamara asked. "Sure, it stings," said Clemens. "I told them I couldn't throw any sliders, but I could get them out with fastballs and fork-balls," Clemens now says. "They told me that if the first couple of hitters got on, they might hit for me."

But memories vary. In the press conference, Gammons reported McNamara said something else. "At the postgame press conference, McNamara clearly implied that Clemens asked out of the game because of the blister. 'My pitcher told me he couldn't go any further,' said McNamara. When George Grande of ESPN later asked Clemens off-camera what McNamara had said, Clemens got upset and started off to confront McNamara. 'Fischer stopped me and told me it was a misunderstanding, that Mac didn't mean it,' recalls Clemens. 'I wanted to pitch the eighth inning, then turn it over to Calvin [Schiraldi] with three outs to go.'"

Though Clemens was Boston's finest homegrown talent, a decade later, Red Sox management was wondering about his future. It was December of 1996, Clemens's Red Sox contract was up, and from spring training on, Clemens had been hinting about the Red Sox offering him a multi-year deal. Duquette, looking carefully at Clemens's record of late—Clemens, 10-13 with a 3.63 ERA last season, was 40-39, 3.76 over the past four. In the previous seven, he had been 136-63, 2.65. At 33, it certainly looked as if his career was headed downhill. Ultimately, Boston offered him a four-year, $20-million deal but just $10 million in guaranteed money. So Clemens went to Toronto, a division rival (sorry, Dan), and he began his amazing eight-year run, four Cy Young Awards, a 148-61 record (from age 34 to 42) with 30-plus starts and seven years of 200-plus innings.

After a brief retirement in 2003, Clemens returned to pitch for the Astros for three more seasons and after the 2006 season, it looked as if the Rocket had been permanently taken off the launching pad. But after a dramatic sev-enth-inning announcement at a Yankee game in May, Clemens decided to come back to pitch for the Yankees and he did OK as a 44-year-old, amassing a 6-6 record with a 4.18 ERA. In the postseason, after the Yankees dropped the first two games of the series, it was up to Clemens to try to turn the tide in Game 3 of the American League Divisional Series vs. Cleveland.

At 44, it was asking too much. Clemens retired Grady Sizemore on a groundout, but Asdrubal Cabrera beat one out to deep short, and Travis Haf-ner drew a 3-2 walk to put two on. Clemens got Victor Martínez to line out to left, but Ryan Garko dropped a single into center field to drive in a run.

After Kenny Lofton popped out, leading off the second, old teammate Trot Nixon tied into a 2-0 fastball and lined one into the right field seats to make it 2–0, Indians. Clemens, approaching 60 pitches already, walked Hafner to lead off the inning and managed, on a full count, to strike out Victor Martínez with a 92-mile-per-hour tailing fastball.

Clemens paused for a moment and walked stiffly toward home plate. Yankee manager Joe Torre called time, and suddenly there was a huddle on the mound, Clemens with his head down, talking animatedly to the trainer. Torre reached up with his left hand and softly, affectionately, patted Clemens on the cheek. He was done.

To a thunderous round of boos and cheer, Clemens stalked off with a slight limp. Head down, he was greeted by pitching coach Ron Guidry at the bottom of the steps. A few Yankees reached out to pat him on the shoulders. Later, it came out a hamstring strain had prompted Roger's exit. The Yankees went on to win the game, but lost the next game and the series.

Roger and out.

Roger Clemens by the Numbers

YEAR	TEAM	W	L	PCT	ERA	G	GS	CG	SHO	SV	IP	H	R	BB	SO
1984	BOS	9	4	.692	4.32	21	20	5	1	0	133.1	146	67	29	126
1985	BOS	7	5	.583	3.29	15	15	3	1	0	98.1	83	38	37	74
1986	BOS	24	4	.857	2.48	33	33	10	1	0	254.0	179	77	67	238
1987	BOS	20	9	.690	2.97	36	36	18	7	0	281.2	248	100	83	256
1988	BOS	18	12	.600	2.93	35	35	14	8	0	264.0	217	93	62	291
1989	BOS	17	11	.607	3.13	35	35	8	3	0	253.1	215	101	93	230
1990	BOS	21	6	.778	1.93	31	31	7	4	0	228.1	193	59	54	209
1991	BOS	18	10	.643	2.62	35	35	13	4	0	271.1	219	93	65	241
1992	BOS	18	11	.621	2.41	32	32	11	5	0	246.2	203	80	62	208
1993	BOS	11	14	.440	4.46	29	29	2	1	0	191.2	175	99	67	160
1994	BOS	9	7	.563	2.85	24	24	3	1	0	170.2	124	62	71	168
1995	BOS	10	5	.667	4.18	23	23	0	0	0	140.0	141	70	60	132
1996	BOS	10	13	.435	3.63	34	34	6	2	0	242.2	216	106	106	257
1997	TOR	21	7	.750	2.05	34	34	9	3	0	264.0	204	65	68	292
1998	TOR	20	6	.769	2.65	33	33	5	3	0	234.2	169	78	88	271
1999	NYY	14	10	.583	4.60	30	30	1	1	0	187.2	185	101	90	163
2000	NYY	13	8	.619	3.70	32	32	1	0	0	204.1	184	96	84	188
2001	NYY	20	3	.870	3.51	33	33	0	0	0	220.1	205	94	72	213
2002	NYY	13	6	.684	4.35	29	29	0	0	0	180.0	172	94	63	192
2003	NYY	17	9	.654	3.91	33	33	1	1	0	211.2	199	99	58	190
2004	HOU	18	4	.818	2.98	33	33	0	0	0	214.1	169	76	79	218
2005	HOU	13	8	.619	1.87	32	32	1	0	0	211.1	151	51	62	185
2006	HOU	7	6	.538	2.30	19	19	0	0	0	113.1	89	34	29	102
2007	NYY	6	6	.500	4.18	18	17	0	0	0	99.0	99	52	31	68
TOTALS		354	184	.658	3.12	709	707	118	46	0	4916.2	4185	1885	1580	4672

BARRY BONDS

ONE LAST LONG OUT

DATE: September 26, 2007

SITE: AT&T Park, San Francisco, California

PITCHER: Jake Peavy of the San Diego Padres

RESULT: Flyout to center field

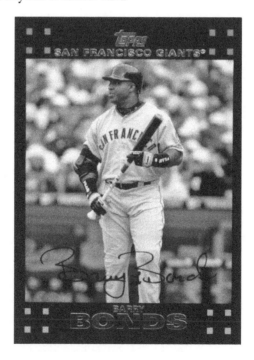

Was Barry Bonds baseball's Hamlet? Undeniably gifted, complex and misunderstood, prone to self-serving soliloquies and "woe-is-me" outbursts that made it seem he was suffering to excel the way he did, rarely has someone been so visible, so dominant for so long and ultimately, unloved. Or so it seemed. Or so it seemed he felt.

Watching him from afar, you could no more imagine Barry Bonds returning a fan's mail-in request for an autograph or smiling for a picture with a kid or joking around with a media member than you could imagine Harry Caray turning down a beer.

On the field, Bonds's game face seemed to alter between a smirk and a scowl. You would think mentioning baseball's all-time home-run king and single-season home-run record holder to most fans would bring a smile and a nod or a story. That does not happen with Barry Bonds.

Never particularly media-friendly, things seemed to worsen for him around the 1998 season. The son of former big leaguer Bobby Bonds and the godson of Giants legend Willie Mays, Barry Bonds was on his way to Cooperstown, or so it seemed in that memorable summer.

Already a three-time MVP, Bonds was in the middle of having a fine season in San Francisco—.303, 37 home runs, 122 RBIs—but two other— well, let's say it, *lesser* players—the Chicago Cubs' Sammy Sosa and the St. Louis Cardinals' Mark McGwire ended up grabbing national headlines all summer with their chase of Roger Maris's single-season record of 61 home runs. It was a thrilling race; the whole nation seemed to be swept up in it. In San Francisco, Bonds wasn't as impressed.

According to Jeff Pearlman's 2006 article in *ESPN Magazine*, Bonds decided he was going to change that in the 1999 offseason. "On an otherwise ordinary night, over an otherwise ordinary meal," Pearlman writes, "(Ken) Griffey, Bonds, a rep from an athletic apparel company and two other associates chatted informally about the upcoming season. With Griffey's framed memorabilia as a backdrop, and Mark McGwire's obliteration of the single-season home run record a fresh memory, Bonds spoke up as he never had before. He sounded neither angry nor agitated, simply frustrated.

"'You know what,' he said. 'I had a helluva season last year, and nobody gave a crap. Nobody. As much as I've complained about McGwire and Canseco and all of the bull with steroids, I'm tired of fighting it. I turn 35 this year. I've got three or four good seasons left, and I wanna get paid. I'm just gonna start using some hard-core stuff, and hopefully it won't hurt my body. Then I'll get out of the game and be done with it.'"

According to Pearlman's article, "Bonds' frustration had peaked on Aug. 23 of the previous season. That was the day he crushed a knuckleball from Marlins lefthander Kirt Ojala into the bleachers of Miami's Pro Player Stadium, becoming the first man in major league history to compile 400 home runs and 400 stolen bases. On the scoreboard, '400/400' flashed in bright yellow letters, and most of the 36,701 fans rose in appreciation. Outside the stadium, however, few people cared.

"Bonds' achievement found its way into every sports section across America—but on the second, third or fourth page," he wrote. "For Bonds himself, the ultimate statistics scavenger, reaching 400/400 was momentous. He had gone beyond his father, Bobby Bonds. He had gone beyond his godfather, Willie Mays. He had gone beyond Babe Ruth and Hank Aaron. In the sort of aw-shucks false modesty he put on from time to time, Bonds told the small number of assembled reporters that he was nothing compared to McGwire and Sammy Sosa, who were in the midst of their epic home run race. 'I have nine writers standing here,' he said. 'McGwire had 200 writers back when he had 30 home runs. What they're doing is huge, phenomenal. Two guys might break the record. I mean, what's the chance of that ever happening again?'"

When Bonds arrived at spring training the next year, some said he looked more like a linebacker than a left fielder. As Pearlman writes: "Within the Giants' clubhouse, Bonds' transformation was met with skepticism. His face was bloated. His forehead and jaw were substantially larger. 'And the zits,' says Jay Canizaro, who played 55 games as a Giants infielder in 1996 and '99. 'Hell, he took off his shirt the first day and his back just looked like a mountain of acne. Anybody who had any kind of intelligence or street smarts about them knew Barry was using some serious stuff.'"

Bonds's 1999 season was disappointing. He played in just over 100 games, posted a low .262 average with 34 home runs and 83 RBIs, nowhere near Bondsian numbers. Beginning in 2000 when he turned 35, Bonds's numbers suddenly became otherworldly, especially for a player approaching 40.

- Age 35 - 2000 - .306, 49, 106, 117 walks, MVP runner-up
- Age 36 - 2001 - .328, 73, 137, 177 walks, MVP (his 4th)
- Age 37 - 2002 - .370, 46, 110, 198 walks, MVP (his 5th)
- Age 38 - 2003 - .341, 45, 90, 148 walks, MVP (his 6th)
- Age 39 - 2004 - .362, 45, 101, 232 walks, MVP (his 7th)

When the book *Game of Shadows* came out in 2006, linking Bonds to the Bay Area Laboratory Co-operative (BALCO) and steroid use, he became radioactive. Though he had hoped to continue playing past 2007, chasing 3,000 hits and 800 home runs, there were no takers.

In November of 2007, Bonds was indicted on felony charges of obstruction of justice and perjury (he claimed in 2003 he had never knowingly used anabolic steroids or human growth hormone). In 2011, Bonds was convicted of obstruction of justice but eventually, the conviction was overturned, the case eventually dropped. His reputation remains tarnished. As well it should be, in the eyes of some baseball aficionados.

How would we view Barry Bonds if he hadn't been tied to BALCO and steroid use? The king stat head Bill James, for example, in 2000 ranked Bonds as the third-best left fielder of all time behind Ted Williams and Stan Musial. By 2003, James considered Bonds as the 28th greatest player of all time. By 2007, after the steroid mess, James refused to rate him at all.

Though his credentials are extraordinary, like Clemens, he's tainted with the stain of steroids.

Unfortunately, that topic never comes up in an otherwise interesting somewhat revisionist 90-minute chatty interview Bonds does with Giants public address announcer Renel Lake-Moon, now available on YouTube.

In it, there are a lot of contradictions; Bonds claiming to have off-the-charts baseball IQ but crediting Bobby Bonilla with telling him it was wrong to drag bunt in the late innings of a one-sided baseball game—a rookie knows that. Later, Bonds claimed his baseball IQ was so great, he saved all his most dramatic home runs for home games. OK. He also said that he wanted to keep playing in 2008 but—"I never got to retire. I never got to do that." When it came to dealing with the press, he admits "I was a brat. You said these nasty things about me and now you want to talk to me?" He also explains he loved playing the villain, being the last one out on the field most games, intentionally making the fans wait, soaking up the boos as inspiration for his next at-bat. The perversity went deeper than that.

When *Sports Illustrated*'s Rick Reilly wrote the famous (or infamous) 24–1 story in August of 2001, pulling back an ugly veil on Bonds's diva-like actions, it was easy to see why so many felt so strongly about him. He knew exactly what he could get away with and did with no shame about it whatsoever. You can imagine how the Giants' front office winced when they read Reilly's *Sports Illustrated* piece, which begins this way: "In the San Francisco Giants' clubhouse, everybody knows the score: 24-1," he wrote. "There are 24 teammates, and there's Barry Bonds. There are 24 teammates who show up to pose for the team picture, and there's Bonds, who has blown it off for the last two years. There are 24 teammates who go out on the field before the game to stretch together, and there's Bonds, who usually stretches indoors with his own flex guy. There are 24 teammates who get on the players' bus at the hotel to go to the park, and there's Bonds, who gets on the bus with the broadcasters, the trainers and the manager who coddles him. There are 24 teammates who eat the clubhouse spread, and there's Bonds, whose nutritionist brings in special meals for him. There are 24 teammates who deal with the Giants' publicity man, and there's Bonds, who has his own clubhouse-roving p.r. guy, a freelance artist named Steve Hoskins, who turned down George Will's request for an interview with Bonds because Hoskins had never heard of him."

Dislike him yet? There's more. "There are 24 teammates who hang out with one another, play cards and bond, and there's Bonds, sequestered in the far corner of the clubhouse with his p.r. man, masseur, flex guy, weight trainer, three lockers, a reclining massage chair and a big-screen television that only he can see. Last week, after Bonds hit his 51st home run in a 13-7 win over the Florida Marlins, most of the players stayed to celebrate the victory, and at least one was gone before the press arrived in the clubhouse: Bonds."

Bonds's fearless/envious (pick one) teammate Jeff Kent explained to Reilly that this is how it was. "'That's Barry,' Kent told Reilly. "'He doesn't answer questions. He palms everybody off on us, so we have to do his talking for him. But you get used to it. Barry does a lot of questionable things. But you get used to it. Sometimes it rubs the younger guys the wrong way, and sometimes it rubs the veterans the wrong way. You just hope he shows up for the game and performs. I've learned not to worry about it or think about it or analyze it. I was raised to be a team guy, and I am, but Barry's Barry. It took me two years to learn to live with it, but I learned.'"

Because of that story and a million others, when Bonds retired at the end of the 2007 season with a pretty lousy San Francisco Giants team, there was no great outcry to keep him in the game. It was as if the game had put up with Bonds for as long as it could. To be or not to be? How about this? Be gone.

Bonds never made any attempt to make peace with the media; in fact, he may have gone as far as he could the other way as he went after the game's home-run record. The chapter heading on Bonds in Ken Burns's *The Tenth Inning*—the sequel to his acclaimed *Baseball*—was "Negative Capability." It fit.

"The problem with me, like my dad told me before he passed away," Bonds recounts in the film, "he said 'The problem with you Barry is every great athlete that has gone on for great records, everyone knows their story. And I'm sorry. I was raised to protect my family, keep my mouth shut and stay quiet. It doesn't make me a bad person. It doesn't make me an evil person. I'm an adult and I take responsibility for what I do, but you know what, I'm not going to allow you guys to ruin my joy.'"

But if there was joy, it was hard to spot and it certainly didn't seem shared. As he approached Aaron's home-run marks, there were nasty signs in stadiums across the National League, most pointing to steroid accusations: "Babe Ruth did it with hot dogs, Hank Aaron did it with class," or most damning, bearing an asterisk. (Maris had an asterisk after his 61 because it came in an 162-game season, not 154 like Ruth's.) "This record is not tainted at all," Bonds said, flatly. "At all. Period."

Few agreed.

"Cheer me, cheer me, boo me, boo me. But they still come to see the show," Bonds said, as if to demonstrate the boundaries of his unlikeability. "And I'm happy. L.A. Dodger Stadium is the best show I ever go to and watch baseball. They say 'Barry sucks' louder than anybody out there. And in left field, you'll see me out there going like this (raising arms, as if to call for more) because you know what, you've got to have some serious talent to have 53,000 people saying you suck. And I'm proud of that."

As dominant as he was—four MVPs in a row!—examining Bonds's career numbers now turns up surprises. His career average? .298! What? How could he wind up at .298 after that .370 season, that .362 season with the 232 walks?

There was more. Surely, a hitter as dominant as Bonds would have 3,000 career hits. Nope, 2,965. Of course, leading the league in walks 11 times, that took a lot of at-bats away. Three of the top four walk totals for a season are Bonds—232 in 2004 (when he was 39!), 198 in 2002, 177 in 2001. One interesting statistic—seldom mentioned—is for the final nine years of his career, he was in single digits for grounding into double plays until his last year (13). Imagine that? Single digits in double plays, just five in over 850 plate appearances in that 2004 MVP season; a .362 average, 232 walks, 45 home runs, and 101 RBIs in who knows how many reduced RBI opportunities?

In all, Bonds retired with a staggering 688 intentional walks, an amazing 120 in 204 when he was a 39-year-old. He led the league 12 separate times, more than twice as many in his career as Albert Pujols, the number two guy.

Yet, when the end came for such a player on a chilly September night at AT&T Park, it seemed a bit of a relief. Like so many other players linked to steroids, it almost seemed good to have him leave before we could find out more about those extraordinary .370 or .362 seasons, the details of his 73-home-run season, or those 762 lifetime home runs that surpassed Hank Aaron's 755. We knew too much already.

The final stretch of his career was a fast fade. His final hit, a single off the Padres' Brett Tomko, came leading off the second inning of a 6–0 loss in San Diego, on September 15. He left the game and you did not see Bonds back on the field until September 26, the final home game of the regular season. His final home run came in early September

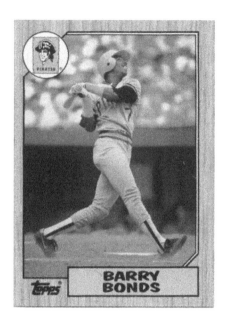

in Colorado (September 5) in the first inning off Ubaldo Jiménez. He didn't play after that September 15 appearance until that home finale.

On that night, he started, played left field, and batted three times against the Padres' Jake Peavy, eventual Cy Young Award winner, and was held hitless.

In the first, he bounced a 2-2 sinker right at first baseman Adrián González. In the fourth, he came up with one out and topped one right back at Peavy for the second out. In the fifth, he misplayed a Khalil Greene single in the middle of a six-run rally for an error on the last ball he handled. It wasn't a good night.

Finally, in the bottom of the sixth, he stepped up to the plate for the final time in his career with 42,926 standing and cheering at AT&T Park. Peavy, up 9–2, fell behind 2-0 and fired a fastball up and in. Bonds put a good swing on it, the ball soared up, up into the chilly San Franciscan night, but dropped in front of the Diamond Walnuts sign in right-center field. Out.

Bonds trotted toward first, then shook hands and embraced Peavy, whispering something to the Padres right-hander before pointing into the stands, waving, and saluting the fans. He was called out of the dugout for a curtain call, keeping his helmet on, waving, then clapping along.

The Giants retired his number 25, also worn by his dad, in an on-field ceremony in 2018. He served as a Marlins hitting coach in 2016 and has, of late, taken up cycling, he told Lake-Moon. She did not bring up the topic of steroids or Cooperstown.

Oddly, two of the game's giants left at the same time. Roger Clemens, one of the game's greatest pitchers, made his final appearance just 11 days after Barry bowed out. Turns out Sammy Sosa's finale came three days later.

Some 13 years later, Bonds and Clemens, the two greatest players of their era at their respective positions, still await the call from the Hall. The pair appeared on the 2020 Hall of Fame ballot for the ninth time and made no headway, each getting around 60 percent, well short of the 75 percent necessary. Steroids may be the only reason, of course. Neither Bonds nor Clemens got enough Hall of Fame votes in their final year on the ballot. From there, their only chance for selection will be from the Veterans Committee. Neither made many friends there. So, two of the greatest players in the history of the game wait to be forgiven for something they say they never did. They both hope to one day be included in the Hall of legends in Cooperstown. It may not ever happen.

Barry Bonds by the Numbers

YEAR	TEAM	G	AB	R	H	TB	2B	3B	HR	RBI	BB	SO	SB	BA	SLG	OBP
1986	PIT	113	413	72	92	172	26	3	16	48	65	102	36	.223	.416	.330
1987	PIT	150	551	99	144	271	34	9	25	59	54	88	32	.261	.492	.329
1988	PIT	144	538	97	152	264	30	5	24	58	72	82	17	.283	.491	.368
1989	PIT	159	580	96	144	247	34	6	19	58	93	93	32	.248	.426	.351
1990	PIT	151	519	104	156	293	32	3	33	114	93	83	52	.301	.565	.406
1991	PIT	153	510	95	149	262	28	5	25	116	107	73	43	.292	.514	.410
1992	PIT	140	473	109	147	295	36	5	34	103	127	69	39	.311	.624	.456
1993	SF	159	539	129	181	365	38	4	46	123	126	79	29	.336	.677	.458
1994	SF	112	391	89	122	253	18	1	37	81	74	43	29	.312	.647	.426
1995	SF	144	506	109	149	292	30	7	33	104	120	83	31	.294	.577	.431
1996	SF	158	517	122	159	318	27	3	42	129	151	76	40	.308	.615	.461
1997	SF	159	532	123	155	311	26	5	40	101	145	87	37	.291	.585	.446
1998	SF	156	552	120	167	336	44	7	37	122	130	92	28	.303	.609	.438
1999	SF	102	355	91	93	219	20	2	34	83	73	62	15	.262	.617	.389
2000	SF	143	480	129	147	330	28	4	49	106	117	77	11	.306	.688	.440
2001	SF	153	476	129	156	411	32	2	73	137	177	93	13	.328	.863	.515
2002	SF	143	403	117	149	322	31	2	46	110	198	47	9	.370	.799	.582
2003	SF	130	390	111	133	292	22	1	45	90	148	58	7	.341	.749	.529
2004	SF	147	373	129	135	303	27	3	45	101	232	41	6	.362	.812	.609
2005	SF	14	42	8	12	28	1	0	5	10	9	6	0	.286	.667	.404
2006	SF	130	367	74	99	200	23	0	26	77	115	51	3	.270	.545	.454
2007	SF	126	340	75	94	192	14	0	28	66	132	54	5	.276	.565	.480
TOTALS		2986	9847	2227	2935	5976	601	77	762	1996	2558	1539	514	.298	.607	.444

DAVID ORTIZ

NO PARTING SHOT FOR BIG PAPI

DATE: October 10, 2016

SITE: Fenway Park, Boston, Massachusetts

PITCHER: Cody Allen of the Cleveland Indians

RESULT: Walk

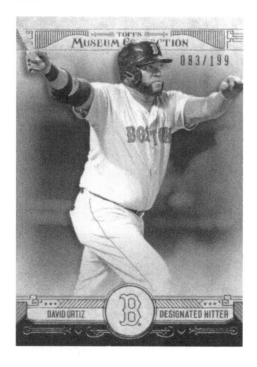

We saw him stand in the same Fenway Park batter's box as those legends of yore: Carl Michael Yastrzemski for 23 seasons, Theodore Samuel Williams for 19 seasons. But somehow, David Américo Ortiz Arias was never in their shadow.

For 14 seasons, Ortiz was a larger-than-life figure in Boston's Fenway Park, helping the Red Sox achieve something Yaz and Ted never could—a world championship. Three of them, in fact. And in building what will surely be a Hall of Fame resume, Ortiz confounded some of the stat heads who seemed to have taken over many of the front offices of the game as his career wound down. The king of the stat gang, in fact, was hired by Ortiz's own front office.

Even as a member of the Boston Red Sox advisory staff, for a long time Bill James insisted that there was no such thing as "a clutch hitter."

As he wrote in 2009, "A reader tells me that I have taken so many positions on the issue of clutch hitting that he has given up hope of following me. Well, for the sake of clarity, I have had only two positions on this issue. First, in following the lead of other researchers, I thought that there was no such thing as an ability to hit in clutch situations. Second, thinking more about the issue, I decided that we had jumped the gun in reaching that conclusion—thereby introducing bias into our research—and that we should have waited and studied the issue more carefully.

"Whether any hitter has an ability to hit in clutch situations is a debatable issue on which I have no position. In any season, however, it is clear that some players come through more often in clutch situations, if only because of luck."

If he had looked up from his abacus, James could well have seen Exhibit A in the famed clutch hitting debate in the prime of his career. It says here that Exhibit A was large, left-handed, wore number 34, and came through so many times "in the clutch," it almost seemed you could write it in the scorebook before he stepped into the batter's box.

Ortiz did it so often and in big spots—the playoffs, the World Series— that it almost seemed he intimidated the opposition into pitching to him in these dramatic spots, thinking, "Well, he can't get a hit every time. This streak of luck is going to change right now." Then it wouldn't.

The numbers, of course, don't back up such an assertion. Ortiz hit .286 for his career with 541 home runs and 1,768 RBI, impressive totals. But if you ask a Boston fan which player they wanted to see walk up to the plate in "a clutch moment"—Yaz, Ted, Manny Ramirez, Jim Rice, Carlton Fisk, Hall of Fame caliber players each, the vote would go to No. 34.

And when it came to baseball's Hall of Fame, the vote went to David Ortiz, too, in January of 2022. Ortiz, like Red Sox legends Ted Williams and Carl Yastrzemski before him, went in on the Hall of Fame's first ballot, earning 77.9 prcent of the votes.

Interestingly, the *Boston Globe's* Hall of Fame columnist Dan Shaughnessy refused to vote for Ortiz, explaining he didn't because his name popped up on the leaked Mitchell Report.

However, Commissioner Rob Manfred said it was unfair to Ortiz's legacy to be tarnished, since it was unknown if Ortiz actually used a performance-enhancing drug and there were at least 10 false positives. There were no other known issues for the rest of his career.

Mark Twain is alleged to have said there are "lies, damn lies and statistics," a quote Mr. James certainly does not have hanging on his computer/abacus/adding machine. From 2003 to 2006, Ortiz had 15 walkoff hits for the Red Sox, including three in the 2004 playoffs alone, then added another one a few years later. And how many unmeasurable hits came to tie games, or bring the Red Sox within striking distance? Numbers may not show the faces of enemy pitchers when they saw Ortiz saunter out of the dugout, spit in his hands, and step into the box.

"Reality is, when I was in the on deck, I was staring at the pitcher, just trying to get in his head, just watching the sequence," Ortiz told Alex Rodriguez on the MLB Channel. "I was thinking about the history, what he was going to attack me with, what did he do before?

"You are not allowed to play baseball with an empty mind," Ortiz said. "The only advantage you have is when you think ahead. You made your game plan before you get here (the batter's box)." And Ortiz knew the impact he had.

"I wanted to make sure that the pitcher know that I was there, walking to the plate," Ortiz said. "That I was going to do some damage. So I was taking my time. A lot of people criticize me for taking my time. It was concentration and focus. When I was in and out, I don't think I was at my best. I was thinking about my homework, what I did before and my game plan. That was when I was at my best."

In the 2013 World Series, Ortiz hit .688, reaching base 19 times in 25 trips to the plate. At age 37. Though an enormous man with a booming laugh, a perennial smile on his face, Ortiz became such a student of the game, seemingly so relaxed in teeth-grinding situations, it was as if he knew the pressure was on the guy with the ball in his hand, not the guy trying to hit it.

"He loves coming up in the big spot," says Theo Epstein, the Red Sox GM at the time, whose experience with Ortiz may have persuaded him to junk the sabermetrics principle that clutch hitting is not a skill. "He makes you rethink the objective analysis. The way he rises to the occasion and the quality of his at bats, the numbers don't reflect that human element."

Ortiz explains it this way. "It's mostly confidence," he told *Sports Illustrated* in 2006. "If you go up there thinking you might not get it done, you're out already. I know I'm going to hit you. And I have confidence all around me here. In Minnesota, if we faced a good pitcher, guys would say, 'Oh, well, I'll get my hits tomorrow.' Here? We don't care who's pitching."

Ortiz's intensity and focus at the plate were quite a contrast to his predecessor in the batting order, the often inexplicable left fielder Manny Ramírez, he of the "Manny being Manny" behavior. Off the field, Ramírez was a workaholic in the cage. On the field, he was liable to do most anything.

For their five years as the latter-day Ruth-Gehrig, Ramírez and Ortiz led the Red Sox to two long-sought World Series championships. When Manny was dispatched to Los Angeles late in 2008, Ortiz continued to be a force in the American League, leading the Red Sox to another title with an extraordinary postseason and a record-setting World Series performance in 2013. And in that amazing season of beards and rallies, an Ortiz speech rings out through the years.

It was after the horrific Patriots' Day bombing at the Boston Marathon and the Red Sox, known for doing these ceremonial things better than anyone, invited some of those victims as well as the health care workers and first responders. It was an emotional day at Fenway, and to close the ceremony, Ortiz was called to speak. He took to the microphone the way he took to a low inside fastball.

"All right, all right, Boston," he said, comfortable at center stage. "This jersey we wear today, it doesn't say Red Sox. It say 'Boston.' We wanna thank you Mayor Menino, Governor Patrick, the police department for the great job they did this past week. This is our fucking city. And nobody gonna dictate it to you. Stay strong. Thank you."

Though Ortiz's profane adjective was later bleeped, the passion behind it endeared Big Papi to the Fenway Faithful even more. Neither Williams, nor Yaz, nor Rice would have ever said such a thing. But emotion was a part of Ortiz's game. Inside that green-walled palace, he was the king. And a benevolent one.

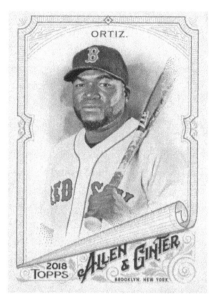

Watching him take batting practice in a nearly empty park, spraying hump-backed liners off and over the walls, it seemed effortless. But there were moments when it looked as if he were done. There was a serious wrist injury and assorted slumps and times when it looked as if the game had passed him by. In 2013, for example, Ortiz missed the team's first 15 games. But when he came back, he was Big Papi again, winding up with a .309 average, 30 home runs, and 103 RBIs, missing 25 games.

Surprisingly, for a guy with no leg hits, facing a ferocious shift that had to cost him 20 points a year, Ortiz hit over .300 in four of his last six seasons, including a stunning .315 in his final year, his third-best career mark with a league-leading 48 doubles and a league-leading 127 RBI as a 40-year-old. It seemed as if he could go on forever, but Ortiz's struggles with an Achilles tendon injury and constant, nagging pain in his legs led him to declare that the 2016 season would be his last before it began.

Later, he admitted he'd wished he hadn't made that declaration public. But it did give baseball fans a chance to take a long last look at Big Papi and a Big Papi farewell tour that earned him gifts and ceremonies in visiting cities.

It also gave them one last chance to wonder at his hitting intelligence, which seemed to deepen as he aged. As Tom Verducci noted in a *Sports Illustrated* article in 2016, Ortiz slugged .603 with two strikes on him. Clutch, indeed.

"The average major league hitter slugs just .278 in all two-strike counts," Verducci wrote. "Just how amazing is that?" Verducci referenced statistics that showed Albert Pujols, at 24, slugged .618 with two strikes and three years later, .615. Next was Ortiz, age 40, at .603. With no leg hits, playing against a shift.

"It's not that easy," Ortiz told Verducci. "But I pay attention. One thing I know: You can't hit trying to cover both sides of the plate. When you know how they pitch you, then you do damage."

Ortiz's Red Sox were hoping to get Big Papi back to a World Series in his final season. They led the American League East for much of the season, but got hot too soon, closing out an 11-game win streak on September 26 as the Ortiz Farewell Tour continued through American League cities. When Boston lost five of its final six games, heading into the postseason and a matchup with former Red Sox skipper Tito Francona, the good ship Red Sox seemed to be taking on water. And after all this time, all these postseason heroics, this time, Ortiz was no help.

After 22-game (and Cy Young Award winner) Rick Porcello was bounced in the opener in Cleveland, David Price was no better in Game 2. Ortiz managed an eighth-inning double off reliever Cody Allen in Game 1, but that was it. He looked exhausted and so did his team. In Game 3 back in Boston before 39,530 at Fenway Park, the Red Sox trailed throughout and Ortiz couldn't do a thing about it. Josh Tomlin walked him leading off the second, he bounced out to first in the fourth, and hit a sacrifice fly lineout in the sixth.

The final trip to the plate came against Allen in the eighth with two out. Allen came in to face Ortiz, giving the Red Sox fans a little extra time to stare at the giant "34" in red on that white background. With the Tribe up a run, Allen was not about to let Ortiz do anything to alter that.

Ortiz settled in at the plate, his baggy white uniform pants extending down over the heel of his cleats. Allen's first pitch was a fastball high and wide.

"Look at this shift. Jason Kipnis is nearly at Pesky's Pole [the right field foul pole, jokingly named for ex-Red Sox banjo-hitting shortstop Johnny Pesky]" came from the TV set. Pitch two was up and in, off the plate.

"Last 32 postseason at-bats," announcer Ron Darling said just before Pitch Three. "Six home runs." An Allen slider broke in, off the plate. 3-0.

"If ever there was a time to swing 3-0," Darling continued, "this is it." A fastball came in, well off the plate and Ortiz took it. The TV monitor mistakenly showed the count as 3-1 as the announcers discussed the call. We looked up and Papi was at first base. There would be no dramatic Ted Williams–style parting-shot home run. Ortiz stood off first for a moment, gesturing with both arms for the crowd to cheer louder, as if their noise might inspire a rally. And it did, Hanley Ramírez lining a single to center, scoring Mookie Betts. Ortiz left the game for pinch-runner Marco Hernández, but when Xander Bogaerts lined out to end the inning, that was it.

Allen gave up a single and walk in the ninth but got Travis Shaw to fly out to end the season and Big Papi's career. A cold Fenway Park seemed unusually somber and chilly. After a few minutes, fans reluctant to leave, Ortiz returned, his bright red uniform undershirt untucked, and walked onto the field, an estimated 25,000 fans still there, some wiping away tears.

Surrounded by dozens of photographers who scurried and scampered around him like glittery horseflies, Ortiz climbed to the pitcher's mound, took off his cap, and held it aloft, turning to all parts of the ballpark, tears welling in his eyes. He stood there for a good three minutes, silently, taking it all in as fans in the stands stood, cheered, wept, some holding Ortiz signs that read "Thanks, Big Papi" and "Goodbye, Big Papi" and "We love you, Big Papi." Then, waving the cap one last time—as Williams had famously refused to—he disappeared into the dugout and, well, into baseball history.

David Ortiz by the Numbers

YEAR	TEAM	G	AB	R	H	TB	2B	3B	HR	RBI	BB	SO	SB	BA	SLG	OBP
1997	MIN	15	49	10	16	22	3	0	1	6	2	19	0	.327	.449	.353
1998	MIN	86	278	47	77	124	20	0	9	46	39	72	1	.277	.446	.371
1999	MIN	10	20	1	0	0	0	0	0	0	5	12	0	.000	.000	.200
2000	MIN	130	415	59	117	185	36	1	10	63	57	81	1	.282	.446	.364
2001	MIN	89	303	46	71	144	17	1	18	48	40	68	1	.234	.475	.324
2002	MIN	125	412	52	112	206	32	1	20	75	43	87	1	.272	.500	.339
2003	BOS	128	448	79	129	265	39	2	31	101	58	83	0	.288	.592	.369
2004	BOS	150	582	94	175	351	47	3	41	139	75	133	0	.301	.603	.380
2005	BOS	159	601	119	180	363	40	1	47	148	102	124	1	.300	.604	.397
2006	BOS	151	558	115	160	355	29	2	54	137	119	117	1	.287	.636	.413
2007	BOS	149	549	116	182	341	52	1	35	117	111	103	3	.332	.621	.445
2008	BOS	109	416	74	110	211	30	1	23	89	70	74	1	.264	.507	.369
2009	BOS	150	541	77	129	250	35	1	28	99	74	134	0	.238	.462	.332
2010	BOS	145	518	86	140	274	36	1	32	102	82	145	0	.270	.529	.370
2011	BOS	146	525	84	162	291	40	1	29	96	78	83	1	.309	.554	.398
2012	BOS	90	324	65	103	198	26	0	23	60	56	51	0	.318	.611	.415
2013	BOS	137	518	84	160	292	38	2	30	103	76	88	4	.309	.564	.395
2014	BOS	142	518	59	136	268	27	0	35	104	75	95	0	.263	.517	.355
2015	BOS	146	528	73	144	292	37	0	37	108	77	95	0	.273	.553	.360
2016	BOS	151	537	79	169	333	48	1	38	127	80	86	2	.315	.620	.401
TOTALS		2408	8640	1419	2472	4765	632	19	541	1768	1319	1750	17	.286	.552	.380

TOM SEAVER

THE KNEE, NOT THE ARM

DATE: September 19, 1986

SITE: Exhibition Stadium, Toronto, Canada

HITTER: Tony Fernández of the Toronto Blue Jays

RESULT: Flyball to right field

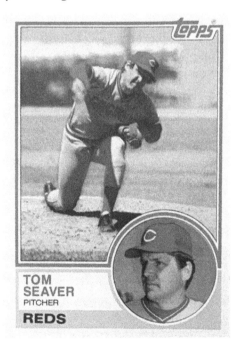

"One thing I've always wanted to do," Tom Seaver says into the camera, looking young, handsome, and impossibly trim in a blue V-necked shirt with a bright white collar. "Pitch to the greatest hitter of all time, Ted Williams."

The camera switches to a smiling Williams, at least a dozen years into retirement, waving the bat without a care in the world. He's seen better. He's seen it all. "Bases loaded," he shouts out to Seaver, "two outs, 3-2, you've gotta concentrate."

The New York Met ace winds and fires and Williams throws up his hands with a hearty laugh. "Ball four," he says, breaking into a broad laugh, throwing up his hands.

Greatest Sports Legends was a syndicated half-hour program that began in 1972. One of the most entertaining episodes of the series was Ted Williams's visit with host Tom Seaver, whose day job as ace of the New York Mets was terrorizing National League hitters. The scene that opens the show is mesmerizing as we see the in-his-prime Seaver take the mound and Williams, long retired, gray at the temples, waving the bat leisurely in a well-worn brown jacket, somehow looking kingly as he stepped into the batter's box. What a matchup! Where did Tom Seaver rank among the game's best? It's a great question.

Seaver's unique blend of power, control, and mound mastery led him to five 20-win seasons, three Cy Young Awards, and 311 wins over a 20-year career that led him to the Hall of Fame with one of the highest vote percentages ever (98.8). Even pitching in the New York media market for the first 12 years of his career, Seaver's brilliance was somewhat overshadowed in his time, an era when the pitcher dominated baseball.

He started in the Mets' rotation in 1967 and before you knew it, it was 1968 and the Year of the Pitcher. The Cardinals' Bob Gibson posted a 1.12 ERA, and the American League had just one .300 hitter, Boston's Carl Yastrzemski. They almost didn't have any. With three games left, Yastrzemski homered in the first, then sliced an opposite field double off Fred Talbot in the fifth inning at Yankee Stadium. He promptly then went 0-for-8, winding up at .301. The next year, they lowered the mound.

Seaver was just getting started. Through those dozen years in New York, you could count on Seaver to make about 36 starts, win from 18 to 25 games, complete roughly half his starts, and essentially, dominate. In a dozen seasons in New York, he was 219-127, posting a 2.51 ERA, leading the league in strikeouts five times, ERA three times.

As Joe Posnanski explained, "Of the six pitchers in his era who won 300 games, Seaver won the fewest (311). Bert Blyleven struck out more batters than Seaver. Jim Palmer won as many Cy Youngs. Nolan Ryan threw seven no-hitters, Seaver threw one (and famously, he didn't even throw it for the Mets). Sandy Koufax's postseason performances are more memorable. Steve Carlton's remarkable 1972 season (when he won 27 games for a terrible Phillies team) is more enduring. So it's easy to think that Seaver was merely one of the great pitchers of his time. But, in my view, he was the best with some space in between.

"And the reason he was the best is that he was a little bit of *all* the other great pitchers. He didn't throw Ryan's fastball or Carlton's slider or Blyleven's curve, no, but he threw a pretty good facsimile of each of them along with several of his own variation pitches. He was a strikeout pitcher with control. He was a wily pitcher with overpowering stuff. He was a student of baseball history, and he nightly brought with him to the mound the lessons of Christy Mathewson and Warren Spahn and Bob Feller."

Seaver put it like this.

"I would like to be a great artist," he said. "I would quit pitching if I could paint like Monet or Rousseau. But I can't. What I can do is pitch, and I can do that very well." Very well, indeed. If you're a WAR fan (Wins Above Replacement), his statistics are historic and way ahead of his peers. Walter Johnson leads with 152, Roger Clemens next at 139, Grover Cleveland Alexander with 116, Lefty Grove with 113, and Seaver with 106 WAR.

And Seaver, like few pitchers before or after him, understood the mechanics of pitching and could explain it, if, say an expert listener like the great Roger Angell just happened to be there. Seaver, like the author who captured his words, was captivating.

"In the clubhouse after his stint, Seaver declared himself satisfied with his work—perhaps more than satisfied. . . . He went over the three innings almost pitch by pitch, making sure that the writers had their stories, and they thanked him and went off. A couple of us stayed on while Tom . . . talked about tempos of early throwing in the first few days of spring—a murmured *'one, two, three-four . . . one, two, three-four'* beat with the windup as his body relearned rhythm and timing. He went on to the proper breaking point of the hands—where the pitching hand comes out of the glove—which for him is just above and opposite his face. Half undressed, he was on his feet again and pitching for us in slow motion, in front of his locker.

"'What you don't want is a lateral movement that will bring your elbow down and make your arm drop out, because what happens then is that your hand either goes underneath the ball or out to the side of the ball,' he said.

'To throw an effective pitch of any kind, your fingers have to stay on top of the ball. So you go back and make sure that this stays closed and *this* stays closed'—he touched his left shoulder and his left hip—'and this hand comes up *here*.' The pitching hand was back and above his head. 'It's so easy to get to here, in the middle of the windup, and then slide off horizontally with your left side. What you're trying to do instead—what's right—is to drive this lead shoulder down during the delivery of the ball. That way, the pitching shoulder comes up—it *has* to go up. You've increased the arc, and your fingers are on top of the ball, where they belong.'"

Angell noted he'd heard pitching coaches urging their pupils to drive the lead shoulder toward the catcher during the delivery.

"'Sure, but that's earlier,' Tom responded, as Angell continued. "He was all concentration, caught up in his craft. 'That's staying closed on your forward motion, before you drive down. No—with almost every pitcher, the fundamentals are the same. Look at Steve Carlton, look at Nolan Ryan, look at me, and you'll see this closed, this closed, *this* closed. You'll see this shoulder drive down and this one come up, and you'll see the hand on top of the ball. You'll see some flexibility in the landing leg. There are some individual variables, but almost every pitcher with any longevity has all that—and we're talking now about pitchers with more than four thousand innings behind them and with virtually no arm troubles along the way.'"

To Angell, an interested audience, Seaver was in philosophical form. "'What is the theory of pitching?' he went on in the Angell piece. "He sounded like a young college history lecturer reaching his peroration. 'All you're doing is trying to throw a ball from here to here.' He pointed off toward some plate behind us. 'There's no energy in the ball. It's inert, and you're supplying every ounce of energy you can to it. But the energy can't all go there. You can't do that—that's physics. Where does the rest of it go? *It has to be absorbed back into your body.* So you have to decide if you want it absorbed back into the smaller muscles of the arm or into the bigger muscles of the lower half of your body. The answer is simple. With a stiff front leg, everything comes back in *this* way, back up into the arm, unless you follow through and let that hand go on down after the pitch.'"

"But isn't that leg kick—' I began" wrote Angell. Seaver had an answer for that, too.

"'The great misnomer in pitching is the "leg kick,"' he interrupted Angell. "'That's totally wrong. Any real leg kick is incorrect. Anytime you kick out your leg you're throwing your shoulders back, and then you're way behind with everything. You've got to stay up on top of this left leg, with your weight right over it. So what is it, really? If it isn't a leg kick, it's a *knee lift*! Sure, you should bend your back when you're going forward, but—' "He stopped and half-shrugged, suddenly smiling at himself for so much intensity. 'I give up,' he said. 'It's too much for one man to do. It's too much even to remember.' He laughed—his famous giggle—and went off for his shower."

The intelligence, the mastery of the form, it was all there, which allowed Seaver to pitch effectively into his 40s. But it wasn't all for the Mets. After a contract dispute with Mets owner M. Donald Grant, Seaver was dealt to the Cincinnati Reds for four players (Doug Flynn, Steve Henderson, Pat Zachry, and Dan Norman). Seaver stayed for six seasons, finished in the top five in Cy Young voting a couple of times, then moved on to Chicago with the White Sox for three seasons, getting traded to Boston in June of the third season.

Seaver came to the Red Sox in a surprising move, thanks in part to an old Red Sox hero. Former Bosox outfielder, golfer, bon vivant, and announcer Ken Harrelson had somehow become the general manager of the Chicago White Sox. Red Sox GM Lou Gorman—he of the famed "The sun will rise, the sun will set, and I'll have lunch" quip after a Roger Clemens spring training contract exodus—convinced Harrelson to ship Seaver to Fenway in exchange for outfielder and one-time baseball analyst Steve "Psycho" Lyons. It was almost a steal.

Lyons hit just .203 with six RBI in 42 games. Seaver made 16 starts, posting a 5-7 record with a 3.80 ERA (with little support from the Red Sox bats), throwing at least six innings in a dozen of his 16 starts, helping stabilize the Red Sox rotation. The Red Sox, remember, memorably came within one out of ending a much-discussed world championship drought against Seaver's old team, the New York Mets. But the 20-year veteran wasn't able to help on the field. In the dugout, though, it was another story.

Shoulda-coulda-been World Series MVP Bruce Hurst had an impressive mentor feeding him invaluable information throughout the Series. Tom Seaver was sitting next to him in the Boston dugout. "Every game I pitched in that Series, Seaver had things to say to me between innings," Hurst recalled to Dan Shaughnessy of the *Boston Globe*. "He was on the bench with us the whole time. He would make these little statements about the absolutes of pitching: get ahead of the hitters, get the first out of the inning. Important things like that. It was like attending the University of Seaver."

Clemens, who was 24-4 that year and the American League MVP, said Seaver's presence helped him. "It was great to have him there with us,"

Clemens told Shaughnessy, looking back. "I take pride in being a power pitcher, and I learned it from Tom Seaver," said Clemens. "Growing up, looking at the guy's mechanics, you could see that he got his strength from his leg drive.

"Then when he came to us, I'd watch him out there and he's 41 years old, throwing 88, 89, and we'd get to the fifth inning and there's trouble—guys on second and third and no outs—and you watch and next thing you know he pumps a couple of 93-mile-an-hour heaters on the outside corner. Because he needed a strikeout."

"That was a special time," Hurst said, who won two games in the Series and was unofficially named Series MVP (it flashed on the Shea Stadium board) before Mookie Wilson, Bill Buckner, and tears in the dugout and thousands of homes all over New England. "Tom Seaver was my idol. I got to pitch in the World Series and sit in the dugout at Shea Stadium with Tom Seaver and Roger Clemens as my teammates. The magic of that was not lost on me."

His finest game in a Red Sox uniform was on August 6 in Detroit when Seaver, at 41, was one out away from a five-hit, nine-strikeout shutout when Johnny Grubb lined a single to right, scoring Lou Whitaker, who'd opened the bottom of the ninth with a double. Seaver won the next two in a row and pitched well down the stretch.

His final game for the Red Sox and in the majors came on September 19 in Toronto, when Boston's magic number had dwindled down to six. On a Friday night before 40,000 fans in Exhibition Stadium, Seaver was matched against the Blue Jays' ace Dave Stieb. The Red Sox staked him to a 2–0 lead, but Seaver weakened in the second, surrendering a Jesse Barfield double and singles by George Bell and Kelly Gruber to tie the game.

Uncharacteristic control trouble plagued the veteran right-hander in the third as he allowed a single run, walking Willie Upshaw and Lloyd Moseby back to back, then a groundball single to left from George Bell gave Toronto a 3–2 lead.

Seaver came out for the fourth, induced Rick Leach to bounce back to him and Kelly Gruber to ground out to second, but in pitching to Manuel Lee, he later said he felt something pop in his knee. He gave up a single before getting Tony Fernández, the final batter Seaver would face in his 20-year career, to hit a flyball to right. Boston's Dwight Evans snared it, and Seaver headed to the dugout and, ultimately, retirement. Reliever Sammy Stewart took over for Seaver in the fifth.

The official explanation for Seaver's departure was a slight tear of a ligament in his right knee—the knee that Seaver famously used to drive off major-league mounds for 4,783 drop-and-drive innings. In a quirky twist of fate, it just so happened that the Blue Jays' team doctor who examined Seaver's knee that night was an old teammate of his from his days with the Mets, Ron Taylor. Seaver headed back to Boston the next day. There was talk Seaver might be back for the postseason, but it didn't happen. Shaughnessy suggests that had he been able to start Game 4 instead of Al Nipper, the Red Sox might have won the Series.

Seaver did not pitch again for the Red Sox. Gorman offered Seaver a one-year contract for $610,000, but Seaver refused, had surgery on his knee, and waited to see what offers would come in. He heard from the Yankees—no particular contract offer—but that was it. His career, it seemed, was over.

Finally, in June, the Mets were struggling and general manager Frank Cashen thought maybe Tom Terrific could lend a hand. Their staff of Dwight Gooden, Bob Ojeda, Rick Aguilera, David Cone, and Roger McDowell were all struggling at various times with injuries, so Cashen called Seaver and asked him to warm up that right arm.

Seaver tried. At the time, Cashen dismissed any notion of sentimentality in re-signing the former Mets icon. "If I didn't think he could pitch, he wouldn't be here," he said then. But Cashen and Seaver's optimism was unfounded. He threw three exhibition games against Mets minor leaguers and was roasted, allowing 32 hits and 19 runs in 12 1/3 innings, including a home run to rookie catcher Barry Lyons. Seaver decided the next day, it was time to retire. "This is a young man's game and to compete on that level, I just did not feel I could do it. . . . I made the decision because I actually felt I was regressing rather than progressing. In my heart, I feel the time has come for me not to play any more. I've used up all the competitive pitches in me."

After his retirement, Seaver remained involved with the game, serving as a color man. That duty brought him to Orlando to broadcast a Mets-Braves spring training game.

It was unseasonably hot, the game was slow, and for one youngster sitting in the stands with an empty glove, it was especially disappointing—no foul balls. About the seventh, one foul ball peeled back directly into the announcer's booth right at the top of the stands. The youngster felt a nudge, "Go up and wave to them," he was told. "Maybe they'll throw the ball to a kid."

The kid ran to the top of the bleacher, waving his left-handed glove up to the booth, wondering if some announcer might see him. Suddenly, Tom Seaver stood up, baseball in hand, and started autographing the baseball. When he was done, Seaver surveyed the hands, gloves and faces all presented to him. He pointed at a seven-year-old, freckle-faced lefty and gently flipped the ball to him. It read "Tom Seaver, HOF '92." The ball remains in our trophy case, right next to the ball that little lefty lined for his first major-league hit on August 16, 2020. We like to think it helped him get there.

Tom Seaver by the Numbers

YEAR	TEAM	W	L	PCT	ERA	G	GS	CG	SHO	SV	IP	H	R	BB	SO
1967	NYM	16	13	.552	2.76	35	34	18	2	0	251.0	224	85	78	170
1968	NYM	16	12	.571	2.20	36	35	14	5	0	278.0	224	73	48	205
1969	NYM	25	7	.781	2.21	36	35	18	5	0	273.0	202	75	82	208
1970	NYM	18	12	.600	2.81	37	36	19	2	0	291.0	230	103	83	283
1971	NYM	20	10	.667	1.76	36	35	21	4	0	286.0	210	61	61	289
1972	NYM	21	12	.636	2.92	35	35	13	3	0	262.0	215	92	77	249
1973	NYM	19	10	.655	2.08	36	36	18	3	0	290.0	219	74	64	251
1974	NYM	11	11	.500	3.20	32	32	12	5	0	236.0	199	89	75	201
1975	NYM	22	9	.710	2.38	36	36	15	5	0	280.0	217	81	88	243
1976	NYM	14	11	.560	2.59	35	34	13	5	0	271.0	211	83	77	235
1977	NYM	7	3	.700	3.00	13	13	5	3	0	96.0	79	33	28	72
1977	CIN	14	3	.824	2.35	20	20	14	4	0	165.0	120	45	38	124
1977	ALL	21	6	.778	2.59	33	33	19	7	0	261.0	199	78	66	196
1978	CIN	16	14	.533	2.87	36	36	8	1	0	260.0	218	97	89	226
1979	CIN	16	6	.727	3.14	32	32	9	5	0	215.0	187	85	61	131
1980	CIN	10	8	.556	3.64	26	26	5	1	0	168.0	140	74	59	101
1981	CIN	14	2	.875	2.55	23	23	6	1	0	166.0	120	51	66	87
1982	CIN	5	13	.278	5.50	21	21	0	0	0	111.1	136	75	44	62
1983	NYM	9	14	.391	3.55	34	34	5	2	0	231.0	201	104	86	135
1984	CHW	15	11	.577	3.95	34	33	10	4	0	236.2	216	108	61	131
1985	CHW	16	11	.593	3.17	35	33	6	1	0	238.2	223	103	69	134
1986	CHW	2	6	.250	4.38	12	12	1	0	0	72.0	66	37	27	31
1986	BOS	5	7	.417	3.80	16	16	1	0	0	104.1	114	46	29	72
1986	ALL	7	13	.350	4.03	28	28	2	0	0	176.1	180	83	56	103
TOTALS		311	205	.603	2.86	656	647	231	61	0	4782.0	3971	1674	1390	3640

TONY GWYNN

GOODBYE, TONY, GOODBYE

DATE: October 7, 2001

SITE: Qualcomm Stadium, San Diego, California

PITCHER: José Jiménez of the Colorado Rockies

RESULT: Groundball to short

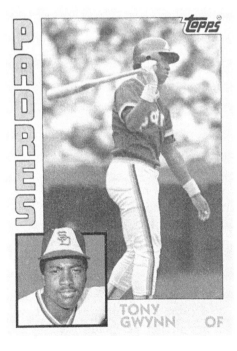

The game, the season, was done.

Two outs away from the end of another disappointing season, 60,013 San Diego Padres fans sat uneasily, peeking into the Padres dugout. They didn't jam Qualcomm Stadium to see two bottom-of-the-barrel NL West teams square off. Or to see much-traveled 42-year-old Rickey Henderson (still two more stops to make!) lead off with a double, score a run, and take himself out of the game. They weren't there to see the final swings of the 2001 National League batting race between Colorado teammates Larry Walker (.350) and Todd Helton (.336). Walker, title safely in hand, had taken the last two days of the season off. Helton played and went 1-for-5 with an RBI double in the fourth in the 14–5 Rockies win.

Those 60,013 were there, it's safe to say, for one reason. To say goodbye to the greatest player in team history, and maybe one of the greatest guys to ever be a part of the game.

Sure enough, the man all those fans waited to see popped out of the Padres dugout one last time, bat in hand. Yes, "Mr. Padre," Tony Gwynn was stepping toward that spot in the batter's box he'd called his own for 20 seasons. Of course, they stood and cheered and roared and wept, many holding signs that read "Thanks, Tony." Then they blinked and it was all over. He hit the first pitch right at shortstop Juan Uribe. One batter later, the season was over and so was Gwynn's career.

As is sometimes the case with even the greatest players of their day, it's difficult to know when it's time to go. For Gwynn, the 2001 season was one last test of his patience and endurance. The chatterbox with the infectious smile and machine-gun laugh had been reduced to a pinch-hitter for this final stretch of his career. Injuries kept him out for most of May and all of June. For most of July and the first part of August, all he could do was pinch-hit. Just one at-bat. On July 11 in Pittsburgh, he decided he'd try to play a whole game and paid for it.

"In 2001, we were playing in Pittsburgh and I started in right field," Gwynn recalled later. "I hit a home run and a double. The next day, everything ached, and I told myself, 'I can't do this any more.'"

From there until the ninth inning of this, the final game of the year, Gwynn's final season consisted of him making 33 pinch-hit appearances (just 5 hits). But no fans of the game asked for any refunds. Just to say they saw Tony Gwynn, it was worth it.

As a lifetime West Coast National League guy, Gwynn probably didn't receive the national recognition he should have. Eight National League batting titles, a .338 lifetime average that certainly dipped a few points with the several-months-long 2001 pinch-hit fest, five Gold Gloves, and eight seasons, including six in a row, when he struck out fewer than 20 times. Some modern hitters would approach 20 strikeouts in a weekend series. One reason for Gwynn's lack of acclaim: He wasn't a home-run hitter, smacking just 135 in 20 seasons.

But as a professional hitter, Gwynn was among the first to use modern technology—video—to perfect his craft. And he did. The proof?

- He reached 3,000 hits in just 2,284 games and 8,874 at-bats.
- Highest lifetime mark (.338) of any player born after 1900.
- Six-straight seasons with fewer than 20 strikeouts.
- Had a .400 or better career average against eight of game's Cy Young Award winners (Greg Maddux, John Smoltz, Bret Saberhagen, Vida Blue, John Denny, Dennis Eckersley, Mark Davis, Doug Drabek).
- Punished the key starters on the Atlanta Braves pitching staff—Greg Maddux (39-for-94, .415), John Smoltz (32-for-72, .444), and Tom Glavine (30-for-99, .303).
- Never fanned vs. Maddux (94 at-bats), Pedro Martínez (35 at-bats), Mike Hampton (33 at-bats), or Hideo Nomo (25 at-bats).

The year everyone mentions with Gwynn, of course, was the strike-shortened 1994 season when Gwynn, collecting nine hits in his last 18 at-bats, had lifted his average to .394 on August 11, when the season was halted. Might he have done it?

He certainly had the league figured out. As Phillies manager and former big-league catcher Joe Girardi said, Gwynn was unstoppable. "When I think of Tony Gwynn, I think of it from a catcher's perspective, how difficult it was to get him out. You look at zones where guys hit the ball, breaking pitches they hit, and there were no cold zones. I mean, the joke used to be, 'Throw it right down the middle, because that's the only pitch he didn't know what to do with.' If you throw outside, he'd hit to left. If you throw it inside, he'd hit it to right. He sprayed the ball all over the place and played a great right field. But he was a gentleman, too. He always had a smile on his face when he played the game. He was a real student of the game. He was a guy who everyone tried to learn from, in a sense, because he was such a good player. You wanted to know his thoughts about the game and hitting."

But as good a player and as nice a guy as he was, a story from that season hinted at the competitive fires that inspired him. After a 5-for-5 night against the Phillies in April that season, Gwynn was riding home with his 11-year-old son, a future big leaguer, and made a prediction.

"They're going to hit me tomorrow," he told his son, Tony Gwynn Jr., who shared that story with Kirk Kenney of the *San Diego Tribune* in 2019. "They think I'm stealing signs."

Sure enough, Curt Schilling drilled Gwynn in the thigh in the first pitch of his first at-bat. In the third inning, Gwynn lined a ball past Schilling for a single. He singled again in the fourth, tying a franchise record with his eighth consecutive hit. After a groundout in the sixth, Gwynn singled again in the eighth, raising his batting average to .448.

"I felt like the incident with Curt Schilling lit a fire," Tony Gwynn Jr. recalled. "I've never seen my dad that upset. Never seen him get up and yell and point. From that point forward, not only was Curt Schilling never going to get him out again, but the rest of the league was in trouble. Because he was just locked in. He was pissed. Pissed."

Gwynn stayed locked in, pretty much, from then on, five times posting the highest average in all of baseball (.351 in 1984, .370 in 1987, .394 in 1994, .368 in 1995, and .372 in 1997 at age 37). Fellow San Diego native Ted Williams—at 38—hit .388 with 38 home runs and 87 RBIs in 1957, impressive numbers for old-timers. They joked about it.

"Ted looked at me and said, 'If I knew that hitting .400 would have been so damn important, I would have done it more often,'" Gwynn said once. "I just laughed. But the more I thought about that, he probably could have hit .400 again if he had wanted." Gwynn actually did hit .400 during the 162-game stretch from August 1, 1993, to May 9, 1995, batting .406 by going 242-for-596. But for an entire season? That was his run at history.

On January 9, 2007, Gwynn learned that he had joined Williams in baseball's most exclusive club, the Hall of Fame in Cooperstown, New York. Video of that morning shows Gwynn, in a sleeveless San Diego State sweater and white shirt, looking heavy and nervous.

He had been telling everyone not to expect the call, even though he'd been tipped off the call would come at 10:30 a.m. When there was no ring, by 10:31, Gwynn was telling everyone around him, "See . . ." Just then, the phone did ring. "This is Jack O'Connell of the Baseball Writers. . . . I'm calling to tell you the baseball writers have elected you to the Hall of Fame. Congratulations."

Whereupon Tony Gwynn nodded three times, rubbed his right eye with his right hand, and started to cry. "I never thought this would happen," he told his wife, Alicia.

A year after he retired, Gwynn brought his love for the game and his experience to San Diego State University, where he took over the baseball program and would likely still be there if salivary gland cancer— Gwynn, like many of his era, was a relentless dipper—hadn't claimed him just five weeks after he had turned 54 in the sad summer of 2014.

GWYNN.

That his career would take him to the Hall of Fame was difficult to imagine. A guy undrafted out of high school, who went to college on a basketball scholarship and didn't even get to play college baseball at first, winds up with eight batting titles, 3,141 hits, and more "what a nice guy" stories than anyone since Stan Musial.

The often-caustic Keith Olbermann said as much in an emotional tribute to Gwynn on TV. When Gwynn and his Padres got to go to Yankee Stadium for the 1998 World Series, Gwynn was delighted to get a chance to play in the Bronx and, to hear Olbermann tell it, just as excited to meet the Yankees' legendary public address announcer Bob Sheppard. When Olbermann told Sheppard this, he said "Take me to him" which Olbermann was happy to. The pair sat and chatted happily for 15–20 minutes, a photo was snapped and later on, Olbermann used the photo in a talking picture frame with Sheppard's hallowed Yankee Stadium introduction of Gwynn: "Now batting for San Diego, number 19, the right fielder, Tony Gwynn, number 19." And Gwynn, sounding so much like a mortal man unexpectedly standing on the shoulders of the game's giants, was beyond excited.

"'It's in my trophy case,' he giggled," Olbermann explained on his Gwynn tribute. "It's with my silver bats (for eight batting titles). I keep pushing

"Play" I'm going to wear the thing out. . . . This is the coolest thing. I'm even trying to say it along with him.'"

"You don't have to have the privilege of knowing him to be heartbroken right now," Olbermann concluded. "What you hoped Tony Gwynn was like, he was like."

Tony Gwynn by the Numbers

YEAR	TEAM	G	AB	R	H	TB	2B	3B	HR	RBI	BB	SO	SB	BA	SLG	OBP
1982	SD	54	190	33	55	74	12	2	1	17	14	16	8	.289	.389	.337
1983	SD	86	304	34	94	113	12	2	1	37	23	21	7	.309	.372	.355
1984	SD	158	606	88	213	269	21	10	5	71	59	23	33	.351	.444	.410
1985	SD	154	622	90	197	254	29	5	6	46	45	33	14	.317	.408	.364
1986	SD	160	642	107	211	300	33	7	14	59	52	35	37	.329	.467	.381
1987	SD	157	589	119	218	301	36	13	7	54	82	35	56	.370	.511	.447
1988	SD	133	521	64	163	216	22	5	7	70	51	40	26	.313	.415	.373
1989	SD	158	604	82	203	256	27	7	4	62	56	30	40	.336	.424	.389
1990	SD	141	573	79	177	238	29	10	4	72	44	23	17	.309	.415	.357
1991	SD	134	530	69	168	229	27	11	4	62	34	19	8	.317	.432	.355
1992	SD	128	520	77	165	216	27	3	6	41	46	16	3	.317	.415	.371
1993	SD	122	489	70	175	243	41	3	7	59	36	19	14	.358	.497	.398
1994	SD	110	419	79	165	238	35	1	12	64	48	19	5	.394	.568	.454
1995	SD	135	535	82	197	259	33	1	9	90	35	15	17	.368	.484	.404
1996	SD	116	451	67	159	199	27	2	3	50	39	17	11	.353	.441	.400
1997	SD	149	592	97	220	324	49	2	17	119	43	28	12	.372	.547	.409
1998	SD	127	461	65	148	231	35	0	16	69	35	18	3	.321	.501	.364
1999	SD	111	411	59	139	196	27	0	10	62	29	14	7	.338	.477	.381
2000	SD	36	127	17	41	56	12	0	1	17	9	4	0	.323	.441	.364
2001	SD	71	102	5	33	47	9	1	1	17	10	9	1	.324	.461	.384
TOTALS		2440	9288	1383	3141	4259	543	85	135	1138	790	434	319	.338	.459	.388

CHIPPER JONES

LESS THAN CHIPPER FINALE

DATE: October 5, 2012

SITE: Turner Field, Atlanta, Georgia

PITCHER: Jason Motte of the St. Louis Cardinals

RESULT: Broken-bat infield hit

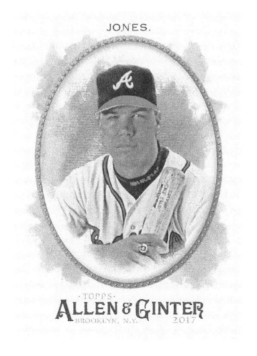

If Clair Bee hadn't already gotten around to creating a character named Chip Hilton for his youthful sports novels in the 1950s and 1960s, he might have chosen Atlanta Braves Hall of Famer Larry Wayne "Chipper" Jones Jr. as his protagonist.

A high school star as a football quarterback and a two-way player in baseball at Jacksonville Bolles, if ever there was a high schooler born to play the game, it was Chipper Jones. All you had to do was watch him play the infield or swing a bat. His father had groomed him for this job, and everybody who watched him play from the time he was a youngster had a two-word assessment: big leaguer.

His dad, who had played at Stetson University, painted a strike zone on the back of a garage and began one-on-one duels with his son as soon as "Chipper"—as in "a chip off the ol' block"—was able. An article from the Society of American Baseball Research explains what those wars were like. "They would play one-on-one games in the backyard, running through the lineup of the Los Angeles Dodgers, father and son's shared favorite team. When Steve Garvey or Ron Cey came up, Chipper would bat right-handed like the real major-leaguers did. When Reggie Smith or Ken Landreaux was up, he would switch to the left side. By the time Chipper was 11 years old, his father could no longer beat him in their backyard games."

The success carried over to high school where scouts were quick to notice his potential. The Turner Field Scouting Report display out behind the left field bleachers talked about his athletic gifts in glowing terms—not something baseball scouts are prone to do.

"Tall, well-proportioned thoroughbred type athletic body," the report began. "Long arms and legs. May fill out some but his body is very impressive. Strong with sloping shoulders."

It continues: "Soft hands. Very smooth fielding and throwing actions. Done everything easy. Excellent instincts for the game. Could be all star in ML."

"Weaknesses: None that I see at present."

Considering the Atlanta Braves made Jones the first overall pick of the 1990 Major League Draft, they evidently agreed with the scout's assessment. You'd have to say, other than Alex Rodriguez, who was the number one pick of the Seattle Mariners three years later, or Ken Griffey Jr., Seattle's number one overall in 1987, Jones has likely paid the most dividends from that number one slot. Some will argue that Hall of Famer Harold Baines, also a number one overall, deserves consideration.

Going back seven years, there hasn't been a real big-league standout so far—other than perhaps Dansby Swanson from that list of number ones—Mark Appel, Brady Aiken, Mickey Moniak, Royce Lewis, Casey Mize, Adley Rutschman, and Spencer Torkelson have yet to make an impact the way Jones did, moving into the Braves' lineup as a 22-year-old and sticking around for 19 impactful seasons.

As Braves GM Frank Wren told Jayson Stark a few years ago, Chipper is the guy who's had "the greatest value to the organization that picked him. How about that? I think you could make that case, from a standpoint of, he's spent his whole career with one organization, and had a Hall of Fame career, whereas other guys haven't necessarily done that."

For the longest time, it seemed if you went to a Braves game, there would be Chipper in the middle of the lineup, hitting around .300, driving in around 100 runs, hitting around 30 or more homers. He was named the NL's MVP in 1999 with these numbers: .319 batting average, 45 homers, 110 RBIs. But he threw up at least eight other years with similar numbers. He was that good.

One of the game's finest switch-hitters since Mickey Mantle, his father's favorite player, Jones was a worthy successor. Jones was amazingly consistent from either side of the plate, hitting .303 for his career overall: .303 from the left side, .304 from the right side. Mantle, for example, hit .330 as a righty, .281 as a lefty. Most switch-hitters favor one side over the other. Chipper was almost identical, though 361 of his 468 homers came from the left side. But with almost twice as many at-bats left-handed, that makes sense.

He was a little more streaky in the middle part of his career. After six years over .300, he dipped to a career low .248 in 2004 but then soared as high as .364 in 2008, earning his only batting title. The next year, 100 points lower. Go figure.

By 2012, as Jones turned 40, he was an old-timer out there. The Braves' dynasty was winding down, finally. Tom Glavine, John Smoltz, and Greg Maddux were gone. So was Manager Bobby Cox and ever-rockin' pitching coach Leo Mazzone. Chipper was just fourth on the team in home runs with 14, just sixth in RBIs with 62. But it was a fine farewell.

"There have been so many cool things that have happened to me this year," he told Jayson Stark then. "The fans' appreciation and [opposing] teams' appreciation, that's been unbelievable in and of itself. And there have just been so many cool things that have happened on the field: My first five-hit game at home [July 3, against the Cubs]. I've never done that before. A couple of walk-offs [two homers that won games the Braves once trailed by six runs] at home. Man, that's the apex. Home run on my [40th] birthday. Home run in my first start of the season, with my parents in the stands. Two homers on my bobblehead day. Just some really, really cool moments where, as the balls are flying out of the park, I'm running down to first, saying, 'You have got to be kidding me. Did that just happen?'"

But the magic faded away. After a dramatic walkoff home run against the Phillies' Jonathan Papelbon on September 2, capping a wild Braves rally, Jones went without another home run, with his batting average dipping from .304 on September 1 down to .287. It seemed, at last, as if all those innings, all those games, almost 9,000 at-bats, had finally worn him down. A writer, interviewing Jones before the final homestand, noted the fatigue, the toll 19 straight 162-game seasons had taken on a major-league regular. He looked ready for a nap and the game was minutes away.

To the average fan, watching games on TV or even from the stands, there's no sense of the personal, physical, or psychic toll playing these endless games in all time zones from February through October takes on an individual. They're handsomely paid, treated as royalty, so they have to work for three hours a day, what's the big deal? Unless you've been through it or knew someone who had, there's no way for you to understand just how exhausting it is.

Jones had considered retiring a couple years earlier but this time, before the 2012 season began, the Braves issued a press release, saying that Chipper would retire at the end of the season. The Braves' regular season concluded in Pittsburgh, but their second-place finish in the NL East earned them a wild card spot against the St. Louis Cardinals back in Atlanta. Chipper would get to play at least one more game at home before Braves fans.

As one of the few one-team players left in the game, there would inevitably be a lot of emotion there, friends and families and long-retired teammates stopping by for the farewell. This was not lost on Chipper Jones, who talked about it in *Chipper Jones, Ballplayer*, his memoir written with Carroll Rogers Walton.

"The last week of the season was a blur," he wrote. "More than fifty thousand fans showed up at Turner Field for a ceremony the Braves held in my honor before our final home series against the Mets. I could look up from my seat on the infield and see fans flashing number 10 posters all over the stadium. I was sitting on a stage with Hank Aaron and Bobby Cox, John Schuerholz, Paul Snyder and Tony DeMacio, the scout who signed me. I had my boys and my parents up there with me. I was emotionally exhausted before the first pitch was thrown. I went 0-for-4 that night and as I told Josh Thole, the Mets' catcher, 'How am I supposed to hit with all this going on?'"

From there, it was on to Pittsburgh where Jones played the first game and went 0-for-3. He came in as a pinch-hitter, leading off the sixth in Wednesday's regular-season finale, and after a generous ovation from the Pittsburgh faithful, all 20,615 of them, then went and promptly lined A. J. Burnett's first pitch into right field for a single, his 2,726th major-league hit.

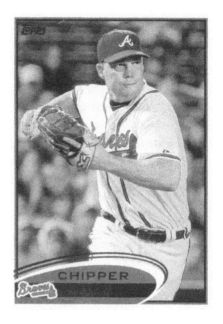

Only 2726? That number shows you how difficult it is to get 3,000 hits. Here's Chipper Jones, a surefire Hall of Famer, a 19-year major-leaguer, an eight-time All-Star and former MVP, and at retirement, he was probably two seasons away from 3,000 hits (274 away!) You could say the same goes for Chipper's home-run total, which, as great a player as he was, wound up 32 homers away from the magical number of 500 (468).

After flying back from Pittsburgh, the Braves sent Kris Medlen (10-1, 1.57) against the Cardinals' Kyle Lohse (16-3, 2.86) in the wild card game under the lights before 52,631 at Turner Field. The Cardinals (88-74) were a well-balanced team, as usual, with five guys with 20 or more homers and a solid pitching staff.

The Braves struck first in the second after Lohse had fanned Jones and Freddie Freeman. Dan Uggla worked a walk and catcher David Ross connected with a two-run homer to stake Medlen to a 2–0 lead. That fell apart in the fourth when Carlos Beltrán lashed a single to right and Matt Holliday a potential double-play ball right to Jones, who hurried the throw and sailed it into right field. An Allen Craig double, an infield out, and a sacrifice fly and it was a 3–2 St. Louis lead.

After Holliday reached Medlen for a solo home run in the sixth, Jones, who had bounced out to end the third, got another chance, but led off the sixth with a popout to second. The Braves infield struggled again in the seventh, and two infield errors led to two more Cardinal runs without the Birds hitting the ball out of the infield.

The Braves rallied in the seventh when pinch-hitter José Constanza tripled and scored on an infield out. Martín Prado singled, chasing reliever Edward Mujica. When Jason Heyward smacked reliever Marc Rzepczynski's second pitch into left field for a double, the stage was set for Jones to do something dramatic. Not this time. He rapped Rzepczynski's second pitch on the ground to second, ending the rally, the Braves' still trailing, 6–3.

In the eighth, the Braves loaded the bases against reliever Jason Motte, but he fanned Michael Bourn to end the inning. That meant Chipper Jones would have one final at-bat at Turner Field in the bottom of the ninth. Reliever Motte got Prado to bounce out and Heyward to fly to left.

Up came Chipper Jones, who talked about this moment in *Ballplayer*. "I've always prided myself on never being the last out of the game," he wrote. "The last game of my career was no different. . . . People can say what they want to say about the infield fly [a weird play that cost the Braves mightily in the eighth] but the most important play in that game was my error. If I had turned the double play, it would have been a completely different game, infield fly or not.

"I put all that in the back of my mind in the bottom of the ninth. We were down to our final out. . . . No way I was going to be the last out."

"I looked over to the visitor's dugout, and all the Cardinals were standing on the top step clapping. Yadier Molina, their catcher, went and stood out in front of home plate, giving the crowd a chance to cheer for me one more time. I tipped my cap to the fans. Then I put my helmet back on and told Yadi 'Let's go, baby.'"

Motte was amped up and threw the first fastball by Jones, who swung and missed. After a pitch away, Motte challenged him again and Jones fouled it back. He was 1-2, one strike away.

"Motte had really good stuff, but guys who throw 95-to-100 mph were right up my alley," Jones said. "The problem was not only did I get 97 when I got to two strikes but it cut."

On the sixth pitch of the at-bat, the Turner Field crowd snapping pictures, screaming and hollering, Jones connected. Well, sort of.

"My bat exploded into pieces on contact, and I thought, *Oh no* and I hit a slow roller up the middle, and second baseman Daniel Descalso made a great jump throw. I almost stopped running, thinking I was out, but the throw pulled Allen Craig off the bag, and I just beat him to it."

Well, maybe. Craig was pulled off the bag but dabbed back with his foot just as Jones was arriving. First base umpire Mike Winters said he was safe. TBS (the Braves' home network) showed a replay but did not slow it down for a particularly careful examination and there did not seem to be any protest from the Cardinals dugout. Call it an infield hit. OK.

The Braves' future MVP, Freddie Freeman, followed with a double to bring the tying run to the plate. But Dan Uggla grounded out, and the Braves' season and Chipper's career had come to an end.

It sure wasn't the kind of goodbye Jones hoped for with his 255th career error (11 in the postseason) and a miserable performance at the plate (0-for-4 before the broken-bat "single"). He hadn't made an error since September 12, when he mishandled a Jeff Bianchi slow roller in a game at Miller Park. At least it wasn't Buckneresque. There was time in that game for the Braves to come back. They just couldn't. And this time, for the last time, Chipper Jones couldn't help them.

Chipper Jones by the Numbers

YEAR	TEAM	G	AB	R	H	TB	2B	3B	HR	RBI	BB	SO	SB	BA	SLG	OBP
1993	ATL	8	3	2	2	3	1	0	0	0	1	1	0	.667	1.000	.750
1994	ATL	0	0	0	0	0	0	0	0	0	0	0	0	---	---	----
1995	ATL	140	524	87	139	236	22	3	23	86	73	99	8	.265	.450	.353
1996	ATL	157	598	114	185	317	32	5	30	110	87	88	14	.309	.530	.393
1997	ATL	157	597	100	176	286	41	3	21	111	76	88	20	.295	.479	.371
1998	ATL	160	601	123	188	329	29	5	34	107	96	93	16	.313	.547	.404
1999	ATL	157	567	116	181	359	41	1	45	110	126	94	25	.319	.633	.441
2000	ATL	156	579	118	180	328	38	1	36	111	95	64	14	.311	.566	.404
2001	ATL	159	572	113	189	346	33	5	38	102	98	82	9	.330	.605	.427
2002	ATL	158	548	90	179	294	35	1	26	100	107	89	8	.327	.536	.435
2003	ATL	153	555	103	169	287	33	2	27	106	94	83	2	.305	.517	.402
2004	ATL	137	472	69	117	229	20	1	30	96	84	96	2	.248	.485	.362
2005	ATL	109	358	66	106	199	30	0	21	72	72	56	5	.296	.556	.412
2006	ATL	110	411	87	133	245	28	3	26	86	61	73	6	.324	.596	.409
2007	ATL	134	513	108	173	310	42	4	29	102	82	75	5	.337	.604	.425
2008	ATL	128	439	82	160	252	24	1	22	75	90	61	4	.364	.574	.470
2009	ATL	143	488	80	129	210	23	2	18	71	101	89	4	.264	.430	.388
2010	ATL	95	317	47	84	135	21	0	10	46	61	47	5	.265	.426	.381
2011	ATL	126	455	56	125	214	33	1	18	70	51	80	2	.275	.470	.344
2012	ATL	112	387	58	111	176	23	0	14	62	57	51	1	.287	.455	.377
TOTALS		2499	8984	1619	2726	4755	549	38	468	1623	1512	1409	150	.303	.529	.401

KEN GRIFFEY JR.

THE KID IS OUTTA HERE

DATE: May 31, 2010

SITE: Safeco Field, Seattle, Washington

PITCHER: Jon Rauch of the Minnesota Twins

RESULT: Groundout to second base

What if William Shakespeare, building to that dramatic swordfight that brings down the curtain on *Hamlet*, saw his main character toss the broadsword to the stage and walk off? And that was the end of the play. No heroics, no drama. Just a bummer for everybody.

In baseball terms, that's about what happened in the ninth inning of Ken Griffey's final appearance on a major-league baseball diamond. A small crowd (19,795), a weeknight game with the Minnesota Twins for a rotten Seattle Mariners team (19-31), and the game drifts into the ninth, the Twins up 5–3, when José López slashed one down the left field line off Twins reliever Jon Rauch and Josh Wilson bounces one through the infield to score López to make it 5–4. And look who's coming up. . . .

Unlike a play, the ending of a professional baseball career can't be scripted. For every Ted Williams, who leaves the game with a dramatic home run on his final swing, there's a Bob Gibson, screaming obscenities at Pete LaCock as he rounded the bases after Gibson surrendered a grand slam on his final big-league pitch. Or the magnificent Babe Ruth, looking wholly out of place in a baggy Boston Braves uniform, limping off the field for the last time after a feeble groundball. Or Jackie Robinson, making the final out of the 1956 World Series chasing a Johnny Kucks sinker in the dirt, the game's only Dodger strikeout, ending a season, a Series, and a career, all on a single pitch.

If there ever was someone who looked born to play the game, it might have been Ken Griffey Jr. Sure, his father was a fine big leaguer (career average .296 over 19 seasons) and yes, he was born in Donora, Pennsylvania on November 21, same day as the great Cardinal Stan "The Man" Musial, and he found himself in the big leagues at 19 years old and got to play alongside his dad in a big-league outfield in August of the next year. Hit back-to-back home runs too, that September 14, only time a father-son ever did that in the big leagues. But forget all that. Just watch him.

It may be unfair and even a bit silly to talk about elegance or style when describing a guy in a baseball uniform running around a field. But there was an easy eloquence to Griffey on the diamond that was impossible not to notice. Other players might have scampered, bolted, dashed for a flyball: Griffey glided.

At the plate, Griffey stood erect and deep in the left-hand batter's box, bat cocked and wiggly. When he launched his majestic swing, a fluid, natural uppercut, it always seemed effortless, never hurried or late. As many have written, he, indeed, looked born to play the game. Which, looking back, perhaps made all of us assume he wasn't ever really giving 100 percent, even when he was. The game looked too easy to him.

For the first 10 years of his brilliant career, who would argue? Through age 30 (November 21, 1999), Griffey had smacked 398 homers, more than anyone else had ever amassed at that age. His career average was a point under .300, he'd won 10 straight Gold Gloves, and seemed to be peaking, averaging over 50 home runs a year over the preceding four years.

But the team was maddeningly inconsistent: 90-72 in 1997, 76-85 in 1998. Despite Hall of Fame talents like Alex Rodriguez, Edgar Martínez, and Randy Johnson, the Mariners could never go anywhere in the playoffs and somehow, Griffey seemed to be the player who caught more of the blame.

After he requested a trade following the 1999 season, he received a death threat in the mail at his Florida home in November. The *Seattle Times* broke the story in early February. Griffey was ready for a change. The player so many fans watched grow up was grown up. And fed up.

"When you get death threats from Seattle fans, then that's bad," he said then. "Something like that is pretty much the last straw as far as me staying in Seattle. You might be able to control where you play, but you can't control what happens to your family. I can." Griffey had agreed to a trade only to his hometown Cincinnati Reds.

"I don't know if I'm gone or not, but I'm not going to worry about it anymore," Griffey said at the time. "It's out of my hands. The way I look at it, I have a job, somewhere, whether it's Seattle or Cincinnati. That's the way it is. I gave the Mariners an option that if they wanted to trade me, they could trade me. But it's got to be where I want to go. And I'm the bad guy in this? I don't get it." New Mariners GM Pat Gillick had discussed a trade with the New York Mets, but Griffey declined. Mariners management was displeased and to Griffey's mind, poisoned the water for him.

"How can I come back there and play?" Griffey told the *Seattle Times*. "You've got everybody pretty much against me. You've got the fans thinking I'm whining, I'm a baby and whatever, because that's what Pat said. Somebody in the front office called me a spoiled brat because I didn't accept the trade to New York. I turned down $140 million from the Mariners. Does that sound like a guy who cares about the money?"

No, it sounds like a guy sick of the fans, the game, the money, all of it. And maybe he was.

Griffey's first year in Cincinnati was successful: 40 home runs, 118 RBIs to go with a .271 average. But you didn't hear any more talk about the joy in his game, him chasing the game's all-time records, about how he made baseball fun. Because it didn't look like fun anymore. And, honestly, it wasn't.

Injuries, particularly to his legs, came one after another. The next year, the numbers dipped to .286, 22 homers, and 65 RBIs in 111 games. The next three years—2002–2004—with the Reds were filled with more injuries, more missed games—70 games, 53 games, 83 games.

His last really strong season was in 2005—.301, 35, 92 with Cincinnati. At age 38, he spent a year with the White Sox, limited to just 41 games and 131 at-bats (.260, 3, 18). Seattle brought him back for old times' sake for two desultory, most un-Griffey-like seasons: 2009 (214, 19, 57) and the sad 2010 (.184, 0, 7 in just 33 games).

It turned out Griffey's final major-league home run, his 630th, came the year before on June 27, in the final game at the Kingdome. The sad, sudden decline in his game altered our perspective of Griffey's place in the game in his prime. In the 1990s, he was an amazing player, perhaps even better than seven-time MVP Barry Bonds over that span:

- Bonds: .302, 361 HR, 299 doubles, 343 steals, 8 Gold Gloves, 3 MVP awards
- Griffey: .302, 382 HR, 297 doubles, 151 steals, 10 Gold Gloves, 1 MVP

That guy, that player, was just a memory when Griffey was summoned from the dugout in the ninth inning on the final night of May in 2010. He got a nice ovation, stepped in, took a strike, then one-handed an offspeed pitch from Rauch on a couple lazy hops to second baseman Nick Punto. Punto fired to second for the force out and when Justin Morneau couldn't pick J. J. Hardy's throw out of the dirt, Griffey was safe at first. He left for pinch-runner Michael Saunders. Casey Kotchman then rapped into a game-ending double play and that night, Griffey decided he'd had enough.

He didn't come to the park the next night or meet the press. As the newspapers reported it: "The 40-year-old Griffey wasn't at Safeco Field on Wednesday. He simply released a statement through the Seattle Mariners—the franchise he helped save in the 1990s and returned to for the conclusion of his career—that he was done playing." Griffey said goodbye after 13 All-Star appearances, 630 homers—then fifth on the career list—and 1,836 RBIs.

"'While I feel I am still able to make a contribution on the field and nobody in the Mariners front office has asked me to retire, I told the Mariners when I met with them prior to the 2009 season and was invited back that I will never allow myself to become a distraction,'" Griffey said in the release. "'I feel that without enough occasional starts to be sharper coming off the bench, my continued presence as a player would be an unfair distraction to my teammates and their success as a team is what the ultimate goal should be.'"

"There will be no farewell tour, just as Griffey wanted," the release continued. "He called Mariners team president Chuck Armstrong and said he was done playing. Mariners manager Don Wakamatsu called his players together before the start of batting practice to inform them of Griffey's decision."

No, "See ya, guys" or hugs in the clubhouse or farewell handshakes. Just a press release. In fact, it was worse than that. More on that in a minute.

His final hit was a dandy, a walkoff single 11 days earlier against Toronto closer Kevin Gregg, winning the game, 4–3, capping a ninth-inning rally. But that same day, sportswriter Larry Larue of the *News-Tribune* reported that Manager Don Wakamatsu did not use Griffey as a pinch-hitter the previous week because he had been asleep in the clubhouse. It caused an uproar. A teammate (Mike Sweeney) challenged anyone to fight him if they continued to say Griffey was asleep. Larue was then boycotted by Mariners players. It was an ugly scene.

So, after that final groundout, Griffey decided he'd had his fill, got in his car, and drove back home across the country to Florida.

Team president Chuck Armstrong found out about Griffey's decision from Griffey's agent the next day, just before game time. Griffey called in from the road to make sure he understood it was over.

It may be understating it to say baseball wasn't fun for Griffey anymore. A decade of injuries, constant disappointment, no World Series appearances, just two All-Star Games over the last 10 years of his career after starting with 10 All-Star invites in a row, and those sliding statistics, left him in a bad place.

Just listen to him talking with a sportswriter near the end.

"People won't understand," Griffey told Terry Mosher in 1997. "How can a 9-to-5 person know what it is like for the 25 guys right here in this clubhouse? How can they understand what I do? Somebody who is making $50,000 a year—then me. They can't. It's numbers, (my stats) that's all it is. That's all they know.

"You guys will write what you want anyway. So why should I say anything? How, for example, would me rating my season dictate what you guys write? It doesn't."

The bitterness, the disillusionment was almost haunting. The chosen one, the favorite of the Baseball Gods seemingly could not get that taste out of his mouth when things went south. Perhaps we should have expected it.

Growing up running around big-league clubhouses with his dad, moving to the major leagues at age 19, having immediate, stunning success, playing 51 games with his dad in the majors, followed by talk of him becoming one of the game's all-timers, how could anyone handle it when the hits stopped coming?

It wasn't until years later that we learned that, as a teenager, Griffey had attempted suicide, swallowing 277 aspirin tablets (isn't it great that we know the precise details?). The desperation in that move, the startling reappraisal of a life that had seemed so charmed was revelatory. Maybe the life was chosen *for* him, not *by* him.

In 2001, in his *Historical Baseball Abstract*, numbers guru Bill James ranked Griffey as the seventh best center fielder of all time, trailing—in order—Willie Mays, Ty Cobb, Mickey Mantle, Tris Speaker, Joe DiMaggio, and Duke Snider. Quite a cast.

Happily for Griffey, the baseball writers focused on the big picture, not the ugly end. In 2016, Griffey was an overwhelming choice for the Baseball Hall of Fame, collecting 99.32 percent of the votes, bettering Tom Seaver's 98.84 mark—both since bettered by Mariano Rivera's unanimous selection in 2019.

Ken Griffey Jr. by the Numbers

YEAR	TEAM	G	AB	R	H	TB	2B	3B	HR	RBI	BB	SO	SB	BA	SLG	OBP
1989	SEA	127	455	61	120	191	23	0	16	61	44	83	16	.264	.420	.329
1990	SEA	155	597	91	179	287	28	7	22	80	63	81	16	.300	.481	.366
1991	SEA	154	548	76	179	289	42	1	22	100	71	82	18	.327	.527	.399
1992	SEA	142	565	83	174	302	39	4	27	103	44	67	10	.308	.535	.361
1993	SEA	156	582	113	180	359	38	3	45	109	96	91	17	.309	.617	.408
1994	SEA	111	433	94	140	292	24	4	40	90	56	73	11	.323	.674	.402
1995	SEA	72	260	52	67	125	7	0	17	42	52	53	4	.258	.481	.379
1996	SEA	140	545	125	165	342	26	2	49	140	78	104	16	.303	.628	.392
1997	SEA	157	608	125	185	393	34	3	56	147	76	121	15	.304	.646	.382
1998	SEA	161	633	120	180	387	33	3	56	146	76	121	20	.284	.611	.365
1999	SEA	160	606	123	173	349	26	3	48	134	91	108	24	.285	.576	.384
2000	CIN	145	520	100	141	289	22	3	40	118	94	117	6	.271	.556	.387
2001	CIN	111	364	57	104	194	20	2	22	65	44	72	2	.286	.533	.365
2002	CIN	70	197	17	52	84	8	0	8	23	28	39	1	.264	.426	.358
2003	CIN	53	166	34	41	94	12	1	13	26	27	44	1	.247	.566	.370
2004	CIN	83	300	49	76	154	18	0	20	60	44	67	1	.253	.513	.351
2005	CIN	128	491	85	148	283	30	0	35	92	54	93	0	.301	.576	.369
2006	CIN	109	428	62	108	208	19	0	27	72	39	78	0	.252	.486	.316
2007	CIN	144	528	78	146	262	24	1	30	93	85	99	6	.277	.496	.372
2008	CIN	102	359	51	88	155	20	1	15	53	61	64	0	.245	.432	.355
2008	CHW	41	131	16	34	53	10	0	3	18	17	25	0	.260	.405	.347
2008	ALL	143	490	67	122	208	30	1	18	71	78	89	0	.249	.424	.353
2009	SEA	117	387	44	83	159	19	0	19	57	63	80	0	.214	.411	.324
2010	SEA	33	98	6	18	20	2	0	0	7	9	17	0	.184	.204	.250
TOTALS		2671	9801	1662	2781	5271	524	38	630	1836	1312	1779	184	.284	.538	.370

NOLAN RYAN

"LIKE A RUBBER BAND"

DATE: September 22, 1993

SITE: Kingdome, Seattle, Washington

HITTER: Dave Magadan of the Seattle Mariners

RESULT: Left with a 2-1 count

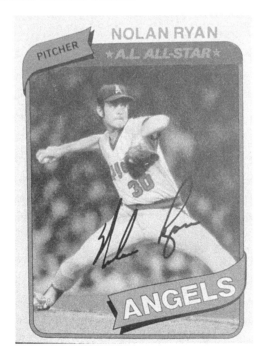

When the third-to-the-last pitch of his career was struck for a first-inning grand slam by the left-handed bat of the somewhat-less-than-immortal Dann Howitt (the fifth and final home run of Howitt's brief career), Nolan Ryan may have had his first inkling that he'd wandered out to a major-league mound one time too many.

At 46, he'd tried and tried and tried to help the Rangers in this, his 27th big-league season, but his body wouldn't cooperate. He missed some 22 days after surgery on his left or landing knee. Missed another 72 days because of a strained hip muscle, another 21 with a strained muscle in his rib cage.

"This whole year has just been a nightmare," Ryan said then. "All I've dealt with all year is frustration. Not only the physical aspect of it, but from the standpoint of not being able to help the club in a pennant race when they really needed me."

With that 5–0 Seattle lead staring back at him from the scoreboard having allowed his eighth career slam, the count 1-1 on Dave Magadan, Ryan did what Ryan had done for 5,386 previous innings, reached back for a little extra—and heard a "pop."

It was the ulnar collateral ligament; "it popped like a rubber band," Ryan said. He threw one more pitch, just to see, called a ball, then left the mound. "It's a hell of a way to end a career," Ryan said. He was right.

For those of us who were fortunate enough to see him pitch in person—and hell, you had 27 years to do it—there was something about the way Ryan threw a baseball that leaving his hand it seemed smaller than anyone else's, more like a dart than a sphere. Even when batters successfully made contact, the ball seemed to be surprised and unable to handle it.

Sure, Ryan gave up quite a few home runs (321); in a 27-year career, you're bound to. But over 5,386 career innings, he allowed just 3,923 hits. So that means he threw 1,463 major-league innings without allowing a hit or roughly the entire career of, say, a Stephen Strasburg to this point.

How many innings was that? Well, if someone ordered Nolan Ryan to throw a nine-inning complete game every day for a team's complete 162-game season, he could have pitched for 3.694 seasons. Just him. Every day. He would have been a team's whole staff for a little over three and a half seasons.

According to the trusty Baseball-Reference.com page, Ryan threw 222 complete games with 61 shutouts. That includes a record seven no-hitters, a dozen one-hitters, 18 two-hitters, and 69 three-hitters. Talk about dominance.

Ryan also, however, managed to walk 2,795 hitters, by far the most of anyone in baseball history. He also threw 277 wild pitches, roughly 10 a year, hit 158 batters, and made 90 errors. According to a recent Joe Posnanski article, Ryan also surrendered 757 steals or 200 more than any other pitcher in the modern era.

Which means Ryan almost certainly cost himself wins with (A.) walks, (B.) bad fielding by himself, (C.) wild pitches, (D.) players getting tired of watching him pitch from the stretch, and (E.) his team not scoring any damn runs for him. And indeed, Ryan lost 292 games, and plenty of them were because of lack of run support. In 1987, for example, as a 40-year-old, he led the National League with a 2.76 ERA. He was 8-16.

He also won 324 games, sometimes pitching, as noted, with pretty bad teams. For 27 seasons, every fourth or fifth day, you could count on something unusual happening when number 34 took the mound.

The baseball seemed to react differently coming out of his hand. If you got close enough, it even seemed to make a different sound. Early in his career, there were stories about Ryan soaking his fingers, particularly his middle finger, in pickle brine to toughen the skin. The middle finger, of course, was appropriate as Ryan's salute to major-league hitters. (The Mets' current fireballer, Noah Syndergaard, stricken with the same middle-finger blister issue, incidentally, tried the Ryan routine and gave it the thumbs down.)

But let's talk about the sound. Sitting in the right field stands on a sunny Sunday afternoon in late June in Detroit's old Tiger Stadium, overlooking the visitors' bullpen, Ryan warmed up for what would be his 315th career win on June 29, 1992. As you watched closely, you could see something of the gunslinger in his manner; you always could, whether he was throwing for the Mets, the California Angels, the Houston Astros (later), or the Texas Rangers (here).

First, there was the peer-in to his target, a steely-eyed, impassive glance homeward, a Clint Eastwood–esque "Make My Day" expression that seemed to say, "whatever I'm dialing up, you have no chance."

When the pitching motion commenced, there was a quick rock back on the right foot, then Ryan's arms—ball in glove—raised up over his head, almost pausing for a second on the back of his neck. As the left leg raises and his hips turn away from the plate, the foot kicks surprisingly high, almost to shoulder height. Ryan tilts his head a little downward as the knee comes to full height and his left shoulder closed as his arms come back down—almost like closing a window—he takes the ball out of his glove, both still hidden from the hitter behind his raised knee.

As he begins the throw, he quickly casts his gaze down at the mound beneath him, *not* his target, which, for someone with almost 3,000 career walks, 277 wild pitches, and frequently terrifying bursts of 100-mile-per-hour-plus velocity, could all be somewhat unsettling to the poor soul standing in either batter's box, just 60 feet, six inches away.

Then, here it comes. The left shoulder opens homeward, the left arm with the glove goes forward as the right arm with the baseball reaches back, almost like an archer drawing a bow. When his left foot lands, wham, here comes a sizzling baseball. And you could hear it from the stands.

Normally, a hard thrower produces a pop, a snapping sort of sound made by the collision of accelerating baseball and resistant catcher's mitt. It's a flat, loud noise. To these ears, Ryan's has more of a buzz to it, almost as if the baseball, launched with enough velocity to really go places, was disappointed to be apprehended after just a 60-foot, six-inch journey.

Since Ryan pitched before spin rate became a topic of conversation and a regularly measured data point, we'll never know technically speaking how his pitches differed from others. But we saw the results.

Having a miraculous arm, of course, is one thing. New York Mets scout Red Murff gushed after seeing Ryan for the first time. "The night before," he said then, "I had seen the two fastest pitchers in the National League at that time, Jim Maloney and Turk Farrell. Nolan Ryan was already faster than both of them by far." In his scouting report, he wrote "BEST arm I ever saw ANYWHERE in my life."

Velocity is only part of the mix, of course. Ryan's arm landed him in the majors rather quickly, but the Mets' staff didn't seem to do much to help him stay there. After spending the first five years of his career with the Mets, posting a 19-23 record despite impressive stats, Ryan reportedly told his wife he'd quit the game if he wasn't traded.

The Mets obliged him and dealt Ryan across the country to the California Angels with three marginal talents (Don Rose, Leroy Stanton, and Frank Estrada) for former All-Star shortstop Jim Fregosi. Fregosi didn't do much in two seasons in New York, while Ryan blossomed into a record-setting hurler.

In his eight years with the weak-hitting Angels, Ryan threw four no-hitters, broke Sandy Koufax's single-season strikeout mark (by one—383) en route to five 300-strikeout seasons, was a 20-game winner twice, and twice won 19 (with no batting support). To beat Koufax's mark, Ryan had to throw all 11 innings of his final start of the year, a 5–4 Angels win. He struck out Rich Reese in the 11th inning for number 383. For the game, he struck out 16, allowed 10 hits and 4 runs, but got win number 21 in his last start of the season.

From there, it was on to Houston for nine seasons, then Texas for five. He won as many as 16 games twice and pitched well, twice leading the National League in ERA (1.69 with an 11-5 mark in 1981 and 2.76 with an 8-16 mark in 1987). But there were no Cy Young Awards, no trips to the World Series, eight All-Star Game appearances, and lots and lots of close losses.

If nobody ever questioned Ryan's velocity, neither did they question his toughness. Nolan's former pitching coach with Texas, Tom House, tells the story of him having trouble in a game and Manager Bobby Valentine sending House out to talk to the fireballer.

"I got to the mound and said, 'Nolan, how you doing?'" House recalled. "He said, 'I'm doing terrible, but it's way better than what you've got going in that bullpen, so get the hell off my mound.' I went back to Bobby and said, 'OK, we're going to have trouble getting him out of there.'

"Bobby went to take him out of the game a couple of innings later. When Bobby said, 'That'll be it, Tex,' Nolan said, 'No it won't. One of us is leaving the mound and it's not going to be me.'" He stayed in and finished the game.

That afternoon at Tiger Stadium, when Ryan picked up his 315th career win, he might have been 45 years old, but his arm seemed years younger. Ryan, twice as old as some of the Tigers who stepped in against him, mowed them down with ease. You never saw so many bad swings, desperate half-swing fouls, and totally intimidated professional hitters.

After the game, an 8–4 Rangers win, a Rangers beat writer was telling Detroit's Tony Phillips that back home, Ryan's 0-3, 4.70 ERA start had Texas fans telling him it was time for him to ride off into the sunset.

Phillips about jumped off his stool. "What?" he said, eyes wide and mouth open. "That's bullshit. The people that say that, they don't have to face him. His fastball still has that good hop. His ball has a lot of movement and he still throws hard. He doesn't look any different to me than the guy we saw last year." Ryan threw his seventh no-hitter around that time.

As Phillips and the rest of the Tigers could testify, that Sunday afternoon before 42,394 fans at the old Tiger Stadium, Ryan was completely in command for seven shutout innings. He mixed a 90-plus fastball with a changeup and a sharp-breaking curveball that he was able to get over at key spots. Like in the third inning.

Just as finely tuned veteran race cars need a little warming up, Ryan always seemed to get stronger as the game went on. But here in the third, he'd walked Phillips and with two outs, Cecil Fielder looped a single to left. Detroit's Mickey Tettleton, as good a fastball hitter as the Tigers had, worked the count to 3-1, expected a good fastball, got it, and fouled it off. Full count. What's next?

The old Ryan would have simply reached back and hummed one. Not this time.

"He came with a 3-2 curve," Tettleton winced at the memory of the pitch which froze him, "and it was a good one. I take my hat off to him."

Nolan Ryan, the fastball king, going to a 3-2 deuce, two out, two on. Nasty.

The funny thing is, boys and girls, despite many recommendations from pitching coaches over the years, Ryan didn't decide to add a changeup to his pitching repertoire until he was over 40. Imagine what those strikeout totals might have been if he had started with that pitch earlier? Hitters everywhere, give thanks.

How many pitches did Nolan Ryan's arm actually have in it? Estimates ran as high as 34,500 pitches, but that seems way too conservative. He had games where he threw over 200 pitches in a single game. It's a mathematical delight. Just counting walks alone, never mind spring training outings, bullpen sessions, and mid-week between-starts tossing, we're talking over 11,000 pitches that were called balls. As for strikeouts—not counting fouls, of course—we're over 16,000 pitches. Add in wild pitches, hit batters, the pitches he threw that turned into 3,923 hits, you're at around 31,000 pitches officially recorded in a major-league scorebook. With 27 years of spring trainings behind, games of outfield catch . . . seems like 50,000 would be more like it. No wonder the ulnar collateral ligament said enough already.

Elected to the Hall of Fame in 1999, Ryan's 98.8 percentage—ranking him fifth all-time behind Mariano Rivera, Derek Jeter, Ken Griffey Jr., and Tom Seaver—showed the baseball writers and major-league hitters had something in common. They both were really impressed by what Nolan Ryan brought to the mound.

Incidentally, Ryan's final game shared something with Cardinals great Bob Gibson's finale. Each guy surrendered a grand slam to the last official batter he faced. Ryan handled his embarrassment a little more gracefully, quietly moving on to the next hitter, Dave Magadan—or trying to, without incident. The fiery Gibson, on the contrary, cursed Pete LaCock all the way around the bases before leaving the mound for the last time.

No, Nolan Ryan did not record a single out in the 773rd and final major-league start of his career. The last of his 5,714 strikeout victims was catcher Greg Myers in the fifth inning of his previous start, September 17. The first of the whiffs was Braves pitcher Pat Jarvis, the very first batter the 19-year-old Ryan faced in his major-league debut on September 11.

In between, there were 5,712 other strikeout victims, including Hank Aaron (4), Dick Allen (11), Wade Boggs (6), Bobby Bonds (10), Barry Bonds (3), George Brett (18), Rod Carew (29), Cecil Cooper (20), Andre Dawson (26), Carlton Fisk (24), Larry Hisle (29), Reggie Jackson (22), Dale Murphy (23), Jorge Orta (30), Dave Parker (23), Jim Rice (19), Pete Rose (13), and Robin Yount (16). Claudell Washington, incidentally, led the way with 39 whiffs.

We also know Ryan threw a record seven no-hitters. But did you know that, but for a few pitches, it might have been 12? Amazingly, there were five other occasions Ryan carried no-hitters into the ninth inning.

- August 7, 1974—One-out single to Dick Allen in a three-hit, 2–1 loss to the White Sox.
- July 13, 1979—One-out single to Reggie Jackson but beat the Yankees, 6–1.
- April 27, 1988—One-out single to Mike Schmidt, game went to extras. No win.
- April 23, 1989—One-out triple to Nelson Liriano. Ryan beat the Jays in a one-hitter, 4–1.
- August 10, 1989—One-out single by Dave Bergman. Rangers went on to win, 4–1.

That was the thing with Nolan Ryan. If he was on the mound, there was a chance he'd throw a no-no or come close. I happened to be in Toronto on April 23, 1989, and lobbied heavily to go to the game but was overruled to head back home. So, listening to the game on the radio, Ryan getting closer and closer to the no-no, things were getting a bit more uncomfortable in the car. Something about opportunities missed, etc. Then up steps Nelson Liriano and he slashes a triple to break up the no-no. I switched off the radio. Heard from the other side of the car: "Now I'm a HUGE Nelson Liriano fan."

Nolan Ryan by the Numbers

YEAR	TEAM	W	L	PCT	ERA	G	GS	CG	SHO	SV	IP	H	R	BB	SO
1966	NYM	0	1	.000	15.00	2	1	0	0	0	3.0	5	5	3	6
1968	NYM	6	9	.400	3.09	21	18	3	0	0	134.0	93	50	75	133
1969	NYM	6	3	.667	3.54	25	10	2	0	1	89.1	60	38	53	92
1970	NYM	7	11	.389	3.41	27	19	5	2	1	131.2	86	59	97	125
1971	NYM	10	14	.417	3.97	30	26	3	0	0	152.0	125	78	116	137
1972	CAL	19	16	.543	2.28	39	39	20	9	0	284.0	166	80	157	329
1973	CAL	21	16	.568	2.87	41	39	26	4	1	326.0	238	113	162	383
1974	CAL	22	16	.579	2.89	42	41	26	3	0	332.2	221	127	202	367
1975	CAL	14	12	.538	3.45	28	28	10	5	0	198.0	152	90	132	186
1976	CAL	17	18	.486	3.36	39	39	21	7	0	284.1	193	117	183	327
1977	CAL	19	16	.543	2.77	37	37	22	4	0	299.0	198	110	204	341
1978	CAL	10	13	.435	3.71	31	31	14	3	0	234.2	183	106	148	260
1979	CAL	16	14	.533	3.59	34	34	17	5	0	222.2	169	104	114	223
1980	HOU	11	10	.524	3.35	35	35	4	2	0	233.2	205	100	98	200
1981	HOU	11	5	.688	1.69	21	21	5	3	0	149.0	99	34	68	140
1982	HOU	16	12	.571	3.16	35	35	10	3	0	250.1	196	100	109	245
1983	HOU	14	9	.609	2.98	29	29	5	2	0	196.1	134	74	101	183
1984	HOU	12	11	.522	3.04	30	30	5	2	0	183.2	143	78	69	197
1985	HOU	10	12	.455	3.80	35	35	4	0	0	232.0	205	108	95	209
1986	HOU	12	8	.600	3.34	30	30	1	0	0	178.0	119	72	82	194
1987	HOU	8	16	.333	2.76	34	34	0	0	0	211.2	154	75	87	270
1988	HOU	12	11	.522	3.52	33	33	4	1	0	220.0	186	98	87	228
1989	TEX	16	10	.615	3.20	32	32	6	2	0	239.1	162	96	98	301
1990	TEX	13	9	.591	3.44	30	30	5	2	0	204.0	137	86	74	232
1991	TEX	12	6	.667	2.91	27	27	2	2	0	173.0	102	58	72	203
1992	TEX	5	9	.357	3.72	27	27	2	0	0	157.1	138	75	69	157
1993	TEX	5	5	.500	4.88	13	13	0	0	0	66.1	54	47	40	46
TOTALS		324	292	.526	3.19	807	773	222	61	3	5386.0	3923	2178	2795	5714

DUSTIN PEDROIA

THE LITTLE ENGINE FINALLY COULDN'T

DATE: April 17, 2019

SITE: Yankee Stadium, New York, New York

PITCHER: J. A. Happ of the New York Yankees

RESULT: Flyball to right field

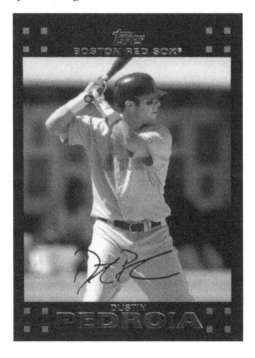

There was something in the way Dustin Pedroia peeled off on his way down to first base that said something was wrong. Real wrong. He'd come to the plate against the Yankees' J. A. Happ in the second inning of a game at Yankee Stadium, hoping to find a way to grind through the 2019 season with a balky left knee that had all but derailed a potential Hall of Fame career. He had taken his Mighty Mouse swing once again at an 0-1 Happ pitch, fouled it off, and felt something. Something bad.

After a feeble flyball to right field, Pedroia headed for the dugout and told manager Alex Cora he was done. At the time, he meant for that game.

"I was surprised that he came up to me and told me that," Cora said after the game. "But at least he was honest. He was down. I haven't seen him like that. Hopefully, it's nothing serious, and it's something that he just got scared."

In an active sense, Dustin Pedroia's major-league career ended with that, his 6,777th plate appearance in his 1,512th career game. But hobbling through just nine games over the last two seasons thanks to that knee, you could say Pedroia's extraordinary big-league run really ended with a 3–2 loss at Fenway Park on September 29 in 2017. The lingering effects of Manny Machado's April 21 spiking of Pedroia's left knee in the eighth inning of a 2–0 loss in Baltimore were too much even for irrepressible Pedroia to overcome. Not that he didn't try with surgery after surgery, rehab after rehab. Nothing worked.

There have been a handful of overachievers who scrapped and clawed their way to the major leagues over the years, David Eckstein probably being the first player you think of. But given his diminutive stature and his extraordinary accomplishments—Rookie of the Year, Most Valuable Player, four Gold Gloves (and there should have been more), a four-time All-Star—Pedroia might have been, along with the Astros' Jose Altuve, one of the best pound-for-pound baseball players we're likely to see in a while.

As the game trends toward power—giant fireballing pitchers and swing-from-the-heels sluggers—there doesn't seem to be a place for the mini-mites. Which, given what Red Sox fans were able to watch throughout Pedroia's 12-year "laser show" seems a great loss for the game. Someone his size has no chance in basketball or football, so baseball seemed the last refuge for the vertically challenged—if you had the skills. And Pedroia had those. More than that, he had the kind of drive that you rarely see these days.

"He was, I don't want to say 'pudgy,' but he wasn't real fast when he came to the big leagues," Terry Francona, Pedroia's first manager in the majors, told the *Boston Globe*'s Dan Shaughnessy. "We pinch ran for him and that just pissed him off. I told him, 'Hey, man, if you run better, I won't.' And the next year he came back and stole 20 bases. That's just him."

"He actually gained some speed," former Red Sox general manager Theo Epstein told Shaughnessy in that same story. "That's almost impossible. I can't ever remember it happening. It always goes in the other direction. No one did more with the physical ability he had. He just absolutely maximized his God-given abilities with sheer determination and great instincts."

Pedroia's size and appearance—he was as bald as a billiard but grew a Grizzly Adams mountain man beard—prompted dozens of mistaken identity stories that only further fueled a guy who always ran hot.

Red Sox fans well remember the story of the Colorado Rockies' security guard who stopped the tiny rookie on his way into Coors Field before Game 3 of the 2007 World Series. "Ask Francis," Pedroia quipped to the security guard, referring to Pedroia's first-inning home run off the Colorado Game 1 starter.

It was always that way. They said he was 5'9", 165, but the scale might have been using the metric system. As Epstein explained to the *Boston Globe*, "that started right in the beginning, even in the draft room. There were some strange looks, because he didn't have the prototypical body to be picked up in the second round.

"When we first signed him and sent him out to Augusta [Ga.] in low A ball to work out with the team and play for a week or two, our coaching staff called and asked if we sent the right guy."

This was something Pedroia had to battle every day.

"He was not impressive physically and never put on a great show in batting practice," continued Epstein. "You expect your first pick to have a little more speed and athleticism, and he had none of those things. He was never going to be a workout warrior, so they were very skeptical.

"Then the games started. Back then, our people would call in and leave game reports on voicemail, and right from the first game, it was, 'Yeah, Pedroia went 3 for 4 with two rocket doubles in the gap and made three diving plays and a heads-up baserunning play and dominated every phase of this game. Yeah, we were wrong. Can't judge this guy by the workouts. He's a pretty good player.'

"It was like that at every level. There was some skepticism and there was doubt until the game started, and then he was the manager's favorite player."

That sort of drive had to come from somewhere, and it may well have come from Pedroia's mom, Debbie, who was tiny, a terrific tennis player and as competitive as her son. Red Sox fans may remember a story, maybe apocryphal, of him going to the hospital after the birth of one of his sons and his mom, having seen him swing and miss at a ball in the dirt in that night's game, getting all over his case in the hospital.

His Red Sox career started slow; he hit just .191 in 31 games in the 2006 season. But from there, it was impressive. He hit .317 with eight home runs and 50 RBIs to win Rookie of the Year in 2007, then in 2008 hit .326, with 17 home runs, 83 RBIs ,and an American League–leading 213 hits, 54 doubles, and 118 runs scored, earning Most Valuable Player honors.

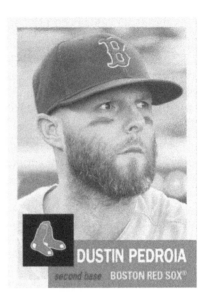

DUSTIN PEDROIA
second base BOSTON RED SOX

He wrapped up the 2016 season with fine numbers: .318, 15 home runs, 74 RBIs, playing in 154 games. But after the injury in April of 2017, he only was able to manage 114 games over the next three seasons before having to announce his retirement in February of 2021.

Those promoting Pedroia's Hall of Fame candidacy note that he is one of only eight players in history who won Rookie of the Year, Most Valuable Player, a Gold Glove (four) and a World Series title (two). In what amounts to a 12-year career, he had 1,805 hits, 140 home runs, 725 RBIs and a highlight reel or three of spectacular plays at second base.

Fans might remember that June night in Colorado—maybe remembering that security guard from three years earlier—when Pedroia went 5-for-5 with three—(count 'em)—three home runs in a 13–11 Boston win. The third homer broke an 11–11 tie in the top of the 13th inning. Clutch.

As it turned out, Pedroia's second-inning at-bat in Yankee Stadium in April of 2019 wasn't the last time he was on a professional baseball field. That came on May 24 when Pedroia suited up with Double-A Portland, facing the Altoona Curve at Hadlock Field. After the Yankee Stadium scare, Pedroia worked with Portland for a bit, worked out with the Red Sox at Fenway, then played five games for Triple-A Pawtucket from May 17 to May 22. Then on the 24th, Pedroia was at the ballpark at 10 a.m., texting a teammate eight hours before the game.

Bobby Dalbec told the *Globe*'s Alex Speier that Pedroia texted him "Wind is blowing out. Let's watch some film and hit early." No, 14-year major leaguers typically don't do that kind of thing. And his physical struggles were evident to everyone. As Mike Antonellis, the radio voice of the Portland Sea Dogs, told Speier: "Just seeing his knee—I was able to see him walking around in shorts. To see what that looked like, to see him hit, to see the pain, to see him come out of games, to see the way his at-bats were, you knew this was not going to be easy."

And it wasn't. Pedroia slapped into a double play in the first inning, then Altoona right-hander James Marvel fanned him on three pitches in the fourth. He took himself out of the game. And The Game.

As it turned out, those extra at-bats on the two-year comeback trail—the 3-for-31 in 2018 and 2019—dropped his lifetime batting average to .299. Though it's only a point, Pedroia's career average would have been precisely at .300 without those desperation at-bats. That point may well matter when it comes to Hall of Fame consideration. Maybe it shouldn't, but it will.

The manager that was his favorite—and the feeling was mutual—seemed to sum up Pedroia's career perfectly. "He was always mad for the right reasons when we lost," Terry Francona said. "It wasn't because he didn't get hits. He cared so deeply about all the right things. He was just such a competitor and he's so much of what's good in our game."

Dustin Pedroia by the Numbers

YEAR	TEAM	G	AB	R	H	TB	2B	3B	HR	RBI	BB	SO	SB	BA	SLG	OBP
2006	BOS	31	89	5	17	27	4	0	2	7	7	7	0	.191	.303	.258
2007	BOS	139	520	86	165	230	39	1	8	50	47	42	7	.317	.442	.380
2008	BOS	157	653	118	213	322	54	2	17	83	50	52	20	.326	.493	.376
2009	BOS	154	626	115	185	280	48	1	15	72	74	45	20	.296	.447	.371
2010	BOS	75	302	53	87	149	24	1	12	41	37	38	9	.288	.493	.367
2011	BOS	159	635	102	195	301	37	3	21	91	86	85	26	.307	.474	.387
2012	BOS	141	563	81	163	253	39	3	15	65	48	60	20	.290	.449	.347
2013	BOS	160	641	91	193	266	42	2	9	84	73	75	17	.301	.415	.372
2014	BOS	135	551	72	153	207	33	0	7	53	51	75	6	.278	.376	.337
2015	BOS	93	381	46	111	168	19	1	12	42	38	51	2	.291	.441	.356
2016	BOS	154	633	105	201	284	36	1	15	74	61	73	7	.318	.449	.376
2017	BOS	105	406	46	119	159	19	0	7	62	49	48	4	.293	.392	.369
2018	BOS	3	11	1	1	1	0	0	0	0	2	1	0	.091	.091	.231
2019	BOS	6	20	1	2	2	0	0	0	1	1	2	0	.100	.100	.143
TOTALS		1512	6031	922	1805	2649	394	15	140	725	624	654	138	.299	.439	.365

2014

DEREK JETER

QUIET FINALE AT FENWAY

DATE: September 28, 2014

SITE: Fenway Park, Boston, Massachusetts

PITCHER: Clay Buchholz of the Boston Red Sox

RESULT: Infield hit

For a storied, legendary New York Yankee franchise that always seemed to be brimming over with All-Stars and All-Timers, the shortstop position had always been just sort of average, other than "The Scooter" Phil Rizzuto, back in the day.

Yeah, Didi Gregorius was pretty good and Tony Kubek was OK and there was Tom Tresh and Gene Michael and Bucky "Bleeping" Dent, not exactly Hall of Famers. Over the years, there were a few other Yankee shortstops who left no footprints on the sands of time.

Which is, odd, for a legendary franchise that always seemed to have one Hall of Famer following another. Babe Ruth to Lou Gehrig to Joe DiMaggio to Yogi Berra to Mickey Mantle to Reggie Jackson and so on.

Over the same time span, the Red Sox went from Joe Cronin to Johnny Pesky to Rico Petrocelli to Rick Burleson to Nomar Garciaparra to Xander Bogaerts. All pretty darn good and memorable major leaguers. You'd certainly take that crew over the Yankee list.

In 1996, that all changed for the Bronx Bombers with the arrival of a 6-foot-3 thoroughbred, a soft-spoken, acrobatic shortstop from Kalamazoo, Michigan. For a generation of Yankee fans, savoring what has lately been their last grasp of extended World Series glory (three titles in a row), it was Derek Jeter manning that spot in the middle of the Yankee infield in what seemed like every damn game, every damn pitch, every damn win.

You can talk about many things about Jeter, The Captain. He was always there. Looking back now, his endurance was extraordinary. Ten full seasons of more than 700 plate appearances—same as Cal Ripken—five times leading the league; a whomping 2,747 career games, 2,674 at shortstop, second all-time to Omar Vizquel's total of 2,709; and Jeter played 372 more games at the position than Iron Man Ripken.

Yes, Jeter was as much a part of Yankee Stadium, it seemed, as those monuments in center field. And yeah, some critics said he had similar range. But with five Gold Gloves, over 3,000 hits, all-around excellence, Jeter was one of those rarities, someone you could spot as an All-Timer the minute you watched him.

For a while, there was the Derek Jeter / Nomar Garciaparra "Who's better?" chatter in Boston and New York, the Athens and Sparta of the baseball world and indeed, Nomar had some spectacular individual seasons. Jeter, however, was on Yankee teams that won. The Red Sox didn't win for the first time until they ditched Nomar in the middle of the season. It may be unfair to suggest that getting rid of him was what the Bosox needed, but that is what happened. Garciaparra was dealt away from Boston on July 31 to the Chicago Cubs, and the Red Sox ended an 86-year World Series drought.

With the preternaturally calm Jeter in the middle of the Yankee infield, the Bombers played in seven World Series, winning five, including three in a row (1998–2000) a feat that had not been achieved since Charlie Finley's A's won three in a row in the 1970s and has not been matched since.

Jeter was remarkably consistent there in postseason, too, playing in the equivalent of another full season—158 games with 20 home runs, 61 RBIs, and a .308 average, just two points lower than his career average of .310.

On the field, there never was a question about Jeter's character, his baseball IQ, or his decision-making. Off the field, his quotes were meticulously non-explosive. He didn't snub the media but wasn't exactly what you'd call insightful. To call him cautious would be generous.

That reserve carried over into his single life as well. Despite being the most eligible single guy playing in the media capital of the world, Jeter's lengthy career only turned up one minor scandal.

According to a *New York Post* article in December of 2011, Jeter had a "gift package" for each of his conquests.

"The next morning, he gets them a car to take them home the next day," the *Post* reported. "Waiting in his car is a gift basket containing signed Jeter memorabilia, usually a signed baseball," the friend dished. "This summer, he ended up hooking up with a girl who he had hooked up with once before, but Jeter seemed to have forgotten about the first time and gave her the same identical parting gift, a gift basket with a signed Derek Jeter baseball," the pal said. "He basically gave her the same gift twice because he'd forgotten hooking up with her the first time!"

Jeter has denied the story. But playing that long in New York City, being *the* most eligible bachelor around, that's not much of a scandal. Playing under that media microscope for that long, Jeter emerged with a remarkably clean image. To sportswriter Joe Posnanski, Jeter was the most seen player of his time.

"He is, I believe, the most *seen* player in baseball history," Posnanski wrote. "What do I mean? Baseball used to be shrouded in mystery. How many people across America actually saw Tris Speaker play? Stan Musial? Frank Robinson? Rod Carew? Even George Brett or Dave Winfield or Lou Brock would appear rarely on television; they were mostly names in box scores (and often shortened names like Mus'l and R'bnsn). They were grainy black and white photographs in the local paper. They were static-speckled images on the Game of the Week.

"Now we can watch any game, see any highlight at any time. We can summon any play in stunning high definition . . . and high-def can look more vivid than reality. Derek Jeter came of age in a game that left nothing to the imagination. He represented that game. He was everywhere, all the time, all of his superpowers and all of his rich flaws magnified and intensified and exaggerated beyond all reason. . . . He came to the plate 734 times in the postseason; that is a full season of Octobers and a record. His flip to beat Jeremy Giambi, his stunt-man leap into the stands, his November home run, his jump throw from the hole, his flares to right field, everybody knows those, they are among the indelible baseball images of our time, making them among the most indelible images of any times.

"But it's more than just that. We saw exactly how he looked in the on-deck circle, how he ran out to the field, how he sat on the bench. We know the models he dated. We know his quotes by heart (though most of them are hardly worth remembering—"We win as a team," "We lose as a team," "Sometimes you have to tip your cap"; Jeter spoke often but purposely said nothing). We can close our eyes and see Jeter doing those things he always did."

So well-mannered, always the consummate professional, Jeter, at times, seemed almost mechanical. One of baseball's first biracial stars, growing up in Michigan, a state known for racial animus, he seemed to have nothing to say about any of that or about much of anything. He just wanted to play.

The interesting thing is, at least one scout, Michigander Dick Groch, saw Jeter's immortal status coming when he was a kid. Back then, the Yankees' scouting director was a guy named Bill Livesey, who worried about offering sixth-round money to Jeter, who, it was feared, might opt to be a Wolverine.

"I hear he's going to Michigan," Livesey reportedly said. "No," countered Groch, "This kid is going to Cooperstown."

The Yankees, who picked number six in the 1992 draft, were concerned that teams ahead of them, Baltimore and Cincinnati, would grab Jeter. But the Orioles grabbed Stanford's Jeffrey Hammonds and the Reds took out-fielder Chad Mottola.

Mottola made it to the bigs, but had a career average of .200 with just four home runs as a journeyman, playing for five different teams. Hammonds had a solid 13-year career, a .272 average with 110 homers, playing for six teams.

The road wasn't all smooth for Jeter. His first year in rookie ball, he hit .210. His next season, he made 56 errors at shortstop. So there was some smoothing out necessary. But after a 15-game trial in 1995, Jeter moved in at shortstop and stuck in a way few have, after a Rookie of the Year season (.314, 10 homers, 78 RBIs) that more or less established what the Yankees could expect from Jeter for nearly the next two decades.

His batting average soared as high as .349 (1999) and .343 (2006), and he was in double figures in home runs every year through 2010 with a high of 24 in 1999. He collected over 200 hits eight separate times with a high of 216 in 2012, his last exceptional season, at age 38.

There were World Series titles in 1996, 1998, 1999, and 2000, playing for Joe Torre. There were World Series losses in 2001 and 2003 before one last Series win in 2009, when Jeter hit .407 to help the Yankees to a 4–2 win over the Philadelphia Phillies.

Had it not been for a postseason injury against the Detroit Tigers in October of 2012, he might have beat his future tenant Tom Brady to the idea of playing until he was 45. At 38, Jeter had one of his finest seasons, playing in 159 games, collecting a career-high 216 hits, batting .316, with 15 home runs and 32 doubles. But the nearly indestructible shortstop finally broke down.

In the opening game of the American League Championship Series, the game went into the 12th inning, Tigers up, 5–4, and Jhonny Peralta slashed one up the middle. Jeter dove and broke his left ankle on the play. Yankee general manager Brian Cashman said the injury would end Jeter's season, but he should be OK for spring training. Or so they hoped.

Sure enough, Jeter reported to spring training a day before pitchers and catchers and was out there, running. So it looked like everything was OK. About midway through the Grapefruit League schedule, Jeter was penciled in as designated hitter on March 9 and a couple days later, was back out at short. The ankle, though, just wasn't up to it and the team put him on the DL to start the season. A little way into the season, it was learned that Jeter had a small fracture in the ankle and he'd be out until the All-Star break.

In July, he played in four minor-league rehab games in Triple-A Scranton/Wilkes-Barre and on the 11th, he was back in the Yankee lineup, batting second. But a pulled quad forced an early exit from that game and here came another stint on the DL. Jeter came back against Tampa on July 28, played for a bit, and found himself back on the DL on August 5.

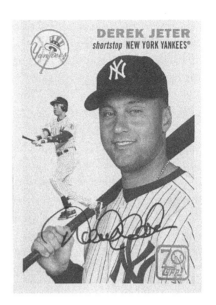

When he returned to the lineup at the end of August, he still wasn't right, and after a weirdly awkward play against the Red Sox on September 5, Yankee management pulled the plug.

As Cashman explained to the *New York Daily News*, "his mobility was definitely becoming more limited with the pain he was receiving so we backed off, and when he's feeling better, we'll turn him loose again. If he was moving around and he was pain-free, he'd be back out there."

But he never was, not until 2014, which turned out to be his final season. He announced in February that this would be it. He turned in a solid year at age 40, playing in 145 games, batting a respectable .256 (was up to .280 on July 29 before a late-summer fade) with four homers and 50 RBIs. His finish, however, was Jeteresque.

The Yankee home schedule closed out with the Baltimore Orioles, and 48,613 showed up for what was the Jeter finale, a Thursday night in the Bronx. And sure enough a so-so Yankee team rumbled into the ninth inning with a 5–2 lead, only to see David Robertson surrender home runs to Adam Jones and Steve Pearce, letting the Orioles tie the game.

But dramatically, as if the Baseball Gods decreed, "Well, we can't let one of our favorite sons leave this way"—the Yankees rallied in the bottom of the ninth against the unfortunately named Evan Meek. Somebody named José Pirela bounced a groundball through the SS-3B hole to open the inning. Brett Gardner put down a sacrifice bunt moving pinch-runner Antoan Richardson to second. Then, with the 48,613 screaming, praying, crying . . . up stepped Jeter.

You heard Bob Sheppard's from-the-crypt introduction (Sheppard had retired in 2007, but Jeter had enough pull to keep his intro for every Stadium at-bat), everyone standing and cheering as number 2 walked up to the plate for the final time.

"Well, the script is there," Yankee announcer Michael Kay said. "The last page is in Derek's hands."

On the very first pitch, Jeter swung and shot a line-drive single into right field. Nick Markakis's throw to the plate was just a little late, and Richardson slid home with the winning run, just like in the movies.

The postgame reaction was interesting as well. After he thrust both arms upward, à la Rocky, Jeter was mobbed by his teammates, then never left the field. He ran out to his position one last time, squatted down, a sea of noise still washing down around him.

He looked up, ran back toward the Yankee dugout only to see many of his old teammates, Andy Pettitte, Jorge Posada, Bernie Williams, grayer, fatter, the boys of summer now heading into the winter of their years, smiling and watching. Derek Jeter, he could see then, was now joining them.

The Schedule Gods of Baseball should have ended it right there and in Jeter's mind, that was the real end to his career.

The statistics will show, however, there were two more games on the schedule in Fenway Park in Boston. Jeter, of course, played in both, and got a hit in each one.

His final hit, number 3,465, was a high chopper off Boston's Clay Buchholz that bounced off home plate and went high in the air, off the hand of leaping Boston third baseman Garin Cecchini, driving in the Yankees' third run of the game.

When Jeter reached first, he looked back into the Yankee dugout at manager Joe Girardi, who made the slicing gesture across his throat, as if to say, is that it? Jeter nodded and trotted in as the Fenway fans stood and cheered. The camera flashed up into the stands to Jeter's parents, Mom in tears. Then back down into the dugout, you saw Jeter taking his batting gloves off, smiling, nodding to his teammates. He looked relieved.

Derek Jeter by the Numbers

YEAR	TEAM	G	AB	R	H	TB	2B	3B	HR	RBI	BB	SO	SB	BA	SLG	OBP
1995	NYY	15	48	5	12	18	4	1	0	7	3	11	0	.250	.375	.294
1996	NYY	157	582	104	183	250	25	6	10	78	48	102	14	.314	.430	.370
1997	NYY	159	654	116	190	265	31	7	10	70	74	125	23	.291	.405	.370
1998	NYY	149	626	127	203	301	25	8	19	84	57	119	30	.324	.481	.384
1999	NYY	158	627	134	219	346	37	9	24	102	91	116	19	.349	.552	.438
2000	NYY	148	593	119	201	285	31	4	15	73	68	99	22	.339	.481	.416
2001	NYY	150	614	110	191	295	35	3	21	74	56	99	27	.311	.480	.377
2002	NYY	157	644	124	191	271	26	0	18	75	73	114	32	.297	.421	.373
2003	NYY	119	482	87	156	217	25	3	10	52	43	88	11	.324	.450	.393
2004	NYY	154	643	111	188	303	44	1	23	78	46	99	23	.292	.471	.352
2005	NYY	159	654	122	202	294	25	5	19	70	77	117	14	.309	.450	.389
2006	NYY	154	623	118	214	301	39	3	14	97	69	102	34	.343	.483	.417
2007	NYY	156	639	102	206	289	39	4	12	73	56	100	15	.322	.452	.388
2008	NYY	150	596	88	179	243	25	3	11	69	52	85	11	.300	.408	.363
2009	NYY	153	634	107	212	295	27	1	18	66	72	90	30	.334	.465	.406
2010	NYY	157	663	111	179	245	30	3	10	67	63	106	18	.270	.370	.340
2011	NYY	131	546	84	162	212	24	4	6	61	46	81	16	.297	.388	.355
2012	NYY	159	683	99	216	293	32	0	15	58	45	90	9	.316	.429	.362
2013	NYY	17	63	8	12	16	1	0	1	7	8	10	0	.190	.254	.288
2014	NYY	145	581	47	149	182	19	1	4	50	35	87	10	.256	.313	.304
TOTALS		2747	11195	1923	3465	4921	544	66	260	1311	1082	1840	358	.310	.440	.377

MARIANO RIVERA

MARIANO'S HIGHER POWER REVEALED

DATE: September 26, 2013

SITE: Yankee Stadium, New York City

BATTER: Yunel Escobar of the Tampa Bay Rays

RESULT: Popout to second base

Whatever you think of Yankees Hall of Fame reliever Mariano Rivera, his unanimous selection to the Hall or his remarkable overall career, you have to remember the guy had a pretty impressive and undeniably powerful pitching coach.

How did he learn the one pitch that made major-league batters weak in the knees, the one pitch that hitters were certain was coming and still couldn't do much with? Let's just say if you had this guy (or gal) on your side, facing a major-league batter would be the least of your worries.

"God gave it to me," Rivera said once. "Again, I didn't discover it. It was given to me by the Lord."

And Rivera, in turn, did the Lord's work (as he sees it) over the next 19 seasons, closing out so many Yankee games he earned his own signature tune, "Enter Sandman," as the guy who put enemy bats (and fans) to sleep. And he did that all the way through the night of September 26, a nondescript Thursday night in the Bronx against the Tampa Bay Rays, when he made his final, emotional trip to the Yankee Stadium mound. Though there were a couple games to go—just as there were for Derek Jeter after his Yankee Stadium finale—Rivera made it clear this was it.

He traveled with the team to the final games in Houston. But it was over.

"I'm done, guys," Rivera told visiting reporters before Saturday's game in Houston. "I'm done."

The story goes that 16 years earlier, the strong-armed, athletic Rivera was playing a game of catch with teammate Ramiro Mendoza in the outfield when he tried a new grip and zing . . . there it was. The birth of the scourge of the American League for the next decade and a half was that simple, that unremarkable.

Over the years, Rivera's out pitch has been labeled, dissected, cursed, and lauded over as "a cutter," which is like calling the ceiling of the Sistine Chapel "illustrated" or Beethoven's Fifth "a neat tune." Plenty of other pitchers throw "a cutter." Then there was Rivera's, which had the finest hitters of a generation flummoxed.

Arizona Diamondbacks outfielder Luis Gonzalez, who authored perhaps the single-most successful and momentous at-bat against the Yankee ace, does not speak of that moment as if he had split the atom or solved an impossible puzzle (a good thing, too, because it was an off-the-fists simple flare over the drawn-in infield, almost predicted by announcer Tim McCarver before the decisive pitch).

With the bases loaded in the bottom of the ninth, score tied 2–2 in Game 7 of the 2001 World Series, the Yankees had turned, as they always did then, to Rivera to get them out of the inning. Announcer Joe Buck called it "the chance of a lifetime" as Gonzalez, who had fanned in his previous at-bat and was hitting an unimpressive .231 in the Series, approached the plate.

"The hardest part about that is you know what he's going to throw you, and I think the more you look for it the more dominant it was," Gonzalez said later. "You knew he was going to throw a cutter in on your hands, and you start looking for it and it seemed like a Pacman, just driving in on your hands every time."

Gonzalez fouled off Rivera's first pitch—up and in. "One problem is," Fox color man Tim McCarver said, "Rivera pitches in to left-handers and left-handers get a lot of broken-bat hits into the shallow outfield."

Rivera threw, Gonzalez swung, and perhaps the most viewed public Rivera failure of all time, unveiled before us as he sliced a ball over a drawn-in Jeter's head to win the World Series for the Diamondbacks.

So how dominant was Rivera? You remember his failures—they were so infrequent—more than the mind-numbing array of saves. If Yankee manager Joe Torre had adopted former Celtics coach Red Auerbach's practice of lighting up a cigar when the win was in hand, the Yankee dugout would have been full of more smoke since the days of chain-smokin' Joe DiMaggio.

Unlike a lot of pitchers and closers in particular, Rivera looked like an athlete. And his calm, "I don't have to worry about signs" demeanor and extraordinary success gave opponents the chill. Even when he lost, which was seldom.

An enterprising young writer named Tim Britton writing for *The Athletic* found out after a lengthy and merry march through the statistics that Rivera had been walked off 24 times by such varied talents as Ichiro Suzuki, David Wright, Moises Alou, Manny Ramírez, Miguel Tejada and some players that, well, only an uberfan would remember, like Bill Selby.

Selby, history will record, happened to step to the plate with the bases loaded on July 14, 2002, the Tribe down 7–6 with two outs in the ninth and Rivera on the mound.

"It got closer and closer, and I just went down to the tunnel and said a quick prayer—'If I'm going to do this, God, you're going to have to help me out,'" he told Britton. "This is the stuff you dream about your whole life. I didn't want to do that without the good Lord by my side."

Having grounded out against Rivera earlier in the series, he took hitting coach Eddie Murray's recommendation to choke up. When he came up, there may have been only about 25,000 fans remaining, but they believed.

"The 25,000 or so that was left in the stadium were as loud as 75,000. You're hearing the drum beat as loud as you've ever heard it," he said. "It happened like a blur." Selby got a 2-2 cutter up and in and managed to get the barrel on the ball—it just cleared the right field wall for a game-ending, game-winning, story-of-a-lifetime grand slam.

In discussing Rivera with those who had been able to beat him (once, at least), their words were respectful.

"His presence alone was something that took the game to another level," Vernon Wells told Britton, recalling his game-winning HR off Rivera on July 20, 2006. "You knew you were facing the best closer of all time anytime he came on the mound. . . . It was an elevated moment in the game."

When Rivera took that Game 7 loss to the Diamondbacks, he reacted with class.

"He handled it like a true champ," Gonzalez told Britton. "This guy just said, 'They got me.' You know what I mean? He could have very easily said, 'I jammed him and he got lucky.' He never made any negative comments toward me or our team. He just said, 'He beat me. They got me.' That's why everybody respects him. He wasn't a talker, he was a doer."

Selby agreed. "I think I would speak for everybody who ever faced him, whether they'd admit it or not: When the ninth inning came and he's jogging out of the bullpen, you're entertaining what's on the (postgame) spread," Selby recalled. "All right, let's figure out tomorrow.' You just associate him with Game Over."

In a 19-year-career, Rivera finished 952 games, saved 652 games, threw 141 postseason innings, and allowed just a pair of postseason home runs, one to Sandy Alomar Jr., one to Jay Payton, finishing with an 0.70 ERA in October baseball.

Like Jeter would a year later, Rivera made sure everyone knew when he was signing off after his 1,115th appearance at the end of the 2013 season. He had announced he would retire before spring training, then went out and had a fine Rivera-like campaign winding up 6-2 with a 2.11 ERA and 44 saves for the Yankees, giving him 652 saves for his career.

Rivera's finale came that final Thursday in September against the Rays. It wasn't your usual Rivera appearance. He came on in the eighth, relieving Dellin Betances, who'd made a mess of the inning with three hits and a walk.

Now, the Yankees trailed 4–0 and he was summoned to face Delmon Young, who had homered off Iván Nova an inning earlier. He got Young to line out to center, and Sam Fuld to bounce back to him.

In the ninth, he got José Lobatón to bounce out, then Yunel Escobar to lift a high popup to Robinson Canó and that was it. Derek Jeter and Andy Pettitte started walking out from the dugout, Pettitte calling time. Rivera spotted them and broke into a wide smile.

Once Pettitte reached the mound, Rivera embraced him, teared up, and did not want to let go. Yankee Stadium's 48,675 didn't want him to go either, and the thunderous noise did not and would not relent, even after Rivera waved to one and all, walked to the dugout, hugged every one of his team-mates, and had a chance to sit down. The cheers continued.

He put his hat back on, went up the steps, and waved to the Yankee nation one last time. That was how to end a career. And he knew it.

When he got to Houston, he explained that to sportswriters. "I think I squeezed every ounce of fuel that I had in my tank, and it's empty," Rivera said then. "I have nothing left. I gave everything that I had. I know that was the perfect moment to leave the game." The perfect finisher had the perfect finish.

Mariano Rivera by the Numbers

YEAR	TEAM	W	L	PCT	ERA	G	GS	CG	SHO	SV	IP	H	R	BB	SO
1995	NYY	5	3	.625	5.51	19	10	0	0	0	67.0	71	43	30	51
1996	NYY	8	3	.727	2.09	61	0	0	0	5	107.2	73	25	34	130
1997	NYY	6	4	.600	1.88	66	0	0	0	43	71.2	65	17	20	68
1998	NYY	3	0	.000	1.91	54	0	0	0	36	61.1	48	13	17	36
1999	NYY	4	3	.571	1.83	66	0	0	0	45	69.0	43	15	18	52
2000	NYY	7	4	.636	2.85	66	0	0	0	36	75.2	58	26	25	58
2001	NYY	4	6	.400	2.34	71	0	0	0	50	80.2	61	24	12	83
2002	NYY	1	4	.200	2.74	45	0	0	0	28	46.0	35	16	11	41
2003	NYY	5	2	.714	1.66	64	0	0	0	40	70.2	61	15	10	63
2004	NYY	4	2	.667	1.94	74	0	0	0	53	78.2	65	17	20	66
2005	NYY	7	4	.636	1.38	71	0	0	0	43	78.1	50	18	18	80
2006	NYY	5	5	.500	1.80	63	0	0	0	34	75.0	61	16	11	55
2007	NYY	3	4	.429	3.15	67	0	0	0	30	71.1	68	25	12	74
2008	NYY	6	5	.545	1.40	64	0	0	0	39	70.2	41	11	6	77
2009	NYY	3	3	.500	1.76	66	0	0	0	44	66.1	48	14	12	72
2010	NYY	3	3	.500	1.80	61	0	0	0	33	60.0	39	14	11	45
2011	NYY	1	2	.333	1.91	64	0	0	0	44	61.1	47	13	8	60
2012	NYY	1	1	.500	2.16	9	0	0	0	5	8.1	6	2	2	8
2013	NYY	6	2	.750	2.11	64	0	0	0	44	64.0	58	16	9	54
TOTALS		82	60	.577	2.21	1115	10	0	0	652	1283.2	998	340	286	1173

MARK MCGWIRE

CALLED BACK TO THE BENCH

DATE: October 14, 2001

SITE: Bank One Ballpark, Phoenix, Arizona

PITCHER: Curt Schilling of the Arizona Diamondbacks

RESULT: Pulled for a pinch-hitter; last at-bat, called strikeout

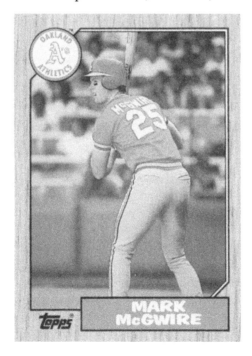

If you needed any evidence how humbling the sport of baseball can be, consider the final major-league game that Mark David McGwire appeared in. In mid-October, it seemed you could barely see him. Batting average below .200, his bat a broadsword that never seemed to catch the flittering, whistling target he chased in vain all season, he was kneeling in the on-deck circle in Arizona's Bank One Ballpark, the fading Cardinals locked in a 1–1 duel with the Diamondbacks' relentless Curt Schilling, when his manager, Tony LaRussa called to him. . . .

Just a few summers earlier, McGwire seemed to stand like the Colossus of Rhodes in every American living room as he and the Cubs' Sammy Sosa pursued Roger Maris's long-standing single-season home-run record with passion, enthusiasm, grace, and class. A giant red-haired hulk from California trying every night—or so it seemed—to one-up a happy, smiling, bulging-out-of-his uniform dark-skinned Dominican who seemed either to be joyously hopping, blowing a kiss to everyone, or running around with an American flag.

It was an unforgettable summer spectacle, one that played out on millions of American TV sets, bringing fans back to a sport that had collapsed in on itself a few years earlier whether the numbers reflect that or not. (Baseball attendance actually didn't change much and went down the next year.) What it did do, undeniably, is put the sport in the news every night.

Network news covered the dramatic home-run chase between these two sluggers, and these two men of different races and markedly different temperaments going head-to-head on a nightly basis grabbed a nation's attention, including the then–Texas governor and soon-to-be-president George W. Bush, who famously said the one decision he regretted the most (at the time) was trading Sammy Sosa back when he was president of the Texas Rangers. Sosa, not politics.

As the season began, there was already talk of records being broken. McGwire had clubbed 58 home runs the previous year. The Seattle Mariners' Ken Griffey Jr. would join in the three-pronged pursuit of Maris's home-run mark of 61, and Sosa as well, after a 20-homer June. The historic diversity of baseball—the first major sport to include Black athletes—was given a national showcase once again and it seemed to unite us as few things have, especially lately.

You had Griffey, a jubilant Black man called "The Kid," from major-league bloodlines, born to it, you might say, able to good-naturedly wear his baseball cap backward and not offend anybody, playing with the joy and abandon of a young Willie Mays. You had McGwire, the whitest of white men, whose stiff intensity and bristly Captain Ahab red beard hinted at obsession and a diamond-sharp concentration that resulted every other night it seemed in scalded long-distance home runs. Finally, you had the excitable, springy Sosa, who always seemed to leap into the air after launching one of his moon-shot home runs over the vines into the Wrigley Field bleachers, the homers never quite as high and majestic as McGwire's but happier, it seemed, as if the ball was enjoying the view and the ride.

McGwire's first home run of the year was a grand slam, hit on Opening Day. And it went from there.... On April 4, for example, listen to Jack Buck's call. "From the stretch. The pitch to Mark McGwire. A long one. Calling air traffic control. Calling air traffic control. A three-run homer for McGwire. He is amazing, dazzling, remarkable, unbelievable. What a guy he's been for the Cardinals!"

As the year went on, the pace intensified and Griffey fell back a little bit and Sosa took over. On August 18, McGwire and Sosa each had 47, Griffey had 42, and Maris's record seemed within reach to all three. But the McGwire-Sosa duel really caught on, baseballs soaring out of major-league parks at a record pace. And the two of them seemed to thrill to the challenge, encouraging each other, joint press conferences, feel-good stories, smiles and fist-bumps and blowing kisses, standing ovations in the other guy's ballpark.

In a memorable August 19 game in Wrigley, Sosa took over the lead in the fifth with number 48, McGwire matched him in the eighth, then took the lead himself with a home run to dead center field for number 49. Players don't often hit home runs to dead center field. McGwire made it look like it was a Little League field. Now that's a race for you.

Later that summer, Steve Wilstein of the Associated Press noticed a bottle of androstenedione in McGwire's locker and asked him about it. At first, McGwire was not concerned at all. In a video clip from the wonderful documentary *Long Gone Summer*, a reporter asks "Why do you do it, how does it help you, why don't you worry about it?"

McGwire says, with a smile, "Well, I don't worry about it because it's legal stuff, sold over the counter, anybody can go in there and buy it," he shrugs, "There's absolutely nothing wrong with it."

Whether he truly thought that in that moment or knew better, imagine how his life—and maybe all of baseball—would be different if he had been more discreet about his use. What if he'd have kept that bottle at home? He must have wondered that a million times.

The chase continued, blow by blow, with the nation clued in on every swing and pitch. Griffey hit a dry spell and fell off the pace. McGwire kept hammering and at the end of August, they were tied at 54. McGwire tied Ruth's mark of 60 on September 5 in St. Louis, and wouldn't you know it, the schedule had the Cubs traveling to St. Louis for a two-game set the next day.

There was a joint press conference, Sosa in blue, McGwire in Cardinal red, and the spirit of friendly admiration and competition was heartwarming and emotional. "I really feel for what Roger (Maris) went through," McGwire said, "all the negative stuff in his life. I wish it didn't happen. Hopefully, the day that I die, after seeing the Lord, I can go see him and Babe Ruth and talk to him."

"Don't forget about me," Sosa said, breaking into a laugh, and it was a delightful moment. How could you not root for either guy, the two of them chasing history together?

And McGwire, ever conscious of history and the sanctity of Maris's home-run record, invited the Maris family to watch the final days of his chase. Sosa was on the field, and the Maris family was in the stands in St. Louis when he hit 61 to tie Maris. It was McGwire's dad's 61st birthday too.

When he hit number 62, a low, knuckling line drive that seemed to not want to leave the park, he embraced the Maris family to the cheers and adulation of millions. He lifted up his son, kissed him. Sosa came over, and he picked him up and hugged him. He went into the stands to hug the Maris contingent.

Aw, the big guy wants to do things right, we all thought. Sosa sent his congratulations, so did the president, and baseball was at a place where it seemed as if when you went to a game, you'd get an American flag, a piece of apple pie, and a puppy.

McGwire wound up with 70, hitting one out in his final at-bat of the season. Sosa, whose Cubs headed for the playoffs, wound up with 66.

One thousand and eighteen days later, just three seasons after his triumphant, record-setting campaign, here was McGwire, late into a Sunday night game—the final night game of the season for the St. Louis Cardinals and the final game of McGwire's career. It had been a rough night for him against Arizona's Curt Schilling. McGwire fanned on four pitches in the second, four pitches in the fourth, and on seven pitches, leading off the seventh.

Opening the Divisional Series on Tuesday, Schilling got him twice on strikes before he grounded out to third in the seventh. In Game 2 in St. Louis, LaRussa called on him to pinch-hit in the bottom of the ninth, the

Cardinals trailing, 5–3, with one out. Byung-Hyun Kim got him to ground into a double play to end the game.

McGwire was back in the lineup in Game 3, but Albie Lopez got him to pop out to short and fly to right before he was able to collect the final hit of his career, a single to center off reliever Brian Anderson. He came up in the eighth against Mike Morgan in that game and took a called third strike.

You could see this ending coming. McGwire's 2001 season was a struggle from the start. His first home run was an opposite-field flyball against Pedro Astacio on April 11 after an 0-for-10 start. Injuries kept him inactive until the end of May when he singled and homered off the Brewers' Paul Rigdon, the only multiple-hit game he had until June 15 against the White Sox when he had four hits, including two home runs to raise his average from .177 to .224.

As his average fell below the Mendoza line on August 2 and stayed there for the rest of the year, he still managed to pump out 29 home runs, including a two-homer game in Houston on September 26. His 583rd and final big-league home run came against Rocky Coppinger, a three-run shot in the sixth in Milwaukee in a Thursday-afternoon game rescheduled because of the 9/11 attack.

Now, the Cardinals' season was on the brink, he'd fanned in five of his last six at-bats against Schilling, and the Diamondbacks ace was mowing them down. He'd allowed a home run to J. D. Drew in the eighth to tie it at 1, but Schilling wasn't coming out of the game, even after allowing a leadoff single to Jim Edmonds.

McGwire had put on his helmet, grabbed his bat, and was in the on-deck circle for what he expected to be his 6,188th career at-bat. LaRussa called him back. Instead, he sent Kerry Robinson up to bunt Edmonds over.

McGwire, the celebrated home-run champion just three years earlier, was pulled for a pinch-hitter. Robinson did bunt him over, but Édgar Rentería and future Cardinal manager Mike Metheny struck out swinging to end the frame.

In the bottom of the ninth, Tony Womack singled in pinch-runner Danny Bautista off reliever Steve Kline and Arizona was a 2–1 walkoff winner. McGwire's season and career, he determined later, was over.

On November 11 in an ESPN interview with Rich Eisen, McGwire said he was done. He had agreed to a two-year, $30 million contract extension in spring training, but after struggling with a sub-.200 average (.187) and a bad knee, it was time.

"After considerable discussion with those closest to me, I have decided not to sign the extension, as I am unable to perform at a level equal to the salary the organization would be paying me," he wrote. "I believe I owe it to the Cardinals and the fans of St. Louis to step aside, so a talented free agent can be brought in as the final piece of what I expect can be a World Championship-caliber team."

But the media wasn't done with McGwire or his accomplishments. In March of 2005, you'd have found him in a suit, granny glasses on, testifying before Congress. In January of 2010, a tearful admission—and apology—to Bob Costas that he'd used steroids on and off for a decade. Unlike many other famous players of the era—Barry Bonds, Sammy Sosa, Roger Clemens—who have refused to admit to intentional steroid use or apologize, McGwire clearly feels he did something he wishes he hadn't. He called Pat Maris, Roger's widow, and apologized. And when Costas noted that Roger's sons considered the 61 the true record, he didn't blink.

"They have every right to," he said. "It was the stupidest thing I ever did. There's no reason to go down that road. It's an illusion."

Which, sad to say, is how future baseball fans may look at that dramatic 1998 McGwire-Sosa home-run race. An illusion.

Mark McGwire by the Numbers

YEAR	TEAM	G	AB	R	H	TB	2B	3B	HR	RBI	BB	SO	SB	BA	SLG	OBP
1986	OAK	18	53	10	10	20	1	0	3	9	4	18	0	.189	.377	.259
1987	OAK	151	557	97	161	344	28	4	49	118	71	131	1	.289	.618	.370
1988	OAK	155	550	87	143	263	22	1	32	99	76	117	0	.260	.478	.352
1989	OAK	143	490	74	113	229	17	0	33	95	83	94	1	.231	.467	.339
1990	OAK	156	523	87	123	256	16	0	39	108	110	116	2	.235	.489	.370
1991	OAK	154	483	62	97	185	22	0	22	75	93	116	2	.201	.383	.330
1992	OAK	139	467	87	125	273	22	0	42	104	90	105	0	.268	.585	.385
1993	OAK	27	84	16	28	61	6	0	9	24	21	19	0	.333	.726	.467
1994	OAK	47	135	26	34	64	3	0	9	25	37	40	0	.252	.474	.413
1995	OAK	104	317	75	87	217	13	0	39	90	88	77	1	.274	.685	.441
1996	OAK	130	423	104	132	309	21	0	52	113	116	112	0	.312	.730	.467
1997	OAK	105	366	48	104	230	24	0	34	81	58	98	1	.284	.628	.383
1997	STL	51	174	38	44	119	3	0	24	42	43	61	2	.253	.684	.411
1997	ALL	156	540	86	148	349	27	0	58	123	101	159	3	.274	.646	.393
1998	STL	155	509	130	152	383	21	0	70	147	162	155	1	.299	.752	.470
1999	STL	153	521	118	145	363	21	1	65	147	133	141	0	.278	.697	.424
2000	STL	89	236	60	72	176	8	0	32	73	76	78	1	.305	.746	.483
2001	STL	97	299	48	56	147	4	0	29	64	56	118	0	.187	.492	.316
TOTALS		1874	6187	1167	1626	3639	252	6	583	1414	1317	1596	12	.263	.588	.394

2007

SAMMY SOSA

SILENT FINISH IN SEATTLE

DATE: September 29, 2007

SITE: Safeco Field, Seattle, Washington

PITCHER: Sean Green of the Seattle Mariners

RESULT: Flyout to right

He played the game with such "Hey, I'm up" excitement and almost a Little League–like enthusiasm, lighting up ballparks across America with a contagious and boundless joy. We all remember the post-home-run hops out of the batter's box, the mugging for the camera, blowing kisses to all of us through the lens religiously following his every move, then the blessing—him pouring the cups of water—always two—over his buoyant, smiling face.

Sammy Sosa, the perpetually happy—and grateful—former Dominican shoeshine boy had as much TV face time as any baseball player in recent memory.

Nowadays, Sammy Sosa's face is all anybody wants to talk about. There he was on national TV, sitting across from ESPN's Jeremy Schaap, his skin a ghastly, almost corpse-like white, clumsily trying to dodge predictable queries about his suspected steroid use with a defensiveness that made each successive answer more questionable than the one that preceded it.

He hasn't been invited back to Chicago—where he surely could have run for mayor and won in a landslide—since he stormed out, leaving Wrigley before the final game of another disappointing season had concluded. How could a guy who seemed to be everything *right* about baseball become yet another symptom of what's bad about it—ego, steroid suspicions, attitude?

Well, there was the corked bat incident on June 4, 2003, against the Tampa Bay Rays where a shattered bat on Sosa's first trip to the plate revealed cork inside it. Sosa immediately apologized "from the bottom of my heart," which evidently was a lot shallower than people dreamed.

It got worse. To quote from "Cubs Insider": "Sosa left early during the Cubs' final game of the 2004 season, a 10-8 win against the Braves at Wrigley that capped a 89-73 third-place finish for the preseason favorites. Sosa reportedly arrived to the ballpark just 70 minutes before the game and bolted shortly after first pitch without ever getting into uniform, leaving nothing but wounded relationships and the apocryphal tale of a smashed boombox in his wake. The disappointing finish and early exit were frustrating for everyone, but Sosa had come to be seen by many as a prima donna who cared more about his numbers than the team's success."

What? Our Sammy? Could *The Game* turn so swiftly on one of its greatest and unexpected heroes who helped restore it to national prominence and importance?

Well, if Mark McGwire's game can skid to the point where he's lifted for a pinch-hitter to get a bunt down in a one-run game, if Bob Gibson can be relegated to the bullpen when he leaves the field, shouting expletives at a less-than-memorable player who'd just turned around Gibson's final pitch for a grand slam, if the magnificent Willie Mays, of all people, can stumble around in the outfield in baseball's annual national showcase, the World Series, it can happen to anyone. Even the irrepressible Sosa, who has lived in a sort of exile ever since he left the game in 2007.

Even after all Sosa had done for the City of Wind—not that far off Jordan territory for a few extraordinary seasons—don't for a moment think the Cubs were going to let him get away with that lousy getaway.

In January, they traded Sosa to the Baltimore Orioles for the immortal trifecta of Jerry Hairston Jr., Mike Fontenot, and Dave Crouthers. They didn't even get the original Jerry Hairston.

Sosa enacted his own sort-of revenge against the Cubs a couple years later, depriving them of what surely would have been a once-in-a-decade marketing experience for the club by hitting his 600th home run *against* them.

And get this, the Cubs, showing bygones will be bygones, as soon as Sosa exited their clubhouse, they gave the very number that Sosa had launched onto a million T-shirts and hats to newcomer Jason Marquis, number 21.

Baseball being what it is, can you guess who happened to be on the mound in Arlington, Texas, a couple years later, wearing that Cubs' number 21 uniform, throwing the pitch that Sosa clubbed into the seats for number 600?

Ah ... baseball.

Sosa broke in as a skinny outfielder with the Texas Rangers in 1989, who had signed him as an amateur free agent at 16 four years earlier. With a wild swing and no strike zone (20 Ks, 0 walks in his first 25 games for the Texas Rangers), he was dealt to Chicago—the White Sox this time (which not everybody remembers) for 33 games.

Sosa hit just three home runs, batted .273 in that tryout, and came back to the Chisox as a 21-year-old regular in 1990, hitting .233 with 15 homers, 70 RBIs, and 150 strikeouts in 153 games. The next year, he barely made it over the Mendoza line—.203, 10 homers, and 33 RBIs with 98 strikeouts.

So nobody was particularly surprised that he was moved—but who expected it would be across town? It was the first White Sox–Cubs deal since the six-player swap on January 25, 1983—Steve Trout and Warren Brusstar to the Cubs for Scott Fletcher, Randy Martz, Pat Tabler, and Dick Tidrow.

It seemed like a great deal for the Chisox; they got All-Star slugger George Bell and gave up a strikeout-prone youngster and a passable lefty reliever in Ken Patterson. But it didn't work out that way. The 32-year-old Bell had a fine first season for the Pale Hose—31 home runs, 97 RBIs, with a .255 average in 155 games. But next year's fade—.217, 13, 49—was final. Troubled with knee issues, Bell retired at 33.

Sosa, meanwhile, was just tuning up. Over the next 13 seasons, he launched 545 homers, won the MVP in 1998 when he hit 66 home runs, earned seven All-Star berths, led the league in home runs twice, and connected on more than 40 home runs over seven different seasons.

And it wasn't just that Sosa hit that many home runs, it was how he came to the park every night. And it was *every* night. Look at these game totals from 1997 to 2001: 162 games (that's *all* of 'em), then 159, 162, 156, 160. You can imagine the groans from National League pitchers in their pregame meetings: "Christ, he's *always* in the lineup." Sosa, who loved the applause, the nightly show, missed just 11 games over that four-year run, remarkable for an overflow of statistics in all shapes and sizes and categories. He still struck out a lot—Sosa led baseball three years running with whiff totals of 174-171-171—no wonder Chicago was the Windy City. But Sosa also drove in runs, lots and lots of them.

Sosa drove in 158 runs in that extraordinary 1998 season, dueling with that big lug from St. Louis. Comparing their stats for that magical year is interesting; McGwire won the dramatic home-run battle of course, 70–66, but also drew 162 walks and 28 intentional. Sosa drew 73 walks, almost double his total from the year before, only eight intentional. He drove in 158 runs to McGwire's 147, numbers as cartoonish as any in that steroid era.

At 34, McGwire was at his peak. Just three seasons later, he was all done. Sosa kept going, driving in 141 runs in 1999, 138 in 2000, and a whopping 160 in a 64-homer season in 2001, the highest in the National League since Hack Wilson's unprecedented, all-time mark of 191 in 1930.

The fans—maybe we should say worshippers—at Wrigley Field understandably grew accustomed to seeing this amazing annual outburst from Sosa, who over that four-year span was a match for anyone in the history of the game, including Babe Ruth, Lou Gehrig, Ted Williams, and Barry Bonds.

Finally, Sosa's numbers started to come back to earth: 49 homers in 2002, 40 in 2003—his corked bat year—and then 35 in his final year in Chicago, when everything fell apart.

As documented by ESPN's Gene Wojciechowski in a column called "Kiss Him Goodbye," it was as ugly as it gets. And sad.

"'Guys stayed late, had a few beers,' says a Cubs official," Wojciechowski wrote. "And there were bats around. These players were exasperated and angry at Sosa, the self-proclaimed 'gladiator' who had betrayed them on a day when none of the Cubs really wanted to be there. Thirteen minutes after Maddux threw his first pitch in that meaningless season finale, Sosa slipped out of the clubhouse, made that brisk walk to the players' lot, fired up his silver Range Rover (Sosa was the only Cub with an assigned space) and gunned it past the surprised attendant, right out the gate. He was gone."

Given Sosa's track record, that was surprising, to be sure.

According to the column, "one of the lingering Cubs, a veteran position player known for his intensity and unselfishness, grabbed a bat and made his way toward the double locker. And there it was, The Gladiator's boom box. Many of the players hated that boom box, mostly because they resented how Sosa used it to mark his territory. This was his house, his team, his city—or so he said. Thirteen years of Cubs service and 545 of his 574 career home runs made it so. But what Sosa didn't understand—still doesn't—is that his power in the clubhouse had eroded. The players, especially some of the veterans, were tired of Sosa's salsa CDs, the way he cranked up the volume, the way he imposed himself on everyone."

In every big-league clubhouse, there are territorial domains. The veterans get certain lockers and are afforded certain privileges and woe be he who intrudes on them. But with Sosa uncharacteristically leaving early, he became an easy target for the Cubs' disappointing year.

As Wojciechowski wrote: "the law of diminishing returns had revealed Sosa for what he was: a fading superstar who spoke of teamwork, but rarely practiced it, a Hall of Famer-to-be who had alienated most of the other Cubs players, as well as key management and support staff. To make matters worse, Sosa lied about sneaking out, insisting he left in the seventh inning. The Cubs would let it be known that a security camera showed otherwise. Once again, he'd been transformed: from shoeshine boy on the streets of San Pedro de Macoris to major leaguer to Hall of Famer to dictatorial diva to . . . quitter."

"So what happened next was no surprise. The teammate stood over the black boom box with a bat and smashed the thing as if it were a hanging curve. In one anger-and-beer-fueled gesture, the coup d'état was complete. This would never be Sosa's house again."

Sosa moved on to Baltimore and played in just 102 games for the Orioles in 2005, hitting just .221 with 14 home runs and 45 RBIs, troubled with a nearly unbelievable assortment of ailments in succession—a staph infection, an abscess, and ultimately, an ailing right big toe that did him in, halting his season on August 25. Or at least that was the rationale. He'd been 5-for-50 over the past 15 games of that season.

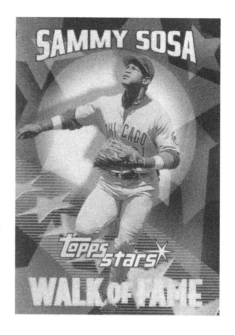

"I'm sure there was a lot of stuff that contributed to his lack of production for us," Orioles manager Sam Perlozzo said at the time. "He was certainly in good enough shape and hits the ball well in batting practice. I look at him and every time he goes to the plate, I feel good that he's going to do something. And it just didn't happen."

In 2006, Sosa marketed himself around, and ultimately turned down a $500,000 offer from the Washington Nationals and took the year off. Very un-Sosa-like.

He returned to the game in 2007 with the Texas Rangers and turned in a most respectable final season, batting .252 with 21 homers and 92 RBIs in 114 games. This time, he made it to the end of the season, playing his final game on a Saturday night in Seattle, a let's-get-it-over-with dentist's visit (2:34)—a 5–1 loss. Sosa, who was DH, batted cleanup and had a quiet night.

He singled off Mariners starter Miguel Batista in the second inning, the 2,408th and final hit of his major-league career. He bounced to short in the fourth, hit a short flare to right in the seventh, and came up for the last time with one out in the ninth, his sad Rangers trailing 5–1, facing reliever Sean Green who quickly got him 0-2. With one last swing, Sosa caught a fastball away and sent it high and deep to right at Safeco Field. But not far enough. José Guillén drifted back and caught it, and Sosa peeled off toward the Rangers dugout. One out later, the season and Sosa's career was over.

What remains puzzling to this day is the Sosa-Chicago split. So much so, former Sosa teammate Doug Glanville was moved to write about it for ESPN.com.

"Maybe I'm missing something, maybe there is some skeleton so large that it is locked away, but if not, we must acknowledge that Sammy Sosa was an integral part of Cubs history," Glanville wrote, perhaps expressing the sentiments of baseball fans everywhere.

"He did a lot of good for the Cubs and the city. What is broken should be repaired. No one has to be blamed, no one has to be wrong or right. There just needs to be a recognition that how it stands does not align with what is and has always been an asset to the Cubs: a tireless loyalty, bigger than self, big-hearted and forgiving, a sentiment that existed well before the 2016 championship."

In the same column, Sosa spoke up.

"Sometimes people make a comment, people talk, but they don't know how I go about my business," Sosa told ESPN.com. "One thing I do not understand: A lot of teammates, I helped them a lot, but they have me like I was one of the worst people in the world. Regardless of what happened, nobody will scratch my number from the board. I have no problem with Chicago or the new front office. It is a surprise [how things are today]. . . . I gave them all my life when I was playing. I asked myself, I really ask myself, 'What have I done so wrong that the people today sometimes treat me like I don't deserve what I did?'"

The two heroes of that magical 1998 summer—Sammy Sosa and Mark McGwire—seem more or less in exile. McGwire had three three-year stints as a hitting coach for the Cardinals, Dodgers, and Padres, a role that seemed sort of belittling to someone who'd done what he had, kind of like asking Houdini to do card tricks. Sosa seems to spend his time traveling, giving the occasional odd interview with Jeremy Schaap, sounding like a man whose house had been burglarized and was still wondering why.

Watching *Long Gone Summer* once again, the thrills of that home-run race will come flooding back to you. In retrospect, knowing that much—if not all of it—was chemically fueled, artificially induced, stings. Still.

Sammy Sosa by the Numbers

YEAR	TEAM	G	AB	R	H	TB	2B	3B	HR	RBI	BB	SO	SB	BA	SLG	OBP
1989	TEX	25	84	8	20	26	3	0	1	3	0	20	0	.238	.310	.238
1989	CHW	33	99	19	27	41	5	0	3	10	11	27	7	.273	.414	.351
1989	ALL	58	183	27	47	67	8	0	4	13	11	47	7	.257	.366	.303
1990	CHW	153	532	72	124	215	26	10	15	70	33	150	32	.233	.404	.282
1991	CHW	116	316	39	64	106	10	1	10	33	14	98	13	.203	.335	.240
1992	CHC	67	262	41	68	103	7	2	8	25	19	63	15	.260	.393	.317
1993	CHC	159	598	92	156	290	25	5	33	93	38	135	36	.261	.485	.309
1994	CHC	105	426	59	128	232	17	6	25	70	25	92	22	.300	.545	.339
1995	CHC	144	564	89	151	282	17	3	36	119	58	134	34	.268	.500	.340
1996	CHC	124	498	84	136	281	21	2	40	100	34	134	18	.273	.564	.323
1997	CHC	162	642	90	161	308	31	4	36	119	45	174	22	.251	.480	.300
1998	CHC	159	643	134	198	416	20	0	66	158	73	171	18	.308	.647	.377
1999	CHC	162	625	114	180	397	24	2	63	141	78	171	7	.288	.635	.367
2000	CHC	156	604	106	193	383	38	1	50	138	91	168	7	.320	.634	.406
2001	CHC	160	577	146	189	425	34	5	64	160	116	153	0	.328	.737	.437
2002	CHC	150	556	122	160	330	19	2	49	108	103	144	2	.288	.594	.399
2003	CHC	137	517	99	144	286	22	0	40	103	62	143	0	.279	.553	.358
2004	CHC	126	478	69	121	247	21	0	35	80	56	133	0	.253	.517	.332
2005	BAL	102	380	39	84	143	15	1	14	45	39	84	1	.221	.376	.295
2007	TEX	114	412	53	104	193	24	1	21	92	34	112	0	.252	.468	.311
TOTALS		2354	8813	1475	2408	4704	379	45	609	1667	929	2306	234	.273	.534	.344

1965

YOGI BERRA

GOODBYE AS A MET?

DATE: May 9, 1965

SITE: Shea Stadium, New York City

PITCHER: Tony Cloninger of the Milwaukee Braves

RESULT: Groundball to second base

He would not pass the eye test. Short, stocky, with those taxi-cab-going-down-main-street-with-its-doors-open ears and a countenance that did not exactly scream intelligence, Lawrence Peter "Yogi" Berra did not look any more like a major-league baseball player than the guy down the street. Until he put a uniform on.

On the almost endless list of New York Yankee greats that stretch back through their decades of baseball dominance, Berra's on-the-field accomplishments are a match for just about any of them.

A three-time American League Most Valuable Player, an 18-time All-Star, a 10-time world champion, Yogi landed in Cooperstown just like Babe Ruth, Lou Gehrig, Joe DiMaggio, Mickey Mantle, and Whitey Ford, acknowledged as one of the game's all-time greats—even if he sure as hell never looked the part.

If you listened to him speak, well, there was another reason to count him out. He was unintentionally, it seemed, comical. He was Forrest Gump in pinstripes, which, of course, belied his extraordinary baseball smarts and on-field decision-making. In media-crazy New York, Yogi was always good copy. Nobody took him seriously—except enemy pitchers.

Why? Well, it's hard to know where to begin talking about Yogi Berra. Some of his missteps were unimaginable, even by a comedy writer. For example, he once signed an anniversary card to his understanding and devoted wife Carmen like this: "Yogi Berra."

"So I could distinguish him from all the other Yogis in my life," she quipped.

No doubt, you know many of these Yogi lines already. Like this one: "Nobody goes there anymore," he said, reviewing a popular restaurant. "It's too crowded." Or "It gets late early out here." Or "If people don't want to come out to the ballpark, nobody's going to stop them." Or when asked what time it was, "You mean now?"

There are countless more, some of which Berra *did* say, some were attributed to him, some might well have been coined by bored New York sportswriters covering a ruthlessly colorless Yankee dynasty, just to pep things up. We will never exactly know.

Always helpful, Yogi offered his own explanation, just to clear things up. "I didn't always say what I said," he explained.

Whether or not the affable Berra actually coined all those phrases or not is impossible to know. But his verbal pretzel logic has, over time, tended to obscure his remarkable career and extraordinary accomplishments, mostly as a player but some as a manager too. If you actually wrote out Yogi's managerial history, it might have been even more improbable than his Hall of Fame career. He won a pennant with the Yankees and the Mets. He was fired by the Yankees twice and once by the Mets.

Even someone with Yogi's sense of the absurd couldn't have imagined this one. After Yogi retired as a player and moved into the manager's seat as manager Ralph Houk moved up to become GM, Yogi steered his Yankees into Game 7 of the 1964 World Series against the St. Louis Cardinals. Then, they fired him. Huh?

That's what happened. Not only did Yogi get fired, but the Yankees went and hired the guy who beat him—and his Yanks—in the World Series, Johnny Keane.

Yogi didn't see this coming—neither did the rest of the world. According to Jon Pessah's *Yogi*, Berra expected to be back. On the charter flight back, he asked Whitey Ford to return as pitching coach. Ford, a shrewd character himself, unknowingly quipped "What makes you think you'll be back?" If he only knew . . .

When Berra met with Houk and Yankee president Dan Topping the next day, he walked in thinking of asking for a two-year deal. Instead, Houk beat him to the punch. "Yogi," Houk says, "we've decided to make a change at manager."

Yankee fans, who already were taking the team's dominance for granted (only 14,879 showed up to watch them clinch yet another pennant), were outraged and probably rightfully so. Rereading the story of Berra's firing now as recorded in the *New York Times* that day seems like a *Saturday Night Live* skit. This is how it appeared in the paper.

"Lawrence Peter (Yogi) Berra was dismissed yesterday as manager of the New York Yankees just one day after losing the World Series. Berra immediately accepted a two-year contract to remain as a 'special field consultant,' a loosely defined, newly created position dealing with scouting and player evaluation.

"Ralph Houk, general manager of the Yankees and Berra's predecessor as field manager, made the announcement at a hastily arranged press conference in the same hotel ballroom used less than a year ago to announce the promotion of Houk and the installation of Berra as manager.

"Upon hearing of Berra's release, Sargent Shriver—who had been sworn in earlier in the day as director of the Government's war on poverty—sought Berra for a top-level position with the bureau's youth program. An aide to the poverty drive chief said Berra turned down the job, with regret."

Hmmm. Sargent Shriver and Yogi Berra? Really? Was there laughter in the newsroom of The Old Gray Lady on that one? There was more.

"Less than two hours before Houk's announcement yesterday, Johnny Keane, manager of the Cardinals, resigned in St. Louis. Keane immediately developed into a leading contender for the Yankee job. Another is Alvin Dark, recently deposed manager of the San Francisco Giants.

"Houk declined to discuss any of the reasons for Berra's dismissal beyond his prepared statement that 'it was better for all concerned.'"

Clearly, newspaper reporters have become a lot more aggressive since then. "Better for all concerned?" Does that include Yogi? The story, written without a byline, continues.

"Then he was asked about possible successors. 'A decision will be made within a week,' he said. 'We have two or three men under consideration.' Was Dark one of them ? Houk hesitated only a fraction of an instant. 'Yes,' he said.

"'What about Keane?' someone asked. 'He's not available, is he?' said Houk. 'He resigned this morning,' the interviewers told Houk. 'I didn't know that when I came into this room,' said Houk, "but if that's so, then I would add him to the list. He would certainly be considered.'"

So, dear reader, we're supposed to believe that Cardinals manager Keane, after winning the World Series, just resigned on his own? With no contact with the Yankees in-between?

The *Times* story goes on: "Houk declared that the decision to replace Berra had been first entertained in mid-August when the Yankees were floundering in third place. The final decision was made before the World Series.

"'The loss of the seventh game had absolutely nothing to do with it,' Houk said. 'We just felt that it would be better for Berra and for the Yankees to have this new arrangement.'

"'Did Berra know that while the Series was in progress?'

"'No,' said Houk, 'it wouldn't have been fair to burden him with that while he was fighting to win. He first learned of it this morning when he met with me and Mr. Topping.'

"Dan Topping, as co-owner of the Yankees and the active executive head of the organization, is Houk's immediate superior. The Columbia Broadcasting System, now in the process of completing the purchase of the Yankees, was not involved in the decision in any way, Houk said.

'It was my decision, with the approval of my president, Mr. Topping,' Houk stated. [Reader note: Doesn't this contradict what he just said?]

"'I wouldn't want to blame it on anybody,' Houk insisted. "I see no need to discuss what made us want to change.'"

A quote later on in the story was a classic. "Yogi isn't exactly being kicked upstairs," said one observer. "He's sort of being kicked sideways."

Not for long. With Gotham seething over the Berra dismissal, Yogi's old boss, Casey Stengel knew how to reach him. Casey decided to hire Berra as a coach for $35,000 a year and Yogi, after a year off, was so happy to have a job, he even decided to strap on the catcher's gear and take a few at-bats for the Mets. It all was hard to fathom. Even for Yogi.

YOGI BERRA
catcher NEW YORK YANKEES

To most baseball fans, Yogi's active career ended in 1963. With Elston Howard taking over behind the plate, Yogi played in just 64 games. It looked as if his final at-bat in Yankee Stadium would come in the regular-season finale vs. the Twins. In the bottom of the ninth, Yogi came up as a pinch-hitter against Bill Dailey and lined out to third.

After the Yankees lost the first two games of the World Series to the Dodgers, Berra came up one last time. Trailing the Dodgers and Don Drysdale, 1–0 in the eighth at Dodger Stadium, Berra pinch-hit for Yankee starter Jim Bouton and lined out to right fielder Ron Fairly.

He did not play in 1964, so that looked like Yogi's final swing until amazingly, for the Amazin' Mets, Berra returned to the active roster at the end of April and pinch-hit and grounded out in a 9–2 loss to the Reds. He actually got two singles in a 2–1 Mets win on May 4, but by May 9, it was clear it was time to retire for good.

Yogi played the first game of a Mother's Day doubleheader against the Milwaukee Braves. He dropped a foul popup for the final error of his career, fanned in his first three at-bats against the Braves' Tony Cloninger, and then hit into a fielder's choice with a groundball to second in the ninth. He announced his retirement as an active player two days later.

He went on to manage those same Mets after the death of Gil Hodges and came back to manage the Yankees again, taking over for former team-mate Billy Martin. He did a creditable job and agreed to manage the team in 1985, provided George Steinbrenner agreed not to fire him during the season. Just 16 games in, Steinbrenner sent general manager Clyde King to Chicago to tell Yogi the bad news. It was another 14 years before Berra would set foot in Yankee Stadium again.

When he did—July 18, 1999—Berra returned to Yankee Stadium for Yogi Berra Day surrounded by many of his former teammates who welcomed the little icon back. Don Larsen threw the first pitch to Berra in front of a packed crowd at the ballpark. And Yogi's return brought with it some Yankee good fortune one last time.

To the delight of Yankee—and Yogi—fans everywhere, Yankee pitcher David Cone threw a perfect game that day, just as Larsen had 43 years earlier. This time, though, Yogi Berra only had to watch. "This was great," Berra told William Rhoden of the *New York Times*, standing in the back of Joe Torre's office. "My day and Don Larsen's here, this was great. Those pinstripes make you do something."

Yogi Berra by the Numbers

YEAR	TEAM	G	AB	R	H	TB	2B	3B	HR	RBI	BB	SO	SB	BA	SLG	OBP
1946	NYY	7	22	3	8	15	1	0	2	4	1	1	0	.364	.682	.391
1947	NYY	83	293	41	82	136	15	3	11	54	13	12	0	.280	.464	.310
1948	NYY	125	469	70	143	229	24	10	14	98	25	24	3	.305	.488	.341
1949	NYY	116	415	59	115	199	20	2	20	91	22	25	2	.277	.480	.323
1950	NYY	151	597	116	192	318	30	6	28	124	55	12	4	.322	.533	.383
1951	NYY	141	547	92	161	269	19	4	27	88	44	20	5	.294	.492	.350
1952	NYY	142	534	97	146	255	17	1	30	98	64	24	2	.273	.478	.355
1953	NYY	137	503	81	149	263	23	5	27	108	50	32	0	.296	.523	.363
1954	NYY	151	584	89	179	285	28	6	22	125	55	29	0	.307	.488	.366
1955	NYY	147	541	84	147	254	20	3	27	108	60	19	1	.272	.470	.349
1956	NYY	140	521	93	155	278	29	2	30	105	64	29	3	.298	.534	.376
1957	NYY	134	482	74	121	211	14	2	24	82	57	25	1	.251	.438	.329
1958	NY	122	433	60	115	204	17	3	22	90	35	35	3	.266	.471	.319
1959	NY	131	472	64	134	218	25	1	19	69	43	38	1	.284	.462	.347
1960	NY	120	359	46	99	160	14	1	15	62	38	24	2	.276	.446	.347
1961	NY	119	394	62	107	184	11	0	22	61	35	28	2	.272	.467	.330
1962	NYY	86	232	25	52	90	8	0	10	35	24	18	0	.224	.388	.297
1963	NYY	64	147	20	43	73	6	0	8	24	15	17	1	.293	.497	.360
1965	NYM	4	9	1	2	2	0	0	0	15	0	3	0	.222	.222	.222
TOTALS		2120	7554	1177	2150	3643	321	49	358	0	700	415	30	.285	.482	.348

GEORGE BRETT

FUN, FUN, FUN

DATE: October 3, 1993

SITE: Arlington Stadium, Arlington, Texas

PITCHER: Tom Henke of the Texas Rangers

RESULT: Groundball single

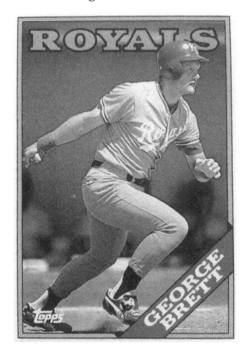

F un?" Dennis Eckersley's voice seemed to rise an octave, responding to Boston Red Sox announcer Dave O'Brien's innocent, time-eating question during yet another dull moment during a 2020 Boston Red Sox telecast on NESN.

"It might have *looked like* I was having fun out there," Eckersley said, instantly conjuring up images of the electric Eckersley, the flowing hair, the dashing Three Musketeers mustache, the fist pumps and the dramatic post-whiff gestures that marked his every appearance throughout his Hall of Fame career. "But that was fear. Fear. I never had fun playing major-league baseball, that was all fear."

"Baseball at this level is just too difficult," agreed ex–Red Sox second baseman and New England folk hero Jerry Remy, also a Red Sox color man. The three of them were calling the game away from an empty Fenway Park, sharing a COVID-19 safe booth in Watertown, Massachusetts, which maybe gave them a different perspective on the sport that made them famous. "I don't know anybody who had 'fun' at this level," Remy concluded.

The two paused for a second, then both said the exact same thing. "George Brett. Ask George Brett." Eckersley blurted and Remy instantly agreed. "George Brett had fun playing major-league baseball."

So it seemed. Twenty-one major-league seasons. Three thousand, one hundred and fifty-four hits, batting titles in three separate decades, a career .305 average, an MVP award, a Gold Glove, and one remarkable run at one of baseball's seemingly unapproachable marks, batting .400. And it wasn't supposed to be him.

If you had asked any number of professional baseball scouts who went to California to watch his older brother or maybe even asked George's father, Jack, they might well have pointed at Ken "Kemer" Brett as the potential Hall of Famer, not George.

Ken Brett could do it all. He was Rick Ankiel plus. A lefty pitcher with 90 plus in his arm, a terrific hitter with power, he might have been the best two-way player coming along in quite a while. Was he going to pitch? Was he going to play center field? Major-league scouts were abuzz.

And then, here was Ken Brett pitching in a World Series for the Boston Red Sox at 19! And he could hit! He was the Brett brother to watch, wasn't he?

The older Brett went on to have a good major-league career. Played for 10 different teams. Made an All-Star team, lasted 14 seasons, and hit 10 major-league home runs, including homers in four consecutive starts as a pitcher, something not even Babe Ruth achieved.

Imagine growing up in that shadow. Imagine trying to follow that opening act. Having a brother in the bigs, well, how did it go for Tommie Aaron? The Alou brothers—Jesús and Matty seemed to be OK with Felipe leading the way. But would Billy Ripken have gotten a chance had it not been for Cal? What about Billy and Tony Conigliaro?

George Brett did show promise, had all the tools and the bloodlines, and the Kansas City Royals did make him a second-round pick. But Brett didn't exactly burst out of the starting blocks.

Beginning his career as a professional starting with the Billings Mustangs in the Rookie League, then the San Jose Bees of the California League, then the Triple-A Omaha Royals, Brett never got his average over .300. Even so, he got the call to the bigs in August of 1973, and he went 5-for-40 in a handful of games. It wasn't as if Cooperstown was clearing a space for him.

But Royals hitting coach Charley Lau saw something in Brett's swing, and the two began to work together, stressing balance, using the whole field, weight shifts. This philosophy ran contrary to the time-honored *Science of Hitting* fundamentals laid out by Hall of Famer Ted Williams, who advocated hip rotation—"hips before hands"—and a slight upswing. Since a pitcher throws from an elevated mound and you want to meet the ball squarely as it comes down, swing up, Ted suggested.

Lau and his prize pupil Brett worked things differently. Brett had no problem with contact, singles, doubles, whatever worked. And groundballs, something Williams disdained, were OK with him. Roger Angell recounted a conversation with an old-time Royals coach talking about Brett. "Everything he hits goes through the infield like a stream of milk."

So it was for American League pitchers for 20 years. When you played the Royals, it always seemed Brett was coming to the plate in a big spot. He was always a difficult out. For example, in his spectacular .390 season, Brett struck out just 22 times in 515 plate appearances. Talk about a throwback player.

In that his MVP season (1980), Brett came just 10 points short of that magic .400, finishing at .390, the highest mark in the major leagues and the greatest challenge to matching Williams's .406 in 1941. In 1981, a strike-shortened season, Tony Gwynn of the San Diego Padres was at .394 when the strike halted the proceedings on August 11. So there were two bids at the .400 mark. There really hasn't been one since.

Brett carried that .400 average deeper into the season. On August 17, a 4-for-4 performance against Toronto raised his average to .401. Three days later, a three-hit performance put him at .406! He kept the average around the .400 mark until September 19 when the A's Matt Keough spun a five-hit shutout at Royals Stadium, holding Brett to an 0-for-4, dropping his average to .396. And it nudged back down to .390 by the end of the year. Reportedly, Brett's dad—a hard-driving, high-expectations sort of guy—hollered at his son when he wound up 10 points shy of the mark.

"You couldn't have found a way to get five more @$$%& hits?"

Yes, Charley Lau's pupil did well for himself. Brett went on to have 11 .300-plus seasons, won three batting titles in three different decades, and also hit lots and lots of doubles (665). He also hit lots of triples (137), along with 317 homers, including seven seasons of 20 homers or more. That's a Hall of Fame player for you.

When most fans think of Brett, the moment they remember more than any other is the famous pine tar game in July of 1983. In the ninth inning of a game at Yankee Stadium, the Royals threatened and fireballing Hall of Famer reliever Goose Gossage was summoned to face Brett. Brett fouled off Gossage's first fastball but connected with the second, sending a soaring drive into the lower deck at Yankee Stadium.

After he crossed home, Yankee manager and first-class irritant Billy Martin protested Brett's bat had too much pine tar on it, citing an obscure rule. Home plate umpire Tim McClelland upheld Martin's complaint, prompting Brett's memorable charge from the dugout, a highlight you've certainly seen a hundred times.

Four days later, American League president Lee MacPhail overruled McClelland. MacPhail let the home run stand and ordered the game resumed at a later date. Brett, however, had been ejected and did not take part in the resumption of the game, which eventually held up as a Royals win.

But for every great player, there comes a time when the competitive juices slow down, the travel, the pressure, all the elements that go into a 162-game season wear you down. So it was with Brett, who, after turning 40, saw the end coming. And said so.

"The game became a job," Brett said then. "It wasn't a game anymore. And baseball shouldn't be treated that way. I wasn't getting that excited when I did something good, wasn't getting that down when I did something bad. I wasn't that happy when we won; I wasn't that sad when we lost. There was something missing."

The next day, a sunny Sunday after-noon, September 26, Brett sent Royals fans home with something to remember him by. Trailing the Angels 3–1 in the fourth, Brett came up with the bases loaded against Angels starter and future Boston Red Sox manager John Farrell. Brett took Farrell's second pitch to deep right-center field for a grand slam. He wasn't done.

After the Angels tied the game and carried it into the 10th, Brett came up against California's Paul Swingle with two out, nobody on. On Swingle's second pitch, Brett launched his 317th and final major-league homer, a walkoff to send the 19,391 Royals fans home happy.

That was about it. The Royals, who weren't going anywhere, had three more games with the Indians, then a road trip to Texas to finish up the year. Brett played in every single game, not wanting to disappoint fans. But he could see the finish line and couldn't wait to get there. By the time Brett reached Arlington, he was just 1 for his last 21. When it came down to that final game, Texas starter Steve Dreyer had retired him three times. He'd lined out to left twice, bounced to second.

But the Baseball Gods set it up for Brett to have one more at-bat. Leading off the ninth inning against Texas reliever Tom Henke, both teams were standing outside their dugout, watching this final spectacle. Brett smiled as he approached the plate, chaw in his cheek. Catcher Iván Rodríguez patted him on the back, and Ranger fans gave him a standing ovation. He fell behind 1-2, then bounced a groundball—and we do mean bounced—*four* times—up the middle into center field, exactly like that stream of milk that coach talked about.

Coach Lee May said something to him and Brett laughed heartily. First baseman Rafael Palmeiro congratulated him, and you could see Brett's expression bore the strain of these last few games. It was over now and he looked relieved and happy. The guy who had convinced American League opponents that he was having the time of his life between the lines gave us a fleeting glimpse of the emotional toll it took for every one of those 2,707 major-league games.

"Every game," he confessed to writer Joe Posnanski, "I thought I would embarrass myself. Every day. I thought, 'What if the ball goes through my legs?' 'What if I strike out and fall down?' I would look up into the stands and see all those people and think about how much it meant to them. What if I let them down? What if we lose because of me? Every day I thought about those things."

Who knew?

George Brett by the Numbers

YEAR	TEAM	G	AB	R	H	TB	2B	3B	HR	RBI	BB	SO	SB	BA	SLG	OBP
1973	KC	13	40	2	5	7	2	0	0	0	0	5	0	.125	.175	.125
1974	KC	133	457	49	129	166	21	5	2	47	21	38	8	.282	.363	.313
1975	KC	159	634	84	195	289	35	13	11	90	46	48	13	.308	.456	.353
1976	KC	159	645	94	215	298	34	14	7	67	49	36	21	.333	.462	.377
1977	KC	139	564	105	176	300	32	13	22	88	55	24	14	.312	.532	.373
1978	KC	128	510	79	150	238	45	8	9	62	39	35	23	.294	.467	.342
1979	KC	154	645	119	212	363	42	20	23	107	51	36	17	.329	.563	.376
1980	KC	117	449	87	175	298	33	9	24	118	58	22	15	.390	.664	.454
1981	KC	89	347	42	109	168	27	7	6	43	27	23	14	.314	.484	.361
1982	KC	144	552	101	166	279	32	9	21	82	71	51	6	.301	.505	.378
1983	KC	123	464	90	144	261	38	2	25	93	57	39	0	.310	.563	.385
1984	KC	104	377	42	107	173	21	3	13	69	38	37	0	.284	.459	.344
1985	KC	155	550	108	184	322	38	5	30	112	103	49	9	.335	.585	.436
1986	KC	124	441	70	128	212	28	4	16	73	80	45	1	.290	.481	.401
1987	KC	115	427	71	124	212	18	2	22	78	72	47	6	.290	.496	.388
1988	KC	157	589	90	180	300	42	3	24	103	82	51	14	.306	.509	.389
1989	KC	124	457	67	129	197	26	3	12	80	59	47	14	.282	.431	.362
1990	KC	142	544	82	179	280	45	7	14	87	56	63	9	.329	.515	.387
1991	KC	131	505	77	129	203	40	2	10	61	58	75	2	.255	.402	.327
1992	KC	152	592	55	169	235	35	5	7	61	35	69	8	.285	.397	.330
1993	KC	145	560	69	149	243	31	3	19	75	39	67	7	.266	.434	.312
TOTALS		2707	10349	1583	3154	5044	665	137	317	1596	1096	907	201	.305	.487	.369

TONY CONIGLIARO

ONE PITCH CHANGED EVERYTHING

DATE: June 12, 1975

SITE: Comiskey Park, Chicago, Illinois

PITCHER: Jim Kaat of the Chicago White Sox

RESULT: Groundball to second base

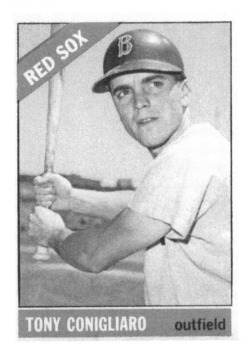

Wwe stood, en masse, as we watched the tall, dark-haired number 25 do something we wondered if we'd ever see again—stand at the plate with a bat in his hand at Boston's Fenway Park. It was April 8, 1975, the first April he'd been in uniform in four years.

After the heart-wrenching and inexplicably abrupt previous endings to the baseball career of Tony Conigliaro, now, he was getting a chance to rewrite it. We were here to see it.

Fenway was slammed—34,055—also to see Hank Aaron play his first American League game, to see the Boston Red Sox open the 1975 season, but for many fans—including this one—getting a chance to see Tony C. back on the field was the main impetus.

It was a chilly, windy day, 52 degrees at game time. And looking at the Red Sox lineup, with Conigliaro penciled in the cleanup spot after four years away from the game, it almost seemed impossible to believe.

Impossible—there's a word that rings out in Red Sox history. Conigliaro was, for much of that Impossible Dream season of 1967, the yin to Triple Crown winner Carl Yastrzemski's yang, a potent right-handed bat whose every swing seemed to take dead aim at Fenway's Green Monster. He was in the middle of another fine season when in the fourth inning of a game against the California Angels on August 18 all of Fenway—if not all of New England—held its collective breath when a Jack Hamilton fastball hit Tony in the face. Watching the handsome young hero carted off the field on a stretcher, it was shocking. But nobody then thought it might be career-threatening.

When Conigliaro was unable to return to the field for the stretch drive and the World Series vs. St. Louis, reports went out about the shattered cheekbone, the damage to his eye. We began to wonder. In spring training, his vision was impaired, he couldn't pick up the baseball. Desperate to return to the game, he spent some of that year trying to become a pitcher, even threw some games in the Winter Instructional League in November.

As he tried to pitch (he was 0-3 and gave up 15 runs in one game), he noticed his vision in his left eye seemed to improve. He got Red Sox coach Sam Mele to throw batting practice and he began stinging the ball again. Doctors found the eye had healed. "It was a miraculous thing," eye specialists said. "Somebody must have said a novena for that kid."

Miraculously, his vision had improved enough by spring training for him to return and Tony C. not only made the team, he had an extraordinary season. His first home run came in the 10th inning of the season opener, and by the end of the season, Conigliaro had 20 home runs, 82 RBIs, and the Comeback Player of the Year Award that now bears his name.

He raised the stakes in 1970 with his finest major-league season, clubbing 36 HR and 116 RBI. His younger brother Billy had himself a fine year too (.271, 18 homers, 58 RBIs) and the Red Sox had a winning record but weren't in the class of the Baltimore Orioles, who won 108 games. Amazingly, Red Sox general manager Dick O'Connell traded Conigliaro as part of a six-player package before the World Series was even over.

Conigliaro, backup catcher Jerry Moses, and pitcher Ray Jarvis were sent west for Ken and Jarvis Tatum (no relation—one a relief pitcher, the other a marginal outfielder) and second baseman Doug Griffin. Looking back, it was a dump. Neither Tatum did much of anything in Boston; Griffin started at second for five seasons, averaging .248.

O'Connell's curious comment to UPI at the time was "the boys are better off separated. I think it's been a liability having them on the same club."

While this certainly made no sense to the average fan—even now, 50 years later—knowing the way baseball management is, particularly then, you can perhaps understand. Problems? What problems? Take them somewhere else.

"It's difficult for me to explain the condition of my eye," Conigliaro told *Sports Illustrated*'s Mark Mulvoy after his abrupt departure from the Angels in the middle of the 1971 season. "I can see the sides of a television screen, but I have trouble seeing the center of it. I can see sidearm pitches pretty well, but not somebody like Sam McDowell coming straight over the top. If I closed my right eye against a pitcher like that, I couldn't see the ball at all.

"I didn't want to tell anyone that the eye was not as good as it should be. I let it get out that my vision in my bad eye was 20-30 in a test, but I cheated on the test. I had studied the chart before with my other eye. I felt that if people in baseball knew my eyesight was as bad as it was, I'd never have made it back. Even last year when I was having a great season, I was scared. I could get hit again by a pitch and maybe get killed. I was risking my life in the outfield. Really. I'd lose the ball and it would reappear, bang, in my glove. But my lawyer, Joe Tauro, convinced me that I should not retire. He said it would not have looked right to retire when I was traded."

So Conigliaro made a tactical error, as he explained to Mulvoy. "At the end of the season I told the Red Sox about my eye trouble. I asked them to move me from right field to left, where the sun wouldn't bother me so much in Fenway Park. But they told me no, because that would admit I had a problem. I really felt great when they said that—and I mean that seriously. I needed support, and I thought they were behind me and that we would be there together for a long time. Then came the trade ...

"When I was traded, I went into shock. I began to think what base-ball was all about. It is big business. I discovered a ballplayer is a machine. When a player is hurt, they grease him, scrub him, oil him and push him onto the field."

It all came apart for Tony C. in an extra-inning game vs. the A's on July 9. Conigliaro fanned four times vs. A's starter Vida Blue (and lined out to shortstop once) en route to an 0-for-8 with five whiffs and an ejection, after swinging at his batting helmet after a strikeout. At 5 p.m., Conigliaro called a hasty press conference and told the press "I've lost my sight and I'm on the verge of losing my mind." He decided it was time to retire, flew back to Boston, thought he was done with baseball for good.

Yet here it was, four years later, Opening Day in Boston, and all that was somehow miraculously in the past. As we looked up, here he was, Tony Conigliaro, standing at the plate, swinging the bat again. When Conigliaro rewarded the Fenway faithful's lengthy and teary standing ovation by lining a Jim Slaton curveball into right field for a single in his first at-bat, it was a wild scene.

When Conigliaro lit out for second with a 2-2 count on Rico Petrocelli, catcher Darrell Porter's throw was off. Shortstop Robin Yount—mindful of Carl Yastrzemski on third—cut the throw off and Yaz, not always the most reliable baserunner, darted home on the double steal. This was not Red Sox baseball, but it sure was exciting.

After Carl Yastrzemski's leadoff double, Tony C. surprise bunted in his next at-bat—out—then bounced out twice. After a hitless second game, he hit a fifth-inning homer off Oriole starter Mike Cuellar, his first home run since a May 30 two-run shot off the Yankees' Mel Stottlemyre four years earlier. That was for the Angels.

With Conigliaro back and two outstanding rookies in the lineup, Fred Lynn and Jim Rice, early April in Boston could hardly have been more excit-ing. But for Tony, the hits weren't coming. With eventual Hall of Famer Rice competing for the DH spot, Conigliaro struggled.

After a 3-for-23 start, Conigliaro didn't play for 10 days. He had a couple of unsuccessful pinch-hit at-bats, then got a start on May 7 in Cleveland and singled in a run off Fritz Peterson for his third RBI of the season. But there wasn't much else. He whiffed in a pinch-hit at-bat three days later, then, after an 0-for-10 in three starts spaced a few days apart against the A's, Royals, and the A's again, his average had dropped to .100. He was starting to sense the end. Again.

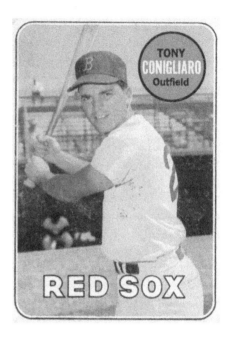

Tony's final multihit game came on a Tuesday night at Fenway against the A's lefty fireballer Vida Blue. Here was his last hurrah, but nobody knew it. Tony singled in Dwight Evans off Blue in the second, then hit his final major-league home run off the lefty, leading off the fourth. Blue, remember, was the same guy who had fanned him four times the last time he faced him in that extra-inning game in California four years earlier. The two hits raised his average to .136.

That was the last big moment. Tony Conigliaro had just 13 more major-league at-bats, his final hit coming off White Sox lefty Jim Kaat in the ninth inning on June 4, a key part of a dramatic rally, a Rick Burleson single off Rich Gossage giving the Red Sox a 7–6 win.

Eight days later, his comeback ended in Chicago. He went 0-for-3, three groundouts including an eighth-inning bouncer to second baseman Jorge Orta off old friend Jim Kaat in a 9–3 loss, and Red Sox management had seen enough. He could retire, go to the minors, and try to regroup, or be released. His final batting average was .123.

He went to Pawtucket for a while, trying to find the magic again. It was gone. He officially retired—again—on August 21. Though it may not seem possible, Tony C.'s luck off the field was even worse. Headed to an interview for a sportscasting position, he suffered a massive heart attack in 1982, suffering irreversible brain damage. He died in 1990.

Bob Ryan of the *Boston Globe* was there that August night in 1967 when everything changed for Tony C. He bought a $3.50 box seat from a scalper and sat over by third base, close enough to see—and hear.

"I have not yet been able to let an Aug. 18 go by without thinking of Tony Conigliaro and the night when his life changed irrevocably," Ryan wrote. "They say it only takes a baseball something like two-fifths of a second to reach the vicinity of home plate after it leaves the pitcher's hand. But two-fifths, three-fifths, a full second, what does it matter?

"What matters is that Tony Conigliaro was unable to get out of the way. A Jack Hamilton fastball did not go where he wanted it to go, and Tony Conigliaro was hit. Baseball players are hit by stray, or even intended-to-hit, pitches all the time, and most of them get up and go to first base. No harm, no foul, you know? This one was very, very different.

"I remember the hush. The sound of silence from 31,027 people is an eerie sensation. There was no hubbub, no low buzzing, as Tony lay at the plate. He wasn't popping up and running to first base. That was obvious. It was also obvious something very bad had just taken place."

Tony Conigliaro by the Numbers

YEAR	TEAM	G	AB	R	H	TB	2B	3B	HR	RBI	BB	SO	SB	BA	SLG	OBP
1964	BOS	111	404	69	117	214	21	2	24	52	35	78	2	.290	.530	.354
1965	BOS	138	521	82	140	267	21	5	32	82	50	116	4	.269	.512	.337
1966	BOS	150	558	77	148	272	26	7	28	93	52	112	0	.265	.487	.330
1967	BOS	95	349	59	100	181	11	5	20	67	27	58	4	.287	.519	.341
1969	BOS	141	506	57	129	216	21	3	20	82	48	111	2	.255	.427	.321
1970	BOS	146	560	89	149	279	20	1	36	116	43	93	4	.266	.498	.324
1971	CAL	74	266	23	59	89	18	0	4	15	23	52	3	.222	.335	.285
1975	BOS	21	57	8	7	14	1	0	2	9	8	9	1	.123	.246	.221
TOTALS		876	3221	464	849	1532	139	23	166	516	286	629	20	.264	.476	.327

MIKE SCHMIDT

ABRUPT END ON THE COAST

DATE: May 28, 1989

SITE: Candlestick Park, San Francisco, California

PITCHER: Mike LaCoss of the San Francisco Giants

RESULT: Walk

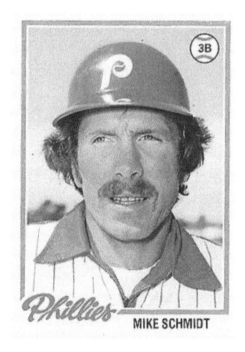

Far away from the City of Brotherly Love, way over on the other side of the country, the idea hit him like a runaway 18-wheeler down a steep incline on the Schuylkill Expressway. Mike Schmidt, future Hall of Fame third baseman, one of the greatest of all time. But here, now, he thought one thing: I don't belong here.

Candlestick Park was in an uproar. A grand slam will do that. With two on and two out, Schmidt had kicked a Robby Thompson groundball to load the bases. His error. Mike Maddux was summoned from the bullpen, and Will Clark had just cleared the bases with one swing. The inning, Schmidt thought, should have been over.

"I don't belong here anymore," Schmidt thought, an idea he'd expound upon the next day in a hastily called press conference. It was Memorial Day in San Francisco and back across the country, in Philadelphia, it was almost as if someone had swiped the Liberty Bell. Though it had taken the city quite a while to warm up to him, after three MVP awards, 10 Gold Gloves, and 548 home runs, they started to realize what they were losing. Philly fans were distraught. And they should have been.

He said goodbye in an auxiliary locker room next to the Phillies locker room in Jack Murphy Stadium. Schmidt swung from his heels one last time.

"Some 18 years ago, I left Dayton, Ohio, with two very bad knees, with a dream to become a major-league player," Schmidt said, breaking into tears and turning away from the microphone. "I thank God this dream came true.

"I was wondering if I could compete with those guys anymore," referring to stars like Kirk Gibson, Will Clark, and Kevin Mitchell. "I'm watching them and feeling like a shadow of the player I used to be. And that was telling me it was time to turn the reins over to somebody else.

"Over the years, I've set high standards for myself as a player. I've always said that when I don't feel I can perform up to those standards, it would be time to retire. My skills to do the things on the field, to make the adjustments needed to hit, to make the routine plays on defense, and to run the bases aggressively, have deteriorated.

"I feel like I could easily ask the Phillies to make me a part-time player, to hang around for a couple of years to add to my statistical totals. However, my respect for the game, my teammates, and the fans won't allow me to do that. For that reason, I have decided to retire as an active player."

It was a bombshell. Sure, the Phillies were struggling, he was struggling, Schmidt's statistics were screaming at him (.203, six homers, 28 RBIs) and here he was, in the middle of a road trip, 46 games into the season, having left—in his mind—a disappointing impression in the minds of 51,498 who had come to watch a Sunday afternoon ballgame vs. the Giants at breezy Candlestick Park. But retiring?

The season had started in promising fashion. The Phils won six of their first eight, Schmidt had homered in the first two games of the season, and it looked like he'd recovered from the rotator cuff injury that had ended his previous season on August 12. But that hot start was just that—a start.

The Phils started to skid, had lost 10 of 13 and Schmidt, so often the answer, wasn't any longer. His average slid to just three points over the Mendoza line, no extra-base hits over his last dozen games and just a couple RBIs. This wasn't the Mike Schmidt we knew.

His last official hit, if you want to call it that, was a seventh-inning bunt off Tim Belcher three days earlier. He left that game for a pinch-runner (Larry McWilliams) and his spot in the lineup came up in the ninth, of course, after the Phillies had pulled within a run. Bob Dernier, hitting in that spot now, lined out to end the game. Normally, there'd have been an uproar; Schmidt not getting a chance to win the game? What?

In a lot of ways, Schmidt's career was as unexpected as his sudden departure. Years later, Schmidt marveled at how it all happened. In a feature story written after he'd retired, he still seemed amazed, as if he'd been in a dream or something.

"I was about the fourth or fifth best baseball player in school—a .250 hitter—and if you don't hit .400 in high school, nobody knows you're alive. I was always the kid with potential. . . ."

But production? According to a story on the SABR website, Schmidt hit just .179 with a single home run as a senior and had to walk on at Ohio University. Imagine that, a Hall of Famer who wasn't even considered good enough to get a scholarship at Ohio University?

Schmidt progressed in college and through the summer leagues, however, and Phillies scout Tony Lucadello convinced the team to take him in the 1971 draft. The Phillies made him a second-rounder, one pick after Kansas City took George Brett. Schmidt signed for $32,500, bought himself a Corvette Stingray, and started his career.

He clubbed his first home run off Balor Moore in a late-September callup in 1972, and played in the majors in 1973, but there were no inklings of Cooperstown in his future. He ended the season with an 0-for-26 slump. Could he play at that level or not?

But in 1974, he emerged with 36 home runs to lead the majors, was second in the NL with 116 RBIs and a .282 batting average, and played a sparkling third base, beginning what ended up being a Hall of Fame career. But the fickle Philadelphia fans were hard on him, even after leading the league in homers three years in a row.

In a way, his treatment by Philly fans was reminiscent of the way Boston Red Sox slugger Ted Williams was covered in Boston. Despite clearly being one of the finest players of his era and all eras, Williams always seemed to be at war with "the knights of the keyboard."

Neither Ted nor Schmidt played in the Twitter era, which is probably a good thing. Their candor might not have gone over well. But ask either team or their fans if they wish they could have each guy start his career right now?

Oddly, two of the finest power hitters of their respective eras had completely different hitting techniques. Schmidt held the bat high, behind his right ear, and swung down on the ball with what he described as "swinging an axe" only to have his powerful right hand or top hand take over as the bat collided with the ball. The result, often enough, was towering flyballs. One, believe it or not, actually hit an overhead speaker 117 feet above the floor in the Houston Astrodome. It was scored a single.

Williams, of course, insisted upon a slight upswing with his left or back hand underneath as he connected with the baseball. Schmidt, who had over 600 more at-bats than Williams, who lost time to two wars, wound up with 548 (not counting that Astrodome near-miss), 27 more than Ted's 521.

But whatever flak Schmidt took in Philadelphia, he excelled on the field. On April 17, 1974, Schmidt pulled off the amazing feat of hitting four home runs in a single game, just the fourth player in MLB history at that point to pull that off. The guy was just amazingly consistent. Look at these home-run totals:

1974	36	1981	31
1975	38	1982	35
1976	38	1983	40
1977	38	1984	36
1978	21 (an off year)	1985	33
1979	45	1986	37
1980	48	1987	35

But despite this remarkable record, Philly fans expected more. The player that no less a baseball expert than Tom Boswell of the *Washington Post* called the best all-around player of the past 15 years and the greatest third baseman of all time wasn't adored.

Schmidt addressed that in his Hall of Fame induction speech. "If I had to do it all over again, I'd do it in Philly," he said. "The only thing I'd change would be me. I'd be less sensitive, I'd be more outgoing and more appreciative of what you expected of me. My relationship with the fans has always been misunderstood. Can we put that to rest here today?"

If you looked closely enough, the hints of Schmidt's demise were surely there. At the start of May, he hit his 548th and final home run off the Astros' Jim Deshaies in the first inning of a Tuesday night game at the Vet. He collected just five more hits—including the bunt—over the next 59 at-bats and 18 games, including a six-day hiatus after an 0-for-17 stretch dropped his average to .220.

Schmidt's final road trip with the Phillies started with a hit. His final outfield hit was a fifth-inning groundball RBI single in a 4–2 win off Fernando Valenzuela on a Tuesday night in Los Angeles, May 23. But then the Phils suffered five straight losses, leading up to the loss to the Giants on that Sunday afternoon.

In what turned out to be his final game, Schmidt flied to center off Rick Reuschel leading off the second, walked in the third, grounded to short in the fifth, and reached on an error in the seventh. He had just one more plate appearance.

With the Giants winning 9–4 heading to the ninth, Tom Herr reached on an infield hit and Von Hayes drew a walk. Manager Roger Craig brought in reliever Mike LaCoss to face Schmidt. He walked on five pitches, and the Phillies went on to lose.

Some time later that stressful day, after phone calls home to his wife, Donna, and friends, Schmidt had made up his mind. He would not play again. It was time to go.

Interestingly, baseball fans weren't ready to let him go yet, almost as if they felt somebody had to make up for the Philly fans' years of indifference. Even though he sported a .203 average, fans voted him onto the National League All-Star team. Schmidt chose not to play but did attend and was in uniform and introduced to the fans in Anaheim.

Happily, they stood, en masse, and did what the Philadelphia fans probably wished they had done a helluva lot more often for Michael Jack Schmidt. They stood and applauded.

Mike Schmidt by the Numbers

YEAR	TEAM	G	AB	R	H	TB	2B	3B	HR	RBI	BB	SO	SB	BA	SLG	OBP
1972	PHI	13	34	2	7	10	0	0	1	3	5	15	0	.206	.294	.325
1973	PHI	132	367	43	72	137	11	0	18	52	62	136	8	.196	.373	.324
1974	PHI	162	568	108	160	310	28	7	36	116	106	138	23	.282	.546	.395
1975	PHI	158	562	93	140	294	34	3	38	95	101	180	29	.249	.523	.367
1976	PHI	160	584	112	153	306	31	4	38	107	100	149	14	.262	.524	.376
1977	PHI	154	544	114	149	312	27	11	38	101	104	122	15	.274	.574	.393
1978	PHI	145	513	93	129	223	27	2	21	78	91	103	19	.251	.435	.364
1979	PHI	160	541	109	137	305	25	4	45	114	120	115	9	.253	.564	.386
1980	PHI	150	548	104	157	342	25	8	48	121	89	119	12	.286	.624	.380
1981	PHI	102	354	78	112	228	19	2	31	91	73	71	12	.316	.644	.435
1982	PHI	148	514	108	144	281	26	3	35	87	107	131	14	.280	.547	.403
1983	PHI	154	534	104	136	280	16	4	40	109	128	148	7	.255	.524	.399
1984	PHI	151	528	93	146	283	23	3	36	106	92	116	5	.277	.536	.383
1985	PHI	158	549	89	152	292	31	5	33	93	87	117	1	.277	.532	.375
1986	PHI	160	552	97	160	302	29	1	37	119	89	84	1	.290	.547	.390
1987	PHI	147	522	88	153	286	28	0	35	113	83	80	2	.293	.548	.388
1988	PHI	108	390	52	97	158	21	2	12	62	49	42	3	.249	.405	.337
1989	PHI	42	148	19	30	55	7	0	6	28	21	17	0	.203	.372	.297
TOTALS			2404	8352	1506	2234	4404	408	59	548	1595	1507	1883	174	.267	.527	.380

1968

ROGER MARIS

HIT 'EM WITH YOUR WALLET, ROG

DATE: October 10, 1968

SITE: Busch Stadium, St. Louis, Missouri

PITCHER: Mickey Lolich of the Detroit Tigers

RESULT: Popout to shortstop

It would be hard to imagine a successful major-league ballplayer wanting to end his career without a headline, but if there ever was one who'd had enough of the spotlight, it might have been Roger Maris.

Every baseball fan knows that it was the sweet-swinging lefty bat of Maris that took advantage of the short right field porch in Yankee Stadium the way that fellow Yankee Babe Ruth did 34 years earlier. In 1961, Maris slammed a record 61 home runs, one better than the Babe's 60 in 1927.

Maris, of course, achieved that milestone in the final game of a 162-game season, connecting for number 61 off Boston's Tracy Stallard in the fourth inning, prompting an asterisk from Major League Baseball commissioner Ford Frick (pronounced with a "p" instead of the "f" in the tri-state area) that Maris had had an additional eight games to break Ruth's mark.

For Maris, the end to his career came after a second trip to the World Series, his seventh Series in a 12-year big-league run. That's a pretty amazing stat right there.

Maris made the last two Series with the St. Louis Cardinals; the first was a seven-game victory over the "Impossible Dream" Boston Red Sox in 1967; the last was a seven-game loss to the Detroit Tigers a year later.

Though just 34, Maris looked and probably felt much older. He'd had a hamate bone injury in his hand in 1965, playing just 46 games, and had suffered an assortment of injuries over the next three seasons that knocked his generally consistent home-run totals down to single digits in each season.

Maris hit just 14 home runs in his two seasons in St. Louis, eight of those solo shots, but he certainly helped the team get to two World Series. His calm professionalism and solid work in right field helped keep things rolling.

On August 5 of that 1968 season, he announced that he'd retire at the end of the season and looked forward to life as a beer baron. Cardinals owner Gussie Busch had given Maris an Anheuser-Busch distributorship. But even that turned out to be gnarly years later. Nothing ever came easy, it seems, for Roger Maris or his family. Except maybe that one season when his swing was so grooved, it seemed everything he hit ended up in the right field stands.

As it turned out, Maris's final Cardinal and major-league home run came off fireballer Don Wilson at the Astrodome on September 15, ending an 0-for-10 streak. The win helped the Cardinals clinch the pennant. Maris looked worn out and wound up his final regular season playing in exactly 100 games, batting .255 with five homers and 45 RBIs. Nothing to write home about. But he was an old pro and St. Louis loved him. It was the opposite of his time in New York.

Maris didn't do much in the Series with Detroit, won by the Tigers in seven games. Maris went 0-for-3 in the Cardinals' 4–0 Game 1 win behind Bob Gibson but sat against ace left-hander Mickey Lolich, the Series' surprise MVP. Most pre-Series experts would have suggested 31-game winner Denny McLain or the always dominant Bob Gibson. It was Lolich who won three games in the Series, including this 8–1 Game 2 win.

In Game 3, Maris looped a pop fly double off reliever Don McMahon, the final extra-base hit of his career. In Game 4, Maris went 0-for-5 as the Cardinals bombed McLain, 10–1. But neither he nor any other Cardinals could really solve the ace lefty Lolich. In Game 5, Maris pinch-hit against Lolich with one out in the ninth in the Tigers' 5–3 win—and whiffed.

In Game 6, Maris managed a pair of harmless singles off McLain in his second and fourth at-bats. It didn't bother McLain, who scattered seven other hits in a 14–1 Tiger win, his 32nd victory of the season. The Series would head back to St. Louis and Busch Stadium for a decisive Game 7, the second straight Cardinals series to go the full seven games.

For Maris, having a chance to wind up his career before the hometown Cardinal fans, it was a great opportunity to let the game go. Though his numbers weren't particularly impressive, there was something about having an old pro helping anchor the outfield, the daily feeling in the Cardinal clubhouse, here was a guy who'd seen it all.

Having the spotlight elsewhere in St. Louis with future Hall of Famers Bob Gibson and Lou Brock in their prime, future Hall of Famer Orlando Cepeda winding down his career, chatty future Hall of Fame broadcaster Tim McCarver always ready to give an interview, Maris was in a great spot. Playing in front of a generally forgiving, rarely inquisitory press, Maris was able to come to the park, play the game, have a beer or two and a Camel or two, then go home to Pat and the kids.

That was certainly not the case in New York, the media capital of the world, even though, in retrospect, the Gotham papers were rarely critical of Maris and his Yankee teammates, who certainly took advantage of their status as honored soldiers in baseball's greatest dynasty. Nosy, yes, but generally not nasty, like in Boston. Nobody criticized Mickey Mantle for not visiting his mother in the offseason, like the Boston papers did with Ted Williams.

Did the New York media drive Maris up the wall? Sure. Coming from Fargo, North Dakota, not exactly a metropolis—especially then—he made his major-league debut with the Cleveland Indians in April of 1957 and collected three hits. It was an OK debut—.235 with 14 home runs, 51 RBIs, nine doubles, and a surprising five triples.

By June the next season, the Tribe sent him, Dick Tomanek, and Preston Ward to the Kansas City Athletics for Woodie Held and Vic Power. Good trivia question. Maris for Vic Power? Know that one?

In the offseason, just a couple weeks before Christmas, the Yankees decide to clean out some old wood for young timber, sending veterans Hank Bauer, Don Larsen, Norm Siebern, and (did you know this one?) Marvelous Marv Throneberry to the Athletics for Joe DeMaestri, Kent Hadley, and Roger Eugene Maris, now playing for his third major-league franchise in three years. It turned out to be a legendary move.

It was yet *another* trade between the Yankees and the Kansas City Athletics who, the *New York Times* was happy to note, had swapped 59 players in 15 deals since the team moved from Philadelphia. That was the only number on the Rolodex, evidently. The only one they needed.

"I know we'll take a lot more ribbing," Yankee general manager George Weiss told John Drebinger of the *Times* announcing the deal, "but it simply got down to where we couldn't close a deal with any other club. We were fairly close to making two with National League clubs, but these still are stalled.

"I hated to see so fine a competitor as Bauer go, and we'll always be indebted to Larsen for his perfect game performance. However, in Maris, we have a young outfielder who should develop into a fine player at the Stadium."

In other words, the shrewd Weiss noticed that the left-handed hitting Maris, a dead-pull hitter, also happened to hit a lot of flyballs, perfect for the 296-foot right field porch "at the Stadium." He couldn't have been more prophetic and neither could Drebinger. "At the Stadium," indeed.

Drebinger was never more correct in his long career. "The 25-year-old Maris definitely was the key man of the deal as far as the Yankees were concerned," he wrote. "Maris started the 1959 season with a great splurge and was leading the league when, shortly before the first All-Star game (they had two that year), he was stricken with appendicitis. Though he recovered quickly, he never regained his former stride and finished the season with a .273 average, 16 homers and 72 runs batted in."

While Maris turned in a terrific 1960 season, winning his first Most Valuable Player Award with a .283 average, 39 home runs and 112 runs batted in, that was just a warmup. In the MVP voting, Maris edged out teammate Mantle, though Mantle got two more first-place votes (10–8). Looking at the MVP vote now, it seems as if it was an odd year: Baltimore's Ron

Hansen was fifth, Al Smith sixth. And just for laughs, note that Baltimore's Chuck Estrada (12th) outpolled Boston's retiring icon Ted Williams (13th). Be honest, are those names you would have expected to see that high on an MVP ballot?

In 1961, Maris had his breakthrough year, won a second MVP, again, barely outpolling teammate Mickey Mantle, who'd hit 54 HR and a higher batting average (.317). Again, Maris got one more first-place vote (7–6) to win. Again, there were surprises in the MVP voting: Baltimore's Jim Gentile (46 home runs, 141 RBIs, tying Maris for the league lead) was third, Detroit's Norm Cash—a phenomenal year (.361, 41, 132)—was fourth, and the Yankees' Whitey Ford and Luis Arroyo were fifth and sixth with Elston Howard 10th, making it five Yankees out of the top 10 MVP candidates. Minnesota's Harmon Killebrew, who also hit 46 homers and drove in 122 and hit .288, was a distant 11th in the MVP voting. East Coast bias, perhaps?

As baseball folks look back, the Mantle-Maris home-run race dominated the year. And Weiss's Delphic prediction about Maris being a great player "at the Stadium" was dead-on. Maris even outdid the Babe, regardless of Ford Frick and his asterisk. Maris found out just how friendly that right field porch was at Yankee Stadium. In 79 games in the Bronx, Maris hit 30 home runs and drove in 73, batting .286. In 1927, when Ruth set the record of 60—"Let's see some sonovabitch beat that!" he said—Babe hit 28 at home and 32 on the road.

Sorry, Ford, Roger did beat The Babe. By two.

In that record year, Maris hit five homers in Cleveland, four in Boston's Fenway Park, four in Washington's Griffith Stadium, three in Baltimore's Memorial Stadium, four in Kansas City's Municipal Stadium, five in Detroit's Tiger Stadium, and five in Chicago's Comiskey Park.

For Maris, that was the fun part of the year, between the lines. The difficult part came *after* the games when instead of facing the American League's best arms, he had to deal with the most persistently annoying mouths of the junior circuit, the New York media. And like a screwballing lefty, he couldn't figure it out.

Now, Maris wasn't a rookie; he'd played in Cleveland and Kansas City, had several seasons under his belt when he came to New York, so he should have known how to deal with the media. And while compared to previous years, the Mantle-Maris home run race that dominated the summer probably attracted more attention than usual, the fact that there were so many writers there, so many stories, you would think a player would adjust. Maris never seemed to understand that when reporters accurately quoted his comments, he would get into trouble. It never occurred to him, evidently, that people would read and comment on what he said.

As quoted in Roger Kahn's discussion of this issue in "The Press and Roger Maris": "Maris came to bat four times and hit no homers. Reporters asked if he'd had good pitches to hit. 'I didn't get too many strikes,' Maris said. 'But they were called strikes. (Umpire Hank) Soar had me swinging in self-defense.'"

Now, this is a standard baseball player bitch. This is not surprising in any way. Every ballplayer since the beginning of the game has complained about the umpiring. But when this quote was shared with the nation's readers, there was backlash.

"The next day's newspapers headlined that casual, typical ball player's gripe," Kahn wrote. "Maris was shocked. Until that moment he had not fully realized the impact his sentences now carried. He had not fully realized the price one pays for being a hero. He was disturbed, upset, withdrawn. Tortured would be too strong a word, but only slightly. He showed his hurt by saying little; his mouth appeared permanently set in its hard line. . . ."

He pouted. Later, Kahn recounts this line: "when asked about the fans in right field—these are Yankee fans—Maris said 'Terrible. Maybe the worst in the league.' He recounted remarks that had been shouted at him and, under consistent prodding, ran down the stadium customers for ten or fifteen minutes. The next day, after reading the papers, he said to me 'That's it. I been trying to be a good guy to the writers, but I quit. . . . From now on I'll tell the writers what pitch I hit but no more big spiels. . . .'"

The writers *quoted what he said.* But it never, evidently, *occurred to him how it would look in print.* After this many seasons in the major leagues. And apparently, nobody in the Yankee PR office thought to explain to Maris that the media wasn't necessarily confrontational, you simply had to think that *what you were saying was going in the newspaper.*

Maris never really figured that out, it seems. And his sullen reputation got around. Remember how he was depicted in Jim Bouton's *Ball Four*— "Talking about Yastrzemski recalled one of the great non-hustlers of all time, Roger Maris. Rodg always went to first base as though he had sore feet. If he hit a home run it didn't matter of course. But every time he popped up or hit a routine grounder, it would take him a half-hour to get to first base—if he got there at all. He'd often just peel off halfway down and head for the dugout.

"So (Manager Ralph) Houk would call a meeting and he'd say, 'Boys, it doesn't look good if we don't run the ball out. I want everybody to show some hustle out there.'

"And Maris would go out there and damned if he wouldn't do the same thing all over again. I could never believe Ralph's patience. I know Maris was sensitive about what was written about him in the papers and I don't know why Houk didn't just blast him to the reporters. But he never did. And Maris continued to loaf."

And this: "Roger fought a lot with the people in the stands, especially in Detroit, where he used to give them the finger. He and the fans would get to calling each other names and then Maris would roll out his heavy artillery.

"'Yeah? How much money are *you* making?' Roger was making $70,000 a year (a LOT of money in 1961). After a while every time Maris got into an argument the guys in the dugout would say 'C'mon Rodg, hit him with your wallet.'"

No doubt Maris would have preferred life in the Joe DiMaggio era where the New York writers, sadly, even the great Red Smith, didn't dare to criticize him. If they did—even once—he was done with them. By Roger's time, rereading these clips, it seems the media had finally stopped kneeling.

Gradually, Maris's numbers fell off. He suffered a hamate injury that ended the 1965 season for him after just 46 games, and in December of 1966, the Yankees dealt him to the St. Louis Cardinals for infielder Charley Smith.

Maris had considered retirement, but Cardinals GM Stan Musial convinced him to play another year. He did, enjoyed being away from the New York maelstrom, and did OK (.261, 9 homers, 55 RBI in 125 games) and the Cardinals won the World Series.

But here in Game 7 of the 1968 Series, the Cardinals were facing Mickey Lolich one more time. And the portly left-hander was just on a roll and neither Maris nor the rest of the Cardinals were a match for him. In just over two hours in a thrilling pitching duel, Lolich held the Cardinals to just five hits, beating Bob Gibson in his own ballpark, 4–1, picking off two Cardinals (Brock, Flood) in one inning.

For Maris, Lolich got him to bounce into a double play in the second, struck him out in the fifth, and in the seventh, the Tigers finally got to Gibson, breaking up a scoreless game with three runs, all after two were out.

Singles by Norm Cash and Willie Horton brought up Jim Northrup, who hit a ball that turned into a triple when the Cardinals' stellar center fielder Curt Flood stumbled trying to run it down.

So, with the Cardinals trailing 3–0, number 9 walked to the plate for what would be the final time. A home run here would be the great reward for the Cardinal fans who cheered Maris on his arrival and never stopped. People said he felt appreciated for what had been a remarkable, record-breaking career and here, if he could just turn back the clock. . . .

Maris worked the count to 2-2, then Lolich fired a high fastball and Maris's swing was late. The popup to shortstop Mickey Stanley ended the inning.

He was on deck in the bottom of the ninth when Tim McCarver popped up Lolich's final pitch to catcher Bill Freehan to end the game and Maris's career.

Even in retirement, we still heard Maris's name. He returned to Yankee Stadium a few times, more notably to great cheers in 1978 as the Yanks celebrated their 1977 World Series win. He returned again in July of 1984 when the Yankees retired Maris's number. But Roger was not well, and cancer claimed him in 1985 at age 51.

We heard his name—and saw his family—in St. Louis when Mark McGwire broke the single-season home-run record, mentioning his name with great reverence, McGwire even running down to hug the family in the Busch Stadium stands in the middle of the game. And behind the scenes, the Busch folks must have been just a little uneasy.

Maris's beer distributorship, given to him and his brother Rudy back in 1967, had grown into a $50 million-a-year franchise after his death. Sadly, a squabble over the distributorship erupted between the Anheuser-Busch folks, and eight years of injunctions and lawsuits and three trials ultimately ended with the Maris family winning an enormous settlement.

Newspaper reports said the Maris family will collect at least $120 million as part of a settlement that ended a defamation trial. Maris's relatives accused the brewer of defamation after company officials publicly said the family sold repackaged, out-of-date beer. The family claimed the brewer had plotted to destroy their reputation. A jury agreed with them.

Now, Roger was gone, but this time, the Maris family fought back against the negative talk. And won big-time. Hit 'em with your wallet, Rodg.

Roger Maris by the Numbers

YEAR	TEAM	G	AB	R	H	TB	2B	3B	HR	RBI	BB	SO	SB	BA	SLG	OBP
1957	CLE	116	358	61	84	145	9	5	14	51	60	80	8	.235	.405	.344
1958	CLE	51	182	26	41	75	5	1	9	27	17	33	4	.225	.412	.287
1958	KC	99	401	61	99	176	14	3	19	53	28	52	0	.247	.439	.298
1958	ALL	150	583	87	140	251	19	4	28	80	45	85	4	.240	.431	.294
1959	KC	122	433	69	118	201	21	7	16	72	59	53	2	.273	.464	.361
1960	NY	136	499	98	141	290	18	7	39	112	70	65	2	.283	.581	.371
1961	NY	161	590	132	159	366	16	4	61	141	94	67	0	.269	.620	.372
1962	NYY	157	590	92	151	286	34	1	33	100	87	79	1	.256	.485	.356
1963	NYY	90	312	52	84	169	14	1	23	53	35	40	1	.269	.542	.346
1964	NYY	141	513	86	144	238	12	2	26	71	62	77	3	.281	.464	.364
1965	NYY	46	155	22	37	68	7	0	8	27	29	29	0	.239	.439	.357
1966	NYY	119	348	37	81	133	9	2	13	43	36	60	0	.233	.382	.307
1967	STL	125	410	64	107	166	18	7	9	55	52	61	0	.261	.405	.346
1968	STL	100	310	25	79	116	18	2	5	45	24	38	0	.255	.374	.307
TOTALS		1463	5101	825	1325	2429	195	42	275	850	653	734	21	.260	.476	.346

JOHN NOGOWSKI JR.

AT LAST, IN THE SHOW

DATE: August 16, 2020

SITE: Guaranteed Rate Field, Chicago, Illinois

PITCHER: Dallas Keuchel of the Chicago White Sox

RESULT: Line-drive single to center field—first major-league hit

The Call. Once you sign a contract to play professional baseball, the next thing you wait for is The Call.

For John Nogowski Jr., my son, the kid I used to play Wiffle Ball with every night on the front lawn, the call finally came in midsummer of COVID-19, as he wryly predicted the moment the disease halted the Cardinals' spring training.

"This would be the perfect time for me to make my debut," he said, tongue firmly in cheek. And he was right.

After six grinding years on the minor-league baseball trail from Vermont to California, Missouri to Tennessee, 2,500 at-bats, two hand surgeries, winter ball in Mexico and the Dominican Republic, more miles, bus rides, bad postgame meals and hotel stays, the phone rang.

Looking back, COVID-19 had not only stalled the start of the 2020 Major League Baseball season, a profusion of positive tests of the Cardinal players had halted their regular season in St. Louis for 17 straight days. On August 14, the Cardinals were to resume the schedule with a slew of double-headers. The call for John came along with instructions for he, along with 24 other St. Louis Cardinal baseball players, to each get in their own rental cars (for COVID social distancing) and to each drive to Chicago, where the Cardinals were to try to resume their regular season the next day.

"They weren't sure they were going to activate me," John said, remembering the initial phone query. "But they wanted me to go to Chicago in case they did." So The Call was only sort of The Call.

On the way to the Windy City, he got another call.

"A clubbie called me and asked if I was OK with uniform number 34. I told him sure. But I added, I wasn't sure they were going to activate me. He said he thought they were.

"Then I got another call from John Vuch (the Cardinals' director of baseball operations), who signed me out of Independent ball in Sioux City. They wanted him to be the guy to tell me they were bringing me up and that I was going to start tomorrow in Chicago."

The next call, of course, came to Mom and Dad. Pandemonium at the house when this second call came in. John was in the bigs! Finally. Wow. If only we could have been there . . .

How John ended up with the Cardinals is a story in itself. Deciding to leave Florida State after his first team, All-ACC junior season, he was picked by the Oakland A's on the third and final day of the Major League Draft in the 34th round. He'd seen his Florida State teammate Jose Brizuela go 18 rounds earlier, and John was beginning to wonder if leaving FSU was the right thing to do.

After two days of waiting by the phone and fielding exploratory calls from the Houston Astros, St. Louis Cardinals, and Toronto Blue Jays, he couldn't take it any longer and headed for the beach. Around the 20th round, the Cardinals called and negotiations began. He had a figure in mind, the Cardinals had a different number, and all along Florida's I-10, they talked while Mom drove him to the Jacksonville Airport to fly up to play in the prestigious Cape Cod League. "Don't get on that plane," the Cardinals' negotiator cautioned. John's figure was firm. He got on board and barely after takeoff, the Cardinals called back. "OK," they said. They'd match his number.

John immediately called to tell us to watch, St. Louis was going to pick him. I went and retrieved a great photo of him in a Cardinal cap from a summer baseball camp taken during the McGwire-Sosa home-run race and was all ready to take a screenshot of both. A keepsake!

Two picks before the Cards were to make their selection—our son—we heard this: "The Oakland Athletics take John Nogowski from Florida State, a first baseman." "What just happened?" my wife Liz asked. John started professional baseball as an Oakland Athletic.

After a couple successful years in High A Stockton, he was nearing the end of spring training when the team awarded him the Gold Glove for being the best defensive first baseman in the organization: no small feat with Matt Olson ahead of him in Triple-A. The very next day, the last day of spring training, Oakland released John and his FSU teammate Jose Brizuela.

Back in Tallahassee, the phone rang off the hook Saturday from independent teams; John picked a great one, the Sioux City Explorers and manager Steve Montgomery. After 34 games, hitting a league-leading .402, the Cardinals' John Vuch signed him and had him join the Springfield Cardinals, who happened to be in Midland, playing the A's Double-A affiliate—what would have been John's next stop out of Stockton if he had remained in the A's organization.

He homered in his first game as a Cardinal against his old A's teammates and went on to hit .300 for the rest of the year. No spring training invite, however. He hit .300 in another season in Springfield, was Player of the Week once, still no spring training invite.

When he finally arrived at minor-league spring training in year three with the Cardinals, he was promoted to Triple-A Memphis with first-year manager Ben Johnson. When he arrived, he was greeted with the following caveat. "You don't really have a position, I'll try to get you some at-bats spelling Rangel Ravelo and maybe an outfield spot, here or there. But as of now, you won't start."

By the end of the year, he was hitting third in the lineup and though he was limited to just 100 starts out of the 140-game minor-league schedule, batted .296, hit 15 home runs (and missed out on most games in the West Coast PCL bandboxes), yet drove in 75 runs. He also was named the Pacific Coast League's best defender at first base by *Baseball America*.

Invited to a second major-league spring training in 2020, he made an impression. Sent to the alternate site after COVID, he hit really well— .583—and for the longest time, was frustrated to see pitchers and other players being summoned to the show before him. Finally, in mid-August, he got The Call.

His first—and as it turned out—only major-league game in 2020 would happen at Chicago's Guaranteed Rate Field. It was a sunny Sunday afternoon; Mom and Dad were at home in front of the television screen. Dallas Keuchel, former Cy Young Award winner, was on the mound for the White Sox and sure enough, with one out in the bottom of the first, the camera swung over to number 34 at first base. Cheers in our living room.

Twenty-three minutes into the broadcast, the Cardinals' nonpareil announcer Danny McLaughlin chimed in over compelling shots of John at first base—charcoal under each eye, socks pulled up high, sporting somewhat of a mustache, a first.

"If you're wondering about John Nogowski, for fans that don't watch a lot of the spring training games," Danny Mac said, "he is a good defender, a plus defender, and you'll see that glove come into play, possibly this afternoon."

"He's a good player," added color man Jim Edmonds. "They're definitely not losing anything at first base."

Of course, any parent would have killed to be in the stands to see their son's first major-league game. But if you couldn't be there, listening to Danny Mac, just the right mix of expertise and enthusiasm and the first-rate coverage of Cardinal baseball was the next best thing. I sat in my recliner, Liz on the couch, our hearts somewhere on the South Side of the city.

Leading off the third inning, 54 minutes into a game we'd been waiting maybe 20-something years to see, came the call.

"Here's another major-league debut, John Nogowski," Danny Mac told us. "Yesterday, Dylan Carlson, Max Schrock, Jake Woodford and now, John Nogowski."

Sure enough, there he was, digging his right foot into the back of the batter's box, right hand up on the visor of his helmet as he focused on Keuchel, held the bat back over his right shoulder, readied for that first pitch.

"This will be a good test of the strike zone," Danny Mac told us as Kuechel's changeup caught the inside corner for strike one. "He's got a good idea up there," Edmonds said.

"Sometimes, he's had more walks than hits," added Danny Mac, referring to John's most unusual stat—more walks than strikeouts for the past three minor-league seasons, a rarity in these days of the whiff.

Keuchel then fired a fastball on the outside corner. John took it. Strike two. "I was waiting for that changeup," John said later. "I knew he was going to come back to it."

Keuchel did, the ball drifted to the outside part of the plate, and John swung, lining it just to the right of second base, headed for the outfield, it seemed.

White Sox second baseman Danny Mendick was perfectly positioned. It kicked up on him but he caught it and made the play. "No major-league experience and they still have a shift on," Danny Mac shrewdly noted.

Leading off the sixth—it's a running joke around our house that wherever John bats in the lineup, he'll end up leading off at least twice—John steps in again. The White Sox have jumped on a succession of Cardinal pitchers and now lead, 7–0. It's clear Keuchel is on his game.

"The Cardinals' offense has been stymied today," Danny Mac says as John takes an 85-mile-per-hour fastball for a strike. "Just one hit so far."

"Be a good time for your first major-league hit," chimes in Edmonds.

Keuchel misses with a breaking ball. "John is just not going to swing at many pitches outside the zone," Danny Mac says. "He kept a journal in spring training, took notes every single day. Conversations with Paul Goldschmidt, coaching staff. At one point, his career took him to Independent ball. And now here he is, in the big leagues."

As if on cue, Keuchel delivers that changeup and John lines it into left-center field. "Base hit, center field. And John Nogowski has his first major-league hit."

Screams in the house! Text messages galore. Tears, hugs, jubilation. John claps his hands together, looks up to the sky. A hit in the bigs. That night, Matt Carpenter bought him dinner. Mom and Dad sent a bottle of Dom Perignon to his room at The Ritz. "Thanks, Mom and Dad," he said that night in a breathless phone call. "We did this. I mean that. WE did this. And the Ritz is really cool. I like the slippers." The next day, Adam Wainwright presents him with the game ball, authenticated and everything. First hit in the show.

Fast-forward to spring training 2021 and John is the talk of camp. Amazingly, he bats .350, leads the team in home runs and RBIs. There are podcasts in St. Louis, "What will it take for John Nogowski to make the team?"

He surprises the world, makes the club. "He just elbowed his way onto the team," Cardinals manager Mike Shildt says.

Mom and Dad are in chilly Cincinnati for the season opener, and in the second game of the year, number 34 is called to pinch-hit. Suddenly I remembered this sweaty, freckle-faced kid sitting across from me after a youth baseball camp, asking if I thought he could be a good player—"Sure," I said then. "You can hit, field, throw. You can be really good."

"I don't wanna be good," he shot back, a steely look in his eye, "I wanna be great."

I looked up and number 34, that young man, my son, was stepping into the batter's box. On the first pitch—yes, we've discussed the wisdom of chasing the first pitch more than once—he lined a 108-mile-per-hour rocket into left-center field. He got to first base and waved. He was in The Show, 2021.

For a while. As the stories you've read preceding this concluding chapter reveal, baseball is a most unforgiving game. While we thought that ringing single in chilly Cincinnati was just a starting place, by the end of June, there were more than a few bumps in the road. There was a fractured hand, misdiagnosed for a few weeks, options up and down to the minors four separate times and finally, as Independence Day rolled around, the Cards traded him to the Pittsburgh Pirates.

What a day that was! John flies to Pittsburgh with just his glove, Mom and Ashley fly to St. Louis to retrieve his truck (filled with his baseball equipment) and drive to the Steel City, and Dad flies up the next day. We had no idea what was in store.

For two amazing, hold-your-breath weeks, John took over first base for the Pirates, rained hits throughout National League outfields, collecting a record-tying 10 hits in his first five games, including a four-hit game against the Atlanta Braves in his third Pirate game. He even came in to throw a scoreless ninth inning in that blowout and for some unforgettable reason, was an instant hit in the Steel City!

"The Legend" or "The Big Nogowski" or "Nogo" seemed to catch Pirates' fans attention from the first at-bat. A few games in, The Pittsburgh Clothing

Company began to offer a Big Nogowski T-shirt, then came another "Big Nogowski" model on shirts, hoodies, and apparel sold in Pirates gift shops. Fans seemed to love him wearing number 69, that his walkup song was Bruce Springsteen's stirring "Born in the USA," and he always seemed to be getting a hit. PNC Park seemed electric whenever he stepped to the plate.

The hot streak continued through a three-game series at New York's Citi Field, yet another three-hit game, and then a dramatic, two outs, bottom-of-the-ninth game-tying single off the Mets' ace closer Edwin Díaz, bringing hisses and boos from 50,000 New York Mets fans. Can a visiting player enjoy anything more than that?

The announcers began to call him "an instant legend" in Pittsburgh just a handful of games into his Pirates career. For those first 33 games, he was driving in runs, playing an immaculate first base and—how about this?—even pitching a few times in blowouts. It could hardly have been more exciting. It is as if all those years in the minors revved his engine beyond belief—he'd do whatever the Pirates needed.

In Arizona, in his 69th at-bat—an event duly noted by Pittsburgh scribes—The Big Nogowski drilled his first major-league home run. "The legend lives," announcer Greg Brown hollered. It was a once-in-a-lifetime moment, a genuine major-league home run. Mom and Dad, watching at home, stood and high-fived, the phones erupted. (Mom got the ball.)

Things slowed after that. There were a couple more big hits but for the next stretch, it seemed like every hard-hit baseball wound up in somebody's glove. It seemed like guys were diving all over the park to stop him. By mid-August, oddly enough, exactly one year after his big-league debut—yes, the same damn day, August 16—he was back in the minors.

He'd have to start the climb all over again. That's baseball. Been there, done that. And he will have to do it all again. This game is tough, relentless.

It's the journey, they say, not the destination that matters. Whoever said that didn't play in the minor leagues. But this kid is not deterred—if he was, he'd have stopped playing a while back.

The journey from my front yard, catching his first flyball on Father's Day at age four to Tallahassee's Dick Howser Stadium playing for Florida State, his first goal, to Busch Stadium, St. Louis—the major leagues!—to incredibly, a starring role in Pittsburgh, where people were buying his T-shirt, calling his name, lining up outside the dugout for an hour after the game, talking about him all over town. "The Big Nogowski!" You heard it everywhere.

Twenty-four years after that first snag, all those miles and throws and ups and downs, there are moments when, as a dad, you just kind of smile, shake your head and remember. . . .

Staying up until 4 in the morning, listening to a radio broadcast from Modesto, California, as first baseman John is throwing his third inning of extra-inning relief, then getting the game-winning hit and the win. Earning his second straight Dizzy Dean World Series MVP in Moody, Alabama, after winning the MVP in Jasper, Tennessee. Or that amazing, record-setting week in Cooperstown, going 30-for-39 and 3-for-3 in the title game, pitching a complete game—his third time on the mound that day—to win his second straight Dreams Park title. (He still has the record—I just checked.)

Like any dad with a kid in the minors, remembering all the late-night calls, the after-game consultations, bad umps, lineouts, video clips, scouting reports, all part of this endless, often unfathomable minors-to-majors baseball trail.

A little while ago, I found one of those old Wiffle Balls under one of our hedges, no doubt some stray line drive that we never recovered. Unless it was supposed to be there to remind me—and him—where it all started. In the front yard. On Father's Day. Maybe it is the journey after all.

Major-League Debut Box Score

Cardinals vs. White Sox 08/16

St. Louis Cardinals	AB	R	H	2B	3B	HR	RBI	PO	A
Wong, 2b	3	0	1	0	0	0	0	2	1
Schrock, 2b	0	0	0	0	0	0	0	0	0
Edman, ss	4	1	0	0	0	0	0	1	1
Bader, cf	0	0	0	0	0	0	0	0	0
Goldschmidt, dh	3	1	1	0	0	0	0		
O'Neill, lf	3	0	0	0	0	0	0	0	0
Carpenter, 3b	4	0	1	0	0	0	2	0	2
Carlson, cf-rf	4	0	1	0	0	0	0	2	0
Knizner, c	4	0	0	0	0	0	0	10	2
Fowler, rf	3	0	1	0	0	0	0	2	0
B. Miller, ss	1	0	0	0	0	0	0	0	1
Nogowski, 1b	4	0	1	0	0	0	0	6	1
Hudson, p	0	0	0	0	0	0	0	1	1
Ramirez, p	0	0	0	0	0	0	0	0	0
Elledge, p	0	0	0	0	0	0	0	0	0
Kaminsky, p	0	0	0	0	0	0	0	0	0
Totals	33	2	6	0	0	0	2	24	9

Chicago White Sox	AB	R	H	2B	3B	HR	RBI	PO	A
T. Anderson, ss	3	2	1	0	0	0	0	1	1
Moncada, 3b	4	1	1	0	0	1	3	1	4
Grandal, c	4	1	1	0	0	1	1	6	0
Abreu, 1b	3	1	1	0	0	1	1	10	1
Jimenez, lf	4	1	2	0	0	1	2	2	0
Encarnacion, dh	4	0	0	0	0	0	0		
Robert, cf	2	0	0	0	0	0	0	2	0
Mazara, rf	3	1	1	0	0	0	0	4	0
Mendick, 2b	3	0	1	0	0	0	0	1	3
Keuchel, p	0	0	0	0	0	0	0	0	0
Cordero, p	0	0	0	0	0	0	0	0	0
Foster, p	0	0	0	0	0	0	0	0	0
Detwiler, p	0	0	0	0	0	0	0	0	0
Totals	30	7	8	0	0	4	7	27	9

St. Louis Cardinals   0 0 0   0 0 2   0 0 0 -   2 6 1

Chicago White Sox   1 0 0   0 6 0   0 0 x -   7 8 0

E-Knizner. LOB-St. Louis Cardinals 7, Chicago White Sox 2. CI-Robert.

HR-Moncada (Ramirez in the 5th with runners on 2nd & 3rd), Grandal (Ramirez in the 5th with the bases empty), Abreu (Ramirez in the 5th with the bases empty), Jimenez (Ramirez in the 5th with the bases empty). SB-T. Anderson. CS-Robert, Mendick.

St. Louis Cardinals		INN	H	R	ER	BB	SO	BFP
Hudson	L	4.0	2	1	1	1	3	15
Ramirez		0.2	6	6	6	1	1	8
Elledge		2.1	0	0	0	0	5	7
Kaminsky		1.0	0	0	0	0	1	3
Totals		8.0	8	7	7	2	10	33
Chicago White Sox		INN	H	R	ER	BB	SO	BFP
Keuchel	W	5.2	4	2	2	2	1	23
Cordero		1.1	1	0	0	1	2	6
Foster		1.0	1	0	0	0	0	4
Detwiler		1.0	0	0	0	0	2	3
Totals		9.0	6	2	2	3	5	36

BB-Hudson (Abreu), Ramirez (T. Anderson), Keuchel 2 (Goldschmidt, O'Neill), Cordero (Wong). SO-Hudson 3 (Abreu, Encarnacion, Grandal), Ramirez (Robert), Elledge 5 (T. Anderson, Encarnacion, Grandal, Mazara, Moncada), Kaminsky (Jimenez), Keuchel (Carpenter), Cordero 2 (Nogowski, Edman), Detwiler 2 (Knizner, B. Miller). WP-Ramirez. Umpires-Tosi, Conroy, Vanover, Barksdale.

OS-Spear. T-2:52. A-0.

mation can be obtained
ting.com
22
IB/1

9 781493 066537